MICROECONOMICS

W0246828

MICROECONOMICS

Theory and Applications

Second Edition

Anindya Sen

OXFORD
UNIVERSITY PRESS

OXFORD
UNIVERSITY PRESS

Oxford University Press is a department of the University of Oxford.
It furthers the University's objective of excellence in research, scholarship,
and education by publishing worldwide. Oxford is a registered trademark of
Oxford University Press in the UK and in certain other countries

Published in India by
Oxford University Press
22 workspace, 2nd Floor, 1/22 Asaf Ali Road, New Delhi 110002

© Oxford University Press 2007

The moral rights of the author have been asserted

Second Edition published 2007
Ninth impression 2015

All rights reserved. No part of this publication may be reproduced, stored in
a retrieval system, or transmitted, in any form or by any means, without the
prior permission in writing of Oxford University Press, or as expressly permitted
by law, by licence, or under terms agreed with the appropriate reprographics
rights organization. Enquiries concerning reproduction outside the scope of the
above should be sent to the Rights Department, Oxford University Press, at the
address above

You must not circulate this work in any other form
and you must impose this same condition on any acquirer

ISBN-13: 978-0-19-568646-3
ISBN-10: 0-19-568646-2

Typeset in Times New Roman 10/12
by Excellent Laser Typesetters, Pitampura, Delhi 110 034
Printed in India by Repro India Limited

Contents

Preface

The first edition of the text has enjoyed reasonable success, particularly among students and teachers who want a clean and uncluttered approach to the subject. Feedback from the users, has over time taken the form of suggestions to enhance the usefulness of the book.

In the second edition I have tried to incorporate many of these practical and structural suggestions. While the original framework has been retained, several new sections—both applied and theoretical—have been added and existing sections expanded. New and topical concepts (opportunity cost of capital, effects of levying different types of taxes, taxation of a monopolist, free trade and tariffs, learning by doing) have been included. There is now a more extended discussion of some of the new developments in the subject (game theory concepts). Relevant real life examples have been included to make the second edition an up-to-date, contemporary, and relevant text.

Examples which have become less relevant have been replaced with more contemporary material. New examples, both applied and numerical, in the contemporary Indian context, have been incorporated in the text. More exercises which I hope will be useful to both teachers and students are now available at the end of each chapter. New appendices have been added in a couple of chapters for those interested in the derivation of advanced concepts. A detailed index has been prepared as a further aid to reading the text.

This volume, much like its predecessor, aims to expose students to the real life applicability of key concepts and theories in microeconomics, and to keep them abreast of the developments in the subject, while providing coverage similar to any standard microeconomics textbook. I hope that the enhanced second edition will continue to find as much favour with teachers and students as did the earlier one.

September 2006   ANINDYA SEN

Acknowledgements

I thank Oxford University Press for allowing me to reproduce sections from my Introduction to *Industrial Organization: A Reader* (1996), in Chapters 7 and 11 of this book.

Work on this book began at the Indira Gandhi Institute of Development Research (IGIDR), Mumbai and was completed at the Indian Institute of Management Calcutta (IIMC), while I was on sabbatical leave from IGIDR at the latter. I am grateful to both these institutes for providing me with all the facilities necessary to write this book.

My wife, Suparna, insisted that the book take priority over all other work; her support and encouragement helped me to complete it in a reasonably short span of time. This book is dedicated to her.

I welcome comments and ideas from readers and hope to draw on them in the future to make the text more accessible and enjoyable to students.

ANINDYA SEN

1 Introduction

1.1 The Scope of Microeconomics

Economics as a discipline exists because resources are *scarce*. Scarcity exists when the necessary resources for producing the things that people desire are insufficient to satisfy all wants. Scarcity occurs both among the rich and the poor. Even a rich person faces a scarcity of time.

The economic concept of scarcity has to be kept distinct from the physical fact that resources are limited. Suppose that there are three chairs in a room and fifty persons having lunch. Is there a scarcity of chairs in the room? If all the fifty people want to have lunch standing, then even three chairs may be in excess supply.

Moreover, even if resources are not limited, the concept of scarcity would exist because human beings have inherent limitations on the ability to consume and enjoy. Such limitations might refer to

- limited income—most of us earn limited amounts of money every month to spend on various things. One then has to choose how much to spend on which item.
- limited time—even if we never sleep, we can get at the most 24 hours each day. In any case, we have to allocate these 24 hours between work and leisure hours. Our lifespans are finite and we must decide what to do during our finite lifetimes.
- limited human faculties—we have limited faculties of hearing, seeing, etc.

Microeconomics studies *how choices are made* at the individual level under *conditions of scarcity*.

Two things about this definition stand out. First, if there were no scarcities, there would be no need to make choices. We can have anything we want.

The second important thing to realize is that choice must be from among alternatives. If there are no alternatives available, then the freedom to choose has very little meaning. There used to be a joke that one was free to choose any colour of the ambassador car in India, so long as it was white.

Choosing a particular alternative means comparing the benefits and costs of that alternative. Let $B(A)$ be the benefits from choosing alternative A, and $C(A)$ the costs of choosing A. Then A should be chosen if $B(A) > C(A)$, not otherwise.

Put this way, the problem of choice seems to be almost trivial. However, there are subtle considerations involved in the calculations of B and C. First, we must define more precisely B and C. These definitions may be expressed as:

B: maximum rupee amount you would be willing to pay to do A or choose A.

C: rupee value of the resources you must give up in order to do A.

1.2 Opportunity Cost

As the definition of C shows, the cost must be calculated with reference to the other alternatives that were forgone, to get a proper idea of the net benefit from the alternative in question. We therefore come to the critical notion of *opportunity cost*.

Definition: The *opportunity cost* of an action refers to the rupee value of the *next best* alternative forgone.

Usually, in choosing an alternative A, a number of alternatives will be forgone, say, B, C, D, etc. It is the next best alternative that should be considered to calculate the opportunity cost of A.

Example 1.1: Suppose you spend an extra hour watching TV. You could have studied either Physics or Mathematics or Botany during this one hour. By studying an extra hour, you would have got 5 more marks in Physics, 6 more marks in Mathematics, and 3 more marks in Botany. The opportunity cost of watching TV for one more hour is therefore the 6 marks you lost by not studying Mathematics during that time, since that is the best you could have done otherwise.

The concept of opportunity cost therefore differs from the ordinary notion of costs in one significant respect: instead of focusing on the alternative chosen, it focuses on the alternatives forgone. Thus, an accountant would concentrate on the cost of running a business. A consumer would consider the cost of a bar of soap as the amount she paid for it. On the other hand, in each of these instances, an economist would ask what else could have been done and what was the benefit associated with the alternative. Instead of running a business, should the entrepreneur take up a salaried job? What else could have been purchased with the amount spent on the bar of soap? And so on.

Some of the benefits and costs are implicit and some do not have any direct monetary valuation. One might easily overlook them in the computation of opportunity cost.

Example 1.2: Suppose you are deciding whether to go to a one-day cricket match between Sri Lanka and India.
   Benefit: The rupee value of the psychic satisfaction from going to the game is Rs 1000 (say).
Costs:

Explicit costs include: Rs 300 (price of a ticket)
       Rs 100 (cost of transportation)
       Rs 50 (cost of a coke and vada pao)
Implicit costs include: Rs 100 (if you had not gone to the game, you could have made this money in the share market)
       Rs 40 (you are a shy reclusive and normally dislike crowds)

Thus total opportunity costs = Explicit + Implicit costs = Rs 590. This is exceeded by the benefits and hence the decision should be to go to the match.
   In this example, the explicit cost element in the total opportunity cost of Rs 590 was easy to measure. The monetary values measure the resources forgone. Not buying the ticket would have freed up Rs 300 that could have been used to buy other things. And so on. One has to be especially careful to include implicit costs, however.

Some costs should not be included in the opportunity cost but often are. People include *sunk costs* in their calculations of the opportunity cost, even though they should not do so. A sunk cost is one that cannot be recovered, for example, the cost of repairing your car which broke down a day before the match. In practice, you might think that having incurred the expenditure, you are under an obligation to go to the match. However, this cost is non-recoverable and hence has no alternative uses. It should enter into the decision to attend the match since 'one should not cry over spilt milk'. Since the cost is non-recoverable, it has no alternative uses and hence its opportunity cost is zero. In other words, the cost of resources forgone here (the cost of repairing the car) cannot have any subsequent bearing on the decision made (to attend the match or not) and should not be included in the cost of taking the decision.

It is well-recognized that most people find it difficult to ignore sunk costs. Watching a movie to the end even after you are convinced that it stinks, just because you have spent money on the tickets, coke, and popcorn, is an example of this tendency. In many companies, once a project is launched, there is a tendency to keep on spending money on the project even long after it is apparent that the project is not going to be economically viable and should be abandoned. Countries suffer from the same sort of 'sunk cost fallacy'. France and Britain continued to invest in the Concorde (a supersonic aircraft no longer in production) long after it became clear that the project would generate little return. Casinos of course utilize this to their advantage, since the longer people keep on putting money in slot machines without any results; the more difficult it is for them to tear themselves away from these machines.

Example 1.3: The Opportunity Cost of Capital

Capital goods like plant or machinery are durable goods that can be used for a number of times. Therefore two problems are associated with the measurement of the cost of capital. One is the problem of allocation of the initial purchase cost over time and the other is that of taking account of changes in the value of capital over time. To take the question of allocation of costs over time, the simplest case is where the capital is rented. Then the rental cost measures the opportunity cost of capital in every period. If capital is purchased, the economist would amortize the cost of capital by working out how much the firm could charge others to rent the capital. Again, the rental cost is the appropriate measure.

The value of capital may change over time because of shifts in the supply and demand curves in the market for capital goods. This can drive a wedge between the historical cost and the actual cost at a point of time. To maximize profit, the firm must measure the cost of capital at its current opportunity cost and not the historical cost. If a firm bought a piece of equipment for Rs 30,000 but can only resell it for Rs 10,000, then the former value is a sunk cost and it is only the latter value that is relevant for the firm's decision.

But do people make such cost-benefit analyses? One answer is that they do so implicitly, sometimes without being aware of it. The other is that they will enrich both themselves and the society if they are more conscious of the costs and benefits from their actions.

We are assuming that people behave (or ought to behave) *rationally*, that is, take decisions on the basis of cost-benefit analyses. But there might be other ways of making decisions, like by simply tossing a coin, or by asking one's parents for advice (in this case, perhaps the person is assuming that the parents are in a better position to do the cost-benefit calculation). Economics takes rationality as a basic principle guiding people's behaviour, to lend generality to its analysis of economic actions and motives.

There might be some disagreement over what rationality really means. Does it refer to the 'self-interest standard of rationality', which says that rational persons assign significant weights only to those costs and benefits that affect directly themselves? This standard would preclude all charitable motives, motives to make other people happy, and so on. (Of course, one might say that charitable motives also flow from self-interest, from the pleasure that charity or its attendant publicity confers, compared with the actual costs of charity.) Or is it the 'present-aim standard of rationality', which requires the person to act efficiently in the pursuit of whatever goals he/she happens to be pursuing at the moment? This standard can accommodate charitable motives, but is too broad, explaining everything tautologically. For example, if a person with a heart condition likes cholesterol-rich food, this is still rational by present-aim standards, so long as the person does not pay more for the food than is necessary.

(contd)

(contd)

Economists have sometimes formalized rationality to mean that agents solve optimization problems, that is, they maximize or minimize certain objective functions subject to certain constraints. In other words, they try to do the best under the limitations faced by them. Thus, for example, they maximize their 'utility' subject to the fact that they cannot spend more than the income they receive. The posing of the individual's problem as one of optimization allows economists to be more precise in their formulations. But the proper specification of the objective function and the constraints is the key to such analysis.

Of late, attention has come to be focused on 'bounded rationality': this concept refers to human behaviour that is 'intendedly rational but only limitedly so' (Williamson). That is, human beings try to behave rationally. However, they are faced with both neurophysiological limits as well as language limits. The former refer to the power of the individuals to receive, sort, retrieve, and process information without error. Language limits refer to the inability of individuals to articulate their knowledge or feelings by the use of words, numbers or graphics in a way that permits them to be understood by others.

Thus, for example, if a supercomputer had access to all the relevant information, then it would do better than a human being in arriving at the best solution, because the latter would simply find it impossible to take advantage of all the information. Of course, a human being might still do better than a computer when *innovative thinking* is required for a solution.

Example 1.4: Consider voting. Each voter might feel that he/she would have no effect on the outcome. On the other hand, voting involves a cost in terms of time and transportation. Therefore, the self-interest standard of rationality dictates that one should not vote and in fact, in many countries voter turnout percentages are poor. How can society overcome this problem? Society can teach people from the childhood that they ought to vote, so that not voting induces a guilty feeling. By voting, one can avoid the guilty feeling and hence get a positive benefit from voting. Voting can also become a social occasion, where people derive pleasure from participating in a fair-like atmosphere and interacting with many other people.

1.3 The Production Possibilities Curve

It is not only individuals who must make choices from among alternatives. The economy at any point of time has a fixed amount of resources, and must decide what to produce and in what quantities with these resources. The opportunity cost of producing more of a commodity x is the bundle of other commodities that could have been produced with the resources used to produce this extra amount of x.

Suppose that a society can produce only two types of goods—'N-bombs' (military spending) and 'rice' (civilian spending). With the society's resources, various combinations of N-bombs and rice can be produced. Some possible combinations are

N-bombs (hundreds)	Rice (millions of tonnes)
100	0
90	40
70	70
40	90
0	100

These combinations can be represented by means of a *production possibilities curve (PPC)*. We notice a number of things about the production possibilities curve in the diagram below.

First, any point like *A inside* the area bounded by the curve is *inefficient*, in the sense that with the society's resources, more of at least one commodity can be produced at a point like *B on* the curve which lies to the northeast of *A*. A point like *B* is efficient because we cannot find a point anywhere inside or on the curve where more of at least one commodity and less of none can be produced compared to the bundle given by *B*.

Second, a point like *C* lying outside the PPC is *unattainable*: it represents a bundle that cannot be produced with the current resources of the society. All points on or inside the PPC (the shaded area) form the *feasible set*, that is, the set of bundles that can be produced with the current resources.

Third, the PPC is concave to the origin, that is, bowed away from the origin. This has an important implication in terms of the trade-offs that the society faces. First, consider a situation where only N-bombs are being produced. Now, the society decides to produce some rice, too, and makes fewer N-bombs, releasing some resources for rice growing. It makes sense to release those resources that are particularly suited for rice-production, for example, agricultural labourers rather than nuclear scientists. Hence, a small sacrifice in terms of N-bombs (1000 bombs) can yield substantial gains in terms of rice production (40 million tonnes of rice). However, as less and less resources are devoted to making bombs, and transferred into rice production, the addition to rice production per unit of sacrifice of bombs falls (if nuclear scientists are forced to produce rice, they turn out, not surprisingly, to be rather inept at it). The sacrifice of 2000 bombs (from 9000 to 7000) does not generate 80 million tonnes of rice, but only an additional 30 million tonnes (an increase from 40 to 70 million tonnes). This is reflected in the concave shape of the PPC. In other words, society faces increasing opportunity costs. As the production of rice increases, for any additional increase in the production of rice, more bombs must be sacrificed.

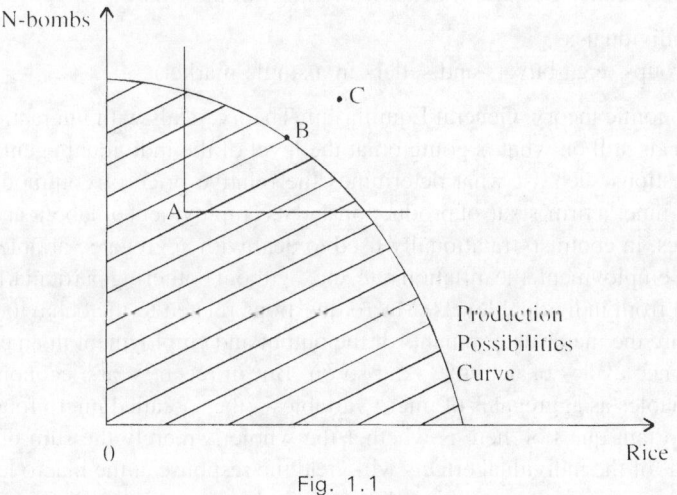

Fig. 1.1

1.4 Absolute Prices and Relative Prices

Prices in the market often act as the starting point for computing opportunity costs. If, for example, I am earning Rs 10,000 per month in a job currently, then my salary (the price of my labour) represents the opportunity cost of switching over to a new job or starting a business of my own. If a pair of Bata shoes is priced at Rs 599.95, then this represents the opportunity cost of purchasing this pair of shoes and not a pair of Arvind denims. But we have to carefully distinguish between *absolute* and *relative* prices. The absolute price is just the price in nominal terms. But in calculating opportunity costs, the price of one good in terms of another or in terms of a basket of goods is what matters. These are the relative prices. Suppose all absolute prices are going up, but the price of edible oil is rising faster than other prices. Then the opportunity cost of buying edible oils is increasing and that of (say) rice is decreasing, even though absolute prices of both edible oils and rice are increasing.

Comparing Absolute and Relative Prices, 1993–4 vs 2004–5

(Wholesale Prices)

Good	1993–4	2004–5	Changes in Absolute Price	Changes in Price Relative to 'All Commodities'
All commodities	100	187	87%	–
Foodgrains	100	177	77%	–10%
Textiles	100	136	36%	–51%
Fuel, power, and lubricants	100	280	180%	+93%

Source: Economic Survey, 2005–6.

An analysis of the index of wholesale prices for India during the years 1993–4 to 2004–5 reveals that while all prices went up in absolute terms, the relative price of foodgrains and textiles showed declines while that of fuel, power, and lubricants increased relative to all commodities.

1.5 Microeconomics and Macroeconomics

In the definition of Microeconomics, we asserted that it deals with choices at the individual level. Microeconomics is so-called because it deals with things in the small:

- behaviour of individuals;
- behaviour of groups (e.g., buyers and sellers in a single market).

A part of microeconomic theory, General Equilibrium Theory, deals with interactions in all markets. However, the focus is still on what is going on at the level of the individual agent. Microeconomics therefore asks questions such as: what determines the relative price of commodities like rice and wheat? What determines a firm's rate of production and its employment of labour and capital services?

Macroeconomics, in contrast, traditionally used to deal with aggregate variables like the GDP of a nation, aggregate employment, the inflation rate, etc., without bothering particularly about how these were to be derived from individual levels. Macro questions related to the behaviour of the economy as a whole. What are the major determinants of the output and employment in an economy? Why do economies experience cycles of activity? And so on. But in recent years, economists are trying to analyse macro variables as aggregates of micro variables—the so-called micro foundations of macro analysis. One important question here is whether the whole is merely the sum of the parts, so that proper 'summation' of the individual effects will yield the response at the macro level. For example, is the aggregate demand curve for a commodity merely the sum of the individual demand curves?

1.6 Positive and Normative Economics

While studying microeconomics, it is useful to keep the distinction between *positive* and *normative economics* in mind. Positive economics deals with causes and consequences, for example, why do people demand less of a commodity when its price goes up, what is the probable effect on cigarette prices of an increase in *bidi* prices, etc. Normative economics is concerned with questions involving value judgements, for example, should mergers between two firms be allowed, should efforts be made to discourage the consumption of tobacco and alcohol, etc. Sometimes, positive and normative elements in an analysis are mixed up and care should be taken to separate out the two. Often, to make normative judgements, one must first carry out a positive analysis to find out what is going to happen. Would the merger between firms have an 'anti-competitive' effect? Would it, on the other hand, result in increased research and development expenditure? After these questions are answered, one can try to assign relative weights to these probable consequences to arrive at a normative judgement about the desirability of the merger.

Topics for Discussion

1. What determines a student's decision to go for higher education (B.Tech to M.Tech M.A. to Ph.D.)? Is there any reason to believe that a higher percentage of students in the Arts streams will be going on to do Ph.Ds compared to those in the Commerce or Engineering streams?
2. Why do banks pay interest to their depositors? Do you believe that usury is an evil practice and should be forbidden?

Exercise

1. You have purchased a personal computer for Rs 40,000. The next week the manufacturer announces a new computer with twice the power for Rs 30,000. You can trade in your old computer for a new one by paying an additional Rs 20,000. What should you do in this situation? Not buy the new computer for a year or so, or accept the trade-in offer?
2. Sanjay and Sujay are planning to go to Goa for summer vacations for one week. Since both are rational economic gents, they have calculated the costs of flying versus driving:

    Flying:
        Airline ticket   Rs 2500 per person
        Car rental   Rs 600 per day

    Driving:
        Petrol   Rs 1000
        Lodging while in transit   Rs 500 for a double room
        Wear and tear on car   Rs 500

(a) The total cost of flying to Goa is Rs _____ and the total cost of driving there is Rs _____. The option which should be chosen is _____ (flying/driving).
(b) If Sanjay dislikes car trips and is willing to pay a maximum of Rs 1500 to avoid a car trip, then the total cost of driving is Rs _____ and the two gents should opt for _____ (flying/driving).

3. Bharat has the option of either working on his own land as a farmer or being employed as a supervisor in Shatrughna's farm. The table below lists the various costs and revenues for the two options in a given period of time:

First option: Self-employment as a farmer			
Revenue		Costs	
Revenue from sales of produce	1500	Seeds and fertilizer	90
		Capital costs	90
		Hired labour	80
Total revenue	1500	Total costs	260

Second option: Employment as a supervisor in Shatrughna's farm			
Salary	1600	Travel costs	500

(a) The opportunity cost of self-employment as a farmer for Bharat is Rs _____.

(b) Self-employment as a farmer generates an economic _____ (profit/loss) of Rs _____ for Bharat. (define economic profit/loss as revenue minus all opportunity costs)

4. A recent engineering graduate turns down a job offer at Rs 30,000 per year to start his own business. He will invest Rs 50,000 of his own money, which has been in a bank earning 7 per cent interest per year. The expenses related to the business will be Rs 65,000 a year. What will be the opportunity cost of running the business?

5. Suppose that random access memory can be added to your computer at the cost of Rs 50 per megabyte. Suppose also that the value to you, measured in terms of your willingness to pay, of an additional megabyte of memory is Rs 200 for the first megabyte and then falls by one-half for each additional megabyte. How many megabytes of memory should you purchase?

6. Ayesha has purchased a Rs 500 ticket to a show featuring Ajay Devgan. On the day of the show, she is invited to a welcome-home party for a cousin returning from abroad. She cannot attend both the show and the party. If she had known about the party before buying the ticket, she would have chosen the party over the show.

True or False: It follows that if she is rational, she will go to the party anyway. Explain.

2 Demand and Supply

Even if individuals in an economy behave rationally, there might be no guarantee that their actions are coordinated and lead to the achievement of social objectives. In fact, rationality would seem to presuppose selfish behaviour which would rule out the attainment of social goals. Adam Smith's great insight was to show that a system of smoothly functioning *markets* could ensure that

- individual economic agents reach their own goals behaving rationally;
- at the same time their actions are consistent with each other and lead to the attainment of social goals.

This is so-called *invisible hand doctrine*: the invisible hand of the marketplace coordinates and guides the numerous unrelated decisions of individual agents towards the achievement of social objectives.

Definition: A *market* consists of the buyers and sellers of a good or service.

Sometimes markets have a specific time and location, for example, the *hats* which meet on certain days of the week for specified time periods in certain locations. On the other hand, the Bombay Stock Exchange does not have a fixed location in the sense those buyers and sellers are dispersed all over India (and even outside India).

In a market, the interaction of buyers and sellers determines the prices that are established and the quantities that are transacted. The two sides of a market are represented through the forces of demand and supply. We now turn to a consideration of these forces.

2.1 The Market Demand Curve

The market *demand schedule* shows the amounts of the commodity per period that buyers are prepared to buy at different prices. The market *demand function* expresses this relationship between quantities demanded and prices in compact functional form. When the relationship between price and quantity demanded is plotted as a graph, we get a *demand curve*.

A demand curve therefore represents in the form of a graph the quantity demanded at each price. Alternatively, it might be thought of as representing the *maximum price* that buyers are willing to pay for each quantity. Remember that the quantity demanded must always be expressed in per period term (quantity demanded per week/per month/per year etc.) though we may not sometimes represent this in our graphs.

Example 2.1: Consider the demand for toothpastes. Let the demand function be $Q^d = 10 - P$, where P is the price per unit and Q^d is the quantity demanded in some units (say number of tubes). Q^d refers implicitly to some period of time. Your demand for toothpastes must be expressed as either one tube per month (say) or 12 tubes per year. The demand schedule then is, for some representative prices, as given below

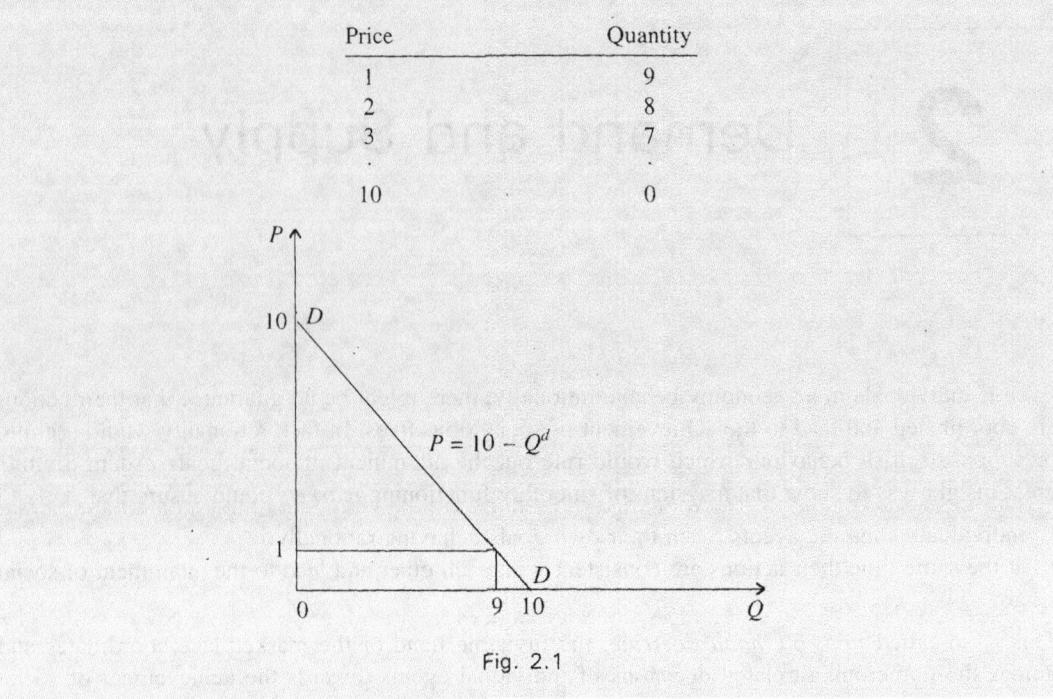

Price	Quantity
1	9
2	8
3	7
.	.
10	0

Fig. 2.1

For reasons of convenience, to draw the demand curve, economists first express price as a function of quantity, thereby deriving the *inverse demand curve*: $P = 10 - Q^d$. One can then measure P on the y-axis and Q^d on the x-axis and represent points on the inverse demand curve by the curve labelled *DD*.

In our example, the demand curve is linear, which means that its slope—given by the first derivative dQ^d/dP—is the same (here it is—1) everywhere on the demand curve, that is, it is independent of P or Q^d. For non-linear curves, the slope of the demand curve will change from point to point on the demand curve. In general, we do not expect the demand curve to be linear, that is, a straight line. However, for illustrative purposes, we will deal with linear demand curves to keep things simple.

The downward sloping demand curve that has been drawn above exemplifies the *law of demand*: Quantity demanded decreases as price increases. The slope is negative (but may not be constant) at all points of the demand curve. Now, remember that we are discussing about the market demand curve that has been aggregated from individual demand curves for different buyers in the market. It will be seen later that it is theoretically possible for individual demand curves to be upward sloping. In practice, such demand curves are a rarity. Even if some individual demand curves are upward sloping, if there are enough buyers with downward sloping demand curves, we expect the market demand curve to be downward sloping.

It is obvious from even casual observation or introspection that demand depends on many things. In general, the quantity demanded is expected to depend on

- own price
- incomes[1]

---

[1] Since we are discussing a market demand curve, which is derived from the demand curves of individual buyers, 'income' here can refer to the average income of these buyers or their total income or some other measure summarizing the effect of the incomes of the buyers.

- tastes and preferences
- prices of 'related' commodities
- expectations, etc.

In functional notation,

$$Q^d = f(I, T, P_r, E, P),$$

where I refers to income, T to some measure of tastes and preferences, P_r to prices of related commodities, and E to expectations.

It is clear that we can express Q^d only as a function of P if we assume that the other things like I, T, etc. are not changing:

$$Q^d = f(P; I = i, T = t, P_r = p_r, E = e),$$

where i, t, p_r, and e are particular values of the variables I, T, P_r, and E respectively.

This is called the assumption of *ceteris paribus* ('other things remaining the same'). It is made not to neglect the effect of all the factors that might affect demand, but to break the analysis of the demand curve into a number of transparent stages. First, we try to find out the effect on demand if the own price, P, alone changes. Then we allow the other variables to change and investigate the effects of these.

It is convenient to refer to Q and P as *variables*, and the others as *parameters*. A parametric change thus leads to a *shift in the entire curve*. In our example, the number 10 captures the total influence on demand of all the other things that are being kept fixed. If any of the 'other things' change, then the *entire demand curve shifts*. It is very important therefore to distinguish between *movements* along an unchanging demand curve and *shifts* in the curve itself. When a movement along the curve is being analysed, it is customary to refer to a change in *quantity demanded*. A *change in demand*, on the other hand, refers to a shift in the demand curve.

How do we expect the 'other things' to influence demand?

- If I (income) increase, we expect more to be demanded at every price for 'normal' goods. However, there may be some 'inferior' goods whose demand falls as income increases. For example, an increase in the incomes of poor farmers might lead them to buy more of rice and wheat and less of coarse cereals like ragi, jowar, and bajra.
- If T (tastes and preferences) change such that buyers like a commodity more, again the same thing will happen.
- If the price of a *substitute* commodity rises, we expect the demand to rise, too (as price of coffee rises, the demand curve for tea shifts upward and to the right). If the price of a *complementary* good rises, we expect the demand to fall (as price of sugar rises the demand curve for tea shifts downward and to the left).
- An expectation that prices will rise in the future shifts the demand curve to the right.

The simple thing to understand and remember is this: a change in commodity's own price by itself can only represent a movement along with the demand curve and not a shift in the curve; however, a change in any of the 'other things' will lead to a shift of the demand curve.

Example 2.2: Suppose that the demand for tea depends on its own price as well as the price of coffee, P_c: $Q_t^d = -P_t + 10P_c$. Initially, suppose that P_c = Rs 4. Then the equation of the demand curve is $Q_t^d = -P_t + 40$. The equation of the inverse demand curve is $P_t = 40 - Q_t^d$ and it is represented by the curve DD. Now, if the price of coffee rises to Rs 5, the demand curve becomes $Q_t^d = -P_t + 50$ and the equation of the inverse demand curve $P_t = 50 - Q_t^d$. It can be seen that the entire inverse demand curve has shifted upwards because of the increase in the price of coffee. The new curve is labelled $D'D'$ in Fig. 2.2.

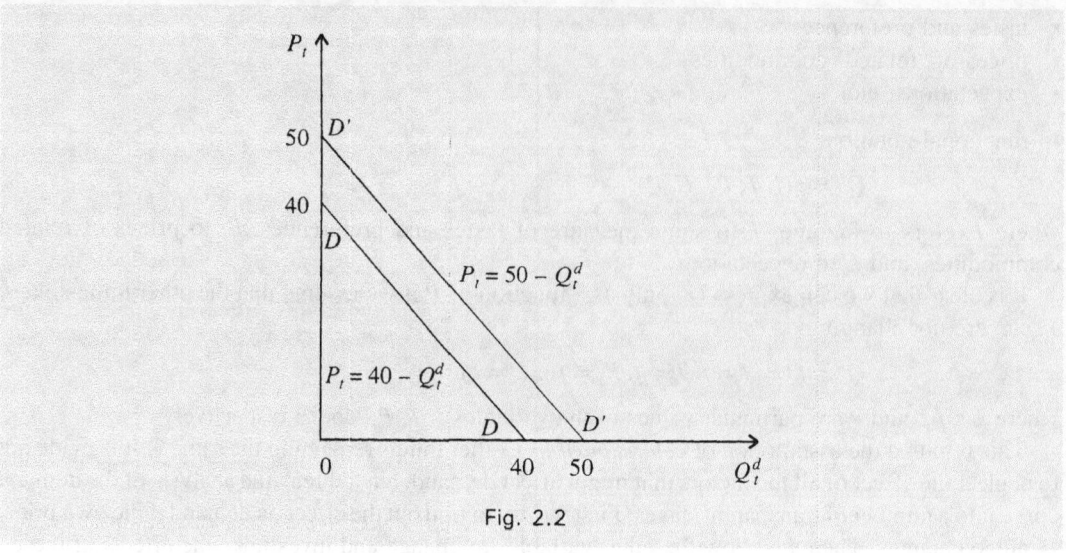

Fig. 2.2

2.2 The Market Supply Curve

The market *supply schedule* shows the amounts of the commodity that sellers are prepared to supply at different prices. The market *supply function* expresses this relationship between quantities supplied and prices in compact functional form. When the relationship between price and quantity supplied is plotted as a graph, we get a *supply curve*.

A supply curve therefore represents in the form of a graph the quantity supplied at each price. Alternatively, it might be thought of as representing the *minimum price* that sellers want for supplying each quantity.

Example 2.3: Let the supply function be $Q^s = P$, where P is the price per unit and Q^s is the quantity supplied in some units (say kilograms). Q^s refers implicitly to some period of time. As before, the supply of toothpastes must be expressed as either one tube per month (say) or 12 tubes per year and the period chosen should be the same as the period chosen for the demand curve.

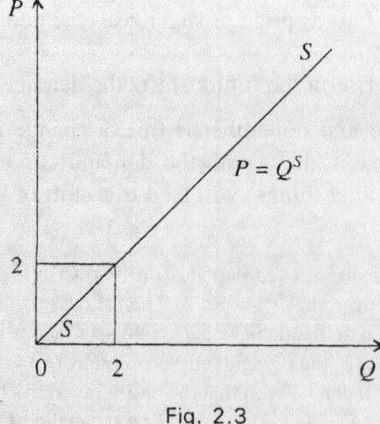

Fig. 2.3

The supply schedule then is, for some representative prices,

Price	Quantity
1	1
2	2
3	3
.	.
.	.
10	10

Again, for reasons of convenience, to draw the supply curve, economists first express price as a function of quantity, thereby deriving the *inverse supply curve*: $P = Q^s$. One can then measure P on the y-axis and Q^s on the x-axis. The curve is labelled *SS*.

The upward sloping supply curve that has been drawn above exemplifies the *law of supply*: Quantity supplied increases as price increases. It will be seen later that it is possible to have supply curves that are *backward bending*, that contain a downward sloping segment, so that quantity supplied falls as price increases.

Like demand, supply also depends on many things. In general, the quantity supplied is expected to depend on

- own price,
- technological knowledge,
- input prices,
- prices of goods that are related in production,
- expectations, etc.

In functional notation,

$$Q^s = g(T_e, P_I, P_R, E_s, P),$$

where T_e refers to technical knowledge, P_I to input prices, P_R to prices of goods that are related in production, and E_s to expectations.

We have to make the ceteris paribus assumption to obtain the supply function:

$$Q^s = f(P; T_e = t_e, P_I = p_i, E_s = e_s),$$

where t_e, p_i, p_r and e_s are particular values of the variables T_e, P_I, P_R, and E_s respectively. In general, even though we do not expect the supply curve also to be linear, for illustrative purposes, we will deal with linear supply curves to keep things simple.

We have again to distinguish between *movements* along an unchanging supply curve and *shifts* in the curve itself. When a movement along the curve is being analysed, it is customary to refer to a change in *quantity supplied*. A *change in supply*, on the other hand, refers to a shift in the supply curve.

Example 2.4: Suppose that the equation of the supply curve is $Q^s = 2 + 3P_I + P$. Initially $P_I = 2$, then $Q^s = 8 + P$. Next, suppose that P_I changes and becomes 4. It can be seen that the equation of the supply curve becomes $Q^s = 14 + P$ and therefore the entire supply curve shifts.

How do we expect the 'other things' to influence supply?

- A change in technology that allows the commodity to be produced more cheaply should shift the supply curve downwards and to the right. This happens when an improvement in technology makes some of the inputs more productive.

- If input prices increase, exactly the opposite should happen.
- Goods may be either substitutes or complements in production. If the price of rice increases while that of wheat remains the same, we expect some farmers to switch from growing wheat to growing rice, and the supply curve for wheat should shift to the left. Wheat and rice are therefore *substitutes* in production. On the other hand, if more crude oil is sought to be produced, the production of natural gas as a by-product would probably increase. Crude oil and natural gas are *complements* in production.
- If firms expect the price of their product to rise in the future, they may withhold some of the good today, reducing the supply of the good in the current period.

In addition, we may note that an increase in the number of firms in the industry or an increase in the productive capacity of firms is likely to result in a rightward shift in the supply curve.

2.3 Market Equilibrium

What will be the actual price in the market and the actual quantity transacted? *Market equilibrium* occurs *when the prevailing price equates quantity demanded to quantity supplied.* The equilibrium refers to the (price, quantity) pair at which this takes place. At such a price, buyers find that they are able to buy exactly the amount that they are demanding at the prevailing price and suppliers are able to sell exactly the amount they are willing to supply at the prevailing price. In other words, there is no incentive for anyone in the market to change their behaviour.

The market equilibrium is therefore solved for by setting $Q^d = Q^s$, and solving for the resultant P. In diagrammatic terms, equilibrium is reached at the intersection of the (inverse) demand and supply curves DD and SS, since at the point of intersection, the quantities demanded and supplied are equal.

> **Example 2.5:** In our earlier examples, $Q^d = 10 - P$ and $Q^s = P$. Setting $Q^d = Q^s$, we get $10 - P = P$; which gives us the equilibrium price $P^* = 5$. The equilibrium quantity then will be $Q^* = Q^d = Q^s = 5$.

What happens if the market price is other than 5? In Fig. 2.4, for any $P > P^*$, we can see that $Q^d < Q^s$, so that there is *excess supply* in the market. For any $P < P^*$ on the other hand, $Q^d > Q^s$, so

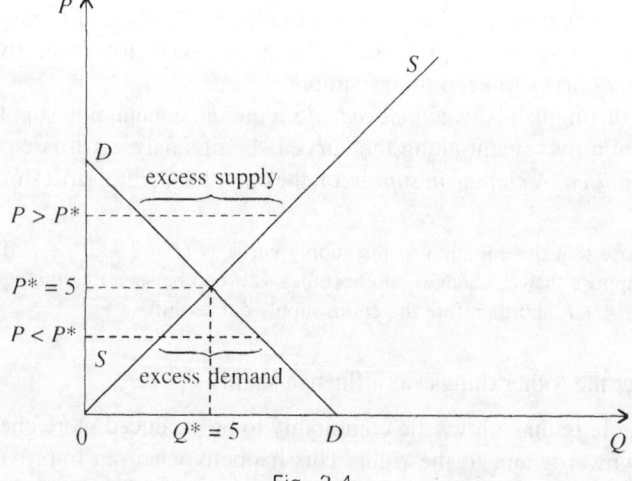

Fig. 2.4

that there is *excess demand* in the market. An excess supply means that suppliers cannot sell off everything they want to at the current market price and some of them will try to reduce prices to sell off their unsold stocks. When there is excess demand, some buyers are unable to satisfy their demand, and will bid up prices to induce sellers to supply them the desired amount of goods. In either case, there are forces in the market pushing the actual price towards the equilibrium price.

We can now examine possible changes in equilibrium. If a market is initially in equilibrium and then certain parameters change, we would like to be able to predict the directions of change. A particular market equilibrium is valid only for a fixed set of demand and supply curves. If these curves shift, then a different equilibrium will obtain. Let us cite at a few examples.

1. In Fig. 2.5, the inverse demand curve shifts from DD to $D'D'$. At the initial equilibrium price P^*, there is an excess demand EA which tends to push up the price. But as the price increases, it induces more supply from the sellers (represented by a movement along the supply curve) and tends to reduce demand. The new equilibrium is reached at the price-quantity pair of (P', Q').

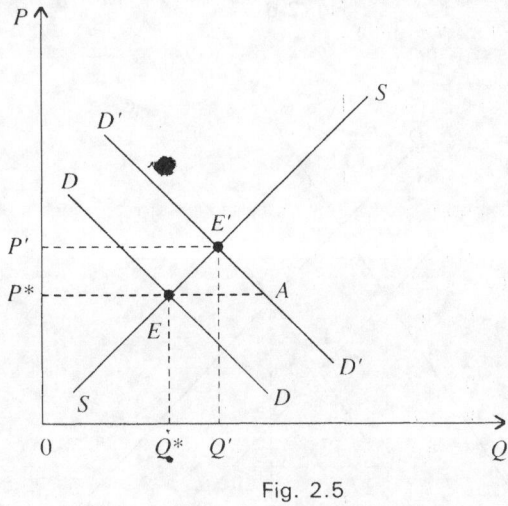

Fig. 2.5

2. Consider a ban on imports of a commodity. Suppose that the government bans the import of poultry from abroad to prevent the possibility of the spread of bird flu. In Fig. 2.6, this shifts the total supply of poultry in the country without a ban (S) to S', which represents domestic supply of poultry alone. As a result, the price increases from P to P' and quantity falls from Q to Q'.

3. Consider the market for apples. Suppose that two things happen together: (a) there is a blight in apple orchards which shifts the supply curve to the left (from SS to $S'S'$) and (b) doctors find that eating apples is not demonstrably good for one's health, so that the demand curve shifts also to the left (from DD to $D'D'$). It can be seen quite easily that these two effects together will always lead to a fall in equilibrium quantity, but the effect on price remains ambiguous. The shift in the supply curve tends to raise the price and the shift in the demand curve tends to lower the price. The final effect on price depends on the relative extent of the shifts in these two curves.

In markets where demand and supply curves are rapidly shifting, the market may not be able to settle down to any equilibrium and actual prices and quantities will continue to be disequilibrium prices and quantities.

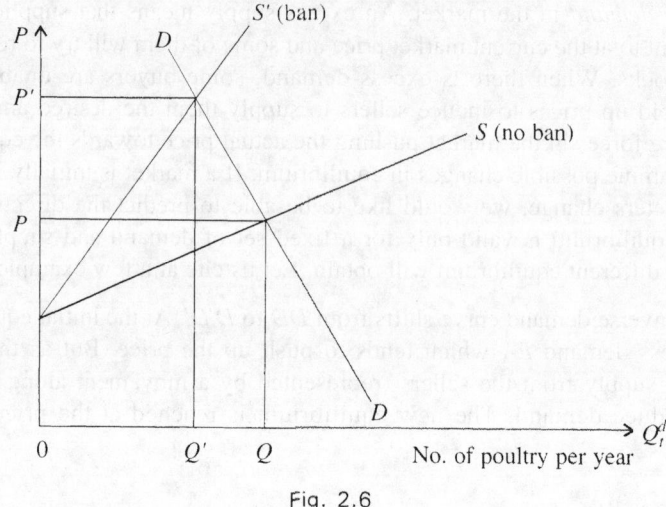

Fig. 2.6

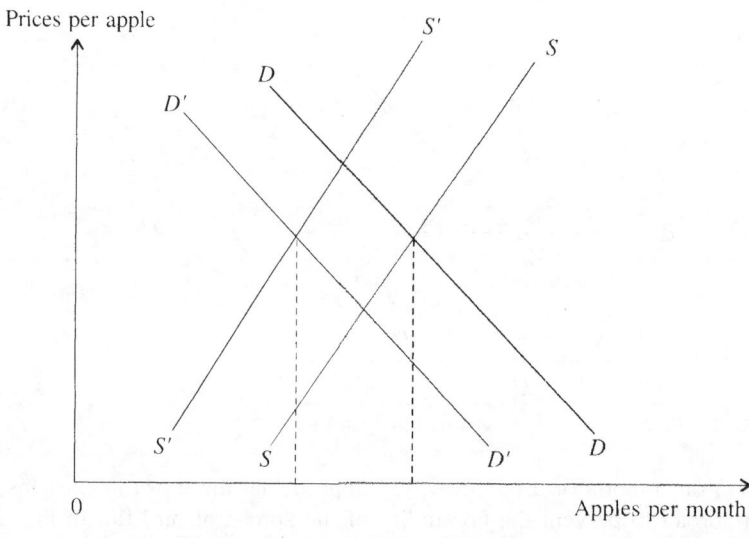

Fig. 2.7

This discussion makes it clear that one must be careful to interpret the demand and supply schedules. The demand schedule, for example, is the result of a hypothetical experiment: it is as if we had taken a list of prices and gone around asking buyers how much they would be prepared to buy at each price. Then, we totalled the quantities given by the different buyers at each price and came up with the demand schedule. But what about the actual quantities bought and sold in the market? If we go to a market, observe different prices at different times, and then add up the actual quantities sold at these prices, then (a) things other then price affecting demand might have changed so that the different price-quantity pairs might represent different demand curves and (b) the actual quantities are the equilibrium quantities, reflecting both demand and supply conditions. The same observations remain valid for supply curves. To emphasize the point once more, the actual transactions in the market are

(contd)

(contd)
the result of both demand and supply forces and cannot (except in special cases) be used to derive either the demand or the supply schedule.

Markets also operate at different levels. Most consumers go to the local grocery store to make their purchases, like they deal with retailers. The retail seller in turn buys from the wholesale trader. Wholesale prices are responsive to many things. When the government tries to impose a service tax and transport operators go on a strike, the effect is first felt at the wholesale level. But retail level prices may take some time to change. The practice of setting fixed, rather rigid, prices, is called *posted-offer pricing*. Prices are not changed often at the retail level because there is a cost to changing prices. If a demand change is temporary, for example, the retailer does not want to run the risk of alienating customers by marking up prices.

Some prices are also set by *bargaining*, for example, vegetable prices in the local market. The seller quotes a price, but buyers recognize that counteroffers may be made and prices brought down from the opening level. When there are many buyers and sellers in the market, there is less scope for bargaining if agents are more or less well-informed about prices. A seller's price is benchmarked against that of others. Both buyers and sellers have the option to deal with others at 'standardized' prices. But in situations where smaller numbers of agents are involved, bargaining takes place, because no price acts as a standard. The extent of bargaining also depends on the opportunity cost of time and money saved. A retired person's opportunity cost of time spent in bargaining is low, and she will spend longer time in bargaining.

From now onwards, we use the terms 'inverse demand (supply) curve' and 'demand (supply) curve', interchangeably, unless it is necessary to clearly distinguish between the two.

2.4 Existence, Uniqueness, and Stability of Equilibrium

One might at this stage ask whether at least one equilibrium will always exist. Fig. 2.8 shows that even if the demand curve is downward sloping and the supply curve is upward sloping, there may not be any equilibrium. The demand and supply curves do not intersect even at zero price they intersect at a negative price, but for most commodities, a negative price does not carry any meaning. Thus no equilibrium might exist.

Fig. 2.9 shows a second possibility. The supply curve is 'backward bending' and as a result, there are two equilibria, that is, two points E_1 and E_2 at which the curves intersect. Equilibrium is not unique, and without further information, one cannot predict what price and quantity will be established in the market.

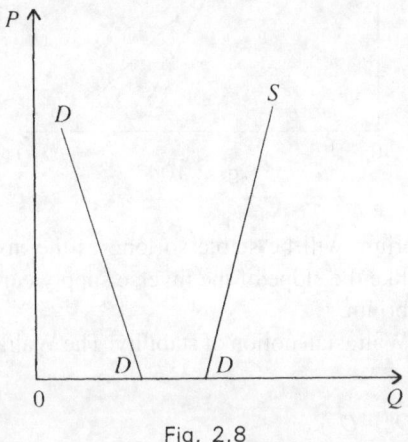

Fig. 2.8

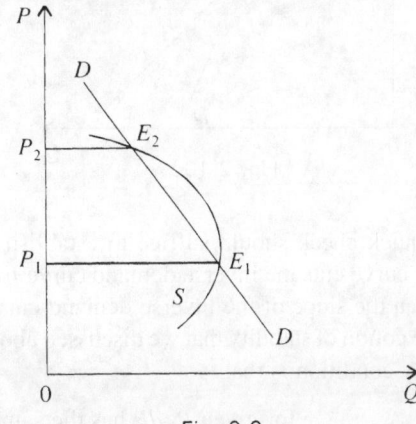

Fig. 2.9

There is, however, one critical distinction between E_1 and E_2. Consider a price P slightly above P_1. At this price, supply is greater than demand and there is a pressure on price to fall and move towards P_1. Similarly, if $P < P_1$, there is an upward pressure on the price. Hence, we say that E_1 is a stable equilibrium: a movement away from the equilibrium sets in motion forces that tend to bring the market back to equilibrium. Next, consider a price P slightly less than P_2. At this price, quantity supplied is greater than quantity demanded, and price tends to fall and move away from P_2. Similarly, the price tends to increase if it is initially greater than P_2. Therefore, E_2 is an unstable equilibrium: any movement away from E_2 is aggravated and the market is pushed further and further away from E_2.

What happens if the demand curve is upward sloping and/or the supply curve is downward sloping? The four possibilities are shown below.

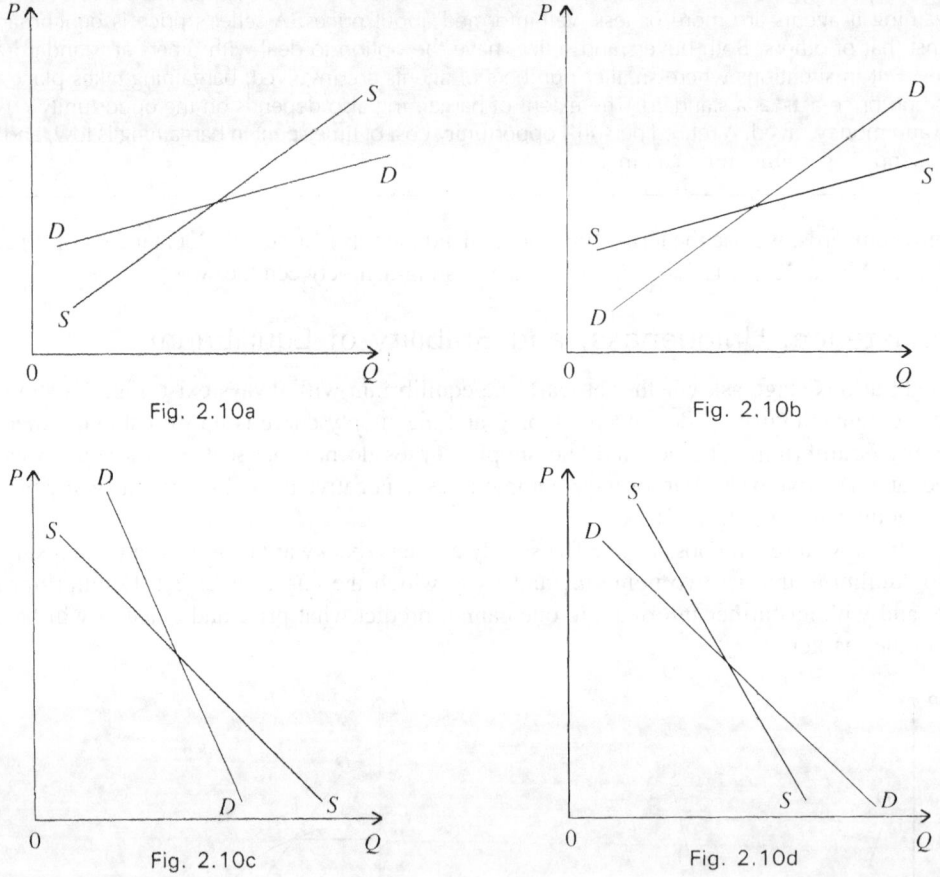

Fig. 2.10a

Fig. 2.10b

Fig. 2.10c

Fig. 2.10d

A quick check should suffice to establish the equilibrium will be stable so long as the inverse supply curve cuts the inverse demand curve *from above*, like the slope of the inverse supply curve is less than the slope of the inverse demand curve at equilibrium.

The notion of stability that we discussed above was the Walrasian notion of stability. The Walrasian stability condition is that

for given P, dP has the same sign as $(Q^d - Q^s)$.

This means that price tends to increase if there is excess demand and fall if there is excess supply. An alternative concept of stability is that of Marshallian stability, which requires that when the demand price is greater (smaller) than the supply price, the quantity supplied will be increasing (decreasing):

$$\text{for given } Q, \, dQ \text{ has the same sign as } (P^d - P^s).$$

Marshallian stability, in contrast to Walrasian stability, requires that the slope of the supply curve be greater than the slope of the demand curve at equilibrium, that is, the inverse supply curve cut the inverse demand curve *from below*. This can be checked from Fig. 2.9 above.

2.5 Welfare Properties of the Equilibrium

Suppose that everything else is fixed and equilibrium is established. This equilibrium will have the desirable property that no reallocation of the commodity can improve some agent's position without harming at least one other agent. The free market equilibrium is therefore *Pareto-optimum* (this notion of optimum or a 'best' state is due to the economist Vilfredo Pareto).

Pareto had realized the difficulty, if not the impossibility, of comparing the well-beings of different persons. However, even without making such comparisons, one can still say that certain situations are superior to others. Thus if starting from a situation Z, it is possible to make at least one person better off and nobody worse off in another situation X, then clearly X is superior to Z. And if no other situation W exists which is superior to X using the same criterion, then X is a 'best' situation in some sense, and is said to be Pareto-optimal.

Compared to the equilibrium at E, any other price-quantity combination will be such that at least somebody can be made better off and nobody worse off merely by redistributing the commodity in question. For example, in Fig. 2.11, start with a price of Rs 2. At this price, only two units will be supplied in the market, and there will be excess demand. If only two units are available in the market, buyers are willing to pay a maximum price of Rs 8 per unit. Now, a buyer in the market can offer to pay a price of Rs 5 for an extra unit. The seller can gain Rs 3 by accepting this offer and supplying one more unit. The buyer gains Rs 3, since she was willing to pay up to Rs 8. Thus the gap between the buyers' price of Rs 8 and sellers' price of Rs 2 creates the possibility of sharing in Rs 6 of gains. Hence there is another price-quantity combination that is *Pareto superior* to the original (2, 2)

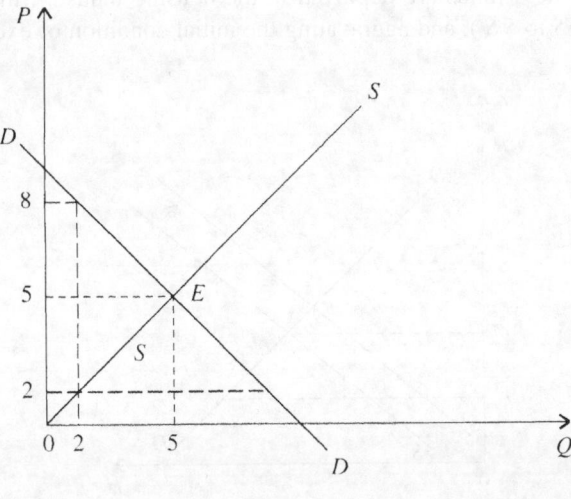

Fig. 2.11

combination. Such transactions are not possible once the equilibrium pair of $E = (5, 5)$ is reached. E is then a Pareto-optimum situation.

But this result definitely does not establish anything about the 'fairness' of the equilibrium. The market demand curve is aggregated from the individual demand curves, and we have seen that each individual demand curve depends on the income level of the agent. Thus each market demand curve presupposes a particular *distribution of incomes* among the agents. The prevailing income distribution might be considered very unfair by society. It might involve most agents having very little incomes and unable to afford the price established in equilibrium.

2.6 Government Interventions and their Effects

Sometimes Governments try to correct this situation by engaging in direct actions aimed at changing the existing pattern of income distribution. They also often try to achieve the results indirectly, by interfering with the market processes. Examples are *rent control laws* and *minimum wage legislation*. Governments also impose *taxation* on the purchase and sale of certain commodities and sometimes impose quotas on importers. We next try to use the tools of demand and supply analysis to get some insights into the probable effects of such government interventions.

2.6.1 Rent Control Laws

Governments sometimes try to set a *ceiling* on rents in the belief that rents in free market equilibrium would be too high for most people to afford renting flats/apartments. Thus in the market for housing, the maximum rent allowed is r' which is less than the equilibrium level $r*$ (see Fig. 2.12).

At r', there will be excess demand for housing. Who gains from this arrangement? The people who are able to get housing at the low rents. But the unsatisfied demand shows up in various ways. First, landlord charge high deposits and 'pugrees'. Second, illegal transactions take place in the form of charging high rents without issuing corresponding receipts. Landlords also might use their discretion to screen applicants, for example, some landlords might rent out flats only to vegetarians.

More importantly, in the long run, the smaller value from housing as an asset might discourage landlords from providing adequate maintenance services. It is not uncommon to see houses in dilapidated conditions when rent control act is enforced vigorously. Over time, funds are switched to other types of investment and less funds are deployed in the housing industry, thus shifting the supply curve to the left (from SS to $S'S'$), and aggravating the initial condition of excess demand.

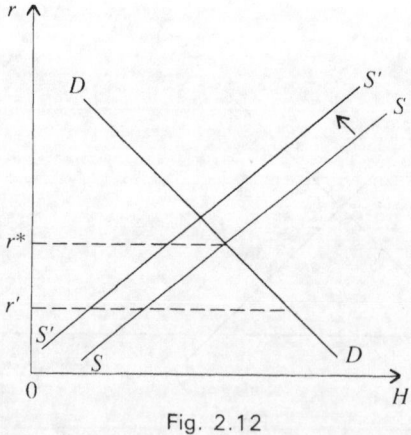

Fig. 2.12

In India, different states have passed different rent control acts. Generally, for pre-war buildings, rents are frozen as of a specified year without any provision for subsequent increases in rents. For post-war buildings, rents are determined on the basis of specified returns on total investment in housing. In many rent acts, there is a provision of a rent control holiday on new buildings for 5–7 years from the date of first letting out. A feature common to various acts is protection provided to tenants against eviction. Normally, if the tenant goes on paying the rent regularly, eviction is possible only if the premises are required for the personal use of the landlord, or the premises become unsafe or unfit for human habitation and repairs cannot be carried out without eviction.

The gross returns that are allowed on post-war buildings vary from 6–8.25 per cent on the total cost of land and building at the time of construction. This is much less than returns from other sources (for example, fixed deposit interest rates till recently could be 12–13 per cent). Moreover, some acts do not allow landlords to recover the increase in local taxes and rates from tenants.

It is clear that construction of housing for rental is strongly discouraged under these acts. In all the major cities in India, housing for long term rental is difficult to get. In Mumbai, for example, a system of 'leave and licence' has developed, under which apartments are rented out for 11 months at a time. Moreover, landlords have the incentive to neglect maintenance, so that the housing becomes unsafe and then can be pulled down and the vacant land sold at a huge profit.

Source: Devendra B. Gupta, 'Urban Housing in India', 1985, World Bank Staff Working Papers, No. 730.

2.6.2 Minimum Wage Legislation

In contrast to rent control laws that set upper bounds on prices, minimum wage legislation is under-taken to ensure that wages paid to workers do not fall below a certain minimum. Hence, in the labour market, a *floor* is set on wages, that is, wages are not allowed to fall below a certain level.

Consider Fig. 2.13. In the absence of government intervention, the equilibrium wage rate would be w^*. But the government decrees that the wage rate cannot fall below w'. At this wage rate, there is excess supply of labour. Since some workers would have been willing to work for lower wages, a 'contract' system of wages tends to develop. Workers are employed for smaller periods or in smaller numbers, so that the minimum wage provision does not apply, or they are not paid other benefits like medical benefits, PF, gratuity, etc. In the longer run, employers might switch to more machine-intensive processes to economize on labour costs.

Note that if $r' > r^*$ or $w' < w^*$, then the price ceiling or floor is not *binding*: the equilibrium price will not violate the constraint imposed by the government, and therefore the government's action is not expected to change the free market outcome substantially.

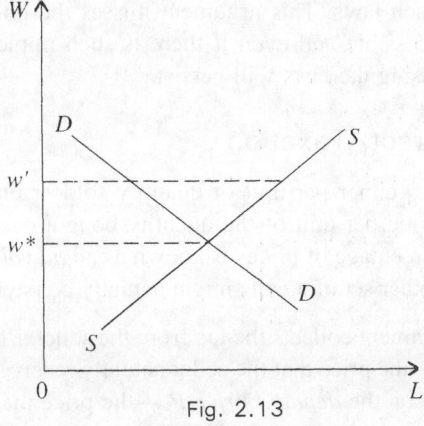

Fig. 2.13

The Central Government in India sets minimum wages for workers in different employments at different rates for different categories of workers (unskilled, semi-skilled, skilled, etc.) The minimum wages also vary by location, being the highest for the major cities. Some illustrative numbers for the Central Government set minimum wages are given below. In addition, the state governments also fix minimum wages for certain employments. There are now 1139 employments for which minimum wages have been fixed, either by the Central Government or by the State Governments.

Name of Employment	Minimum Wages for Lowest Unskilled Worker in Area A
Agriculture	Rs 56.09
Construction	Rs 34.96
Stone breaking or crushing	Rs 34.96

There is evidence to believe that an increased 'casualization' of workers is taking place in India. Mukhopadhyay (1992) quotes NSS figures to show that the percentage of 'casual' workers in urban areas of India increased from 10.1 per cent in 1972–3 to 14.6 per cent in 1987–8; in rural areas it increased from 22 per cent to 31.4 per cent during the same period. However, it has yet to be established that such casualization is due to the existence of minimum wages alone. Other factors seem to be equally important, one especially important factor being the absence of a so-called 'exit policy'. The latter refers to the near-impossibility of retrenching 'regular' labour in organized industry.

Sources: Ministry of Labour, Government of India, Annual Report, 1996–7.
Swapna Mukhopadhyay, 1992, Casualization of Labour in India: Concept, Incidence and Policy Options, *The Indian Journal of Labour Economics*, Vol. 35, No. 2.

The foregoing analysis should not be taken to mean that interventions in the forms of price ceilings or price floors are always undesirable. There is some gain from each of these actions and there are some losses, and these must be balanced by society against each other. For example, in developing countries, the productivity of unskilled workers tends to be low because they are poor and cannot afford minimum amounts of food, clothing, and shelter. But their low productivity prevents them, form earning increased incomes, so that they continue to remain poor. On way out of this vicious cycle of poverty would be to give them 'minimum wages'. But as we have seen, when markets are not allowed to operate freely, forces build up that tend to bypass regulations, with unintended and undesirable outcomes.

It is often argued that these outcomes could have been avoided if only the acts and laws had been strictly enforced, and therefore, rather than giving up intervention, the government should focus on stringent implementation of such laws. This argument misses the point that in fact such stringent implementation is usually impossible and even if there is such implementation, there will still be losers and the forces for bypassing the laws will persist.

2.6.3 Commodity (Indirect) Taxation

The government can levy taxes either per unit of quantity sold or on the price. Let us consider a quantity tax which is a tax levied per unit of the quantity bought or sold. This is also known as a *specific tax*, while a tax as a percentage of prices is known as an *ad valorem tax*. The tax is collected from one set of agents, but another set of agents might actually be paying the tax (partly or wholly).

Case 1. Suppose that the government collects the tax from the sellers. Then the amount supplied will depend on the *supply price* P^s—the price that the seller actually receives after paying the tax, and the amount demanded will depend on the *demand price* P^l—the price that buyers actually pay.

We know that $Q^d = f(P^d)$ and $Q^s = g(P^s)$. Also, $P^s = P^d - t$, where t is the tax per unit. Then $Q^d = Q^s \Rightarrow f(P^d) = g(P^s) \Rightarrow f(P^d) = g(P^d - t)$.

Example 2.6: Let $Q^d = 10 - P^d$ and $Q^s = P^s$. In equilibrium, $Q^d = Q^s = Q$ and $P^d = P^s = P$ (since the sellers get exactly the price that buyers pay). Solving, we find that $Q = 5$ and $P = $ Rs 5. The government now levies a tax of 10 paise per unit, that is, $t = 0.1$. This means that $P^s = P^d - (0.1)$. Now $Q^d = Q^s \Rightarrow 10 - P^d = P^d - 0.1$. In the new equilibrium, $P^d = $ Rs 5.05 and $Q = 4.95$. Note that even though sellers have to pay a tax of 10 paise on every unit they sell, the price has gone up by 5 paise. Thus 5 paise of the tax is actually being paid by the buyers. In the diagram (Fig. 2.14), the supply curve shifts up since the new inverse supply curve is $P^s = Q^s + (0.1)$ (before tax, the quantity supplied was 10 when price was 10; after tax, the quantity will be $10 - t$, because the supply will depend on what the seller actually gets). In the new equilibrium at E_2, there is a wedge between the supply price and the demand price. Buyers pay Rs 5.05, while sellers receive Rs 4.95 after paying 10 paise in tax to the government.

Case 2. Suppose that the tax is collected from the buyers. Then $P^d = P^s + t$. In this case, in the new equilibrium, the price will be reduced to Rs 4.95. Buyers will pay Rs 5.05, again in effect, paying half the tax per unit (see Fig. 2.15).[2]

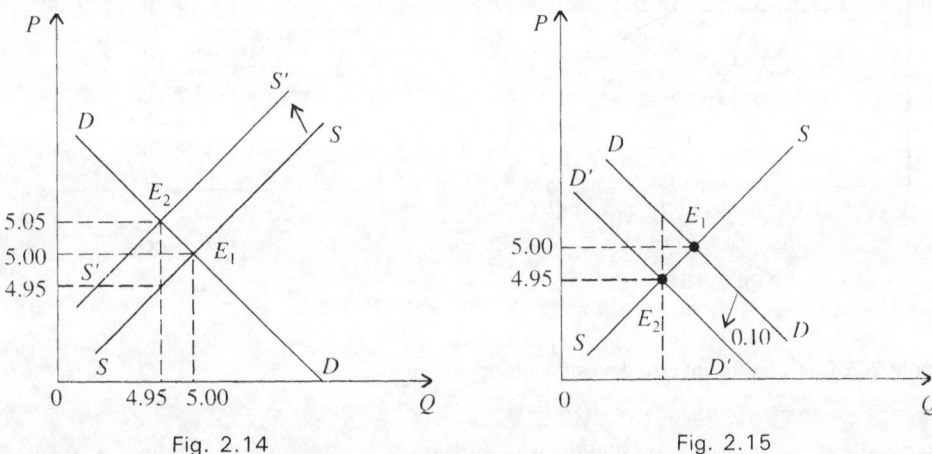

Fig. 2.14   Fig. 2.15

2.7 Comparative Statics

To investigate the effect of the imposition of specific duties on the market equilibrium, we were employing the method of comparative statics. Samuelson (1947) defined the method of comparative statics as '…the investigation of changes in a system from one position of equilibrium to another without regard to the transitional process involved in the adjustment'. That is, when there is a parametric change, either one or both the curves shift and a new equilibrium is established. Comparative statics relates to the comparison of the two equilibria, without consideration of the actual process (dynamics) of convergence to the new equilibrium. Since we often do not have complete quantitative information about the nature of the demand and supply curves, the emphasis is on deriving qualitative results, that is, the direction of change of the different variables. However, Samuelson has

[2] See Chapter 8 for further discussion of the effects of taxation on price and quantity.

established a fundamental Correspondence Principle: the assumptions made about the nature of the adjustment, particularly that of stability of equilibrium enable us to get unambiguous/meaningful results from comparative statics.

First consider the effect on quantity demanded. We need to sign the denominator. The concept of Marshallian stability will be useful here. We have already discussed the fact that the market will be stable in the Marshallian sense if and only if at equilibrium, the supply curve cuts the demand curve from below. This implies $dD/dQ - dS/dQ < 0$. Hence we can conclude that the new equilibrium quantity will be higher.

If we try to find out the effect on price, we need one piece of additional information—the sign of the slope of the supply curve. The new equilibrium price will be higher if the supply curve is positively sloped, and lower if it is negatively sloped.

These results are confirmed by the diagrams given below:

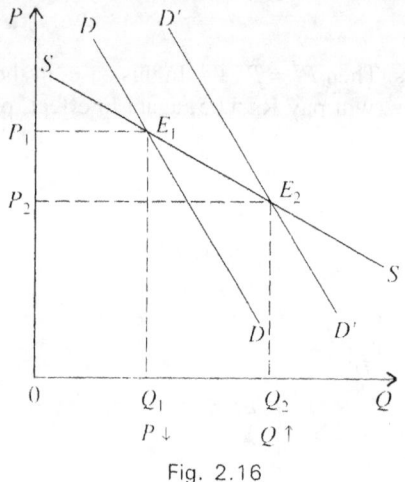

Fig. 2.16

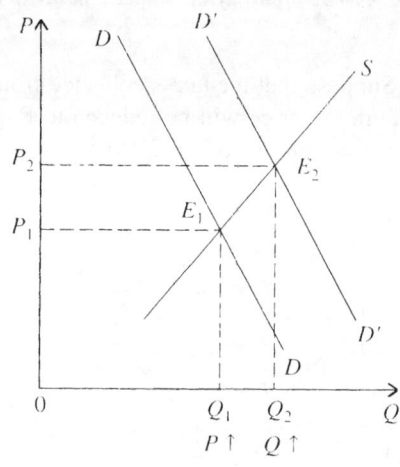

Fig. 2.17

Example 2.7: Consider the inverse demand and supply equations

$$p = D(Q, a) \text{ and } p = S(Q).$$

There is only one parameter a affecting the demand equation; a stands for 'incomes', say. An increase in a shifts the market demand curves upward and to the right, that is, $dD/da > 0$. Initially, let the value of a be a^0. The initial equilibrium values of Q and P depend on a^0. Let these be $Q^0 = f(a^0)$ and $P^0 = g(a^0)$.

What is the effect of a 'small' increase in a on equilibrium value of P and Q? To answer this question, we employ the techniques of differential calculus. Differentiate both the demand and supply equations with respect to the parameter (everything being evaluated at the original equilibrium values) to get

$$(dD/dQ)(dQ/da) - dP/da = -dD/da, \text{ and}$$
$$(dS/dQ)(dQ/da) - dP/da = 0.$$

By substitution, we get

$$dQ/da = -(dD/da)/[dD/dQ - dS/dQ] \text{ and}$$
$$dP/da = -(dS/dQ)(dD/da)/[dD/dQ - dS/dQ].$$

By assumption of the nature of the shift, $-(dD/da) < 0$.

Topics for Discussion

1. What is wrong with the following statement?
'If at the initial price there is excess demand, the price will rise. The increase in price has two consequences: it shifts the demand curve down since people buy less at a higher price; and it shifts the supply curve up because producers find it profitable to produce more at a higher price. Price will continue to adjust until there is no longer any excess demand.'

2. Governments sometimes introduce price-support programmes to keep agricultural prices at levels higher than the free market equilibrium levels. The government buys the excess supply from the farmers at the higher price.
If the excess stock is expected to be resold in the market, prices are expected to come down. How can the government prevent resale? If the price-support programme were to be continued over time, how would you expect the supply curve for this commodity to be affected? Would this make it easier or more difficult for the government to carry on with the programme?

3. Public policy towards Indian agriculture in recent years has been characterized by the following:

   (i)   Subsidies on fertilizer, power, and irrigation.
   (ii) Declining trend of investments made by the government in agriculture.
   (iii) Opening up and liberalization of domestic and foreign trade in agricultural produce.

   Discuss the probable effects of these policies in terms of supply and demand analysis.

Exercise

1. Let the equations for the demand and supply curves of a particular commodity be $Q^d = 8096 - 3596P$ and $Q^s = 500 + 4000P$. Represent these curves graphically and solve for the equilibrium price and quantity.

2. The market for audiocassettes has inverse supply and demand curves given by $P = 2Q^s$ and $P = 42 - Q^d$, respectively.

   (a) What will be the price and quantity in equilibrium?
   (b) How many units will be traded at a price of Rs 35? At a price of Rs 14? Which participants will be dissatisfied at these prices?
   (c) Suppose that the government levies a tax of Rs 21 on each cassette sold collected from sellers. What quantity of cassettes will be sold in equilibrium? What price do buyers pay? How much money goes to the government?
   (d)* What should be the tax per unit if the government is trying to maximize its tax revenue?
   [Hint: The government tries to maximize $T = tQ$, subject to the condition that $P^s = P^d - t$. Note that in equilibrium after tax, we must have $Q^s = Q^d \Rightarrow P^s/2 = 42 - P^d \Rightarrow (P^d - t)/2 = 42 - P^d$. From this, we can express P^d as a function of t so that T is expressed as a function of t. The first order condition for maximization can then be applied.]

3. The equation of the demand function for potatoes is $Q^d = 28 - 0.04P$ and the equation of the supply curve for potatoes is $Q^s = -2 + 0.16P$.

   (a) What will be the equilibrium price and quantity in the market for potatoes?
   (b) Next, the Potato Growers Association begins a nationwide advertising campaign to promote potatoes. As a result, the demand curve for potatoes now becomes $Q^d = 40 - 0.05P$. Supply is unaffected by the advertising campaign. What will be the new equilibrium price and quantity of potatoes? Represent the original and new equilibrium in a diagram.

4. The demand function for a good X is $Q^d = 1800 - 20P + 0.06M - 50P_R$, where M is the (average) consumer income and P_R is the price of a related good Y. Then good X is _____(normal/inferior). The commodities X and Y are _____ (substitutes/complements).

5. Using diagrams show what changes in price and quantity would be expected in the following markets under scenarios given:

   (a) *Crude Oil:* As petroleum reserves in Bombay High decrease, it becomes more difficult to find and recover crude oil.

   (b) *Air Travel:* Continuous disruption of flights caused by agitations by ATCs and others cause travellers to shy away from air travel.

   (c) *Rail Travel:* Continuous disruption of flights caused by agitations by ATCs and others cause travellers to shy away from air travel.

   (d) *Hotel rooms in Goa:* Continuous disruption of flights caused by agitations by ATCs and others cause travellers to shy away from air travel.

   (e) *Milk:* Newly repaired roads cause the cost of delivering milk to come down.

6. Not since the halcyon days of the late 1990s has M&A activity been so robust.

   Lawyers may be in tight supply, but the pipeline of people who can run the numbers appears downright dry. 'There is a general shortage of accountants right now, especially those who have knowledge in the M&A arena', said Steven Krug, a business-valuation expert in the Atlanta office of Grant Thornton LLP.

   Recruiters who specialize in the financial field say orders for financial jobs are flowing faster than they can find people to fill them. Something has to give, and more often than not, it's the employer's payroll.

   'We see a lot more signing bonuses, performance bonuses, and we see some huge vacation packages being negotiated', said Andrea Jennings, a vice-president at Lucas Group, one of the nation's largest executive search firms.

   Draw a supply-demand diagram, correctly labelling each axis, to explain the phenomena noted above.

3

The Theory of Consumer Choice

The market demand curve is an aggregation of individual demand curves. In this chapter, we analyse how the principle of rational choice allows us to derive the demand curve for an individual. This analysis is in two steps:

1. First, given the consumer's income and the prices of the commodities available in the markets, we can find out all the bundles of commodities that the consumer can afford to buy. This defines the *feasible set* facing the consumer.
2. Next, we assume that the consumer has well-defined *preferences*. Given these preferences, the consumer chooses a point in her feasible set.

3.1 The Feasible Set

Suppose that the consumer's income is fixed at Rs I per period. She purchases only two commodities—'food' (quantities of which are denoted by F) and 'clothing' (quantities of which are denoted by C). Any bundle then is represented by the pair of quantities (F, C).

The consumer believes that her purchases will have no impact on the market prices of food and clothing. These prices are denoted by P_F and P_C, respectively. Then the total expenditure on a bundle (F, C) will be $P_F F + P_C C$. This cannot exceed the consumer's income:

$$I \geq P_F F + P_C C.$$

The feasible set for the consumer is then defined as all bundles (F, C) such that $I \geq P_F F + P_C C$ and $F \geq 0$, $C \geq 0$. To represent this feasible set, we first define the budget line.

If the consumer spends her entire income on these two commodities, then

$$I = P_F F + P_C C.$$

This is called the equation of the *budget line*. On the budget line, any point represents a combination of food and clothing that exhausts the entire income I. For example, if $F = 0$, that is, no food is being bought and only clothing is being purchased, the maximum amount of clothing that can be bought is I/P_C. On the other hand, when $C = 0$, $F = I/P_F$. In Fig. 3.1, these two possible combinations are shown as points B' and B respectively, that is, the intercepts on the two axes.

The feasible set then consists of *all* points on the triangle OBB'. It consists of all points below the budget line (where not all the income is being spent) and all points on the budget line (where all the income is being spent). It is bounded by the two axes because only non-negative quantities are being considered.

The equation of the budget line can be written in two alternative but equivalent forms:

(a) $I = P_F F + P_C C \Rightarrow 1 = (P_F F)/I + (P_C C)/I \Rightarrow$
$\qquad 1 = F/(I/P_F) + C/(I/P_C).$

Example 3.1: Let I = Rs 1000, P_F = Rs 10, P_C = Rs 5. Then the equation of the budget line is $1000 = 10F + 5C$. When $F = 0$, $C = 200$. When $C = 0$, $F = 100$. Therefore $(0, 200)$ and $(100, 0)$ are two points on the budget line and hence in the feasible set. If, on the other hand, the consumer purchases the bundle $(50, 20)$, then she is not spending her entire income. The bundle $(50, 20)$ is in her feasible set. In fact, all points satisfying $1000 \geq 10F + 5C$, and $F \geq 0$, $C \geq 0$, lie in the feasible set (the shaded area).

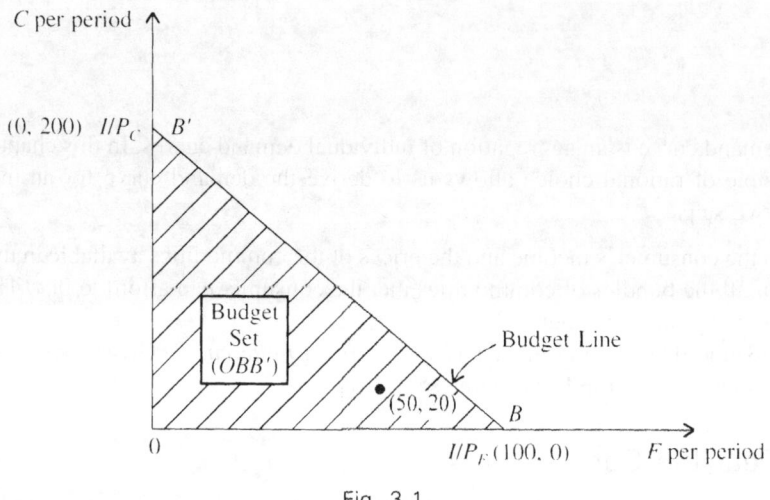

Fig. 3.1

In this formulation, (I/P_F) and (I/P_C) represent the maximum amounts of food and clothing, respectively, that can be bought with the limited income I and are the intercepts on the F- and C-axis respectively.

(b) Transpose terms to write the budget equation as $P_C C = I - P_F F$.

After dividing both sides by P_C, we can write the equation as

$$C = -(P_F/P_C)F + (I/P_C).$$

This is an especially useful way of writing the budget line. The first term within the brackets represents the *slope* of the budget line and the second term within brackets the *intercept*.

Example 3.2: Given the numbers above, we can write the equation of the budget line as either $F/100 + C/200 = 1$ or $C = -2F + 200$. The latter expression shows that the slope is -2 and the C-intercept is 200.

The slope of the budget line has a special significance. It gives the rate at which the consumer can exchange one commodity (food) for the other (clothing) in the market:

Rs P_C buys one unit of clothing
Re 1 buys $1/P_C$ units of clothing
Rs P_F buys P_F/P_C units of clothing

If the consumer buys one unit less of food, she saves Rs P_F and can buy P_F/P_C units of clothing, instead. Thus the slope gives the rate at which food can be exchanged for clothing in the market.

3.2 Shifts in the Budget Line

We can now investigate how the feasible set changes when parametric changes occur. The parameters determining the feasible set in this simple model are the income of the consumer and prices.

1. Suppose that the income of the consumer increases from I to I'. The equation of the new budget line is $C = -(P_F/P_C)F + (I'/P_C)$. The slope does not change, but the intercept on the C-axis increases. This leads to a *parallel*, outward shift of the budget line. The feasible set is thereby enlarged from OBB' to Obb'.

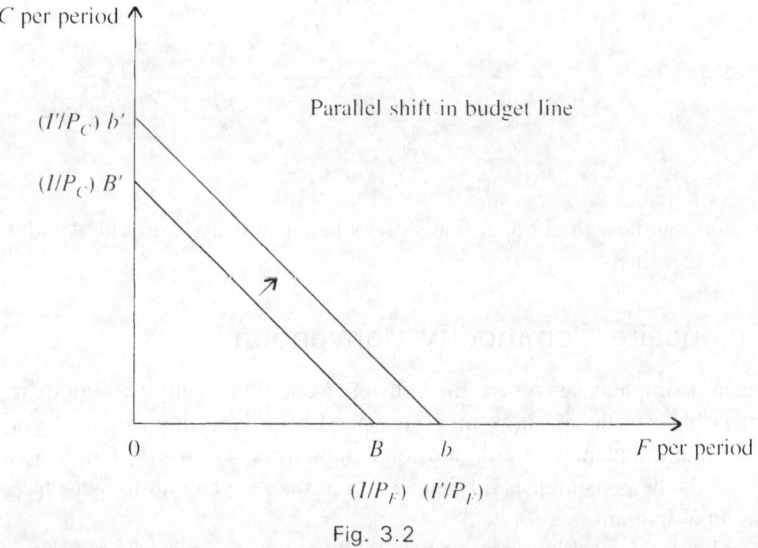

Fig. 3.2

Example 3.3: In the example above, let the consumer's income increase to Rs 2000 per period from Rs 1000 per period. The equation of the budget line now is $C = -2F + 400$.

2. Next consider the effect of a change in price(s). To keep things simple, assume that only P_F falls, I and P_C remaining constant. Let the new price of F be P_F', $P_F' < P_F$. The new equation of the budget line is $1 = F/(I/P_F') + C/(I/P_C)$. Thus the C-intercept does not change while the F-intercept is larger. The budget line rotates outward, keeping the C-intercept fixed. The new slope is $-(P_F'/P_C)$.

It is interesting to note that the effects of taxes and subsidies can be expressed as changes in prices.

First, consider a specific tax of t per unit of clothing (say). Then the equation of the budget line becomes $I = P_F F + (P_C + t)C$—the budget line rotates *inward*, keeping the F-intercept fixed. The new slope is $-\{P_F/(P_C + t)\}$.

Next, consider the imposition of an ad valorem tax on clothing. Such a tax is expressed as a percentage of the sales value or price. If the rate is r, then the equation of the budget line becomes $I = P_F F + (1 + r)P_C C$. Again, the budget line rotates inward, keeping the F-intercept fixed. The new slope is $-\{P_F/(1 + r)P_C\}$.

A subsidy is the opposite of a tax. In case of a quantity subsidy s given on food, the equation of the budget line becomes $I = (P_F - s)F + P_C C$. If the subsidy is an ad valorem subsidy (on food), then the equation of the budget line becomes $I = (1 - m)P_F F + P_C C$, where the subsidy is given at the rate m.

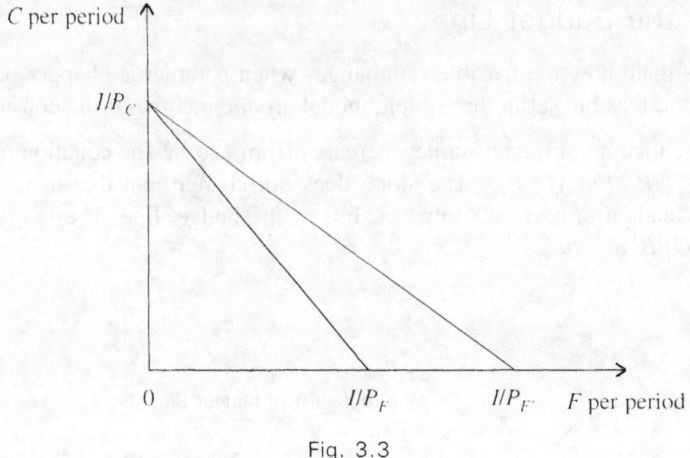

Fig. 3.3

You can easily work out how the budget line shifts when a subsidy is provided and what happens to the slope of the budget line.

3.3 The Composite Commodity Convention

We have considered simple cases where the consumer could buy only two goods in the market. In reality, consumers have to decide how much to spend on a large number n of goods. With three goods, the budget line is a plane in a 3-dimensional diagram: $I = P_F F + P_C C + P_X X$, where F, C, and X are the three goods the consumer is buying. If $n > 3$, then we can no longer represent the budget line/hyper plane in a diagram.

One way of solving this problem is to reduce the number of commodities to two by considering one commodity and the amount of income spent on all other goods. The equation of the budget line can now be written as

$$I = P_X X + Y,$$

where Y is the income spent on all goods other than X. Therefore all commodities other than X are being treated as a 'composite commodity'. The 'price' of the composite commodity is 1. The equation of the budget line can now be written either as

$$1 = X/(I/P_X) + Y/I, \text{ or as } Y = (-P_X)X + I.$$

A Kinked Budget Constraint

The budget lines that we have considered so far have all been straight lines. However, we can think of situations where the line will be kinked. As an example, suppose that a consumer spends all her income on two goods—'electricity' and a composite commodity. The Electricity Supply Corporation charges Rs 2 per unit for the first 100 units of consumption per month and Rs 4 per unit for any consumption above 100 units. The consumer's income is Rs 800. Then, her budget line equation is:

800 = 2E + Y for E ≤ 100, and 800 = 4E + Y for E > 100,
i.e. 1 = E/400 + Y/800 for E ≤ 100, and 1 = E/200 + (Y − 200)/800 for E > 100,
i.e. 1 = E/250 + Y/1000.

(contd)

(contd)

(We have to subtract 200 from Y because the consumer has already spent at least 200 on Electricity, leaving that much less money to be spent on other things.)

The kinked line BAB, which is obtained from the two equations given above, then represents the budget line.

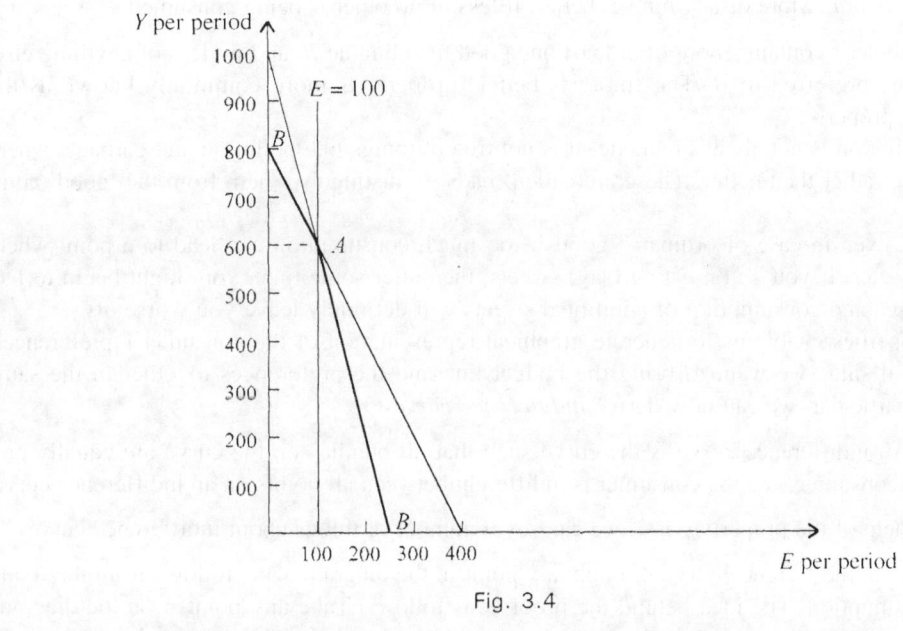

Fig. 3.4

3.4 Preferences

The budget line enables us to identify the bundles that are *available* to the consumer for any set of prices and income. The bundle that will be *chosen* will depend on the consumer's subjective *preferences* over different bundles. It should be noted that the preferences are assumed to depend only on the bundles selected, not the prices and the income. (This assumption is violated if consumers, for example, judge the quality of a good by its absolute price.) The preferences allow the consumer to rank different bundles in order of preference.

A *preference ordering* is a scheme that enables the consumer to rank different bundles of goods in terms of their desirability or order of preference. While different consumers generally will have different systems of preferences, we assume that all preference orderings possess certain properties in common:

1. *Completeness*: The consumer can rank in order of preference any two bundles A and B. Thus, our consumer can always make up her mind when confronted with choices.

Given any two bundles A and B,
either A is preferred to B (we write this as A P B),
or B is preferred to A (we write this as B P A),
or the consumer is indifferent between A and B (we write this as A I B).

2. *Transitivity*: The preference ordering is such that
if A is preferred to B and B is preferred to C, then A is preferred to C.
That is, A P B and B P C ⇒ A P C.

Also, if the consumer is indifferent between A and B and between B and C, then she will be indifferent between A and C. That is, $A \, I \, B$ and $B \, I \, C \Rightarrow A \, I \, C$.

The transitivity property implies that the consumer's choices must be consistent in some sense. If the consumer prefers two vada paos to two idlis, and two idlis to one masala dosa, she should not prefer one masala dosa to two vada paos.

3. *More is Better*: More of anything is better, if less of no other is being consumed.

Thus if bundle A contains more of at least one good than bundle B, and no less of anything else, then A will be preferred to B. The 'more is better' property is more commonly known as the *monotonicity* property.

This assumption is not always realistic. It is not true of things like pollution and garbage, where more is worse rather than better. These are called 'bads' to distinguish them from the 'good' commodities.

Moreover, even in case of ordinary 'goods', too much consumption can lead to a point where more is not better. If you go on eating (say) sweets, then after some time, you might begin to feel physical nausea and consumption of additional sweets will definitely leave you worse off.

These properties enable us to generate graphical representation of the consumer's preferences. This is helpful since we want to bring the budget line and the preferences together in the same diagram. In particular, we can now derive *indifference curves*:

Definition: An indifference curve is the curve such that all bundles on the curve are equally preferred by the consumer, i.e., the consumer is indifferent between all points on an indifference curve.

With the help of the properties 1–3, we can say a number of things about indifference curves:

1. There is an indifference curve through any point in the diagram. This follows from the 'completeness' assumption. The idea behind the proof is as follows. Take any point A on the diagram. Then points to the northeast of A (in the region a) are preferred to A and A is preferred to those to the southwest of A (in the region b).

Take a bundle Z that is preferred to A and a point W such that $A \, P \, W$. Join W and Z by a straight line. Then between W and Z, there must be a point B that is as well preferred as A (by 'continuity' of preferences). Next, starting with B, we can find a point C such that $B \, I \, C$. Proceeding in this way, we can find all the points/bundles that are as preferred as A and label them as the indifference curve I_2.

We can fill up the diagram with indifference curves to get an *indifference map*, which will then represent the consumer's preferences. Some of these are shown in Fig. 3.5.

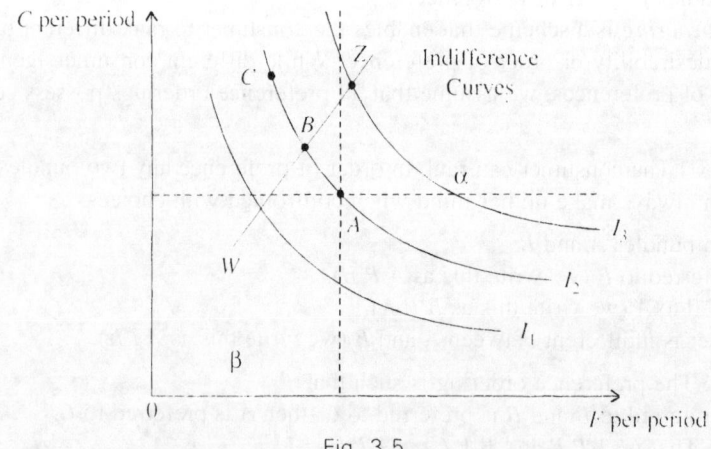

Fig. 3.5

2. Each indifference curve must be downward sloping. We rule out indifference curves that are upward sloping, horizontal or vertical. Why is this so? A moment's reflection tells us that the 'more is better' property is violated in these cases. For example, consider a horizontal indifference curve as in Fig. 3.6. On this curve, we can identify two points such A and B such that $A = (F, C)$ and $B = (F', C)$, where $F' > F$. So the consumer cannot be indifferent between A and B (she should prefer B to A) and yet A and B are on the same indifference curve, which is a contradiction.

You should make sure to go through the same reasoning when the indifference curves are upward sloping or vertical.

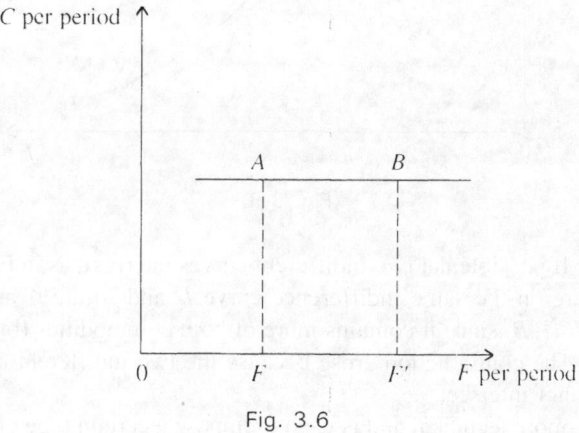

Fig. 3.6

3. Higher indifference curves represent higher levels of utility. This again follows from the 'more is better' property. In Fig. 3.7, A on the higher indifference curve I_2 contains more of at least one commodity compared to B (on the lower indifference curve I_1).

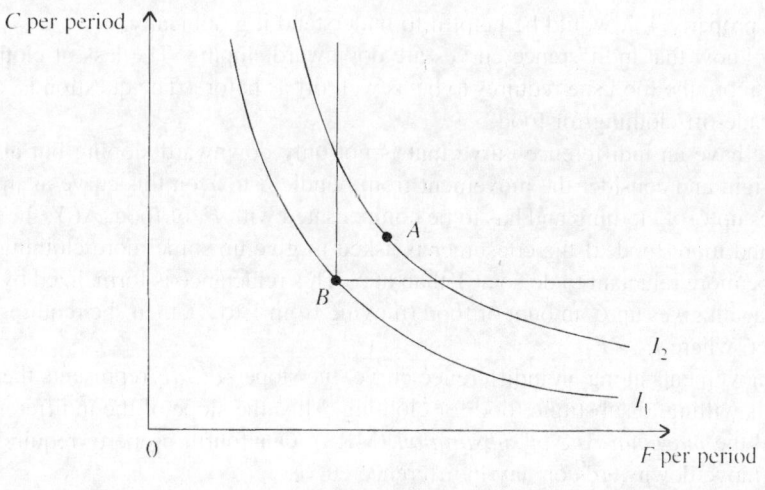

Fig. 3.7

4. Two indifference curves cannot cross each other. This follows from the 'transitivity' and 'more is better' properties taken together.

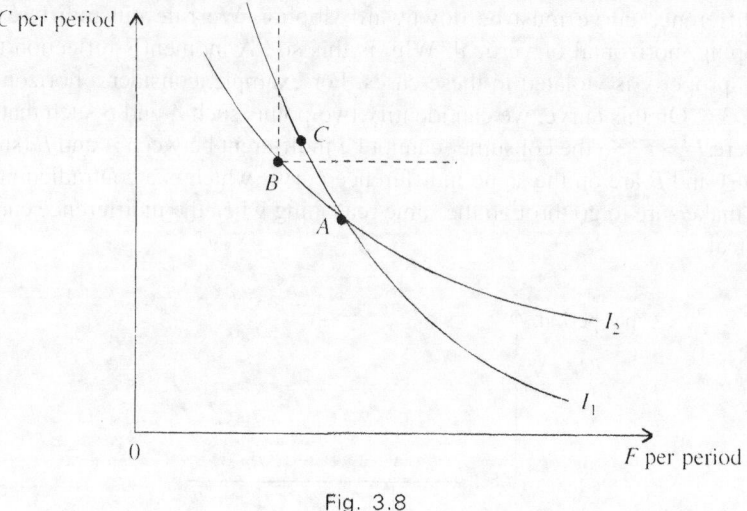

Fig. 3.8

The proof is simple: If possible, let two indifferent curves intersect, as in Fig. 3.8. Then $A\,I\,B$ and $A\,I\,C$ since A and B are on the same indifference curve I_2 and so are A and C (on I_1). Then by transitivity, $B\,I\,C$. But $C\,P\,B$, since it contains more of both commodities (by 'more is better'), and this is a contradiction. The contradiction arose because the two indifferent curves crossed. Hence, indifference curves cannot intersect.

The next property is more technical and is used to impose a certain type of curvature on indifference curves. It guarantees the *convexity* of indifference curves, i.e. that an indifference curve would be bowed out toward the origin.

3.5. Law of Diminishing Marginal Rate of Substitution

Before stating property 4, it would be helpful to understand it graphically.

We already know that indifference curves are downward sloping. The less of clothing (say) the consumer has, more the food she requires to be as well off as before. The question is, at what rate is she ready to trade-off clothing for food?

Suppose we have an indifference curve that is not only downward sloping but also bowed out towards the origin and consider the movement from bundle X to Y on this curve as in Fig. 3.9. The consumer gives up C of clothing and has to be compensated with F_1 of food. At Y, the consumer has less clothing and more food. If the consumer is asked to give up some more clothing for food, we expect her to be more reluctant to do so at Y than at X. This reluctance is formalized by saying that if the consumer again gives up C amount of food (moving from Y to Z), then she requires F_2 of food to compensate her, where $F_2 > F_1$.

For small movements along an indifference curve, the slope $-dC/dF$ represents the rate at which the consumer is willing to substitute food for clothing. This, the slope of the indifference curve at a point, is called the *marginal rate of substitution* (MRS). Our fourth property requires the MRS to decline as we move downwards on any indifference curve.

The law of diminishing MRS ensures that the indifference curves are *convex*. If any two points on an indifference curve are joined by a straight line, all points on the straight line (except the two end-points) lie above the indifference curve. Now, these points represent weighted averages of the end-points, that is, they represent weighted averages of the bundles given by the end-points. For example,

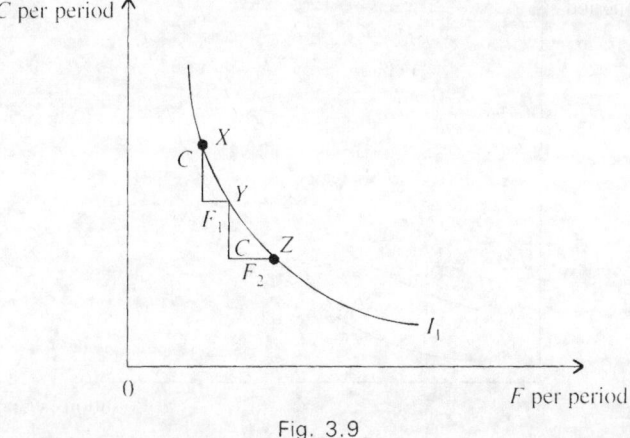

Fig. 3.9

if the end-points are (100, 50) and (70, 80), then the point midway on the line is (0.5 × 100 + 0.5 × 70, 0.5 × 50 + 0.5 × 80), or the bundle (85, 65). Since such points lie above the original indifference curve, we know that each of them lie on a higher indifference curve. Therefore the consumer prefers average bundles to extreme bundles. Rather than having a great deal of one good and a little bit of the other, she likes to have moderate amounts of both.

We should note at this stage that different people have different preference orderings, so that we expect that the indifference maps will be different for different individuals. In Fig. 3.10 (a and b) below for Bijoy and Bijoya, the indifference curves are steeper for Bijoya. This reflects the fact that for any amount of fish curry, Bijoya is willing to give up less dal than Bijoy—she likes dal relatively more than Bijoy. Moreover, if the preferences change, then the entire indifference maps changes. We assume that preferences for any individual are given and do not change frequently or erratically.

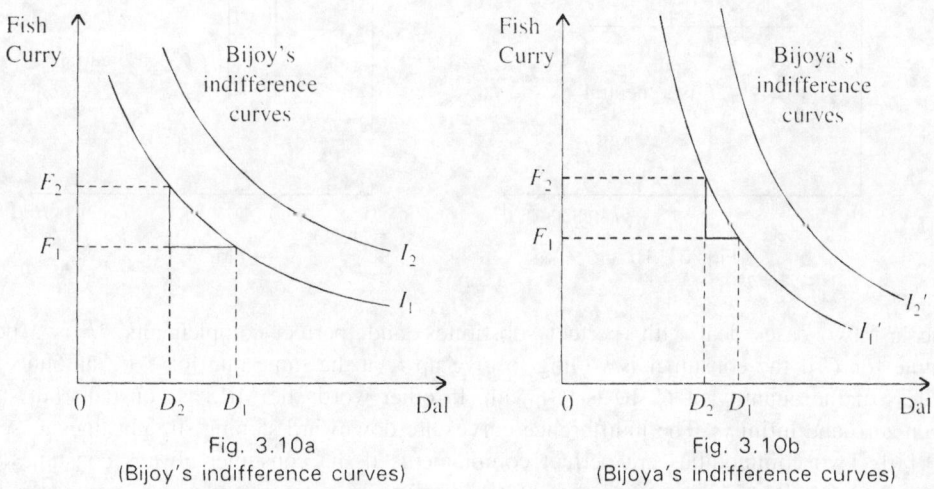

Fig. 3.10a
(Bijoy's indifference curves)

Fig. 3.10b
(Bijoya's indifference curves)

Some other types of indifference curves are shown below. They all violate one or more of the four properties that were discussed above. In Fig. 3.11a, one of the commodities is pollution, for which the monotonicity property is violated. More of pollution is worse, not better. Hence pollution is a 'bad'. The indifference curves are upward sloping.

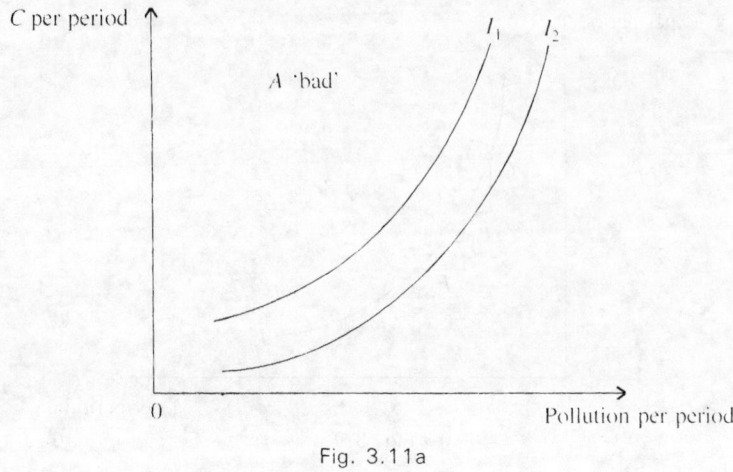

Fig. 3.11a

In Figs 3.11b and 3.11c, one of the goods is a 'neutral' good. More of the commodity leaves the consumer as well off as before, so that the indifference curves are horizontal or vertical straight lines. The consumer's preference ranking over bundles is determined by only one commodity in the bundle. Also, the MRS is either infinity (for vertical curves) or zero (for horizontal curves).

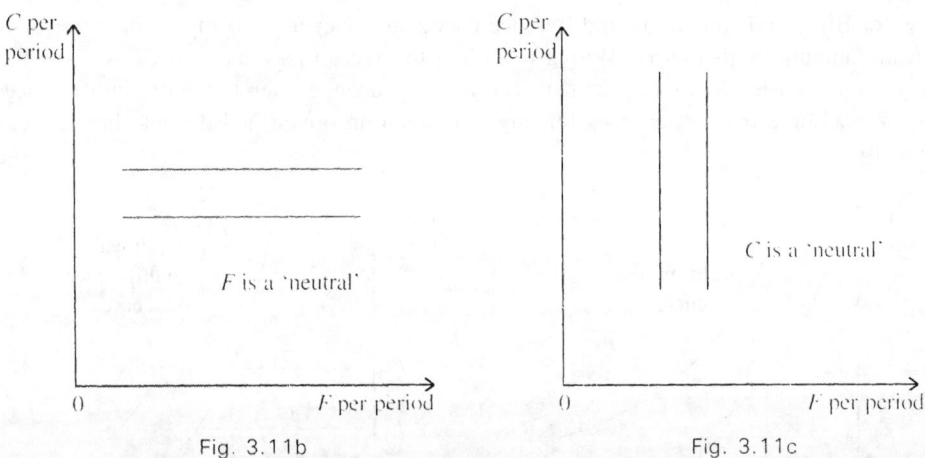

Fig. 3.11b   Fig. 3.11c

The last two cases deal with 'perfect substitutes' and 'perfect complements'. F is a perfect substitute for C if the consumer is willing to give up C at the same rate for extra amounts of F, regardless of the quantity of C she is left with. In other word, the MRS is constant (but strictly between zero and infinity). The indifference curves are downward sloping straight lines as seen in Fig. 3.11d. Two commodities are perfect complements if the consumer always consumes them together in a fixed proportion. One cup of tea requires two spoons of sugar, say. More sugar (in a sugar pot) provided with each cup of tea does not affect the consumer in any way. Nor does extra tea with every two spoons of sugar. The resulting indifference curves are L-shaped as Fig. 3.11e shows. The MRS is not defined at the corner of the L. Everywhere else it is either zero or infinity.

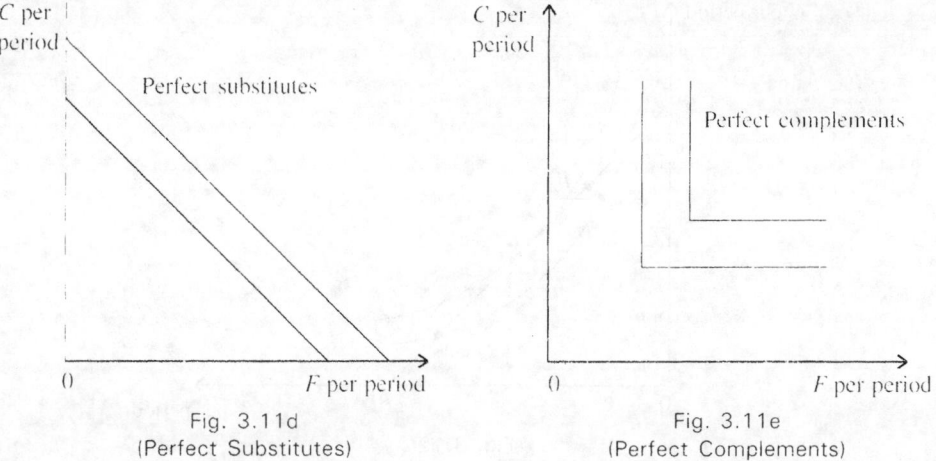

Fig. 3.11d
(Perfect Substitutes)

Fig. 3.11e
(Perfect Complements)

3.6 The Consumer's Choice

We now have all the tools required to analyse the consumer's choice problem. The budget line delimits all the bundles that the consumer can afford to buy, given her income and the prices of the commodities. The indifference curves represent her preference ordering, that is, her ranking of the bundles in order of preference. The consumer's problem is to choose the most preferred affordable bundle (the 'best' bundle, in short).

A point below the budget line cannot be such a bundle. The reason is that at such a point, the consumer is not spending all her income. Starting from such a point, she can spend more and buy more of at least one commodity which makes her better off by the 'more is better' principle. Hence, the best bundle must be chosen from the budget line. (Any of the points above the budget line represent bundles to purchase which the consumer would have to spend more than her given income. These points are therefore *unattainable*.)

A point on the budget line can be of either two types. It can be such that an indifference curve *cuts through* the budget line, or it can be a *point of tangency* between the budget line and some indifference curve.

Consider the first possibility. In Fig. 3.12, *A* is a point where the budget line is cut by an indifference curve. This means that the slopes are not equal. The slope of the indifference curve is the MRS and the slope of the budget line is $-(P_F/P_C)$. Let MRS = 3, which means that the consumer is willing to give up three units of food for one unit of clothing. Let the price ratio be 2, that is, in the market, the same amount of money will buy either two units of food or one unit of clothing. Then the consumer can buy two units less of food, get one unit of clothing with the savings, and reach a higher indifference curve. Why? The rearrangement of her purchase gives her one unit of food and one unit of clothing for three units of food, whereas she would have been contented to have received just one unit of clothing in return. This means that a point like *A* cannot be the best point. The consumer can make herself better off by reallocating her budget—buying less food and more clothing.

The consumer will, therefore, reach her best choice bundle at the point of tangency of the budget line with one indifference curve—the point *E*. At this point, MRS = $-(P_F/P_C)$, so that there is no further scope for attaining a higher indifference curve through reallocation of expenditure.

A different way to realize this is to note that any indifference curve that cuts the budget line must pass through a point like *D* below the budget line. Hence there will be points like *B* on the budget line that are more preferred to *D* and therefore the point of intersection.

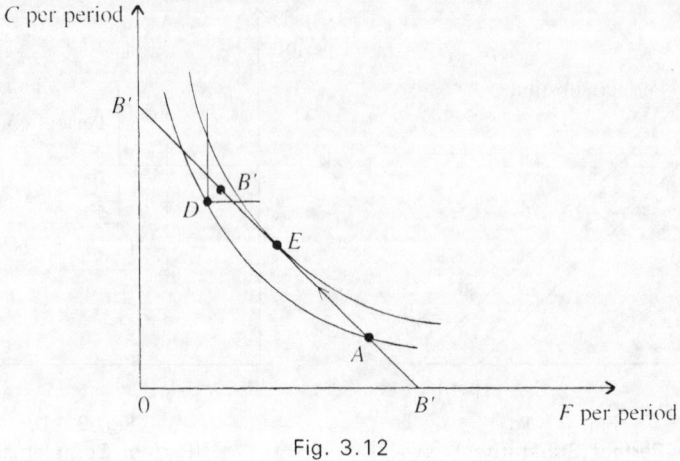

Fig. 3.12

In the solution to the consumer's choice problem shown in Fig. 3.12, the consumer ends up buying both commodities. This will happen if the indifference curves are *nicely behaved*, that is has adequate curvature. We call such solutions *interior solutions*. However, we can think of situations where the consumer will decide to purchase only one commodity. The solution is then called a *corner solution*. In Fig. 3.13a and 3.13b, the indifference curves are downward sloping and convex, but the MRS is everywhere greater, or less, than the slope of the budget line. The consumer purchases at either of the intercepts of the budget line. In Fig. 3.13a, she purchase only clothing and in Fig. 3.13b, she purchases only food. The indifference curves are not sufficiently convex—they are more like straight lines than curves.

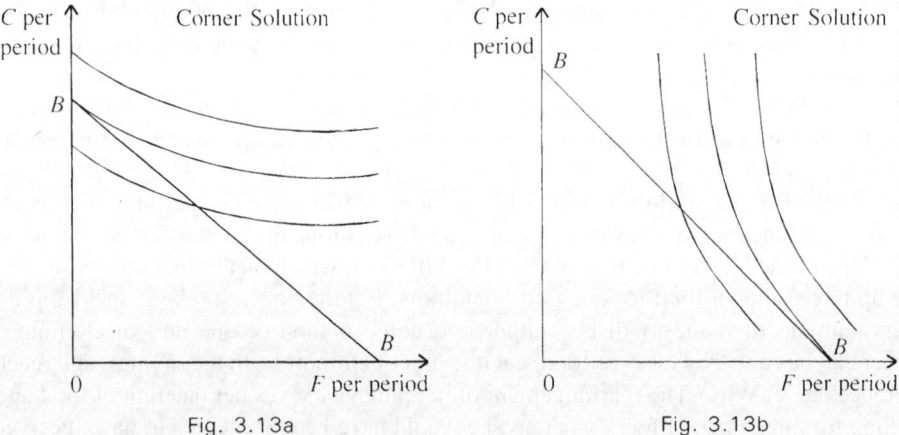

Fig. 3.13a   Fig. 3.13b

If the property of diminishing MRS does not hold, then again corner solutions occur as in Figs 3.14a, 3.14b, 3.14c, and 3.14d (in each case, the arrow shows the direction of increase of utility).

3.7 The Utility Function Approach

So far, in our treatment of the consumer choice problem, we have assumed that the consumer can rank bundles in order of preference. This means that given any two bundles A and B, the consumer

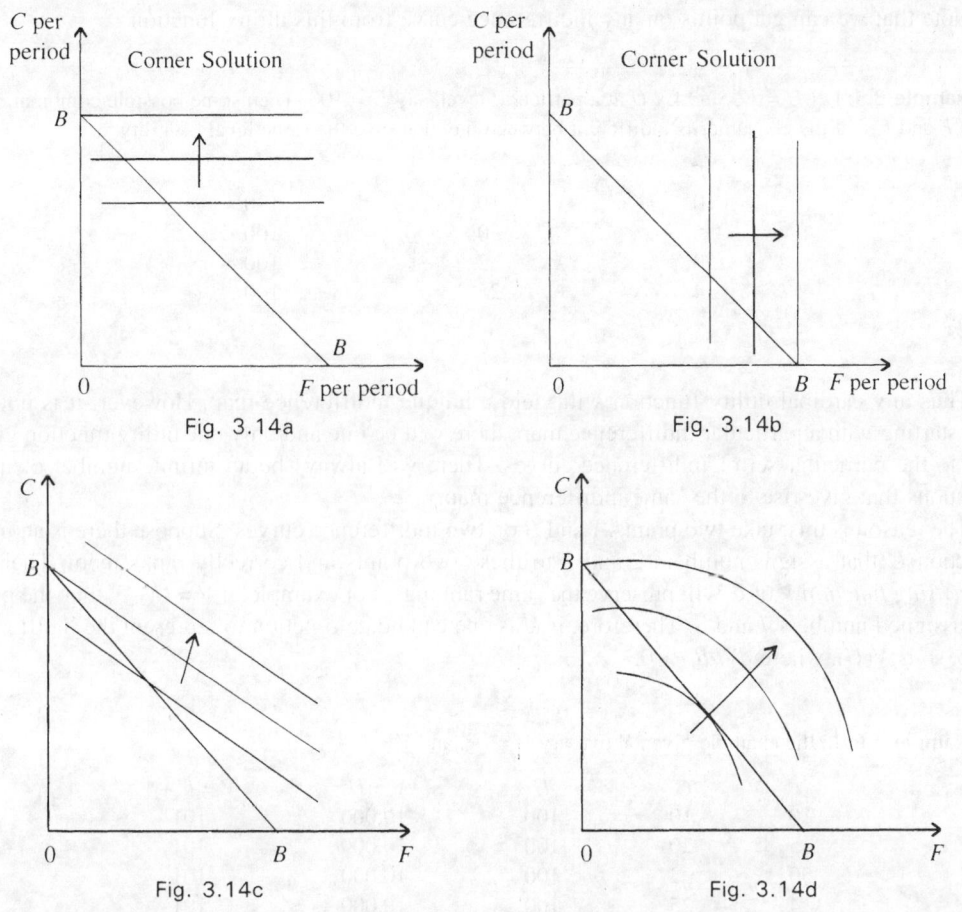

Fig. 3.14a

Fig. 3.14b

Fig. 3.14c

Fig. 3.14d

can assign two numbers that express her relative preference between the two bundles. For example, if she associates a number 2 with *A* and a number 5 with *B*, this tells us that she prefers *B* to *A*.

However, we do not require the consumer to tell us *by how much* she prefers *B* to *A*. The numbers 5 and 2 do not have any special significance. The consumer could have assigned the numbers 8 and 1 or 39 and 14. So long as she assigns the numbers consistently, this is all the information that we need to solve the choice problem.

Such an approach is called the *ordinal utility* approach. The ordinal approach is contrasted with the nineteenth-century *cardinal utility* approach, which required the consumer to be able to assign a precise numerical value to any bundle to denote her satisfaction from that bundle. The function which assigned the numbers to the bundles is called a utility function: $U = U(F, C)$.

Example 3.4: Let $U = FC$. Then some possible combinations of *F* and *C* and the corresponding utilities are:

F	C	U
1	2	2
5	7	35
50	20	1000
100	25	2500

etc.

Note that we can get points on any indifference curve from this utility function:

Example 3.5: Let $U = FC$ and fix U at a particular level, say $U = 100$. Then some possible combinations of F and C that the consumer is indifferent between, i.e. that give the same level of utility, are:

F	C	U
10	10	100
5	20	100
50	2	100
4	25	100

etc.

Thus any cardinal utility function will yield a unique indifference map. However, it is not true that starting with a particular indifference map, there will be one and only one utility function giving rise to the particular set of indifference curves. There will always be an infinite number of utility functions that give rise to the same indifference map.

The reason is this: take two points A and B on two indifference curves. Suppose there is an utility function U that assigns numbers 2 and 3 to these two points and correctly ranks them. Then *any increasing function V* of U will preserve the same rankings. For example, if $V = U + 5$, then the points are assigned numbers 7 and 8. Therefore, if U is one candidate function to represent the indifference map, so is $V(U)$, where $dV/dU > 0$.

Example 3.6: In the example given above, try $V = U^2$, and $V = U + 1$.

F	C	U	$V = U^2$	$V = U + 1$
10	10	100	10,000	101
5	20	100	10,000	101
50	2	100	10,000	101
4	25	100	10,000	101

etc.

Thus, these bundles are on the same indifference curve, regardless of whether $U = FC$ or $U = (FC)^2$ or $U = FC + 1$.

Economists prefer to use the ordinal utility approach because it requires much weaker assumptions. However, the cardinal utility approach provides a convenient and accessible method for summarizing our results and we shall often be using it.

Suppose that the utility function for the consumer is $U = U(F, C)$, as before. Then the additional utility from consuming an extra unit of F or C is called the *marginal utility* of F or C. In mathematical notation, $MU_F = \partial U/\partial F$, that is, the first partial derivative of U with respect to F. Similarly, $MU_C = \partial U/\partial C$. The 'more is better' property can then be restated in terms of marginal utilities. It requires all marginal utilities to be strictly positive:

$$\partial U/\partial F > 0, \ \partial U/\partial C > 0.$$

There is an interesting relationship between MRS and the marginal utilities. The MRS is the slope of the indifference curve at a point, and is given by $-dC/dF$. Now, take the utility function $U = U(F, C)$. Totally differentiating both sides, we get $dU = (\partial U/\partial F)dF + (\partial U/\partial C)dC$. But on any indifference curve, total utility U does not change, so that $dU = 0$. This means that $-dC/dF =$

$(\partial U/\partial F)/(\partial U/\partial C)$, that is, MRS $= MU_F/MU_C$. Therefore, the absolute value of the slope of the indifference curve at a point is the ratio of the slope of the marginal utilities at that point.

Example 3.7: Again, let $U = FC$. Then $MU_F = C$ and $MU_C = F$. Therefore, MRS $= C/F$ at any point. Also note more generally for any $n > 0$ that if $U = F^n C^n$, then MRS $= C/F$.

This relationship between the MRS and marginal utilities enables us to give an equivalent but more intuitive interpretation of the best choice solution. At such a solution, MRS $= (P_F/P_C)$. Then $MU_F/MU_C = P_F/P_C$, which can be written as

$$MU_F/P_F = MU_C/P_C.$$

This condition can be interpreted to mean: at the best choice position, *the marginal utility per rupee of expenditure on food must be equal to the marginal utility per rupee of expenditure on clothing.* If these are not equal, the consumer can attain a higher indifference curve by spending one rupee less on the commodity which gives less marginal utility per rupee and spending that rupee on the commodity that gives more marginal utility per rupee.

Example 3.8: Let $U = F^{0.5}C^{0.5}$. Then MRS $= C/F$. To determine the best choice point we use two equations. One is MRS $= P_F/P_C$, so that $C/F = P_F/P_C \Rightarrow P_C C = P_F F$, implying that the consumer spends exactly the same amount on both food and clothing. The second condition is the equation of the budget line since the best choice point lies on the budget line. Substituting $C = (P_F/P_C)F$ in the budget line and solving for F, we get $2P_F F = I$. We can then write $F = I/2P_F$, which is the demand curve for F for given I. Next, solving for C, we get the demand curve for C as $C = I/2P_C$.

More generally, (see Appendix) for a Cobb-Douglas utility function $U = F^a C^{1-a}$, $1 > a > 0$,

$$F = aI/P_F, \ C = (1 - a)I/P_C.$$

These are the equations of the two demand functions. Note that for given I, both demand functions will be downward sloping. Moreover, $P_F \cdot F = aI$ and $P_C \cdot C = (1 - a)I$. Thus, irrespective of the price level, a fixed proportion of income will be spent on F and the rest on C. Note also that in these special cases, the demand for each commodity depends only on the own price.

3.8 Changes in Income

The best choice point is characterized by the tangency of the budget line with an indifference curve. The position of this point depends on (a) the budget line and (b) preferences that determine the shape and location of indifference curves. The budget line in turn depends on prices and the income of the consumer. We next investigate what happens to the best choice point when the income of the consumer changes.

Let the initial income of the consumer be I and the corresponding best choice point E. Now consider an increase in income to I'. We know from earlier discussion that the budget line will shift upwards, parallel to the old line, as a result of this increase. The new budget line will have a point of tangency with one indifference curve and call this point E'.

In this way, by taking different income levels, we can get different budget lines and corresponding best choice points. Joining all these best choice points, we get an *income-consumption curve*. If this curve is upward sloping, this means that when income increases, consumption of both commodities increases. Both commodities are *normal goods*.

However, it is also possible that the income-consumption curve will have a downward sloping segment in which the consumption of one good decreases when income increases. This good then becomes an inferior good. In Fig. 3.15, as income increases, the demand for food falls (compare E with E').

Note that when there are two goods, both cannot be inferior. If both are inferior, any increase in income will mean that less of both goods will be purchased and so not all the income will be spent. We know that this situation is ruled out by the 'more is better' assumption. If the consumer is purchasing many commodities, of course some, but not all, might be inferior.

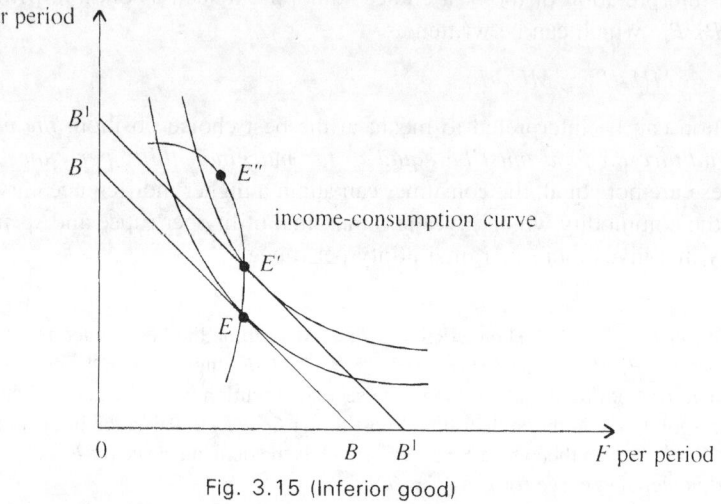

Fig. 3.15 (Inferior good)

One should be careful in using the concepts of normal and inferior goods:

(a) No commodity is intrinsically normal and inferior; whether a commodity is normal or inferior depends on individual tastes and preferences. The same commodity might be normal for some and inferior for others. One person might switch over to CDs from audiocassettes as his income increases; another might start buying audiocassettes.

(b) The same good may be normal at one income level and inferior at another, for the same consumer. As a poor man's income increases, he might buy less of bajra and switch to rice. The Engel curve will be concave to the income-axis.

(c) The concept of inferior goods should be clearly distinguished from the concept of 'bads'. A 'bad' is a commodity like pollution for which the marginal utility is negative. An inferior good is one whose purchase falls as income increases.

We can take a commodity and plot its consumption against different income levels to get the Engel curve for this commodity.[1] An Engel curve is the graph of the demand for one of the goods as a function of income, with all prices held constant. An upward sloping Engel curve implies that we are dealing with a normal good, while a downward sloping Engel curve implies that we are dealing with an inferior good.

[1] The Engel Curve is named after a German Statistician Ernst Engel (1821–96) who first studied the relationship between family incomes and quantities demanded of different goods. Based on a budget study of 153 Belgian families, Engel concluded that the lower a family's income, greater the proportion of it spent on food. This came to be known as Engel's Law.

An Engel curve can also be obtained by expressing total expenditure on a good as a function of income, again holding prices constant. A luxury is then defined as a good that takes up a larger share of income as income rises and a necessity as one which takes up a smaller share.

Example 3.9: Let $U = F^{0.5}C^{0.5}$. Example 3.8 shows that the equation of the Engel curve for F is then $F = I/2P_F$ keeping P_F fixed. It is a straight line through the origin with slope $I/2P_F$, which is positive, indicating that F is a normal good. Alternatively, the equations for Engel curves are $2P_F F = I$ and $P_C C = I/2$. The shares of the two commodities in income remain constant.

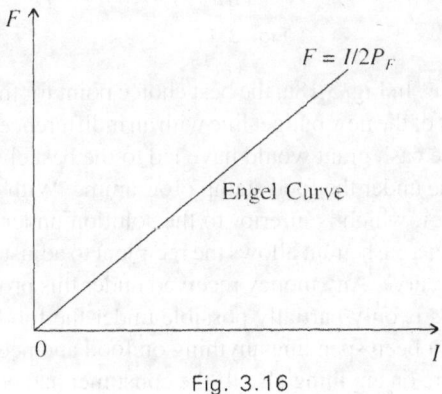

Fig. 3.16

Example 3.10: Engel curve with quasilinear preferences

Quasilinear preferences can be represented by a utility function of the form $u = v(x_1) + x_2$: the function is linear in good 2, but (possibly) non-linear in good 1. Maximize this utility function subject to the usual budget constraint $p_1 x_1 + p_2 x_2 = I$. From the budget constraint, $x_2 = (I - p_1 x_1)/p_2$, and therefore, substituting into the utility function, we get $u = v(x_1) + (I - p_1 x_1)/p_2$. The utility can therefore be maximized with respect to x_1, and the first order condition yields $dv/dx_1 = p_1/p_2$. Since v is a function only of x_1, this tells us that the demand for x_1 is a function only of the ratio of prices, and not income. In other words, the Engel curve will be a line vertical to the I-axis.

3.8.1 Food Stamp Programmes

For the poor and needy, some countries often have *food stamp* programmes. Under such programmes, poor people are given stamps with a certain face value (say Rs 100) which can be exchanged for food of equal value. The alternative is to give *cash grants*, that is, give the poor Rs 100 in cash. How do these two programmes compare?

Let us use the composite commodity model. The consumer's budget constraint is $I = P_F F + Y$, where Y is the expenditure on 'other goods'. In the food stamps programme, the consumer gets Rs 100 which can only be spent on food. Therefore the maximum amount that the consumer can spend on food increases by this amount. The F-intercept increases to $(I + 100)/P_F$. But the maximum amount that can be spent on other things is still Y. On the other hand, in the cash grant programme, the individual's income increases to $I + 100$. The maximum Y he can purchase is $(I + 100)$.

In Fig. 3.17, the new budget line with the food stamp programme is BAB', while that for the cash grant programme is $B'B'$. Is there any difference between the two programmes?

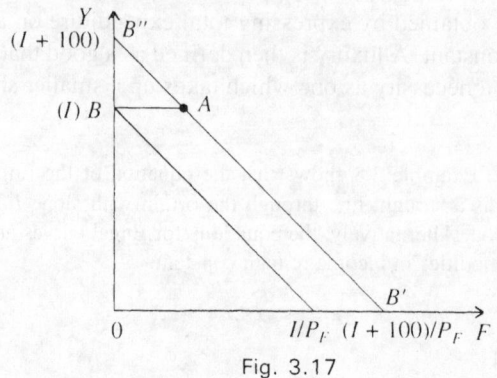

Fig. 3.17

Fig. 3.18 shows two situations. In Fig. 3.18a, the best choice point for the two programmes coincide at E', because the tangency point of the new budget line with an indifference curve occurs in the segment AB'. However, in Fig. 3.18b, the cash grant would have led to the best choice point E' in the segment $B'A$. This segment is unavailable under the food stamp programme. With the food stamp programme, therefore, there is a solution at A, which is inferior to the solution under the cash grant programme.

The point here is quite simple: a cash grant allows the recipient to adjust the allocation of her income and reach a higher indifference curve. Any money received under this programme can be spent either on food or on other things. This is only partially possible under the food stamp programme. At one extreme, if the consumer had not been spending anything on food and needs to buy at least Rs 100 on food, then she cannot spend more on anything else. If the consumer had been spending Rs 10 on food, then she can release only Rs 10 under the food stamp programme to be spent on other things. And so on.

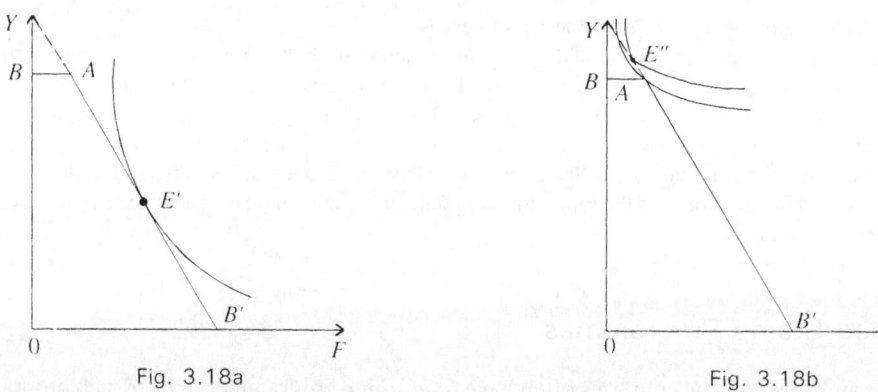

Fig. 3.18a   Fig. 3.18b

Why do governments still favour food stamp programmes over cash grant programmes? One justification is that a cash grant might be spent on 'undesirable' items like alcohol. The food stamp programme forces the recipients to increase the spending on food, at least to some extent.

The same type of analysis seems to be applicable to foreign aid to developing countries that are earmarked for certain projects. Countries providing such aid want to make sure that the aid is not spent under 'undesirable' heads like military expenditures or staff expenses.

3.9 Options

When the income of the consumer increases, the budget line shifts outward and the feasible set expands. The consumer has more options to choose from. She reaches a higher level of utility with her income. We know that with the increased income, the consumer always has the option of selecting the original best choice bundle, so that she is sure of obtaining at least the original level of utility. In general, she can increase her utility level because of the expansion in her feasible set.

Does an increase in the set of options always make an individual better off? It has been seen that an increase in options can have detrimental effects. As individuals, we are sometimes prepared to give up options if others also gave up those alternatives. For example, we accept speed limits on the roads which limit our options in driving if others also do so.

There are other options that we might not want for ourselves, independently of whether they are made available to others or not. Thus the teenager might not want to take drugs with her friends. The option is not agreeable to her, but not taking it, once it is available, might involve a loss of face. Game theory has highlighted the fact that having less options might represent commitments. If an army does not have the option of retreating, its threat to fight may be more credible (see Chapter 11 for related discussion).

Individuals are not super-rational beings. If one has options, one can make a mistake. Psychologically, bygones are not bygones, and having an alternative and making a wrong choice seems to be worse than reaching the same outcome having no choice at all. Individuals also dislike having to spend time and effort to choose among alternatives.

Topics for Discussion

1 In what respects does the custom of gift-giving differ from the ordinary market exchange process?
   The analysis of the food-stamp appears to show that getting more resources in money rather than in kind is better, because it enlarges the set of options. However, gifts are often given in kind. Instead of cash, people gift flowers, cards, candies and toys. Does this mean that except for strictly monetary presents, the custom of gift-giving is socially inefficient?
2. In India, a large portion of the incomes of senior level employees both in the private and the public sector is in the form of 'perks' (perquisites). In this context, Basu (1991) argues that 'This is ...an undesirable institution which leads to wastage and inefficiency...'. Examine the pros and cons of this statement.

Exercise

1. Antara gets an allowance of Rs 9 per week which she spends entirely on chanachur and bhelpuri. Chanachur costs Re 1 per 100 gm and bhelpuri costs Rs 1.50 a helping. X denotes the quantity of chanachur and Y denotes that of bhelpuri.

   (a) If Antara spends her entire allowance on chanachur only, she can buy _____ gm of chanachur and if she spends her entire allowance on bhelpuri only, she can buy _____ helpings of bhelpuri.
   (b) Antara's budget equation is

   $$Y = _____ \cdot X + _____.$$

   (c) The slope of the budget line is _____ which means that the opportunity cost of a helping of bhelpuri is _____ of _____(chanachur/bhelpuri).
   (d) Suppose that with the same income and prices, Antara chooses to consume 4 helpings of bhelpuri and 300 gm of chanachur per week. Is she on her budget line? _____(Yes/No).
   (e) Consider the four possible cases:
      (i) Only the price of bhelpuri increases to Rs 3 a helping, price of chanachur and income remaining the same. Antara's budget equation now is

      $$Y = _____ \cdot X + _____.$$

(ii) Only the price of chanachur increases to Rs 2 per 100 gm, the price of bhelpuri and allowance remaining the same. Antara's budget equation now is

$$Y = \underline{\hspace{2cm}} \cdot X + \underline{\hspace{2cm}}.$$

(iii) Antara's allowance is increased to Rs 18 a week, even though prices of bhelpuri and chanachur do not change. Antara's budget equation now is

$$Y = \underline{\hspace{2cm}} \cdot X + \underline{\hspace{2cm}}.$$

(iv) The price of bhelpuri doubles to Rs 3 a helping and the price of chanachur doubles to Rs 2 per 100 gm. To help her out, Antara's father decides to double her allowance to Rs 18 per week. Antara's budget equation now is

$$Y = \underline{\hspace{2cm}} \cdot X + \underline{\hspace{2cm}}.$$

(f) Graphically represent the four cases in (e). In each case, draw the original budget line and label it *BB*. Indicate for all lines the quantities associated with the intercepts on both axes.

2. Rekha spends all her income attending plays and movies. Her utility function is given by $U = 3P + M$, where P represents the number of plays and M the number of movies.

   (a) Draw her indifference map below (draw at least two indifference curves).
   (b) Rekha earns Rs 120 a week from tutoring. If play tickets cost Rs 12 each and movie tickets cost Rs 5 each, draw her budget line in the same diagram, clearly labelling the two intercepts.
   (c) Label the best choice for Rekha as *E* in the diagram. She will watch ____plays and ____ movies evry week.

3. Vikram budgets Rs 18/week for his coffee with milk consumption throughout the week. He prepares his coffee with 4 parts of coffee to one part of milk. Coffee costs $1/oz, and milk costs $0.50/oz. Let C and M denote the quantities of coffee and milk respectively.

   (a) The equation of Vikram's budget line is $C = \underline{\hspace{2cm}} \cdot M + \underline{\hspace{2cm}}.$
   (b) Vikram will buy _____oz of coffee and _____oz of milk every week.
   (c) In a diagram, draw his budget line and three indifference curves. Represent his best choice point by *E* on the budget line.

4. Madhuri's utility function is $U = F \cdot C + F$, where F stands for food and C for clothing. The prices of food and clothing are P_f and P_c respectively. M stands for income.

   (a) The MRS at any point of an indifference curve for Madhuri will be $-(dC/dF) = \underline{\hspace{2cm}}.$
   (b) The equation of the Engel curve for food will be $M = \underline{\hspace{4cm}}.$
   (c) The equation of the Engel curve for clothing will be $M = \underline{\hspace{4cm}}.$
   (d) For Madhuri, food is a _____ (normal/inferior) good and clothing is a _____ (normal/inferior) good.

5. A consumer consumes two commodities, whose amounts are denoted by F and C. The following information is given:

$$P_F = \text{Rs } 5, \quad P_C = \text{Re } 1, \ M \text{ (Income)} = \text{Rs } 40.$$

If MRS $= (40 - 5F)/(30 - C)$, find the best choice bundle for the consumer.

6. A consumer is willing to trade 1 kg of sugar for 3 kg of atta. He currently is purchasing as much sugar as atta per month. The price of sugar is twice that of atta. Should he reduce his consumption of atta and increase sugar consumption or should he reduce his consumption of sugar and increase atta consumption? Briefly explain your answer.

7. A consumer has the utility function $U = X^2Y^2$, and the budget constraint $M = P_xX + P_yY$.

   (a) Set up the constrained maximization problem and derive the first-order conditions.
   (b) Derive the consumer's demand for X and Y in terms of the parameters.
   (c) Derive the indirect utility function for the consumer.

8. In exercise 5, the demand for each commodity depends only on its own price. Check whether this is true for a consumer who has the utility function $U = (X + 2)(Y + 1)$ and the budget constraint $M = P_xX + P_yY$.

Appendix A

We can use differential calculus to solve the consumer's problem. Let us look at two equivalent approaches.

1. Let the consumer's utility function be given by $U = U(F, C)$. The consumer wants to maximize total utility U, but is constrained by the fact that the choice must be from within the budget set: (F, C) must satisfy $I \geq P_F F + P_C C$. Given the 'more is better' property, the individual must choose a point on the budget line. Hence, the consumer's problem is:

$$\max_{(F, C)} U(F, C) \text{ subject to } I = P_F F + P_C C.$$

From the budget constraint, $F = \{I - P_C C\}/P_F$. Then $U = U\{(I - P_C C)/P_F, C\}$. Employing the first order condition for maximizing U with respect to C, we get

$$dU/dC = (\partial U/\partial F)(-P_C/P_F) + (\partial U/\partial C) = 0 \Rightarrow (\partial U/\partial F)/(\partial U/\partial C) = P_F/P_C,$$ which is the condition we derived above.

2. The second method is to form a Lagrangean

$$L = U(F, C) + \lambda(I - P_F F - P_C C),$$

and maximize L w.r.t. F, C, and the Lagrange multiplier λ.

The first order conditions are:

$$\partial L/\partial F = \partial U/\partial F - \lambda P_F = 0$$
$$\partial L/\partial C = \partial U/\partial C - \lambda P_C = 0$$
$$\text{and } \partial L/\partial \lambda = I - P_F F - P_C C = 0.$$

Manipulating the first two conditions, we get back our marginal utility per rupee condition for best choice.

Example: Suppose that the utility function is of the Cobb-Douglas type: $U = F^a C^b$, $a + b = 1$, $0 \leq a, b \leq 1$.

Method 1. Since $F = \{I - P_C C\}/P_F$, $U = [\{I - P_C C\}/P_F]^a C^b$. We can then differentiate this expression with respect to C to solve for the best choice bundle. An easy way of doing this is to note that a logarithmic transformation would be an increasing function of U and should give us the same solution. Then $\ln U = a\ln(I - P_C C) - a\ln P_F + b\ln C$, where ln represents the natural logarithm. Differentiating $\ln U$ w.r.t. C, and setting equal to 0, we get $[a/(I - P_C C)]P_C + b/C = 0$. This yields $(a + b) P_C C = bI$, and therefore $C = bI/P_C$. We can then solve for F to get $F = aI/P_F$. Note that $P_C C = bI$, so the amount spent on $C(F)$ is a constant $b(a)$ fraction of the income I.

Method 2. Again, take $\ln U$ instead of U, and set up the Lagrangean:

$$L = a\ln F + b\ln C + \lambda(I - P_F F + P_C C). \text{ Then}$$
$$\partial L/\partial F = a/F - \lambda P_F = 0,$$
$$\partial L/\partial C = b/C - \lambda P_C = 0, \text{ and}$$
$$\partial L/\partial \lambda = I - P_F F - P_C C = 0.$$

Using all three equations, one can show that $\lambda = 1/I$, and the solution follows.

Appendix B

The indirect utility function

In the Lagrange method, we are solving for 3 variables $-F$, C, and λ. As we have seen, these three variables can be solved for with the help of three equations:

$$\partial U/\partial F - \lambda P_F = 0,$$
$$\partial U/\partial C - \lambda P_C = 0$$
$$\text{and } I - P_F F - P_C C = 0.$$

It is obvious that the solutions can be expressed in terms of the parameters P_F, P_C, and I. Thus the demand functions are

$$F = F(P_F, P_C, I)$$
$$C = C(P_F, P_C, I)$$

These are called the *ordinary* or *Marshallian* demand functions. The Lagrange multiplier can be solved for by setting either $\partial U/\partial F - \lambda P_F = 0$ or $\partial U/\partial C - \lambda P_C = 0$.

If we substitute F and C with these functions in the utility function, then the maximized value of the utility function can also be expressed in terms of the parameters:

$$V = U[F(P_F, P_C, I), C(P_F, P_C, I)]$$

This is called the *indirect utility function*.

Example: If $U = F^{0.5}C^{0.5}$, then $F = I/2P_F$, $C = I/2P_C$. These are the Marshallian demand functions. The Lagrange multiplier can then be solved for by setting $\lambda = (\partial U/\partial F)/P_F = I/(4P_F P_C)^{0.5}$.

Putting the F and C functions in the utility function, we get the indirect utility function:

$$V = (I/2P_F)^{0.5} (I/2P_C)^{0.5} = I/(2P_F^{0.5}P_C^{0.5})$$

Two results

1. The indirect utility function allows us to derive a rather nice economic interpretation of the Lagrange multiplier λ:

$$\lambda = \partial V/\partial I$$

The Lagrange multiplier therefore tells us by how much the maximized value of the utility function will change for a small change in the income of the consumer.

Proof: $\partial V/\partial I = (\partial U/\partial F)(\partial F/\partial I) + (\partial U/\partial C)(\partial C/\partial I)$
$= \lambda P_F (\partial F/\partial I) + \lambda P_C (\partial C/\partial I)$ (from the first order conditions)
$= \lambda[P_F (\partial F/\partial I) + P_C (\partial C/\partial I)]$ (*)

Also, from the equation of the budget line, taking the partial derivative with respect to I, we get

$$P_F (\partial F/\partial I) + P_C (\partial C/\partial I) = 1 \quad (**)$$

Combining (*) and (**) we get the required result.

2. Roy's Identity

Given the indirect utility function, can we recover the ordinary demand functions? The answer is provided by Roy's Identity:

Let $x^0 = x^0(P_F, P_C, I)$, $x = F, C$ be the ordinary demand functions. Then

$$x^0 = -(\partial V/\partial P_x)(\partial V/\partial I), \quad x = F, C.$$

Proof: The proof utilizes the first order conditions. We know that

$$V(P_F, P_C, I) = U[F^0(P_F, P_C, I), C^0(P_F, P_C, I)].$$

Let us prove the result with respect to F. Differentiating both sides w.r.t. P_F and I, we obtain

$$\partial V/\partial P_F = (\partial U/\partial F)(\partial F^0/\partial P_F) + (\partial U/\partial C)(\partial C^0/\partial P_C)$$
$$\partial V/\partial I = (\partial U/\partial F)(\partial F^0/\partial I) + (\partial U/\partial C)(\partial C^0/\partial I)$$

But we know that by first order conditions, $U_x = \lambda P_x$, $x = F, C$. Therefore these two expressions can be written as

$$\partial V/\partial P_F = \lambda P_F(\partial F^0/\partial P_F) + \lambda P_C(\partial C^0/\partial P_C)$$
$$\partial V/\partial I = \lambda P_F(\partial F^0/\partial I) + \lambda P_C(\partial C^0/\partial I)$$

Also, $P_F F^0 + P_C C^0 = I$. Then,

$$F^0 + P_F (\partial F^0/\partial P_F) + P_C (\partial C^0/\partial P_F) = 0$$
$$P_F (\partial F^0/\partial I) + P_C(\partial C^0/\partial I) = 1$$

Hence,

$$\partial V/\partial P_F = -\lambda F^0$$
$$\partial V/\partial I = \lambda$$

From these two expressions, we get our result.

The expenditure function

We have so far been discussing the representative consumer's problem of maximizing the utility function subject to the budget constraint. Let us now turn to a slightly different problem. Suppose that the utility level of the consumer is fixed at a level U'. One can then ask the question: given prices, what is the minimum amount the consumer must spend to attain the level of utility U'?

In other words, the consumer's problem is now posed in the following manner:

$$\text{Minimize } P_F F + P_C C$$
$$\text{subject to } U(F, C) = U'$$

In diagrammatic terms, this means that a particular indifference curve corresponding to $U = U'$ is first fixed. Since $P_F F + P_C C = R$ is the equation of a straight line for any R, the 'indifference curves' for the objective function can be represented by means of a family of parallel straight lines. The point at which the lowest such straight line is just tangent to the fixed indifference curve U' provides the best choice bundle.

It can be readily seen that the solutions are in terms of the three parameters of the problem—the prices and U':

$$F = f(P_F, P_C, U')$$
$$C = C(P_F, P_C, U')$$

These are called *compensated* or *Hicksian* demand functions. If we substitute these expressions in the objective function, we obtain the *expenditure function*:

$$M = P_F F + P_C C = P_F f(P_F, P_C, U') + P_C C(P_F, P_C, U')$$

Example: Consider the problem – min $P_F F + P_C C$ subject to $U' = FC$. Set up the Lagrangean

$$\mathcal{L} = P_F F + P_C C + \mu(U' - FC)$$

The first order conditions yield

$$\partial\mathcal{L}/\partial F = P_F - \mu C = 0,$$
$$\partial\mathcal{L}/\partial C = P_C - \mu F = 0, \text{ and}$$
$$\partial\mathcal{L}/\partial\mu = U' - FC = 0.$$

From the first two conditions, $C/F = P_F/P_C \Rightarrow C = F(P_F/P_C)$. From the third equation, this allows us to solve for F : $F = [U'(P_C/P_F)]^{0.5}$. Next, $C = [U'(P_F/P_C)]^{0.5}$. Finally, we can get the expression for the expenditure function:

$$M = 2[(P_F.P_C)U']^{0.5}.$$

Appendix C

Duality

The indirect utility function and expenditure function capture two different but closely related ways of looking at the individual's problem. We use the term duality to refer to these two perspectives. First, consider the utility-maximization problem. The solution to this problem identifies the indifference curve associated with the highest level of utility that the consumer can attain with her limited income. In Fig. 3.19, this is the indifference curve marked I. The best choice point is E and the associated demands for the two goods are F^* and C^*.

Now let us ask a different question. What is the minimum amount of income (given the same set of prices) that will allow the consumer to attain the level of utility represented by I? You should be able to see that the answer to this problem gives us the expenditure function. Also, since the prices are the same, the 'iso-income lines' are parallel to the budget line in the utility maximization problem. Hence, the point of tangency of one of these lines with I will occur at precisely point E. *The best choice point will be the same for the two problems.*

To see this, consider again the problem

Minimize $P_F F + P_C C$
subject to $U(F, C) = U'$

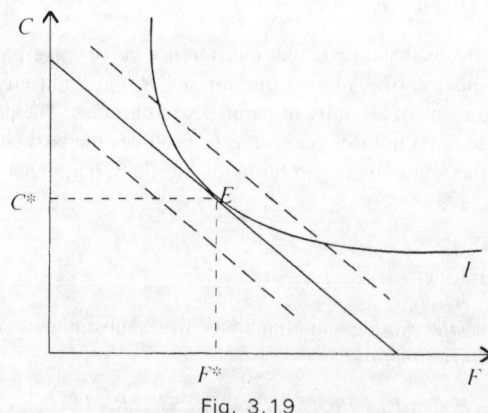

Fig. 3.19

Form the Lagrangean $\mathcal{L} = P_F F + P_C C + \mu(U' - U(F, C))$ and derive the first order conditions:

$$\partial\mathcal{L}/\partial F = P_F - \mu\partial U/\partial F = 0,$$
$$\partial\mathcal{L}/\partial C = P_C - \mu\partial U/\partial C = 0, \text{ and}$$
$$\partial\mathcal{L}/\partial\mu = U' - U(F, C) = 0.$$

From the first two equations,

$$\mu = [P_F /\partial U/\partial F] = [P_C/\partial U/\partial C] = 1/\lambda.$$

Moreover,

$$P_F/P_C = (\partial U/\partial F)/(\partial U/\partial C)$$

This shows that the cost-minimizing choice of F and C is the same as the utility-maximizing choice of F and C, *if the utility level is fixed at the maximum level of the first problem and prices remain the same.*

Example: Let $U = F^{0.5}C^{0.5}$. To obtain the expenditure function we form the Lagrangean

$$\mathcal{L} = P_F F + P_C C + \mu(U' - F^{0.5}C^{0.5}).$$

The solutions are

$$P_F = \mu U'/2F$$
$$P_C = \mu U'/2C$$

Then

$P_F F + P_C C = \mu U' \Rightarrow \mu = I/U'$, where $I = P_F F + P_C C$ is the cost-minimizing expenditure. This means that

$$P_F = I/2F \Rightarrow F = I/2P_F$$
$$P_C = I/2C \Rightarrow C = I/2P_C$$

thus demonstrating that the best choice bundle is the same as in the utility-maximization problem.

4

From Consumer's Choice to Individual and Market Demand Curves

4.1 The Individual's Demand Curve for a Commodity

We now have all the ingredients for deriving an individual agent's demand curve for a particular product. As before, suppose that the consumer has a fixed income M that can be spent on either of two commodities—food and clothing. The consumer's preferences are represented graphically by a system of indifference curves.

Given a set of prices P_C and P_F, the consumer's best choice point is E' and she demands F' amount of food at this point. In a diagram with coordinate axes P_F and F, this point is represented by point D'. Next suppose that the price of food decreases to $P_{F''}$ with the price of clothing remaining the same. The budget line rotates to BB', and the new best choice point is E''. The new combination of food price and food demand at this price is represented by point D''. In this way, by considering the demand for food associated with the different possible prices of food, we get the curve DD which represents the consumer's inverse demand curve for food. By joining the points like E' and E'', we get a *price-consumption curve* for food.

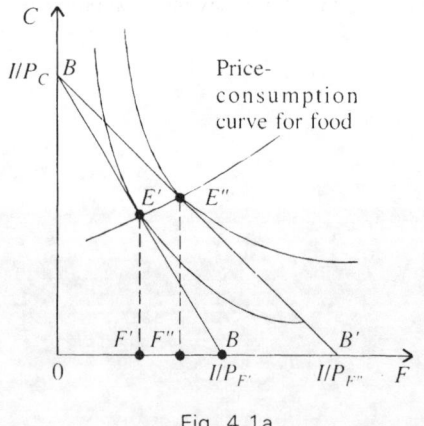

Fig. 4.1a

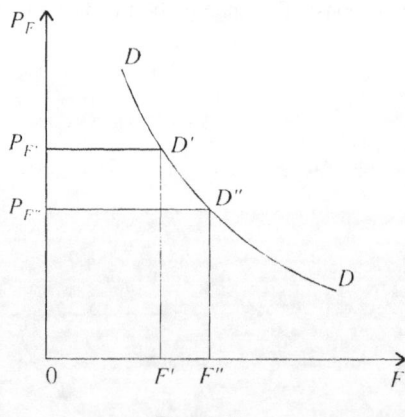

Fig. 4.1b

Example 4.1: Suppose that the utility function is $U = F \cdot C$. The consumer tries to maximize U subject to the budget constraint $P_C C + P_F F = M$. The consumer's fixed income is Rs 100. We know that the best choice points would be given by $F = 50/P_F$ and $C = 50/P_C$. The equation of the inverse demand curve for F is then $F = 50/P_F$. The points on the inverse demand curve for F are obtained by considering different values of P_F:

P_F	F
1	50.0
2	25.0
4	12.5
5	10.0

etc.

The equation of the price-consumption curve can be obtained by dividing the expression for F by C, so that $F/C = P_C/P_F$.

There are a number of features of this process for deriving the demand curve that are important. (Henceforth, we will be using the terms 'inverse demand curve' and 'demand curve' interchangeably, unless it is important to distinguish between the two.)

1. The price of clothing and the income of the consumer remain fixed when a particular demand curve is being derived. If any of these things change, then the entire demand curve would shift. For example, suppose that the income of the consumer is Rs 100 rather than Rs 50. Then for each value of P_F the demand for food is higher, and the demand curve lies further out to the right.
2. While the price of clothing and the income of the consumer remain the same when a demand curve for food is being derived, the associated demand for clothing can vary.
3. The demand curve is derived on the basis of a *fixed indifference map*. This indicates that the consumer's tastes and preferences are assumed to be unchanging during the derivation of the demand curve.
4. Since each point on the demand curve is obtained from the best choice points, at each point on the demand curve MRS = P_F/P_C. If, instead of clothing, the commodity other than food had been the 'composite commodity', then its associated price would have been 1. In that case, MRS = P_F at every best choice point, and the height of the demand curve for food would also represent the MRS at each point.

The specific form of the utility function that we considered in the previous example generated a downward sloping demand curve: lower prices were associated with larger amounts of quantity demanded. However, we can also visualize situations where the demand curve would be upward sloping. The investigation of the situations where such upward sloping demand curves are likely yields important insights into the forces determining a consumer's demand for a commodity.

4.2 The Substitution Effect and Income Effect of a Price Change

The demand curve is derived by varying the price of the commodity and observing the effect on the quantity demanded. We now carry out a thought experiment in which the effect of a price change is broken down into two components:

1. The *substitution effect*: When the price of food goes down, food becomes cheaper relative to other commodities and consumers tend to substitute food for other commodities. This *always* tends to increase the quantity demanded of food.
2. The *income effect*: A fall in the price of food represents an increase in the income of the consumer, because the consumer can now reach the same indifference curve with a smaller income. The extra income has to be allocated between food and other commodities and this income effect can lead to a reduction in the demand for food.

In Fig. 4.2a, the initial best choice point is A. Next, a lower price of food, $P_{F'}$, is considered and the budget line swings out to BB'. The new best choice point is E. The movement from A to E can be conceptually broken down into two segments:

1. The fall in the price of food allows the consumer to attain the initial indifference curve with a smaller income. Consider a budget line $B''B''$ with prices P_C and $P_{F'}$ that just touches the initial indifference curve II. It is parallel to the new budget line BB', but lies below it, showing that a smaller amount of income need be spent to reach the same indifference curve as before. The best choice point associated with $B''B''$ is B. The movement from point A to point B is called the *Hicksian substitution effect of the price change*. The substitution effect will *always* lead to an increase in the demand for food when the price of food goes down. Why? Because the indifference curves are strictly convex by assumption, that is, the law of diminishing MRS is assumed to hold. A fall in the price of food means that the price ratio P_F/P_C falls. Hence the equality of MRS with the price ratio requires the MRS to be lower, too, which is possible only at a point like B that lies to the right of A. The demand for food increases from F_A to F_B.

2. The movement from B to E is called the *income effect of the price change*. Note that the budget lines $B''B''$ and BB' are parallel, showing that the movement from B to E represents an increase in income, rather than a change of price. However, we know that the effect of an increase in income on quantity demanded is ambiguous. We can then distinguish between three possibilities:

   (i)   If food is a *normal good*, then the income effect also leads to an increase in the demand for food, so that the overall effect on the demand for food is unambiguous. In Fig. 4.2b, $F_E > F_B > F_A$. The demand curve is downward sloping.

   (ii) If food is an *inferior good*, then the income effect leads to a reduction in the demand for food, to (say) F_E. That is, there is a movement from F_B to a point to the left of F_B. However, still $F_E > F_A$, so that the total effect is to increase the demand for food: the demand curve is again downward sloping (Fig. 4.2c).

   (iii) Finally, if food is an inferior good and the income effect is so strong that $F_E < F_A$, then a fall in the price of food leads to a fall in the quantity demanded of food. The demand curve is upward sloping. In this case, the commodity is called a *Giffen good* (Fig. 4.2d).

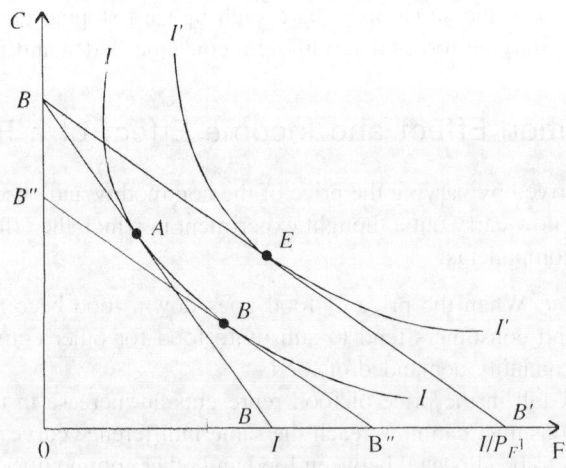

Fig. 4.2a

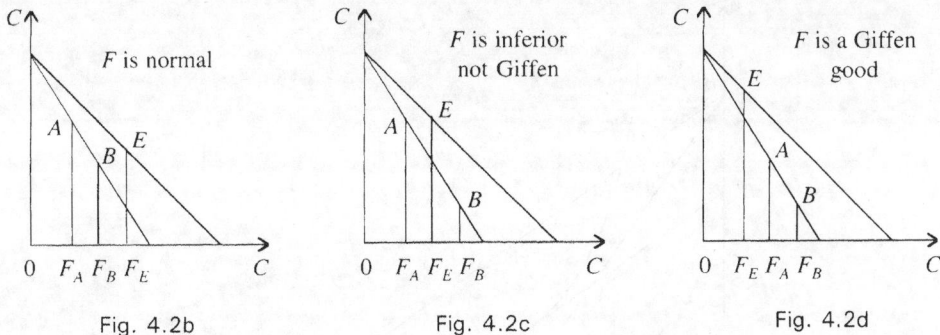

Fig. 4.2b   Fig. 4.2c   Fig. 4.2d

Since the substitution effect of a price change always acts to increase the demand for a good when its price falls, the Giffen good must be one for which the income effect not only acts against the substitution effect but is strong enough to overpower it. A much-cited example of a Giffen good was potato during the Irish potato famine of the nineteenth century. The idea was that potatoes were such a large part of the poor man's budget to begin with that an increase in the price of potato severely reduced his real income. As a result, many families responded by cutting back on meat and other more expensive foods and buying even more potatoes.

Even though modern historians dispute whether potato ever was a Giffen good, the potato story does illustrate the characteristics that a Giffen good would have to possess. First, it must be an inferior good. Second, it must account for a large share of the consumer's budget for the income effect to be significant and overwhelm the substitution effect. In practice, it is difficult to think of goods that exhibit both characteristics at once.

In India, foodcrops like ragi, bajra, and jowar probably are inferior goods. As incomes increase, people shift from the consumption of these to rice and wheat. They also account for a large share of the budget. However, the substitution effects are unlikely to be small relative to the income effects because each of these goods, by itself, has substitutes. And if they are considered together, then it is unlikely that the resultant good would be inferior. We therefore expect to find downward sloping demand curves for these commodities.

There is another useful way of separating out the substitution effect and the income effect that was first proposed by Slutsky. Consider again a fall in the price of food. Then, instead of drawing a budget line $B'B'$ that is tangent to the original indifference curve, draw a budget line based on the new price that passes through the *original best choice bundle*. This then is a budget line based on the lower price of food that allows the consumer to buy the initial bundle and hence make her at least as well off as before. However, on this new budget line, the individual will usually be able to move to a higher indifference curve by reallocating her budget. Label this new best choice point B. Then the movement from A to B is again the substitution effect and that from B to E is the income effect.

It can be shown that for 'small' price changes, this procedure for separating out the substitution and income effects is equivalent to the procedure outlined earlier. See Milton Friedman's 'Price Theory: A Provisional Text' for a discussion of the relationship between the two procedures.

Example 4.2: Suppose that the consumer's problem is to maximize $U = F.C$ subject to the budget constraint $F + 2C = 100$. The initial prices are therefore Re 1 and Rs 2.

Let us first derive the initial best choice point A. Here MRS $= C/F$ and $P_F/P_C = \frac{1}{2}$. Then $F = 2C$ and putting this in the budget equation, we get $C = 25$ and $F = 50$. Hence $A = (50, 25)$.

Now let us suppose that the price of food falls to Rs 0.5. $P_F/P_C = \frac{1}{4}$. To purchase the initial bundle, the consumer needs an income $M = 50 \times (0.5) + 25 \times 2 = $ Rs 75. The consumer's problem is now to maximize

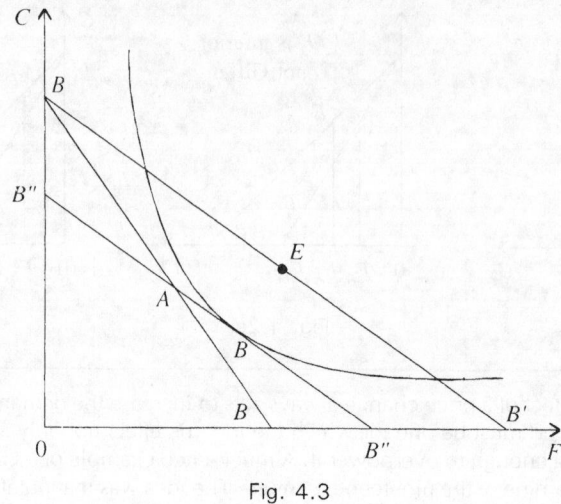

Fig. 4.3

$U = FC$ subject to $0.5F + 2C = 75$. It can be easily shown that the solution to this problem is $F = 75$, $C = 18.75$, that is, $B = (75, 18.75)$. Note that the substitution effect is the increase in the demand for F from 50 to 75, while the demand for C falls.

Finally, consider the problem: maximize $U = F \cdot C$ subject to $0.5F + 2C = 100$. It can be shown that the solution is $F = 100$. The income effect is then the increase in demand for F from 75 to 100.

4.2.1 Perfect Substitutes and Complements

It would be useful at this stage to analyse cases where goods are either perfect substitutes or perfect complements. When two goods are *perfect substitutes*, the indifference curves are parallel straight lines, that is, the MRS is the same at any point of an indifference curve.

In this situation, there are three possibilities; the slope of the budget line determined by the price ratios (a) is equal to MRS, (b) is greater than MRS or (c) is less than MRS. Start from a price P_F such that P_F/P_C is greater than MRS. Then no food would be demanded and the demand curve would coincide with the price-axis. As the price of food falls, at some stage P_F/P_C will be equal to MRS and the budget line will coincide with an indifference curve. Then any point on the indifference curve might be demanded and the demand curve has a horizontal segment at this price. If price falls further, then only food will be demanded and we expect to get a downward sloping segment.

In the case of *perfect complements*, the indifference curves are L-shaped and the commodities are always demanded in fixed proportions; the best choice point is reached when the budget line touches the kink of an indifference curve. As the price of food falls, the budget curve swings out to the right and the quantity demanded of food increases, generating a downward sloping demand curve. Notice that when the goods are perfect complements, the substitution effect is zero because there are no substitution possibilities (see Fig. 4.4a and 4.4b).

4.3 From the Individual Demand Curves to the Market Demand Curves

The procedure for deriving an individual agent's demand curve for food (say) has just been described. It is now a simple matter to derive the market demand curve for food. At each price, the

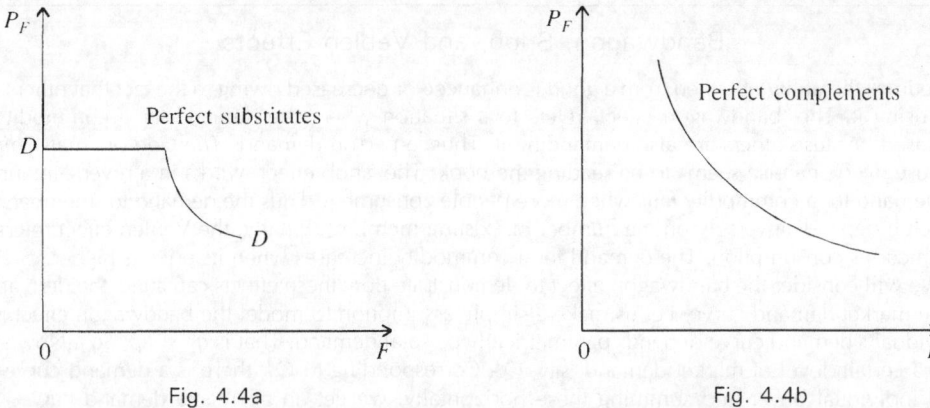

Fig. 4.4a   Fig. 4.4b

quantities demanded by all the individual buyers in the market must be summed to get the market demand. The market demand curve is therefore obtained by *laterally* or *horizontally* summing up all the individual demand curves.

Fig. 4.5 illustrates this procedure. There are just two buyers in the market, Ms A and Mr B. At the price P_F, their respective demands are F_A and F_B. The market demand at this price is then $F_A + F_B$, which is shown in panel *c*. By summing up the quantities demanded in panels *a* and *b* for each price, we generate the market demand curve.

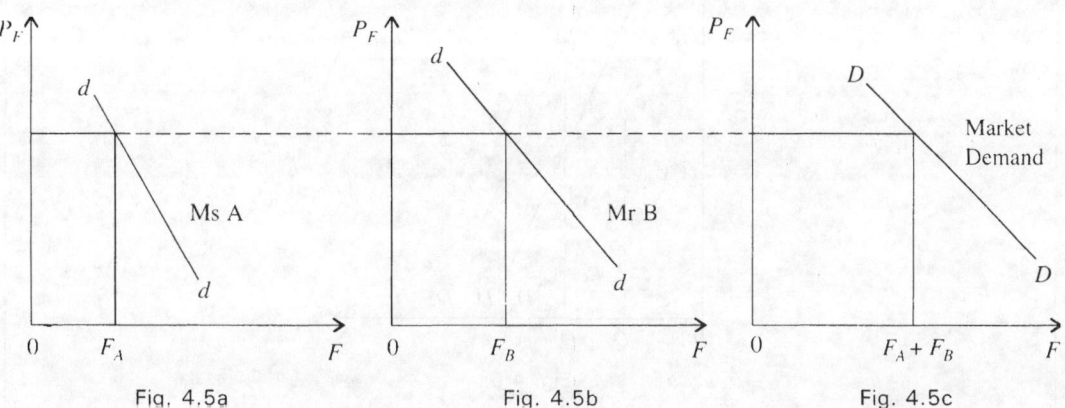

Fig. 4.5a   Fig. 4.5b   Fig. 4.5c

Example 4.3: Let the demand equations for A and B be

$$q_d^A = 10 - P \text{ and } q_d^B = 20 - 4P.$$

Note that for $10 > P \geq 5$, only A demands the commodity. Then the equation of the demand curve will be

for $10 > P \geq 5$, $Q = q_d^A = 10 - P$ and
for $P < 5$, $Q = q_d^A + q_d^B = 30 - 5P$.

The market demad curve will have a kink in this case. But if there are many buyers in the market, we expect the kinks to disappear and the market demand curve to be a smooth curve.

Bandwagon, Snob, and Veblen Effects

Sometimes the utility obtained from a good is enhanced or decreased owing to the fact that others are also using it. The 'bandwagon effect' refers to a situation where the demand for a commodity is increased because others are also demanding it. Thus, a person demands *The God of Small Things* because everyone else seems to be reading the book. The 'snob effect' works in a reverse manner: the demand for a commodity falls when more people consume it. Thus the demand for membership of a club depends inversely on the number of existing members. Finally, the Veblen effect refers to conspicuous consumption. The demand for a commodity increases when its price is higher.

We will consider the bandwagon effect to demonstrate how these effects can affect the derivation of the market demand curve. Let us make a simple assumption to model the bandwagon effect: the individual's demand curve depends parametrically on total demand. That is $q_i^d = f(p; Sq_i)$. Now start with a certain level of market demand, say, Q^a. Corresponding to Q^a, there is a demand curve for each individual buyer and summing these horizontally, we get an aggregate demand curve, Sq_i^a (labelled as D_a). However, only one point on this aggregate demand curve is consistent with Q^a, the market demand that generated the individual demand curves in the first place. This is the point a, which is given by the intersection of the D_a curve with the vertical line at Q^a. Considering other such Q's, we can generate a set of points a, b, c, etc. and joining these together we get the real or equilibrium demand curve DD. Given that the consumers possess accurate market information, only points on DD can be sustained.

Note that the curve DD is flatter than any of the Sq_i curves (it may be downward or upward sloping). When the price of the commodity falls, a bandwagon effect gets added on to the price effect. As total demand increases, this in turn will shift each of the demand curves to the right.

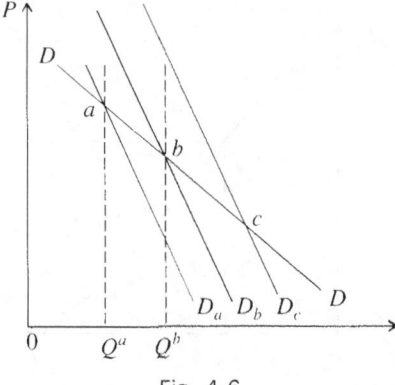

Fig. 4.6

The other two effects can be incorporated in our analysis in a similar manner.

Source: Harvey Leibenstein, 1950, 'Bandwagon, Snob, and Veblen effects in the theory of consumer's demand', *Quarterly Journal of Economics*.

4.4 The Income-compensated Demand Curve

The individual demand curves considered so far have taken into account both the substitution and income effects. However, this might not be appropriate in certain cases. Suppose that the price of petrol increases but to neutralize the increase, the government decides to pay more dearness allowance to its employees. Then for a government employee, the demand curve for petrol should take account of only the substitution effect.

A demand curve generated by considering only the substitution effect is called an *income-compensated demand curve*. Remember that for a normal good, the income effect of a fall in the price is to increase the quantity demanded. Hence, for a normal good, the compensated demand curve will be *steeper* than the ordinary, uncompensated demand curve: when price falls, the increase in quantity demanded is greater when the income effect is taken into account in addition to the substitution effect. For an inferior good, it will be flatter. (What happens when the good is a Giffen good? One must remember that the demand curve is upward sloping in this case.)

4.5 Revealed Preference

The discussion of the demand curve till now has been based on the assumption that the consumer's tastes and preferences, more specifically her rankings over different commodities, are known. But one might argue that such knowledge is impossible to obtain. The best that one might do is to observe the consumer's actual choices in the market and try to deduce conclusions from such observations. Paul A. Samuelson proposed an elegant model for doing just this. In fact, he showed that if certain conditions are satisfied and a sufficient number of observations are available, then one can even generate a consumer's indifference map. Samuelson's approach is known as the *revealed preference approach* since it takes the position that the consumer's preferences are revealed through her choices in the marketplace.

To simplify the discussion, we will assume that in each price-income situation, one and only one best bundle is chosen. The revealed preference approach is then based on one important axiom:

Weak Axiom of Revealed Preference (WARP): *The consumer's choices are consistent in the sense that if the bundle A is once revealed preferred to bundle B, and the two bundles are not the same, then it can never again be revealed inferior to bundle B.*

Let us discuss this assumption in some more detail. The important thing here is to understand when a bundle is revealed preferred to another. Bundle A is revealed preferred to bundle B if A is chosen when B could have been purchased. This means that bundle A was at least as expensive as bundle B, but was chosen over B. Now consider another situation when the consumer is observed to have chosen bundle B. This can only happen if, in the prevailing price-income condition, bundle A was more expensive and, therefore, unattainable. Otherwise, the consumer's choices in the two situations would be inconsistent with each other. In other words, if I buy one apple rather than one banana when I could have bought both, the apple is revealed preferred to the banana. Consistency requires that when both are again available to me (I can purchase both), I should not end up buying a banana rather than an apple. If I am observed ever to be purchasing a banana, this must be because I could not afford an apple.

All these can be compactly written as follows. Suppose the bundle $X^1 = (x_1^1, x_2^1)$ is chosen when prices are $P^1 = (p_1^1$ and $p_2^1)$, and the bundle $X^2 = (x_1^2, x_2^2)$ is chosen when prices are $P^2 = (p_1^2$ and $p_2^2)$. In the first situation, X^1 is revealed preferred to X^2 if and only if $p_1^1 x_1^1 + p_2^1 x_2^1 \geq p_1^1 x_1^2 + p_2^1 x_2^2$, that is, if and only if $P^1 X^1 \geq P^1 X^2$. On the other hand, if X^2 is chosen when prices are as in P^2, then it must be that X^1 cannot be purchased with prices P^2: $p_1^2 x_1^1 + p_2^2 x_2^1 > p_1^2 x_1^2 + p_2^2 x_2^2$, otherwise WARP is violated.

$$\text{Thus } P^1 X^1 \geq P^1 X^2 \text{ must imply } P^2 X^1 > P^2 X^2.$$

Of course, if the consumer's tastes and preferences change significantly between the two situations, there would be no inconsistency in the choice of A over B in one situation and B over A in another. The notion of consistency presupposes that the consumer's preferences are stable over the time period for which we observe her behaviour.

The notion of consistency can be extended in another sense. Suppose that the bundle A is revealed preferred to B, which in turn is revealed preferred to a bundle C. Then we should never observe a sequence of choices under which C would be revealed preferred to A.

Strong Axiom of Revealed Preference (SARP): *If A is revealed preferred to B (either directly or indirectly) and B is different from A, then B cannot be revealed preferred to A directly or indirectly.*

Revealed preference theory allows us to derive some of the results obtained earlier. While the results are the same, we get the benefit of simpler proofs. Moreover, the methodology employed is often found useful in proving other results.

As an example, we prove that the substitution effect always leads to an increase in demand. Suppose that the consumer chooses the bundle $X = (x_1, x_2)$ when the prices are $P = (p_1, p_2)$ and the bundle $Y = (y_1, y_2)$ for some prices $Q = (q_1, q_2)$. Also assume that the consumer is indifferent between the two bundles. Such a situation is shown in Fig. 4.7.

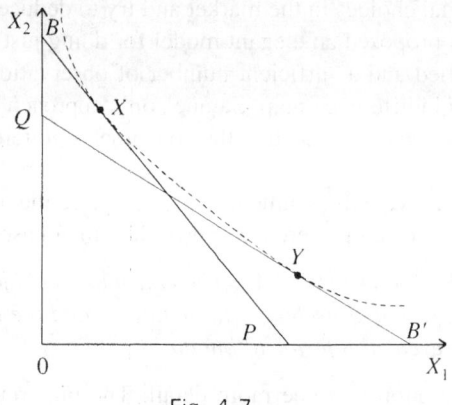

Fig. 4.7

Thus neither bundle can be revealed preferred to the other. From revealed preference theory, we know that the following two inequalities cannot hold:

$$P \cdot X > P \cdot Y$$
$$Q \cdot Y > Q \cdot X$$

Hence the following inequalities *must* hold:

$$P \cdot X \leq P \cdot Y$$
$$Q \cdot Y \leq Q \cdot X$$

Adding both sides we get

$$P(X - Y) + Q(Y - X) \leq 0$$

that is

$$-P(Y - X) + Q(Y - X) \leq 0$$

or

$$(Q - P)(Y - X) \leq 0.$$

The last expression can be written out as:

$$(q_1 - p_1)(y_1 - x_1) + (q_2 - p_2)(y_2 - x_2) \leq 0$$

Consider a change in the price of commodity 1 only, so that $q_2 = p_2$. Then we get

$$(q_1 - p_1)(y_1 - x_1) \leq 0$$

that is

$$\Delta p \cdot \Delta x \leq 0$$

That is, the substitution effect is negative.

The revealed preference approach also allows us, in principle, to construct a consumer's indifference map if sufficient observations on her market behaviour are available. Consider Fig. 4.8. Suppose that the consumer is observed to select the bundle A when the price line is PP'. Therefore A is revealed preferred to every point on or below PP'. It is also apparent that every point like G, which lies to the northeast of A in the region KAL, should be revealed preferred to A because such points contain more of at least one commodity. Therefore the indifference curve through A must lie below KAL and above PP'. This shows that at least near A, the indifference curve must have a negative slope (because it cannot enter the area KAL) and must be convex to the origin.

We can continue further using this approach. Suppose that the point B is chosen when the price line is RR'. B is then revealed preferred to a point like E. But since A was revealed preferred to B, it is now revealed preferred to E. The indifference curve through A must lie above E, and so on.

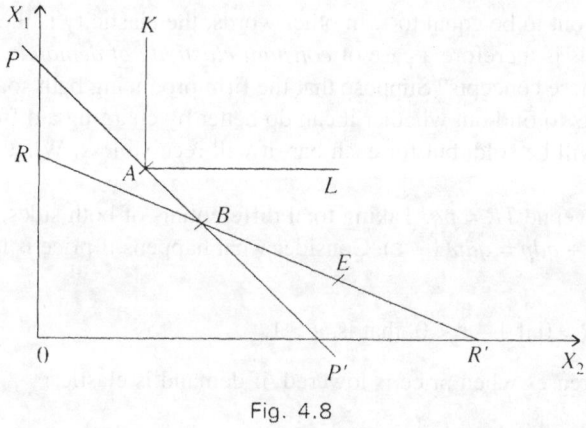

Fig. 4.8

4.6 Elasticities

The quantity demanded depends on prices and income. When prices or incomes change, the quantity demanded changes, but the responsiveness of quantity demanded to price or income changes varies from commodity to commodity. The concept of elasticity, which summarizes this responsiveness, is useful for a variety of problems.

Consider the market demand for a commodity, q, and let it depend on a factor y (which might be its own price, or the price of a related good, or income). Then the *elasticity* of demand for q with respect to y is defined as the percentage change in q that results from a 1 per cent change in y. It is the percentage change in q divided by the percentage change in y. Since percentage changes are pure numbers, the elasticity measure will always be a unit-free pure number. It will not depend on the unit in which quantity is measured, for example, kilograms or pounds.

Mathematically, elasticity of q with respect to y is $(dq/q)/(dy/y) = (dq/dy) \times (y/q)$. It is useful to note here that this is also equal to $d\ln q / d\ln y$ (where ln denotes the natural logarithm), since $d\ln q = dq/q$ and $d\ln y = dy/y$.

4.6.1 Price Elasticity of Demand

The (own) *price elasticity* measure is used extensively in the literature. For downward sloping curves, prices and quantities move in opposite directions, so that the elasticity value is negative. To avoid this problem, we consider the absolute value of the elasticity. Noting that the percentage change for quantity demanded is $(dq/q) \times 100$ while that for price is $(dp/p) \times 100$, we can write the price-elasticity measure as

$$\varepsilon = - [(dq/q)/(dp/p)] = -(p/q) \times (dq/dp).$$

Since price-elasticity is being measured at a point on the market demand curve, we are assuming that all the other factors that affect market demand are remaining fixed. For example, distribution of incomes among consumers, their tastes and preferences, prices of related commodities, etc., are all assumed to be constant. *In this sense, the elasticity measure really refers to partial derivatives rather than total derivatives.*

If the percentage change in q > the percentage change in p, then ε > 1, and we have *elastic* demand. If the percentage change in q = the percentage change in p, ε = 1 and we say that demand is *unit elastic*. If the percentage change in q < the percentage change in p, so that ε < 1, demand is said to be *inelastic*.

An interesting case arises when the demand function is of the form $q = Ap^{-r}$. Then $dq/dp = -rAp^{-r-1}$, and ε turns out to be equal to r. In other words, the elasticity is the same at each point on the demand curve. This is therefore a case of *constant elasticity of demand*.

Why do we need these concepts? Suppose that the firm producing bath soap is selling each bar at a certain price. It wants to find out whether it can do better by charging a different price. If it lowers the price, more bars will be sold, but for each bar, it will receive less. What will happen to its total sales revenue?

Now, total sales revenue $TR = pq$. Taking total differentials of both sides, we get
$dTR = d(pq) = pdq + qdp = qdp(1 - \varepsilon)$. Consider what happens if price is lowered, so that $dp < 0$. Then

$$dTR > 0 \text{ if } 1 - \varepsilon < 0, \text{ that is, } \varepsilon > 1.$$

(Total revenue increases when price is lowered, if demand is elastic.)

$$dTR = 0 \text{ if } 1 = \varepsilon.$$

(Total revenue is not affected if demand is unit-elastic.)

$$dTR < 0 \text{ if } \varepsilon < 1.$$

(Total revenue falls when price is lowered, if demand is inelastic.)

The use of differentials makes the concept of elasticity precise. However, in real life, we must consider finite price and quantity changes, not changes that are infinitesimally small. Suppose that we have the following two observations on price and quantity:

Situation 1	Situation 2
p_1 = Rs 10	p_2 = Rs 9
q_1 = 100	q_2 = 105

Instead of considering differentials, we consider the finite changes in prices and quantity. $\varepsilon = -[\Delta q/\Delta p] \times [p/q]$, where $\Delta q = q_2 - q_1 = 5$ and $\Delta p = p_2 - p_1 = -1$. However, there is now an ambiguity relating to which set of values to use for p/q. There are three possibilities.

1. Point-elasticity measures.

We can use the price-quantity values from either of the two situations:

(a) $\varepsilon = -[\Delta q/\Delta p] \times [p_1/q_1] = -(-5) \times (10/100) = 5/10 = 0.5$
(b) $\varepsilon = -[\Delta q/\Delta p] \times [p_2/q_2] = -(-5) \times (9/105) = 9/21 = 3/7 = 0.42$

For 'small changes' in price, there will not be too much of a difference between the two values thus obtained. But for larger changes, the differences become substantial, as our example shows.

2. Arc-elasticity measure.

To get rid of this ambiguity, we can take an *average* of the values in the two situations:

$$\varepsilon = -[\Delta q/\Delta p][(p_2 + p_1)/2]/[(q_2 + q_1)/2]$$
$$= -[\Delta q/\Delta p][(p_2 + p_1)/(q_2 + q_1)]$$
$$= 5(19/205) = 0.46.$$

4.6.2 A Straight Line Demand Curve

If the demand curve is a straight line, then it is particularly easy to get the price-elasticity value at a point. Consider the demand curve AB in Fig. 4.9. Then price-elasticity at a point C on the demand curve = $(EB/CE)(CE/OE) = EB/OE = (BC/CA)$ (by property of similar triangles).

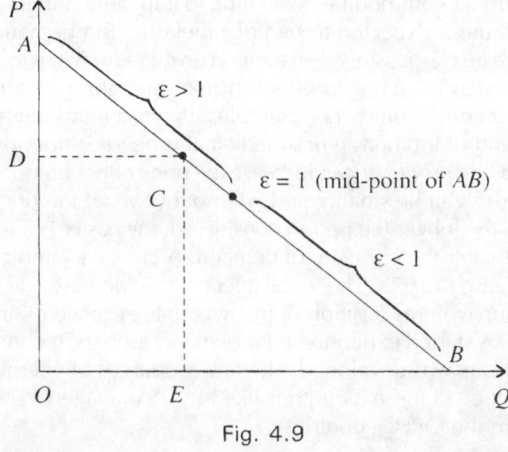

Fig. 4.9

It is obvious that at the mid-point of the demand curve, $\varepsilon = 1$. All points above this have elasticity greater than 1, and demand at all points below the mid-point is inelastic.

Two special types of the straight line deserve mention at this stage. If the (inverse) demand curve is a horizontal straight line parallel to the quantity axis as in Fig. 4.10a, then the slope of the demand curve is infinity (the slope of the inverse demand curve being 0) and the price-elasticity measure goes to infinity. We say that demand is perfectly elastic. On the other hand, if the (inverse) demand curve is a vertical straight line as in Fig. 4.10b, then $e = 0$ and demand is said to be perfectly inelastic.

It is also to be noted that the value of price-elasticity generally (but not always) varies from point to point on the demand curve. An example of a demand curve that is iso-elastic (has the same elasticity everywhere) is $q = p^{-a}$. It can be easily checked that $\varepsilon = a$ at every point of the demand curve. For example, if $q = 10p^{-1}$, then price-elasticity = 1, and we can expect that total revenue will not change when price changes. This is obviously true because $TR = pq = 10$, which is a constant.

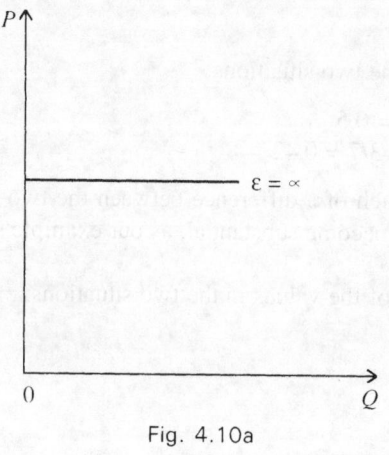

Fig. 4.10a

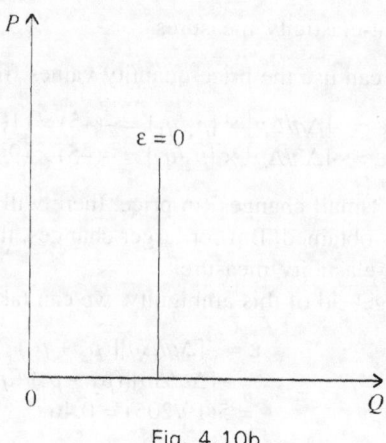

Fig. 4.10b

Among other things, the price-elasticity will depend on

1. Availability of close substitutes—if close substitutes are available, then an increase in the price will lead to large fall in demand, since consumers can easily and quickly shift to other commodities. On the other hand, if the commodity is a close substitute for other commodities, a fall in its price will lead to consumers of similar commodities switching to it in large numbers. A commodity like salt that has no close substitute is expected to be price-inelastic. But demand for a particular type of toothpaste is expected to be elastic, since consumers can quickly switch to other types of toothpaste. An aim of advertising often becomes to establish the uniqueness of a particular commodity as opposed to other, similar commodities. For example, advertisements might try to convince customers that a particular brand of toothpaste has medicinal properties not possessed by other brands. Once this is established, the producer can increase the price of her brand, secure in the knowledge that the quantity response will be smaller and will not outweigh the price effect on revenue.
2. Time period involved—the longer the period considered, the easier is it for buyers to make adjustments and hence the greater the elasticity of demand. A classic example of this was the effect of the OPEC oil price increase in 1973. The initial effect of this increase was to have a severe adverse effect on the balance of payments position of many countries, since oil import bills soared. However, over time, countries started exploiting their own oil reserves; technology for making smaller and more fuel-efficient cars was developed; alternative sources of energy like solar power began to be tapped. As a result of all these, countries like the US managed to considerably reduce their dependence on oil from the OPEC countries.

4.6.3 Other Elasticity Measures

We have already seen that the demand for a commodity depends, among other things, on

(a) own price;
(b) incomes;
(c) other 'related' prices.

Just as we derived the measure for the own-price elasticity of demand, we can derive elasticity measures related to the other factors affecting demand.

4.6.4 Income-elasticity of Demand

The individual demand curves depend on the income that each consumer has. Since the market demand curve is aggregated from the individual curves, it depends on the distribution of income between consumers. If the income distribution changes, then the market demand curves will shift. For example, if the government taxes the richer persons and subsidizes the poorer sections, this represents a distribution of incomes from richer to poorer sections. We then expect the market demand curves for commodities like food to shift to the right, since poorer people spend most of their incomes on things like food and housing. On the other hand, the demand curves for 'white goods' like refrigerators are expected to shift to the left.

If all consumers were exactly alike and had the same incomes, then this income is also the average income and the effect of 'income change' on market demand can be accounted for completely. But if this is not the case, the changes in the average income will not adequately represent the effect of changes in the distribution of income. However, sometimes it is still useful to calculate the income-elasticity of demand with reference to the *average income*. If M is the average income of consumers in the market, the *income-elasticity* of demand is defined as

$$\varepsilon_m = (dq/dM)(M/q).$$

In the case of a normal good, $\varepsilon_m > 0$, while for an inferior good, it is < 0. If $0 < \varepsilon_m < 1$, then the good is called a *necessity*, otherwise it is a *luxury*. Income elasticity, like price-elasticity of demand, can be measured either at a point or over an interval as an arc-elasticity measure.

Reddy and Bose have calculated the income-elasticity of tea consumption in India. They considered the following regression model: $\ln y = b_0 + b_1x_1 + b_2x_2 + b_3x_3 + u$, where y is the tea consumption variable, x_1 is the percentage of households consuming tea, x_2 is the natural logarithm of per capita monthly expenditure and x_3 is a measure of urbanization. Finally, u is the error term. Among other things, using data for 1987–8, they find that in the rural areas every 1 per cent rise in per capita consumer expenditure led to a 1.25 per cent rise in the per capita consumption of tea at home (in gm). Tea is therefore a luxury good. For urban areas, this variable is not significant; it appears that the percentage of households consuming tea is a major determinant of tea consumption at home and also outside of home in both rural and urban areas.

Source: V.N. Reddy and A. Bose (1995), 'Domestic Consumption of Tea in India: A State Level Analysis', A Project Sponsored by Tea Board, Calcutta.

4.6.5 Cross-price Elasticity of Demand

We know that the demand for a particular commodity also depends on prices of related products. If the price of Coke increases, we expect the demand for Pepsi to increase. If the price of sugar increases, this might not only reduce the demand for sugar, but also the demand for tea, since sugar is used in the preparation of tea.

The *cross-price elasticity* of the commodity x with respect to the price of y is defined as $\varepsilon_{xy} = (dx/dp_y)(p_y/x)$. If this is positive, x and y are said to be *substitutes* (Coke and Pepsi), while if this is negative, the commodities are said to be *complements* (tea and sugar).

Example 4.4: Suppose that the equation of the demand curve is

$$Q = 250,000 - 500P - 1.5M - 240P_R.$$

The values of P, M, and P_R are respectively 200, 60,000, and 100.

To calculate the income-elasticity of demand, we note that $dQ/dM = -1.5$ and that $Q = 36,000$. Then $\varepsilon_m = (-1.5)(60,000)/(36,000) = -2.5$.

The cross-price elasticity of demand is $(dQ/dP_R)(P_R/Q) = (-240)(100)/(36,000) = -0.67$.

4.7 Consumer Surplus

People engage in voluntary market transactions only if they gain from such activities. Otherwise, they would not have engaged in such activities. (We are assuming that people are not being coerced into 'voluntary' transactions; that is, farmers in India often have to sell commodities like wheat and sugar at pre-determined prices to the government.) It is then necessary to develop a measure of the rupee value of the gains from market transactions. The demand curve provides an easy way of doing this.

Consider the inverse demand curve DD in Fig. 4.11 and suppose that the market price of the commodity is Rs 3. The height of the inverse demand curve can be interpreted to represent the maximum amount that the consumer is willing to pay for any quantity, rather than go without the commodity. Thus for the first unit, the consumer is willing to pay Rs 14, but has to pay only Rs 3. Her surplus/gain for this unit is Rs 11. For the second unit, she is willing to pay a maximum of Rs 13, so her gain is Rs 10. In this way, we can calculate the total gain for the consumer. If small changes are considered, the *consumer surplus* is represented by the triangle *DAB* above the price line of Rs 3 and bounded by the inverse demand curve.

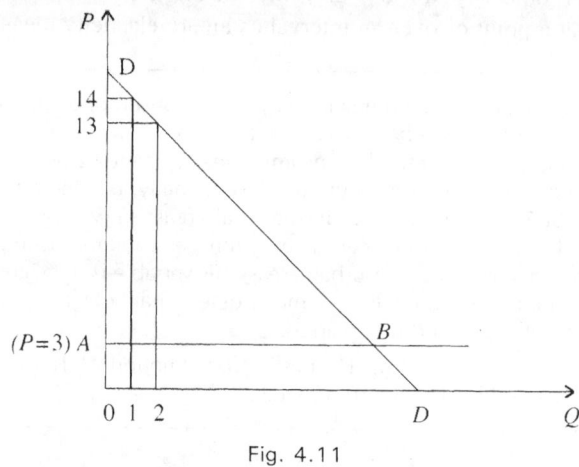

Fig. 4.11

One must sound a note of caution here. This willingness-to-pay interpretation is strictly valid if and only if the demand curve is the compensated demand curve. If it is the ordinary demand curve, then it incorporates the income effect. In that case, if the consumer has already purchased the first unit, then she is poorer by Rs 14 when she considers purchasing the second unit. Hence her willingness to pay will be smaller than Rs 13 because of the income effect. However, if income effects are small, then no great harm is done by employing the ordinary demand curve rather than the compensated demand curve.

4.8 Applications

4.8.1 Choosing Taxes

The consumer behaviour theory developed above can be used to analyse the choice between specific taxes and income taxes. First let us see how the imposition of a specific tax can affect a consumer's decisions. Initially the equation of the budget line is

$$p_1 x_1 + p_2 x_2 = I$$

and the consumer's best choice bundle is at the point A. The imposition of a specific tax at the rate t on the first commodity changes the equation of the budget line to

$$(p_1 + t)x_1 + p_2x_2 = I.$$

As Fig. 4.12 shows, the budget line rotates inwards and the best choice point now is B $(x_1{}^*, x_2{}^*)$. Since this point must satisfy the new budget constraint, $(p_1 + t)x_1{}^* + p_2x_2{}^* = I$ and the tax revenue is $R^* = tx_1{}^*$.

Instead of imposing a specific tax, the government can try to raise the same amount of revenue by means of a lump sum tax of R^* on income, where $R^* = tx_1{}^*$. The equation of the budget line now is

$$p_1x_1 + p_2x_2 = I - R^*.$$

or

$$p_1x_1 + p_2x_2 = I - tx_1{}^*.$$

One can note two things about this budget line. First, it is parallel to, but lies below the original budget line $p_1x_1 + p_2x_2 = I$. Second, it passes through the point B since the bundle $(x_1{}^*, x_2{}^*)$ satisfies the equation $p_1x_1 + p_2x_2 = I - tx_1{}^* = (p_1 + t)x_1{}^* + p_2x_2{}^* = I$.

It then follows that when an income tax is imposed on the consumer, her optimal bundle C will in general lie on an indifference curve higher than the one passing through B. Therefore, the income tax turns out to be definitely superior to a specific tax from the point of view of the consumer in the following sense: an income tax that raises the same amount of tax revenue as a specific tax leaves the consumer better off than under the specific tax.

One must of course remember that this conclusion is valid only for a lump sum tax on income. Further, if there are many consumers, then a uniform specific tax will translate into different equivalent income taxes for different consumers because they will have different preferences and hence different optimal bundles under the same specific tax. If a uniform income tax has to be imposed on all consumers, then this will generally not be better than a uniform specific tax.

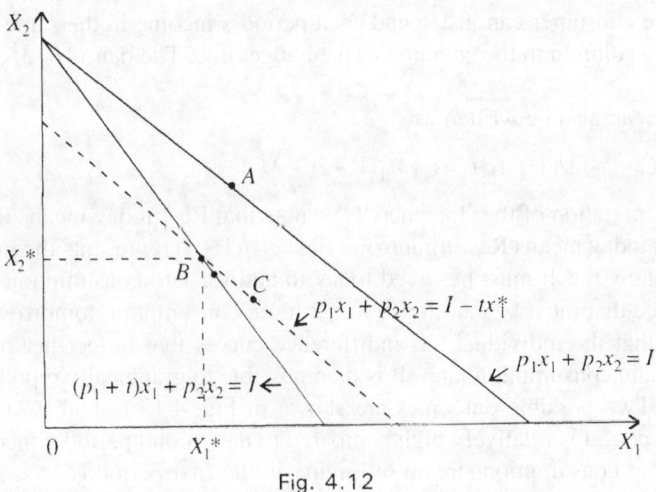

Fig. 4.12

4.8.2 The Decision to Save or Borrow

Instead of analysing the consumer's problem of allocating income between different commodities, we can consider the consumer's intertemporal problem of allocating life-time income between consumption in different time periods. We want to keep our analysis simple, so we assume that the consumer survives for just two time-periods—periods 1 and 2. The consumer gets incomes M_1 and M_2 in the two periods and consumes C_1 and C_2. The consumer can reallocate consumptions between the two periods by saving or borrowing. All borrowings must be repaid by the end of period 2. The consumer is assumed not to leave anything behind for her heirs.

	C_1	C_2
Saving	Falls	Increases
Borrowing	Increases	Falls

For simplicity, the ruling interest rate is i. The consumer can borrow any amount at the rate i; if she borrows Rs X in period 1, she must repay Rs $X(1 + i)$ in period 2.

To draw the intertemporal budget line for the consumer, it is helpful to find out the two intercepts, that is, the maximum amounts of consumption possible in the two periods. The maximum consumption in period 2 is max $C_2 = M_1(1 + i) + M_2$. This requires the consumer to save all the income in the first period and lend it out at interest rate i.

What is max C_1? The consumer can consume all of the first period's income, plus borrow an amount that can be repaid with period 2's income. The consumer can then borrow a maximum of Y such that $Y(1 + i) = M_2$, that is, $Y = M_2/(1 + i)$. Then max $C_1 = M_1 + M_2/(1 + i)$.

The equation of the budget line then is

$$1 = C_1/[M_1 + M_2/(1 + i)] + C_2/[M_1(1 + i) + M_2]$$
$$\Rightarrow C_1(1 + i) + C_2 = M_1(1 + i) + M_2$$
$$\Rightarrow C_2 = -C_1(1 + i) + [M_1(1 + i) + M_2]$$

The second term represents the C_2-intercept. The slope $-(1 + i)$ represents the 'price' of consumption today relative to the price of consumption tomorrow. Every rupee of consumption today that is forgone enables one to consume Rs $(1 + i)$ tomorrow.

In particular, the consumer can just spend each period's income in the same period, that is $C_1 = M_1$ and $C_2 = M_2$ is a solution to the equation of the budget line. The pair (M_1, M_2) is called the initial endowment point.

The budget line can also be written as

$$C_1 = -\{1/(1 + i)\}C_2 + \{M_1(1 + i) + M_2\}.$$

What is the interpretation of the slope here? We note that Re 1 today means Rs $(1 + i)$ tomorrow, that is, Re $1/(1 + i)$ today means Re 1 tomorrow. Hence $1/(1 + i)$ represents the present cost of future consumption, i.e., how much must be saved today to add Re 1 to consumption tomorrow. In other words, it is the price that must be paid today to get more consumption tomorrow.

Let us assume that the individual has indifference curves that reflect her preferences between consumption now and consumption later. It is then possible to graphically represent the consumer's best choice point. Two possible outcomes are shown in Fig. 4.13 (a and b). In the first case, the income in the first period is relatively high compared to the second period's income. The consumer then smooths out her consumption stream by saving in the first period ($C_1^* < M_1$) and consuming more in the second period. In the second case, the income in the second period is relatively higher. The consumer consumes more than her first period's income by borrowing against the second period's income.

One can now attempt some comparative static exercises. First, consider a fall in the second period income, M_2. This leads to a downward, parallel shift in the budget line. If consumptions in both

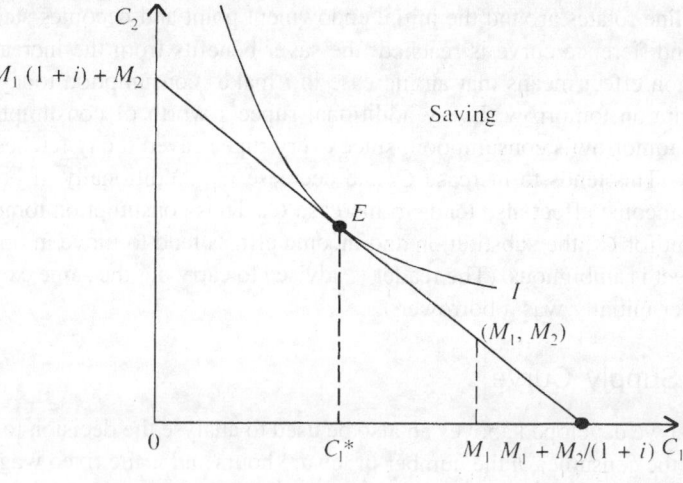

Fig. 4.13a

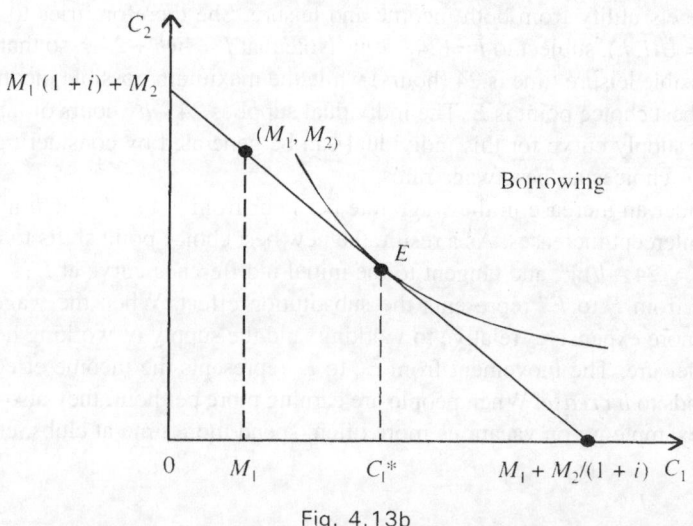

Fig. 4.13b

periods are normal goods, then both C_1 and C_2 will fall. Since the income in the first period is unchanged, this means that first period savings will increase. This emphasizes the point that first period savings depend not only on current income, but also on future income. Moreover, the adjustment to a fall in M_2 is made in both periods, that is, the loss is spread over both periods.

Next, consider an increase in i. This of course changes the slope of the budget line, making it steeper. However, there is now an added effect on income. The lifetime income depends on i through the intertemporal tools of saving and borrowing. It can be seen that even with incomes in the two periods unchanged, the maximum possible consumption tomorrow—$M_1(1 + i) + M_2$—goes up. Hence the budget line rotates inwards around the initial endowment point. The maximum consumption possible today goes down.

What can we say about the new best choice point? We need to know something about the initial best choice point before we can answer this question. Suppose that the consumer was saving in the first period, that is, the initial endowment point on the budget line lay to the right of the best choice point. The budget line rotates around the initial endowment point and becomes steeper. It is easy to see that a higher indifference curve is reached: the saver benefits from the increase in the interest rate. The substitution effect means that an increase in i makes consumption today more expensive relative to consumption tomorrow. Every additional rupee's worth of consumption today means higher sacrifice of tomorrow's consumption, since every rupee saved today fetches more in interest earnings tomorrow. This tends to increase C_2 and decrease C_1. Additionally, if both C_2 and C_1 are normal goods, the income effect also tends to increase C_2. Thus consumption tomorrow unambiguously increases. But for C_1, the substitution and income effects tend to move in opposite directions, and the overall effect is ambiguous. (The reader is advised to carry out the same exercise for the case where the consumer initially was a borrower.)

4.8.3 Labour Supply Curve

The techniques that we developed above can also be used to analyse the decision to suply labour. Let I be the income of the consumer, h the number of leisure hours and w the fixed wage rate per hour of labour supplied. Since there are 24 hours in a day, $I = (24 - h)w$, where $24 - h$ is the number of working hours.

The individual gets utility from both income and leisure. She therefore tries to maximize some utility function $U = U(I, h)$, subject to $I = (24 - h)w$. Note that $I = -wh + 24w$, so that the slope is $-w$. The maximum possible leisure time is 24 (hours) while the maximum possible income is $24w$ (when $h = 0$). The initial best choice point is E. The individual supplies $24 - h^*$ hours of labour at the wage rate w. The labour supply curve for this individual can be generated by considering different wage rates and the labour choices at these wage rates.

Therefore consider an increase in the wage rate per hour from w to w'. The h-intercept does not change, but the I-intercept increases. As a result, the new best choice point shifts to E'. We can draw a line parallel to $I = (24 - h)w'$, and tangent to the initial indifference curve at E'.

The movement from E to E'' represents the substitution effect. When the wage rate increases, leisure becomes 'more expensive' relative to working, and the supply of working hours is increased at the expense of leisure. The movement from E'' to E' represents the income effect. If leisure is a normal good, it tends to *increase*. When people are earning more per hour, they also will want to buy more leisure, for example go on vacations more often, spend more time at clubs, etc.

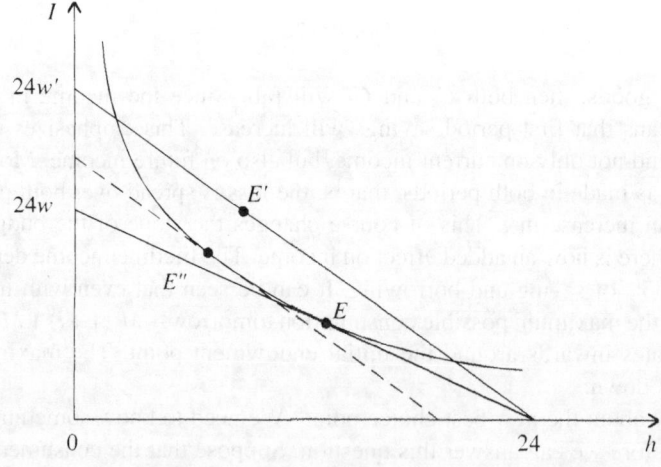

Fig. 4.14

The total effect on the supply of labour is therefore ambiguous. There is the possibility that as the wage rate goes up, this will result in lower supply of labour. Typically, we expect this to happen when the wage rate is sufficiently high. We can then get a 'backward-bending' labour supply curve. In Fig. 4.15 below, for wage rate above w^*, the labour supply curve becomes downward sloping.

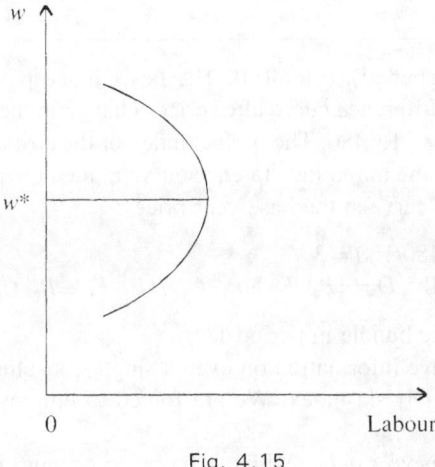

Fig. 4.15

4.8.4 Index Numbers

In any economy, there are many commodities being produced and sold, each with its own price. Over time, these prices change, but usually in different proportions. To get a single measure of the overall price change, we must consider some weighted average of the prices. Changes in this *price index* then serve as a measure of the overall price change.

Example 4.5: Suppose that there are only two consumer goods, food, and clothing. Prices in periods 0 and 1 are as follows:

Period	Food	% change	Clothing	% change
0	2		4	
1	4	100	10	150

The overall increase in prices then lies somewhere between 100 per cent and 150 per cent.

The construction of the price indices depends on the weights being employed. The exact construction of a price index can be a sensitive matter. In India, the consumer price index is used to determine the cost of living and hence the Dearness Allowance that is paid to government employees to neutralize some of the increases in the cost of living. On the other hand, the government uses the Wholesale Price Index to measure the rate of inflation from year to year. Fixed weights are used to weigh prices of different types of commodities to get these measures.

We will now show how to construct an index (the *Divisia index*) that measures exactly changes in the cost of living. Next, we show that the Laspeyre and Paasche indices that are widely used for practical reasons are biased compared to the Divisia index. To keep matters simple, assume that all consumers are alike, so that we can consider a 'representative consumer' and her indifference curves.

We use some numbers to illustrate all these.

Period	Price of Food	Quantity of Food Purchased	Price of Clothing	Quantity of Clothing Purchased
0	$P_F^0 = 10$	$F_0 = 10$	$P_C^0 = 20$	$C_0 = 3$
1	$P_F^1 = 60$		$P_C^1 = 24$	

In period 0, the consumer spent S_0 = Rs 160. The best choice point was $E_0 = (3, 10)$. If the consumer stays on the same indifference curve after prices change in the second period, she chooses $E_1 = (10, 4)$. She has to spend S_1 = Rs 480. The perfect index of the cost of living is called the Divisia index. It is the cost of attaining the initial indifference curve at the new prices divided by the cost of attaining the same indifference curve at the base year prices:

$$D = S_1/S_0 = 480/160 = 3$$
$$\text{More generally, } D = \{P_F^1 F_1 + P_C^1 C_1\}/\{P_F^0 F_0 + P_C^0 C_0\}.$$

where (C_1, F_1) is the best choice bundle in period 1.

Unfortunately, we do not have information on even a single consumer's indifference curves and therefore cannot construct the Divisia index. We are forced to employ imperfect alternatives that exhibit biases.

Let us first consider the *Laspeyres index*, which is based on changes in the cost of purchasing the initial best choice bundle at the new prices. Let $S_L = P_F^1 F_0 + P_C^1 C_0$. Then the Laspeyres index is

$$L = S_L/S_0 = \{P_F^1 F_0 + P_C^1 C_0\}/\{P_F^0 F_0 + P_C^0 C_0\}.$$

In terms of our numerical example, $L = (24 \times 3 + 60 \times 10)/160 = 672/160 = 4.2$.

Compared to the Divisia index, the Laspeyre index overstates the increase in the cost of living. The reason is apparent from Fig. 4.16 below. At the new prices, the Laspeyres index employs a budget line $B'B'$ passing through the initial best choice bundle. However, the consumer could have rearranged her purchase and attained the same indifference curve by spending less, as the line $B''B''$ parallel to $B'B'$ shows. In fact, the consumer can attain a higher level of indifference at point E_L on $B'B'$.

The other commonly employed cost of living index is called the *Paasche index* and it is based on a comparison of the cost of buying the *new* best choice bundle at current and old prices. Let $S_P = P_F^1 F_1 + P_C^1 C_1$ and $S_1 = P_F^0 F_1 + P_C^0 C_1$. Then the Paasche index is

$$P = S_P/S_1 = \{P_F^1 F_1 + P_C^1 C_1\}/\{P_F^0 F_1 + P_C^0 C_1\}.$$

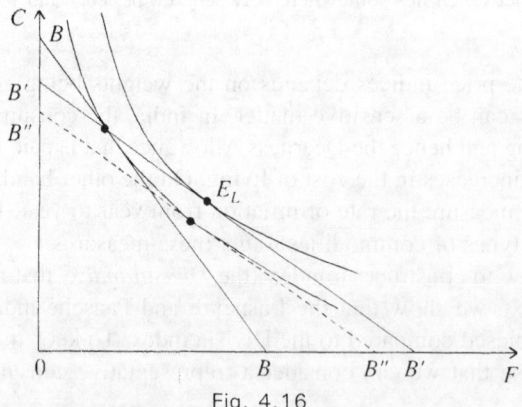

Fig. 4.16

In Fig. 4.17, the best choice bundle at the new prices is $E \equiv (7.5, 3)$. Then it can be calculated that $P = 360/180 = 2$. Therefore, the Paasche index gives a smaller value than the Divisia index and *understates* the increase in the cost of living. The reason is obvious from Fig. 4.17. At the old set of prices, the consumer could have attained a higher level of indifference curve (at E'). Alternatively speaking, she could have attained the current bundle earlier at a lower cost, at the point E'.

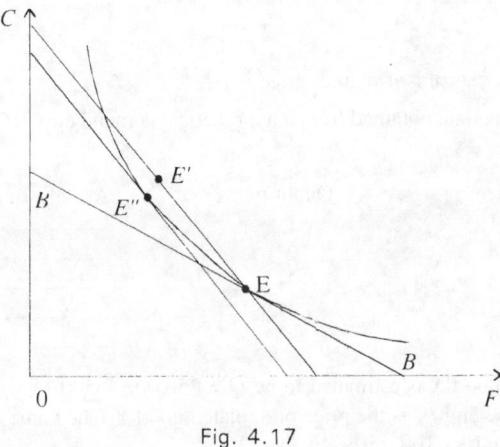

Fig. 4.17

From our earlier discussion, it should be clear that the difference between the three indices will be small when (1) changes in relative prices are small and/or (2) the goods are complements.

Topics for Discussion

1. If the government lowers the tax rates, do you think that this will lead to larger tax compliance? On what factors will the elasticity of tax revenues with respect to a change in tax rates depend?
2. In the text, we posed the consumer's intertemporal decision as one of saving versus borrowing. A related question is in what form savings are made. In India, people often keep their savings in the form of gold. Discuss the reasons for this phenomenon. Can you link up your conclusions with the availability of loans from different sources?

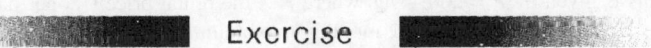 Exercise

1. A consumer tries to maximize $U = F \cdot Y$, subject to the budget constraint $P_F + Y = M$. Find the equation of the price-consumption curve. Diagrammatically represent the P–C curve.
2. Suppose that the consumer's problem is to maximize $U = F \cdot C$ subject to the budget constraint $2F + C = 100$.

   (a) Derive the initial best choice point A.
   (b) Suppose that the price of food falls to Re 1. What is the substitution effect for F? The income effect? (Use Slutsky approach to calculate the substitution effect and income effect.)
3. Suppose that the quantity of good X demanded by individual 1 is given by

$$X_1 = 10 - 2P_X + 0.01M_1 + 0.4P_Y$$

and that the quantity of X demanded by individual 2 is

$$X_2 = 5 - P_X + 0.02M_2 - 0.2P_Y.$$

Also, let $M_1 = M_2 = $ Rs 1000 and $P_Y = $ Rs 10.

(i) Graph the two individual demand curves and the market demand curve.
(ii) What is the market demand function?

4. The equation of an inverse demand curve is $P = a \times Q$.

   (i) At the mid-point of the demand curve, $P^* = $ _____, $Q^* = $ _____.
   (ii) Find the price-elasticity of demand at
   (a) $(0.5P^*, 1.5Q^*)$
   (b) $(1.5P^*, 0.5Q^*)$
   (iii) Calculate the consumer surplus if market price is P^*.

5. You are given the following data obtained from a hypothetical demand curve. Calculate the arc elasticities of demand.

Price	Quantity	Arc-elasticity
21	1	_____
18	2	_____
15	3	_____
12	4	_____
9	5	_____

6. The demand function for good X is estimated to be $Q = 250,000 - 500P - 1.5M - 240P_R$, where M is the (average) consumer income and P_R is the price of a related good Y. The values of P, M and P_R are expected to be Rs 200, Rs 60,000 and Rs 100, respectively.

   (a) Calculate the price-elasticity of demand, income elasticity of demand and the cross-price elasticity.
   (b) Is the demand for X elastic, unit-elastic or inelastic? How would a small increase in P affect total revenue?
   (c) Is the good X normal or inferior? Are the goods X and Y substitutes or complements?

7. Suppose that the demand for crossing the Howrah Bridge is given by $Q = 10,000 - 1250P$, where Q is the number of crossings and P is the toll collected from those who cross the bridge.

   (a) At $P = $ Rs 4 and $Q = 5000$, demand is price-inelastic.
   (b) At $P = $ Rs 6 and $Q = 2500$, demand is price-elastic.
   (c) At $P = $ Rs 5 and $Q = 3750$, the price-elasticity of demand is equal to unity.
   (d) All of the above are true

8. *True or False*: For a budget spent entirely on two goods, an increase in the price of one will necessarily decrease the consumption of both, unless at least one of the goods is an inferior good. Explain.

9. The only video rental club available to you charges Rs 20 per movie per day. If your inverse demand curve for movie rentals is given by $P = 200 - 9Q$, where P is the rental price (Rs per day) and Q is the quantity demanded (movies per month), what is the monthly maximum membership fee you would be willing to pay to join this club?

10. Vinay lives in a world with two time periods—today and tomorrow. At the beginning of each period he receives an income of Rs 210. If the interest rate, expressed as a fraction, is 0.05 per time period, what is the present value of his lifetime income? Draw his intertemporal budget constraint.

    If his utility function is $U = C_1C_2$, what is his optimal allocation of lifetime consumption?

11. Your utility function is $U = XY$. Your incomes and prices in two periods are as follows:

Period	Income	Price of X	Price of Y
1	100	10	10
2	100	10	25

Calculate the Divisia, Laspeyres, and Paasche indices for period 2.

5 Production

In Chapter 2 we saw how the interaction of demand and supply forces led to the establishment of equilibrium price and quantity in the market. The next two chapters showed how to obtain the market demand curve starting from an analysis of the tastes and preferences of the individual consumer. In this chapter and the next two, we turn to the other side of the market and show under what conditions the market supply curve can be derived, starting from an analysis of the behaviour of individual firms.

A firm has to take account of its costs and revenues in deciding how much to produce and supply in the market. We begin by looking at costs. We can use some common principles to analyse the nature of costs independently of the prevailing market structure. On the other hand, revenues depend critically on market structure, that is, the type and extent of competition in the market. Economists have identified a range of market structures, with perfect competition (many sellers) at the one end and monopoly (one seller) at the other end, with imperfect competition ('few' sellers) in between.

Costs can again be conceptually broken up into two components. There is, first, the *physical relationship* between inputs and outputs, and we shall begin by considering these. Second, inputs have to be purchased at some prices, and this enables us to express costs in *monetary terms*. We consider costs in the next chapter.

5.1 Production

Economists define *production* in quite general terms. Production is defined as any activity that transforms *inputs* into *outputs*. Among inputs, economists have traditionally included land, labour, capital and organization/entrepreneurship and more recently, technology and energy. Inputs are also called factors of production. Outputs are those that confer utilities. Examples of outputs are goods like cars and steel, and services like the services of barbers or housewives.

In the real world, there are often a number of stages in the process of production. Iron ore is first mined, then made into pig iron, then into steel, and finally into commodities like cars. In each stage, production takes place. However, we will be implicitly assuming, for the sake of simplicity, that all such 'intermediate' stages are collapsed into a single stage. If necessary, one can take any one of these intermediate stages, and consider the supplier (seller of iron ore) vis-à-vis the user (maker of pig iron), applying the same definition.

Note that finished goods can often be used as inputs rather than for consumption. The use of a car by company executives is an example of the former.

5.2 The Production Function

At any point of time, in any place, a firm's production possibilities are circumscribed by the nature of technology available and its resource endowments. We assume that the firm's technology options have been analysed by engineers who have chalked out a blueprint of the technology that is currently available.

While a firm can, and usually does, produce many outputs, we shall restrict our attention to the case where only one output is produced employing several inputs. The blueprint of technology is then summarized by the production function. When a certain amount of output can be produced from certain amounts of inputs, we say that this is a *feasible technique* for the firm.

Definition: A *production set* consists of those combinations of inputs and outputs such that the corresponding amount of output can be produced from the given inputs. A *production function* is the relationship between inputs and output such that inputs are combined to produce the output in the most efficient way.

Efficiency here has a simple meaning. If it is possible to produce more of the output with the same amount of inputs, then the firm is operating inefficiently. If it is possible to produce the same amount of output employing less of at least one input, again, the firm must be operating inefficiently. When these situations are ruled out, we are left with only the efficient techniques of production. The production function consists of only those techniques that are efficient. But the firm has the option of using the inefficient techniques, that is, these techniques are part of its production set.

Assume that output Q is produced with the help of two inputs, 'capital' K and 'labour' L. K is measured in 'machine-hours' and L in 'man-hours'. In other words, L and K refer to the flow of services provided by stocks of the two inputs. Then we can write $Q = F(K, L)$, where F is the production function. The production set is $\{Q \geq 0 \mid Q \leq F(K, L)\}$.

Example 5.1: Let $Q = KL$ (note the similarity with $U = FC$).
For various amounts of the inputs, we can generate the highest amount of output possible:

		L			
		1	2	3	4
	1	1	2	3	4
K	2	2	4	6	8
	3	3	6	9	12
	4	4	8	12	16

In this example, 6 units of output can be produced with 2 units of labour and 3 units of capital. If, instead, only 4 units are produced, this will be an inefficient situation, because 4 units could have been produced with 1 less unit of capital, that is, with 2 units of labour and 2 units of capital. Hence $L = K = 2$ and $Q = 4$ cannot belong to the production function. However, the combination of 4 units of output and 2 units each of labour and capital is in the production set.

Again, 6 units of output can be produced with either 2 units of labour and 3 units of capital or 3 units of labour and 2 units of capital. Neither of these is inefficient; when more labour is used, less capital is used and vice-versa. Both these combinations form part of the production function.

This technological view of the firm has sometimes been called the 'black-box' view of the firm. It can be represented as follows:

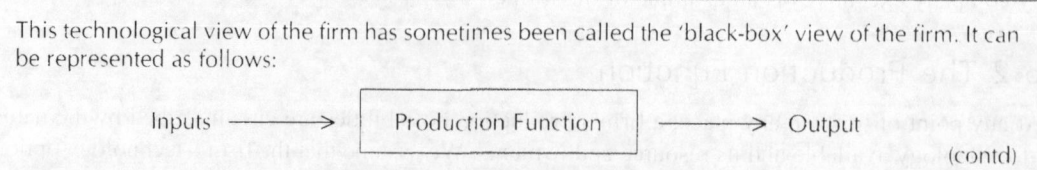

Inputs ⟶ Production Function ⟶ Output

(contd)

(contd)

Inputs are put into a 'black-box' called the production function and the output comes out at the other end. The firm is identified with the production function. We do not enquire into what goes on inside the box—what exactly is the process whereby inputs are transformed into outputs.

It has come to be felt that this view of the firm is too narrow. In reality, firms are very complex entities. The way firms are organized, for example, into semi-autonomous departments or divisions, the relationships of authority and subordination within firms, the nexus of contracts between various stakeholders, etc., all have bearing on the nature of operation of the firm. The technological aspects are not the sole determinants of the firm's activities.

To understand just how complex the working of modern corporation is, let us take a look at some of the decisions that have to be made within the firm. We are told that any economy must solve the problems of WHAT (commodities to produce and in what quantities), HOW (to produce) and FOR WHOM (particular goods to produce). From the firm's viewpoint too, it helps to classify the decisions in this way.

WHAT—The questions of what to produce and in what quantities relate to the *scope* and *scale or size* of the firm. In economic theory, goods are identified not only by their physical characteristics, but also by their spatial ('where available') and temporal ('when available') properties.

HOW—This relates not only to the choice of a *production technology*, but also to the choice of the entire *organizational structure* of the firm.

The organizational structure refers to the hierarchy of decision-makers within the firm and to the entire network of relationships between them. It refers, among other things, to—the design of incentives (salaries, bonuses, perks, etc.), lines of authority (who takes orders from whom), communication channels (who reports what to whom), organizational rules.

The firm has also to decide—accounting conventions to be followed and measures of performance to be emphasized; method of financing (debt versus equity); skill levels of employers; capital equipment to be employed; inputs to be purchased; R&D; technology to be used.

FOR WHOM—This becomes the general question of what markets to enter, both as a buyer and a seller. In the product markets, the firm must identify its potential customers and target its product at them. Market research is undertaken to identify customers and wholesale and retail distribution channels are developed to reach them. The firm can undertake advertising, sales promotion measures, product design, discount pricing etc. to capture market segments. Similarly, the firm must enter various input markets as buyers—capital markets to obtain funds for investment, labour markets to hire personnel, other factor markets to purchase various inputs, etc.

No single theory of the firm can attempt to address all these issues. However, any useful theory of the firm must address some or all of these issues.

Source: Daniel F. Spulber (1995), 'Economics and Management Strategy: A Survey', Part 1, *Journal of Economics and Management Strategy*.

5.3 Short Run and Long Run

The flexibility of a firm, that is, its ability to adjust production, depends on the nature of the inputs it employs. A *fixed input* is one whose quantity cannot be changed in some given time period. An example of a fixed input is specialized heavy machinery. Once such machinery is installed, it is not possible for the firm to add to such machinery quickly. The firm has to place new orders for such machinery to its specifications and the suppliers generally need some time to produce the machines to order. On the other hand, a *variable input* is one whose quantity can be varied in the given time period.

One can then analytically distinguish between short run and long run. The *short run* for a firm is the time period during which at least one of the inputs is a fixed input. A *long run* is a time period during which all inputs are variable.

The actual length of short run and long run will vary from firm to firm. For a small 'stall' on the street selling egg rolls or batata vadas, even a day can be a long run. All inputs are easily variable.

The seller can purchase more or less of ingredients like eggs and potatoes; if necessary more labour can be hired or the existing labour laid off; people eat the food standing on the pavement, hence there is no problem of space. On the other hand, for large steel plants, plant and machinery are specialized and the short run can be as long as 3–4 years because such equipment cannot be changed quickly.

5.4 The Short Run

We begin with a more detailed consideration of the short run. Suppose that the output Q is produced with L and K, but that in the short run, $K = K_0$, that is, the quantity of capital cannot be varied. Hence $Q = F(K_0, L)$.

Since K is fixed, we can plot a relationship between Q and L. This curve is called the *total product curve*. For the given value of K, the production function is represented by all points on the curve, while all points below the curve in the first quadrant together with all points on the curve represent the production set.

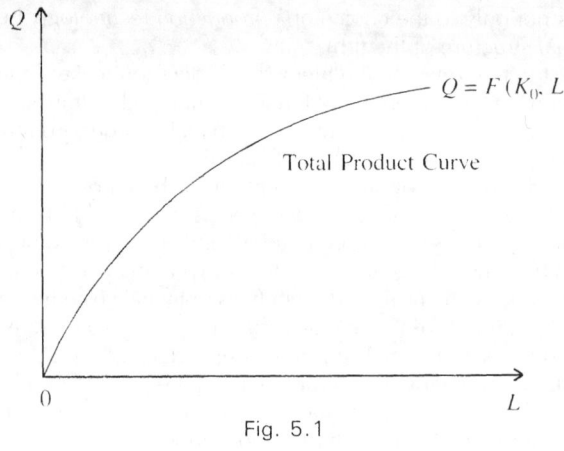

Fig. 5.1

Example 5.2: Let $Q = K^{0.25}L^{0.75}$, and in the short run $K = 16$. Then $Q = 2L^{0.75}$. This is the equation of the total output curve.

The *marginal product of labour* (MP_L) is defined as the change in Q divided by the change in L. Remember that in the short run, we are assuming that K is fixed. If K had been variable, then we would have defined the marginal product of labour as the extra output per extra unit of labour, *keeping K constant*. Graphically, the MP_L at any L is represented by the slope of the tangent to the total product curve at this L.

$$MP_L = dQ/dL \ (K = K_0).$$

The marginal product is assumed to be positive, that is, the addition of an extra unit of labour always adds to the output. That is, we are assuming that $dQ/dL > 0$ in the range of values we are considering.

In the example just given, $MP_L = 1.5L^{-0.25} = 1.5/L^{0.25}$. For $L > 0$, $MP_L > 0$.

The *average product of labour* is the output per unit of L, that is,

$$AP_L = Q/L.$$

The average product of labour at a point on the total output curve is given by the slope of the ray from the origin to that point.

In terms of our example, $AP_L = 2/L^{0.25}$.

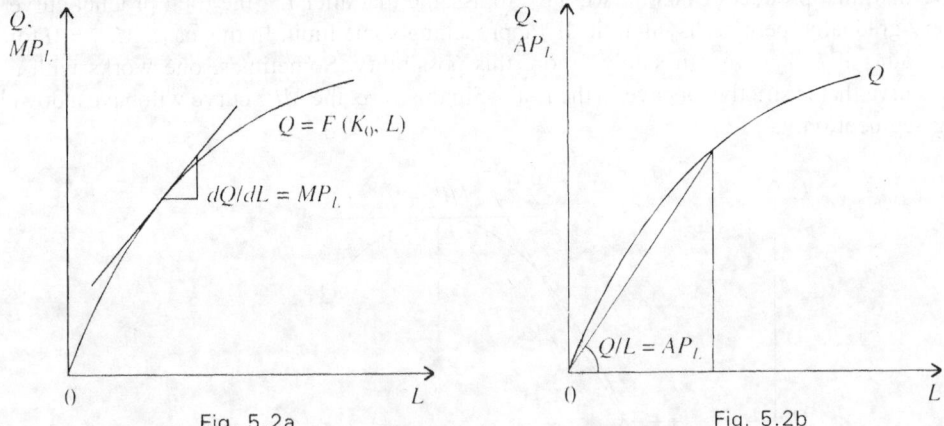

Fig. 5.2a   Fig. 5.2b

The marginal product and average product curves are obtained by plotting the marginal product and average product of labour, respectively, against L. The positions of these two curves, as well as that of the total product curve, are determined by the level at which K is fixed. A change in the value of K leads to a shift in all three curves.

To proceed further with our analysis, we need to assume something about the relationship between Q and L. Economists appeal to the law of diminishing returns to provide some structure to this relationship:

The *Law of Diminishing (Marginal) Returns* states that if at least one input is a fixed input, then the marginal product of any other input will, eventually, decrease as more of that input is applied. That is, in our model, since K is fixed, after a point, MP_L will decrease as more of L is used. Hence $dMP_L/dL = d^2Q/dL^2 < 0$ eventually. As more and more of labour is applied, the additional output per extra unit of labour goes down after a point. One should remember that by its very definition, the law of diminishing returns is applicable only in a short run situation.

Example 5.3: Consider the following hypothetical production function.

L	dL	Q	dQ	dQ/dL
1		10		
	1		1	1
2		11		
	1		3	3
3		14		
	1		3	3
4		17		
	1		2	2
5		19		

The total product curve is sometimes drawn as an inverse-S shaped curve. Since the MP_L curve is the slope of the total product curve at the corresponding points, it can be seen from Fig. 5.3 that an inverse-S shaped total product curve implies that (a) the MP_L curve is at first rising (till $L = L^*$), (b) then it has a downward sloping segment, where the law of diminishing returns applies. However, it is still positive. At L^{**}, $MP_L = 0$, and (c) after L^{**}, it becomes negative. If we want to rule out a negative marginal product of labour, we have to assume that after L^*, the total product curve rises only very gradually, perhaps asymptotically approaching some limit. In this case, $MP_L = 0$ for such a large value of L that we can safely ignore this possibility. Sometimes, one works with a total product curve that is strictly concave to the L-axis. In this case, the MP_L curve will have a downward sloping segment only.

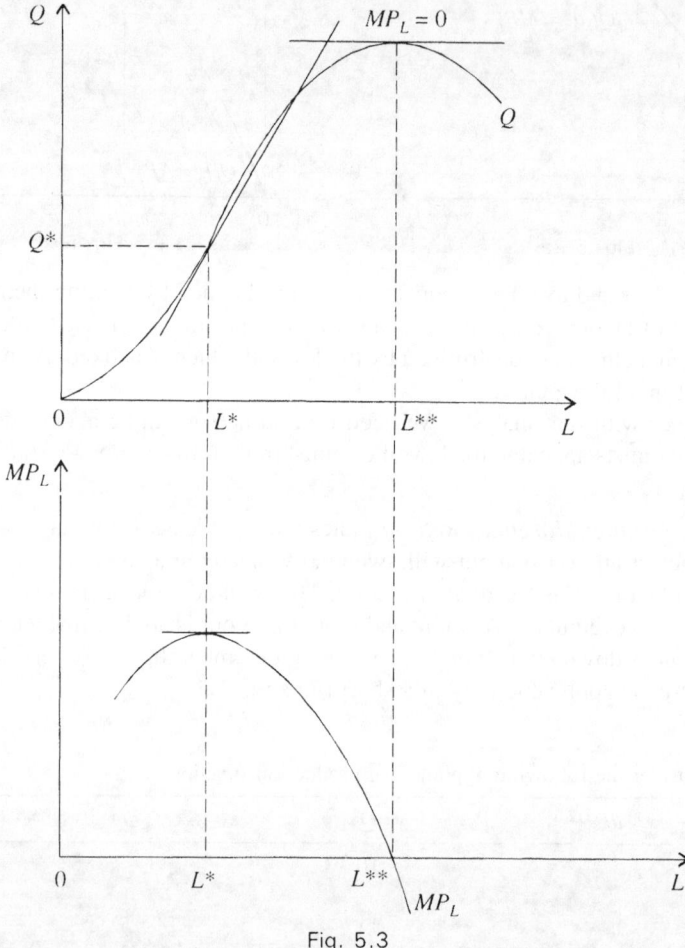

Fig. 5.3

The observation of diminishing marginal returns came from agriculture. In agriculture, a farmer has a certain plot of land that is fixed in size. This constitutes the fixed input of production. On this land, labour is employed to produce crops. With a few labourers, the land is not fully utilized, and the application of extra labour results in more effective tilling, ploughing and harvesting. Hence, in the initial stages, the extra output from each extra unit of labour goes on increasing. However, after a point, there are too many labourers working on the (fixed) plot of land and they tend to get in each other's way. At this point, the law of diminishing returns comes into operation.

5.4.1 Relationship between MP_L and AP_L

We should note at this point a very important relationship between the average product and marginal product of labour.

Now, $AP_L = Q/L$, by definition. That is, $Q = AP_L \times L$. Differentiating both sides with respect to L, we get $dQ/dL = (dAP_L/dL)L + AP_L$. The expression on the left hand side is nothing but MP_L. Hence, rearranging terms, we get

$$dAP_L/dL = (MP_L - AP_L)/L.$$

This means that

$$MP_L > AP_L \Rightarrow dAP_L/dL > 0.$$
$$MP_L = AP_L \Rightarrow dAP_L/dL = 0.$$
$$MP_L < AP_L \Rightarrow dAP_L/dL < 0.$$

When the marginal product of labour is greater than the average product of labour, the average product is rising; when it is equal, the average product remains unchanged and when it is lower, the average product is falling. Fig. 5.4 represents this relationship, assuming that the law of diminishing returns holds beyond the output level Q^*, so that the marginal product of labour curve has a negative slope beyond L^*.

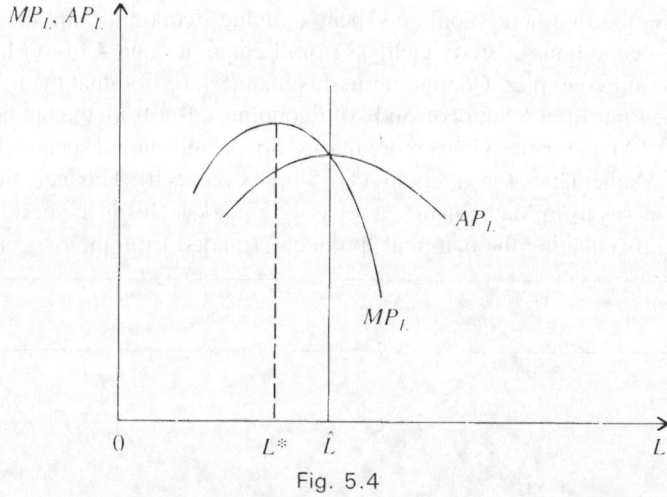

Fig. 5.4

The intuition behind this relationship can be quickly captured if the reader thinks of exam grades. Suppose that till now, Ms Ahana is getting an average grade of B on the papers she has taken. She sits for another exam, say in English. If she gets a grade above B in English, this marginal grade pulls up her average grade and makes it higher than B. If she gets B in English, her average grade remains unchanged at B. If she gets less than B in English, then her average grade falls below B.

5.4.2 Application

The concept of the marginal product provides a basic tool for analysing the optimal allocation of resources. Let us see how marginal analysis can be used if there is a fixed amount of a certain resource that must be 'optimally' allocated between competing ends. Suppose that Anand has 10 hours of study time left before exams. He has to study only two subjects, Economics and Mathematics. He has a fair idea of the marks he will get in each subject given the time he spends studying each.

Example 5.4: $Q = K_0 L^{0.5}$, $K_0 = 2$.

L	Q	dK	dQ	AP_L	MP_L
1	2			2	
		3	2		2/3
4	4			1	
		5	2		2/5
9	6			2/3	
		7	2		2/7

In this example, the marginal product is diminishing throughout. When it is less than the average product (e.g. 2 > 2/3), it pulls down the average product (average product becomes 1).

This information is provided in the table below. M_L and M_M refer to the total marks from Economics and Mathematics, respectively. Anand's aim is to obtain the maximum marks from the two papers *together* in his 10 hours of study.

In this example, note that for any number of hours spent, the total marks from Economics is always greater than Mathematics. It would, however, be a mistake to conclude that Anand should only study Economics. He should compare the marks from an extra hour's study of each subject. Starting from zero hour of study, the first hour of study yields 9 from Economics and 4 marks from Mathematics. Hence, the first hour should be spent studying Economics and the last column notes this. Similarly, the second hour of study yields 8 from Economics and 4 from Mathematics, so this too should be spent on Economics. Continuing in this manner, we find that the marginal gains from both subjects are the same after 5 hours of study of Economics. But from the 6th hour onwards, each extra hour of study of Mathematics yields more marks. So, Anand should spend 6 hours on Economics and 4 hours on Mathematics (or, alternatively, 5 hours on each). This nets him 39 marks from Economics and 16 marks from Mathematics, a total of 55 marks. This is the best he can do, and this solution is obtained by equating the marginal 'products' (marks) from the two subjects.

Number of Hours Spent Studying	M_L	M_M	$d M_L$	$d M_M$	
1	9	4			Economics
			8	4	Economics
2	17	8			
			7	4	Economics
3	24	12			
			6	4	Economics
4	30	16			
			5	4	Economics
5	35	20			
			4	4	Eco/Maths
6	39	24			
			3	4	Mathematics
7	42	28			
			2	4	Mathematics
8	44	32			
			1	4	Mathematics
9	41	36			
			0	4	Mathematics
10	41	40			

This was, of course, a simplified example. Anand might have to take into account the fact that he must score pass marks in each subject. For example, if he has to score more than 40 marks in Economics to pass, then he has to spend at least 7 hours studying Economics.

5.5 The Long Run

In the long run, both K and L can be varied. We can then define isoquants, in analogy with indifference curves.

Definition: An *isoquant* is a locus of those combinations of inputs that produce the same amount of output.

The word 'iso' is of Greek origin and means 'equal' or 'same'. An isoquant is a curve along which the quantity is the same.

Example 5.5: Let $Q = KL$. Fix $Q = 50$ (say). Then some of the combinations of K and L that will produce this amount of output are

K	L
5.0	10
10.0	5
12.5	4

etc.

All these combinations lie on the same isoquant. It is helpful to draw the analogy between isoquants and indifference curves. An indifference curve refers to a fixed level of utility while an isoquant refers to a fixed level of output. Indifference curves and isoquants behave similarly. A higher Q leads to a higher isoquant. The isoquants are downward sloping, because an upward sloping isoquant would imply inefficiency: more inputs would be used to produce the same amount of output. On the isoquant, therefore, one can either use more labour and less capital (that is, labour-intensive techniques) or more capital and less labour (that is, capital-intensive techniques). Moreover, two isoquants cannot cross each other, because this would again mean that two levels of output can be produced with the same combination of inputs, which is ruled out by the requirement of efficiency in production.

Since both inputs can be varied in the long run, it is possible to define the marginal products of both L and K in the long run. The marginal product of any input is the extra output per additional unit of that input, *keeping the amount of the other input fixed*. It is the partial derivative of the output with respect to the input. In the example given earlier, where $Q = LK$, $MP_L = K$ and $MP_K = L$.

In Fig. 5.5, we have a situation in which the firm can vary the proportion in which K and L can be combined. Such a proportion is given by the slope of the ray from the origin to any point on the isoquant. We have *variable proportions*. Sometimes, however, K and L can be combined only in a *fixed proportion*, as Fig. 5.6 shows. The general form of a fixed proportion production function is $f(L, K) = \min(aL, bK)$.

In consumer behaviour theory, the slope of the indifference curves at each point represented the consumer's marginal rate of substitution between the two commodities. Similarly, the slope of the isoquant at a point represents the *marginal rate of technical substitution* (MRTS), which is the rate at which L has to be substituted for K to keep output constant.

Like indifference curves, we assume that isoquants are strictly convex to the origin. The MRTS is assumed to become smaller as more and more L is substituted for K. That is, as L increases and K falls on an isoquant, it becomes more and more difficult to substitute L for K.

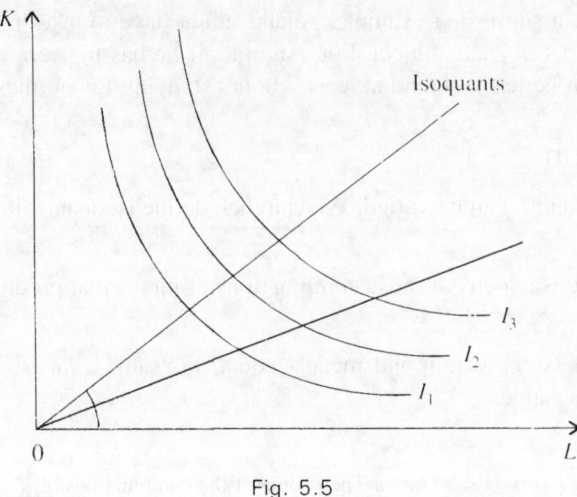

Fig. 5.5

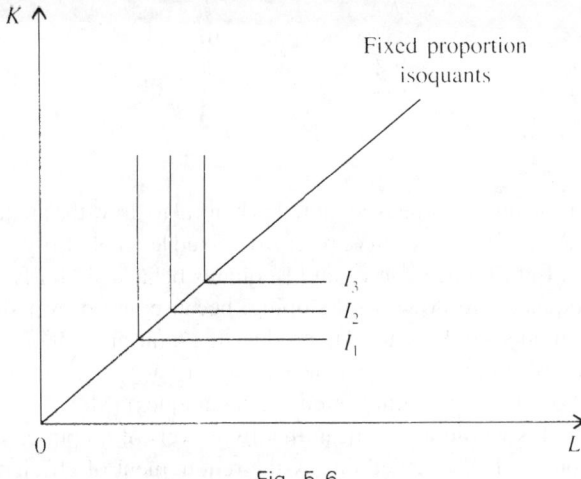

Fig. 5.6

The MRTS at a point is equal to $-(dK/dL)$. Now,

$$dQ = (\partial Q/\partial K)dK + (\partial Q/\partial L)dL = MP_K\, dK + MP_L\, dL.$$

But on an isoquant, $dQ = 0$. Hence, we find that

$$\text{MRTS} = -(dK/dL) = MP_L/MP_K.$$

The MRTS is equal to the ratio of marginal products. When $Q = KL$, MRTS = K/L.

As more and more of units of an input are used, its marginal product keeps on falling. If the marginal product becomes negative after a point, then the isoquant will come to have a positive slope and become backward bending. Fig. 5.7 illustrates this possibility. With more than K_2 units of capital, MP_K is negative. Similarly, beyond L_2 units of labour, MP_L is negative. However, it makes little sense to hire an input whose marginal product is negative. In Fig. 5.7, both input bundles C and D can produce the same amount of output. But C needs the use of more K than D and therefore it will be more expensive to produce the output at C rather than at D. Hence points like C and E can be ruled out. Once all such points which lie on the backward bending portions of the isoquant are ruled out, what remains is called the *economic region of production*. In Fig. 5.8, lines like OAB and ONM that pass through the points where MRTS = infinity or zero are called *ridge lines*. The area bounded by the ridge lines is the economic region of production.

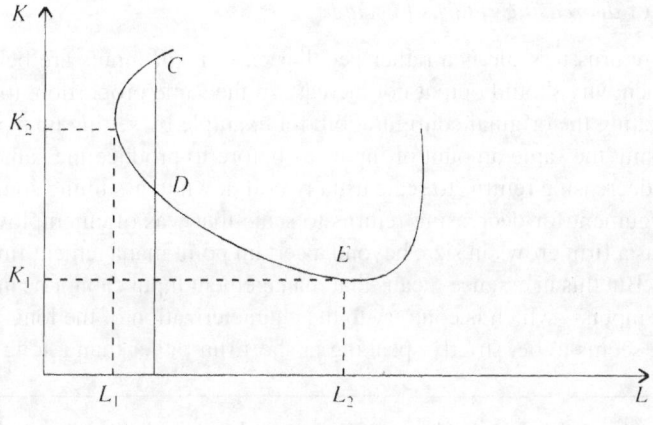

Fig. 5.7

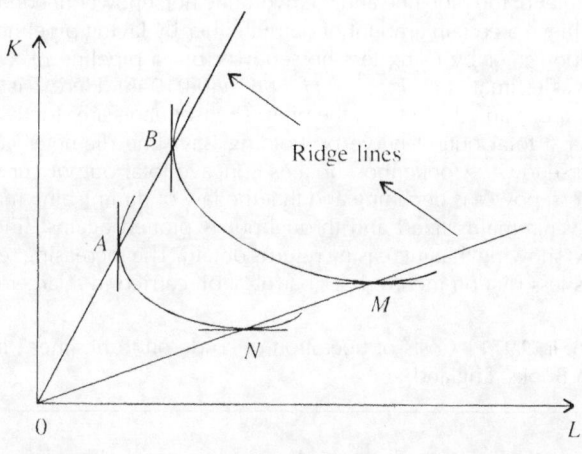

Fig. 5.8

5.5.1 Returns to Scale

In the short run, one input is fixed and we examined what happened to the output when more of the other input is applied. We also discussed the law of diminishing marginal returns in this context. In the long run, all inputs are variable. We can then ask the following question: if all inputs are increased in the same proportion, does output increase in the same proportion? That is, if we consider an input bundle (aL, aK), is the resultant output greater than, equal to, or less than aQ?

Three cases are possible:

1. $F(aL, aK) = aF(L, K)$, for all $a \geq 0$, that is, output increases in exactly the same proportion as inputs. If both inputs are doubled, for example, output will also be doubled. Similarly, if both inputs are halved, the output will also be halved. This is the case of *constant returns to scale*.

2. $F(aL, aK) > aF(L, K)$, for all $a > 1$, that is, output increases more than in proportion to the inputs. This is the case of *increasing returns to scale*. An example would be the use of a pipeline to carry oil. Doubling the radius of the pipe increases cost by a factor of 2, since the required circumference also doubles. But the carrying capacity of the pipe goes up by a factor of 4, as the volume quadruples.

3. $F(aL, aK) < aF(L, K)$ for all $a > 1$, that is, output increases more than in proportion to the inputs. This is the case of *decreasing returns to scale*.

The decreasing returns to scale is a rather peculiar case. If *all* inputs are being increased in the same proportion, then why should output not increase in the same proportion, too? We always have the choice of replicating the original configuration, for example by setting up a plant identical to the one existing and using the same amount of inputs as before to produce the same amount of output. The arguments for decreasing returns to scale usually boil down to assuming some input that is fixed in quantity. One argument for decreasing returns to scale that was often employed was shortage of managerial talent; as a firm grows in size, beyond a certain point management finds it difficult to run the firm efficiently. But this in essence means that management input cannot be increased in the same proportion as other inputs—which is contrary to the characterization of the long run. Hence decreasing returns to scale seems to be, strictly speaking, a short run rather than a long run phenomenon.

L. Cookenboo, Jr estimated the production function for crude oil trunk lines. The output is the 'through-put', which refers to the volume of liquid carried per unit of time. The throughput depends on two inputs: the inside diameter of the pipe line and the hydraulic horsepower needed to pump oil through the pipes. One can achieve a certain amount of output either by laying pipeline of a lower diameter but using more horsepower or by using less horsepower but a pipeline of a larger diameter. The production function was estimated as $T^{2.735} = (H)(D^{4.735})/(0.01046)$. Here T is the throughput, H is the horsepower and D the inside diameter of the pipe. The isoquants are strictly convex to the origin. One can also consider a total output curve by holding (say) line diameter constant, and plotting throughput against horsepower. Cookenboo obtains concave total output curves, showing that the marginal product of horsepower is declining and that the law of diminishing marginal returns holds. However, if horsepower remains fixed and throughput is plotted against line diameter, the total output curve is *convex*, showing that increasing returns obtain. The increasing returns are attributable to the fact that there is less friction incurred per barrel of oil carried in a larger-diameter pipe than a smaller-diameter pipe.

Source: L. Cookenboo, Jr, 1971, 'Costs of operation of crude oil trunk lines', in H. Townsend (ed.) *Price Theory*. Penguin Books, England.

A constant returns to scale case (say) is perfectly consistent with diminishing returns to the inputs. Returns to scale describes what happens when all the inputs are increased, while diminishing returns describes what happens when at least one input cannot be increased.

5.5.2 The Cobb-Douglas Production Function

One of the most widely used forms of production function is the Cobb-Douglas production function. It can be written as $Q = AL^a K^b$, where a and b are parameters lying between 0 and 1. 'A' is a constant defining the scale of production.

For the C-D production function,

$$MP_L = AaL^{a-1}K^b, \text{ and } MP_K = AbL^a K^{b-1}.$$

Hence, MRTS = MP_L/MP_K = $(a/b)(K/L)$. Note that on any isoquant, as L is increased and K is decreased, the MRTS falls.

What type of returns to scale exists depends on $(a + b)$. If $a + b = 1$, there is constant returns to scale. In this case, if both L and K are increased by a proportion of t, then $A(tL)^a(tK)^b = At^{a+b}(L^aK^b) = At(L^aK^b) = tQ$. By similar reasoning, one can show that increasing returns to scale exists when $a + b > 1$, and decreasing returns when $a + b < 1$.

Let $a = b = 2/3$. It can be seen the law of diminishing returns holds with respect to both L and K. If K is kept fixed, then MP_L falls as L is increased. Similarly for MP_K. But $a + b = 4/3 > 1$, which means that there is increasing returns to scale.

5.5.3 Elasticity of Substitution

The marginal rate of technical substitution measures the slope of an isoquant. It is also useful to have a measure of the curvature of an isoquant. The curvature can be measured by calculating the response of the input ratio to a change in the slope of the isoquant. If a small change in the slope gives rise to a relatively large change in the input ratio, the isoquant must be relatively flat.

The *elasticity of substitution* is then defined as follows:

$$r = \frac{d(K/L)}{d\text{MRTS}} \times \frac{\text{MRTS}}{(K/L)}$$

In logarithmic terms,

$$r = d\ln(K/L)/d\ln\text{MRTS}$$

Example 5.6: Consider the Cobb-Douglas production function $Q = K^a L^{1-a}$, $1 > a > 0$. MRTS $= [(1 - a)/a]$ (K/L). We can then see that $(K/L) = A$MRTS, where $A = a/(1 - a)$. Hence $d(K/L)/d$MRTS $= A$, and $r = A$MRTS/AMRTS $= 1$.

Example 5.7: The Cobb-Douglas production function is a special case of the Constant Elasticity of Substitution (CES) production function:

$$F(K, L) = (K^\rho + L^\rho)^{1/\rho}$$

In this function ρ is a constant. MRTS $= MP_L/MP_K = (L/K)^{\rho-1} = (K/L)^{1-\rho}$. We can then write K/L in terms of MRTS:

$$K/L = \text{MRTS}^{1/(1-\rho)} = \text{MRTS}^\sigma, \text{ where } \sigma = 1/(1 - \rho)$$

Noting that $d(K/L)/d$MRTS $= \sigma\text{MRTS}^{\sigma-1}$, we can show that the elasticity of substitution is

$$r = \sigma = 1/(1 - \rho)$$

The elasticity of substitution is a constant in this case.

Topics for Discussion

1. Think of some of the productive activities that you are familiar with and try to estimate the lengths of the short run and long run for such activities. You should try to identify the fixed inputs in the short run.
2. Discuss how the distinction between short run and long run is relevant for analysing the effects of the government's industrial policies.

Exercise

1. Graph the short run total product curves for each of the following production functions if K is fixed at $K_0 = 2$. Graph the marginal and average product curves in the corresponding diagrams.

   (a) $Q = 4K + 5L$
   (b) $Q = K(L)^2$
   (c) $Q = K(L)^{0.5}$
   (d) What is the marginal product of labour for $L = 8$ in the production function $Q = (K)^{2/3}(L)^{1/3}$, if K is fixed at 27?

2. The average marks gained by a Srinath from Biology is $20 - 12r_1$ where r_1 is the fraction of time spent studying biology. His average gain in marks from Mechanics is $10 - 8r_2$, where r_2 is the fraction of time spent studying mechanics.

   (a) The total marks gained by Srinath from Biology is $G_1 =$ _____. (Express as a function of r_1)
   (b) The total marks gained by Srinath from Mechanics is $G_2 =$ _____. (Express as a function of r_2)
   (c) The marginal marks gained by Srinath from Biology is $M_1 =$ _____.
   (d) The marginal marks gained by Srinath from Mechanics is $M_2 =$ _____.
   (e) What is the optimal fraction of time spent in studying Biology if Srinath's aim is to maximize the total marks gained? [Hint: Remember that $r_1 + r_2 = 1$]

3. (a) Complete the following table.

L	Q	AP_L	MP_L
0	0	–	
1			1
2			2
3			3
4			4
5			5
6			6
7			5
8			4
9			3
10			2

   (b) Draw the total, average, and marginal product curves.

4. The following table shows the amount of total output produced (in italics) from various combinations of labour and capital:

Units of labour	Units of capital			
	1	2	3	4
1	50	120	160	180
2	110	260	360	390
3	150	360	510	560
4	170	430	630	690
5	160	480	710	790

Calculate the marginal product and average product of labour when capital is held constant at 2 units. When does diminishing returns set in?

5. The average product of labour when three workers farm an acre of land is 150 bushels of wheat and the marginal product of the fourth worker is 75 bushels. What is the total output with four workers?

6. If the equation of the total product curve is $TP = 6 + 2L$, where L denotes the amount of labour input, then what is the marginal product of labour for $L = 3$?

7. Consider the cubic production function $Q = aK^2L^2 - bK^3L^3$, where $a > 0$, $b > 0$. In the short run, $K = K'$.

   (a) If $A = aK'^2$ and $B = bK'^3$, derive the average product and marginal product of labour in terms of A and B.

   (b) Find the level of labour usage beyond which diminishing returns sets in.

   (c) Find L for which average product of labour is at maximum.

8. Fill the gaps in the table below:

Quantity of variable input	Total output	Marginal product of variable input	Average product of variable input
0	0	–	–
1	200		
2			250
3		130	

9. Two managers were overheard arguing about the following statement: 'A manager should never hire another worker if the new person causes diminishing returns'. Is this statement correct? If so, why? If not, explain why not.

10. Determine whether the following production functions exhibit increasing, decreasing or constant returns to scale:

   (a) $Q = 50K^{0.3}L^{0.5}$

   (b) $Q = 14K^{0.5}L^{0.5}$

   (c) $Q = 300K + 25L$

   (d) $Q = 2K^{0.4}L^{0.5}E^{0.15}M^{0.1}$

6 | Costs

The production function delineates the most efficient input combinations that are available to the firm to produce any amount of output. However, to decide how much to produce and using which particular input combination, the firm must consider the prices of inputs and the price of the final output. In other words, it has to find out the costs and revenues associated with a particular production plan. In this chapter, we analyse costs.

The notion of cost that economists use is that of opportunity cost, which has already been discussed. From the point of view of the entire economy, we are interested in the best allocation of scarce resources among their alternative uses. The firm must also strive to use the resources at its command in the best possible way. To do this, it has to balance the costs and benefits of different courses of action. If it is making losses, should it continue to produce or close down? How does it decide to enter a particular market and not any other? And so on.

The calculation of opportunity costs forces us to take into account both implicit and explicit costs. Examples of implicit costs include

(a) the owner of the firm working for the firm but getting no salary, and
(b) the cost of funds invested in the firm that could have been used elsewhere.

Matters are simplified by assuming that the firm treats the market prices of labour and capital services as fixed. The market prices therefore reflect the opportunity costs of these resources.

The price of labour services is w, the wage rate. We are assuming (contrary to all evidence) that all labour services are homogeneous, that is, the same. All differences in skills and aptitudes are being abstracted from. If the owner of the firm works for the firm, she is assumed to provide the same type of labour service as any other worker, and a wage rate of w must be imputed to her services. Similarly, all capital services are homogeneous. Capital can be either hired or owned. In either case, the rental rate of r must be assigned per unit of capital services. Therefore the total cost of producing any level of output Q is $wL + rK$, where $Q = F(L, K)$.

One rupee saved is one rupee gained. We assume that the firm tries to produce each level of output at the minimum cost. In other words, its tries to select that input combination that minimizes the cost of producing any level of output.

More formally, the firm tries to minimize total cost $(C) = wL + rK$, subject to $Q = F(L, K)$, fixing Q at some level.

6.1 The Short Run

In the short run, at least one input is fixed in quantity. It is conventional to assume that K is fixed in the short run, that is, $K = K_0$. Then the minimum amount of L needed to produce some Q is obtained by solving $Q = F(L, K_0)$.

Example 6.1: Suppose $Q = KL$, and $K = 100$ in the short run. Then, from the definition of the production function, the minimum amount of L needed to produce any Q is $L = Q/100$.

Therefore, *total cost* in the short run is $C = wL + rK_0$.
Note that this total cost has two components:

Total fixed cost (TFC) $= rK_0$. This part of the cost does not change when output level is changed.
Total variable cost (TVC) $= wL$. This part of the cost is dependent on the level of output, since the minimum L required to produce any Q changes when Q changes. To indicate this dependence, we can write TVC = TVC(Q).

Therefore, $C(Q) = \text{TFC} + \text{TVC}(Q)$.
Note that $C = C(Q; w, r)$, that is, the total cost also depends on the input prices. However, we will often suppress the input prices and write $C = C(Q)$.

Example 6.2: Let $Q = L^{0.5} K^{0.5}$. This means that $Q^2 = LK$, or $L = Q^2/K$. Let $K = 2$ in the short run, $w =$ Re 0.50 and $r =$ Re 1. Then $C = 1 \times 2 + 0.5(Q^2/2) = 2 + Q^2/4$. The total fixed cost is 2 and the total variable cost is $Q^2/4$.

Corresponding to each of these total cost concepts, we can define an average cost concept, that is, the cost per unit of quantity produced. The definitions are all similar:

Average total cost (AC) $= C/Q = (wL + rK_0)/Q$.
Average fixed cost (AFC) $= \text{TFC}/Q = rK_0/Q$.
Average variable cost (AVC) $= \text{TVC}/Q = wL/Q = w/(Q/L) = w/AP_L$.

Note that AC = AFC + AVC.
Next, we have to define marginal cost, which will play a crucial role in subsequent analysis. The marginal cost MC at any level of output is the extra cost incurred per additional unit of output:

Marginal cost (MC) $= dC/dQ$.

Therefore MC $= d(\text{TFC} + \text{TVC})/dQ = d\text{TVC}/dQ$, since total fixed cost by definition does not change when output changes. In our two inputs case, MC $= d(wL)/dQ = w(dL/dQ) = w/(dQ/dL) = w/MP_L$.
All the costs, it should be noted, depend parametrically on the input prices and the fixed level of K.

Example 6.3: Let us continue with $Q = L^{0.5} K^{0.5}$. Let $K = 2$ in the short run, $w =$ Re 0.50 and $r =$ Re 1. Hence $L = Q^2/K = Q^2/2$. Hence TVC $= Q^2/4$.

Q	L	TVC	TFC	C	AC	AVC	AFC	MC
1	½	¼	2	2.25	2.25	0.25	2.00	
								0.75
2	2	1	2	3.00	1.50	0.50	1.00	
								1.25
3	4.5	2.25	2	4.25	1.41	0.75	0.66	
								1.75
4	8	4	2	6.00	1.50	1.00	0.50	

6.1.1 Shapes of Short Run Cost Curves

Let us begin with the simplest concept—that of the total fixed cost curve. It is fixed, hence it is represented by a horizontal straight line at the height of rK_0. The average fixed cost, on the other hand, always falls as more and more output is produced and asymptotically approaches the Q axis (since it never becomes 0).

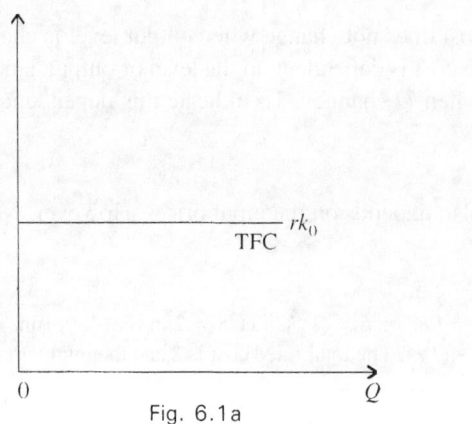

Fig. 6.1a

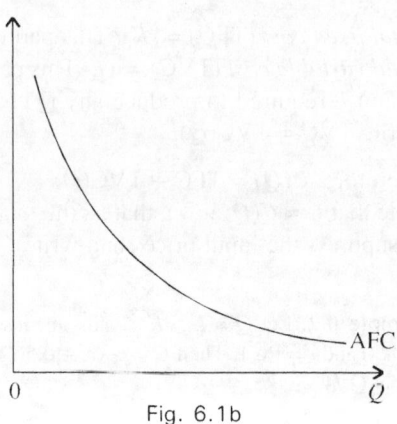

Fig. 6.1b

The definitions of AVC and MC curves show us that there is an intimate relationship between these cost curves and the curves representing average and marginal products of labour. Refer again to Fig. 5.3. We assume diminishing returns beyond Q^*, so that the marginal product of labour curve is falling beyond this point.

First consider the MC curve. Remember that MC = w/MP_L. If the MP_L curve is first rising and then falling beyond Q^*, then the MC curve must be first falling and then rising beyond Q^*. So it must have a U shape. But the marginal cost curve represents the slope of the TVC curve. The shape of the TVC curve that is consistent with the shape of the MC curve is shown in Fig. 6.2b.

From the shape of the TVC curve, three things follow.

1. The C curve will be just the vertical summation of the TFC and TVC curves. Given that the TFC curve is a horizontal straight line, the C curve will have exactly the same shape as the TVC curve, though it will lie above the TVC curve. The vertical distance between the two at any Q will equal TFC.

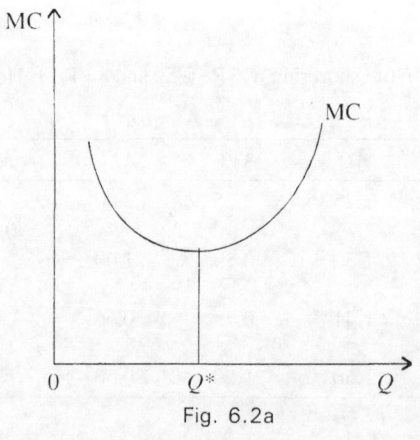

Fig. 6.2a

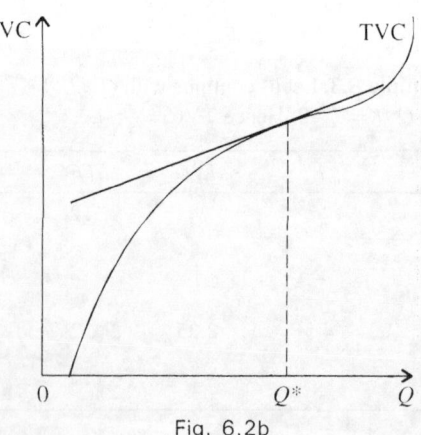

Fig. 6.2b

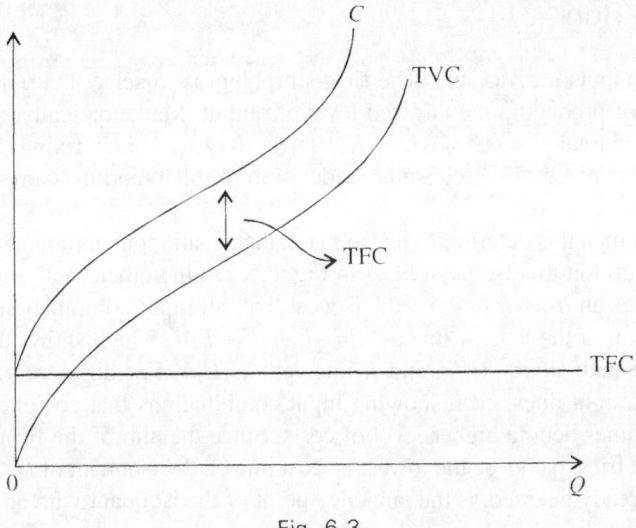

Fig. 6.3

2. The AVC for any Q is the slope of the ray from the origin to the TVC curve at that Q. Hence, given the shape of the TVC curve, it follows that the AVC curve is also U-shaped.

3. The AC curve, which represents the slope of the ray from the origin to the C curve at any Q, will be U-shaped. It can also be represented by the vertical summation of the AFC and the AVC curves. Note that AC − AVC = AFC, that is, the distance between the AC and AFC curves represents the AFC curve. Since the AFC curve asymptotically approaches the Q axis, the vertical distance between AC and AVC curves grows smaller as output is increased.

Finally, we note the interesting fact that the MC curve cuts both the AC and the AVC curves at their lowest points. The proof is simple. MC = dC/dQ = $d(\text{AC}\cdot Q)/dQ$ = AC + $Q\cdot d\text{AC}/dQ$. Hence $d\text{AC}/dQ$ = (MC − AC)/Q. At the lowest point of the AC curve, $d\text{AC}/dQ = 0$, which implies that MC = AC at this point. The reader is advised to carry out the same exercise noting that MC = $d\text{TVC}/dQ$.

The relationship between all the average and marginal cost curves are shown in Fig. 6.4.

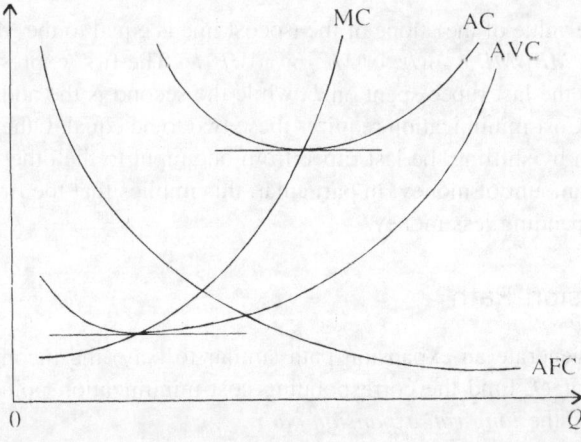

Fig. 6.4

6.2 The Long Run

In the long run, all inputs are variable. The firm's problem is to select that input combination that minimizes the cost of producing the targeted level of output. Mathematically, as already noted, the firm tries to minimize total cost $(C) = wL + rK$, subject to $Q = F(L, K)$, fixing Q at some level. This problem is the mirror image of the consumer's decision problem and the same graphical technique can be employed.

If we fix $Q = Q^*$, then this determines an isoquant, that is, all input combinations that can produce this amount of output. Let this isoquant be II in Fig. 6.5. On the other hand, set $wL + rK = E_1$, say. Given E_1, this defines an *isocost line*: on the isocost line, all input combinations cost the same. We can write the equation of the isocost line as $K = -(w/r)L + E_1/r$, which shows that it is a downward sloping straight line with slope $-(w/r)$ and K-intercept as E_1/r. For different values of E, we get a family of parallel straight lines, each showing input combinations that cost the same amount. Further, higher isocost lines denote higher level of costs. Since the aim of the firm is to produce Q^* at the minimum cost, it tries to choose the lowest isocost line on the isoquant of Q^*. The solution, as the reader must have already guessed, is the tangency point of the isoquant with an isocost line. Denote this point by P^*.

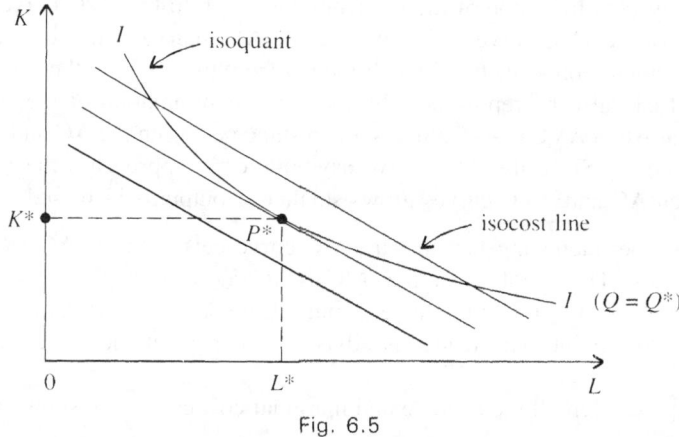

Fig. 6.5

At P^*, the (absolute value of the) slope of the isocost line is equal to the MRTS. Hence, MRTS = w/r which implies that $MP_L/MP_K = w/r$, or $MP_L/w = MP_K/r$. The first expression is nothing but the additional output from the last rupee spent on L, while the second is the additional output from the last rupee spent on K. Cost minimization requires these two to be equal. Otherwise, one can readjust the expenditure pattern by shifting the last rupee from one input to the other, and thereby get more output from the same amount of money. In particular, this implies that the firm could have obtained the earlier output by spending less money.

6.2.1 The Expansion Path

It is now possible to generate an expansion path similar to (say) the income-consumption curve. Take different levels of Q. Find the corresponding cost-minimization points and join them. The resultant curve is called the *long-run expansion path*.

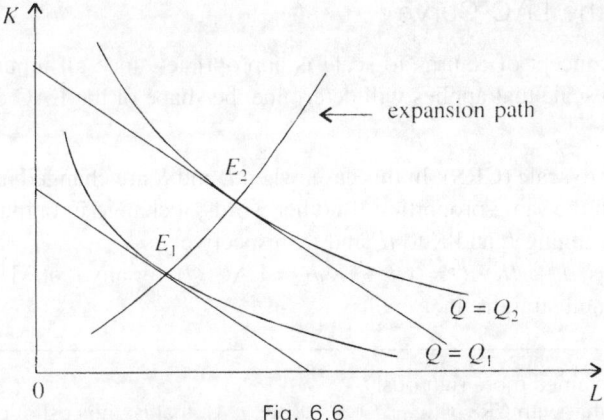

Fig. 6.6

Example 6.4: Consider the C-D production function $Q = L^{1/2}K^{1/2}$. It can be shown that MRTS = K/L. At the input combination that minimizes cost, $K/L = w/r \Rightarrow L = rK/w$. Then from the production function, for any given Q, we can eliminate L. We get $Q = (rK/w)^{1/2}K^{1/2} = (r/w)^{1/2}K$. This means that $K = (w/r)^{1/2}Q$ and hence $L = (r/w)^{1/2}Q$. The equation of the long run expansion path is $K/L = (w/r)$, that is, $K = (w/r)L$. Given the C-D production function, the expansion path is a straight line through the origin. Finally, the total cost can be expressed as $C = w(r/w)^{1/2}Q + r(w/r)^{1/2}Q = 2(wr)^{1/2}Q$. Therefore, the total cost depends parametrically on both the level of output Q and the input prices w and r. An increase in any of these three increases total cost. Note that the average total cost is AC = $2(wr)^{1/2}$, which is fixed so long as the input prices do not change.

6.2.2 Long Run Costs

In the long run, the total cost LC = $wL + rK$, where L and K are solved from the conditions MRTS = w/r and $Q = F(L, K)$. There are no fixed costs in the long run; all costs are variable. Hence LC = LVC (long run variable cost). This in turn implies that the average total and average variable costs coincide, that is, LAC = LAVC, where LAC = LC/Q and LAVC = LVC/Q.

The long run marginal cost (LMC) is defined as dLC/dQ. Noting that LC = $Q \cdot$LAC, we can show that dLAC/dQ = (LMC – LAC)/Q. Thus the LMC curve lies below the LAC curve when the latter is downward sloping, intersects it at its lowest point, and lies above it when LAC is upward rising (Fig. 6.7).

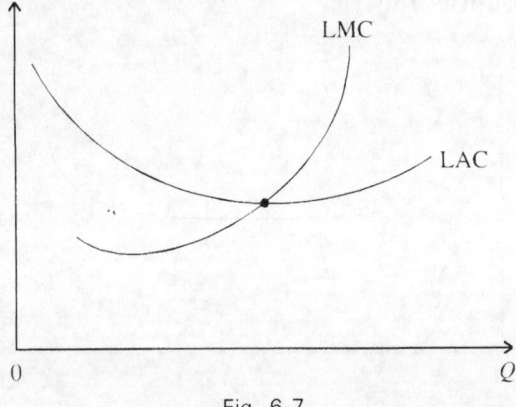

Fig. 6.7

6.2.3 Shape of the LAC Curve

In the long run, the concept of returns to scale is appropriate, since all inputs are freely variable. The type of returns to scale that applies will determine the shape of the LAC curve. Remember that $LAC = (wL + rK)/Q$.

1. Constant returns to scale (CRS): In this case, when L and K are changed in the same proportion, output also changes in the same proportion. In other words, a change in output from Q to tQ, $t > 0$, can be achieved by changing L and K to tL and tK respectively.

Hence $LAC(tQ) = (wtL + rtK)/tQ = (wL + rK)/Q = LAC(Q)$, for any $t > 0$. The LAC curve, plotted against Q, is a horizontal straight line.

This result can be obtained more rigorously.

It can be proved that with CRS, $C(w, r, Q) = QC(w, r, 1)$, that is, the cost of producing Q amount of output is simply Q times the cost of producing one unit of output. The proof runs as follows.

First, suppose that (L^*, K^*) is the least-cost input combination for producing one unit of output so that $C(w, r, 1) = wL^* + rK^*$. By constant returns to scale, Q amount of output can be produced with (QL^*, QK^*). Is this the least-cost combination for producing Q?

Suppose not, and let (L', K') be the least-cost combination. Then $wL' + rK' < w(QL^*) + r(QK^*)$. This inequality can be written as $w(L'/Q) + r(K'/Q) < wL^* + rK^*$. But if (L', K') can produce Q, by CRS $(L'/Q, K'/Q)$ can produce one unit. The inequality therefore says that $(L'/Q, K'/Q)$ can produce one unit of output at a lower cost than (L^*, K^*), which is a contradiction.

Hence $C(w, r, Q) = QC(w, r, 1)$, which means that $LAC = C(w, r, Q)/Q = C(w, r, 1)$, which is a constant because it only depends on the fixed input prices.

---

2. Increasing returns to scale (IRS): In this case, when L and K are increased in the same proportion, output increases by a larger proportion. In other words, a change in output from Q to tQ, $t > 1$, can be achieved by changing L and K to $t'L$ and $t'K$ respectively, where $t' < t$.

Then $LAC(tQ) = (wt'L + rt'K)/tQ = LAC(Q)(t'/t) < LAC(Q)$, for any $t > 1$. Hence when IRS prevails, the LAC declines as output is increased; the LAC curve is downward sloping.

Decreasing returns to scale (DRS): When L and K are increased in the same proportion, output increases by a smaller proportion. It is easy to show that the LAC curve will be upward rising in his case.

Economists usually work with a U-shaped LAC curve. Implicitly they are assuming that when the firm produces more and more in the long run, it first faces a condition of IRS, then CRS (when the curve reaches its minimum) and finally DRS. The minimum point of the U-shaped LAC curve is called the *minimum efficient scale* (MES).

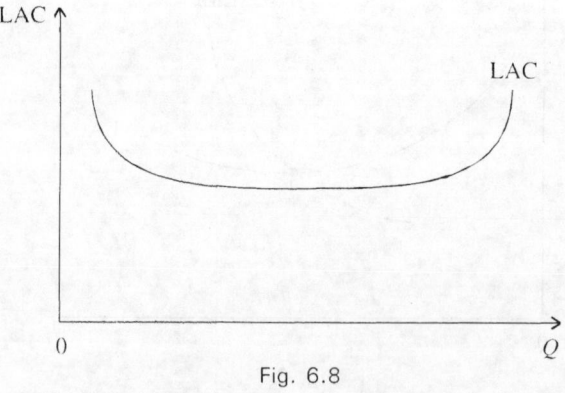

Fig. 6.8

Empirical studies sometimes suggest that the LAC is a flat-bottomed curve, that is, there is a range of outputs for which condition of CRS prevails.

Finally, note that a natural measure of scale economies seems to be s = LAC/LMC. If $s > 1$, then LAC > LMC, and LAC is falling, which means that IRS exists. If $s = 1$, then CRS characterizes production and if $s < 1$, then there is DRS.

6.3 The Relationship between Short Run and Long Run Cost Curves

In the long run, the firm is free to vary all inputs. Therefore it has more flexibility and in general achieves a lower cost of production than in the short run. In Fig. 6.9, the firm chooses a combination (L^*, K^*) in the long run to achieve a total cost of C^* associated with the isocost line that is tangential to the isoquant at point E^*. In the short run, the capital input is given at K' and the firm has to choose L' on a higher isocost line. Hence the short run cost C' is greater than the long run total cost C^*.

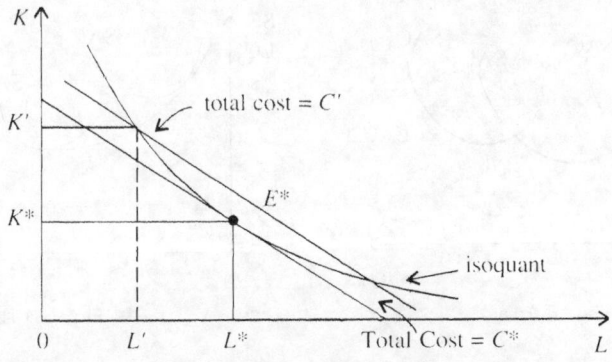

Fig. 6.9

The relationship between the long run and short run cost curves can be analysed as follows. Consider three possible levels of K. Each of these determines a particular short run total cost curve. In the short run, given the level of K, the firm is stuck to one of these curves. However, in the long run, the firm is free to choose the level of K that minimizes a particular level of output. In Fig. 6.10, the level of K that minimizes the total cost from 0 to Q_1 is K_1, from Q_2 to Q_2 is K_2 and from Q_2 onwards, it is K_3. The long run total cost curve is then obtained by joining the corresponding segments of the short run total cost curves. It is the *envelope* of the short run cost curves, denoted by the thick curve.

Similarly, the LAC curve is the envelope of the SAC curves (Fig. 6.11a). If there is a continuum of short run curves, then the long run cost curves become smooth curves (Fig. 6.11b). Note that in this case, each SAC curve touches the envelope LAC curve only once. Moreover, the point of tangency, in the upward and downward sloping segments of the LAC curve, is *not* the minimum point of the SAC curve. It is the minimum point of a SAC curve only when there is CRS in the long run, that is, at the minimum point(s) of the LAC curve.

What happens to the long run marginal cost curve, LMC? It is build-up from the corresponding SMCs. Take a particular output and consider the corresponding point on the LAC curve. It is a point of tangency with some SAC curve. At that point, the LMC is nothing but the corresponding short run

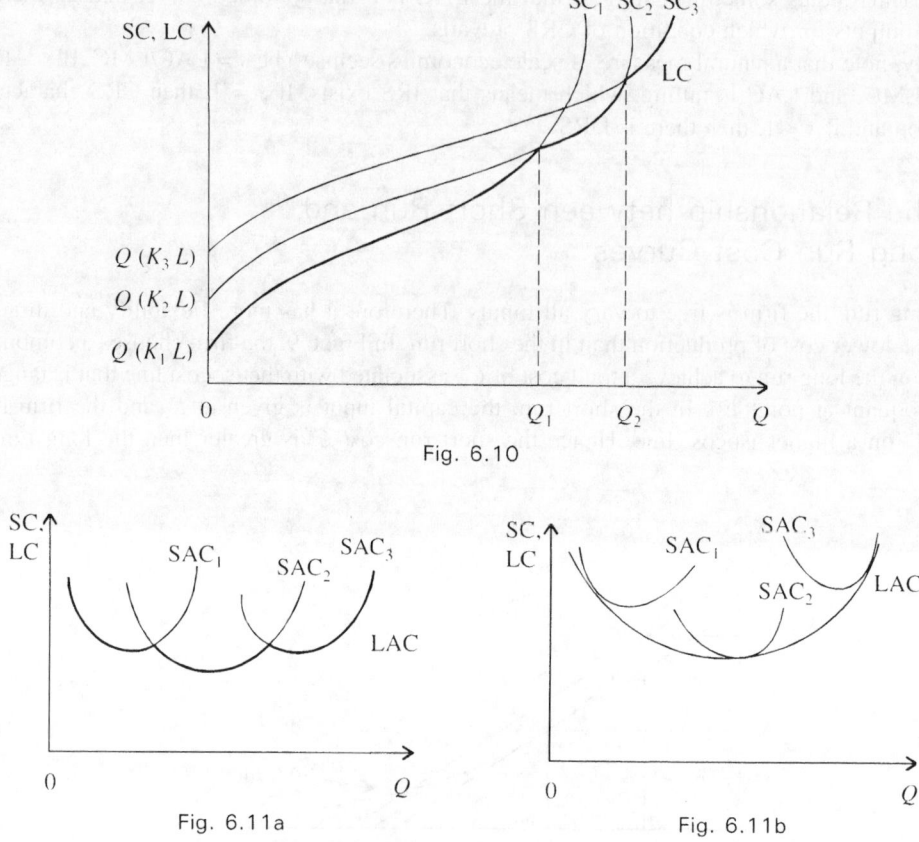

Fig. 6.10

Fig. 6.11a   Fig. 6.11b

marginal cost (point A). Hence, the LMC curve is obtained from the points on SMC curves at different levels of Q, the SMC curves corresponding to the SAC curves that minimize short run average costs at those Q.

If there is CRS for every level of production, then the LAC curve is a horizontal straight line and coincides with the LMC curve.

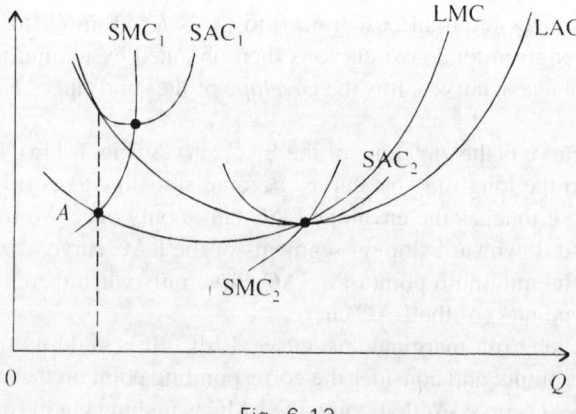

Fig. 6.12

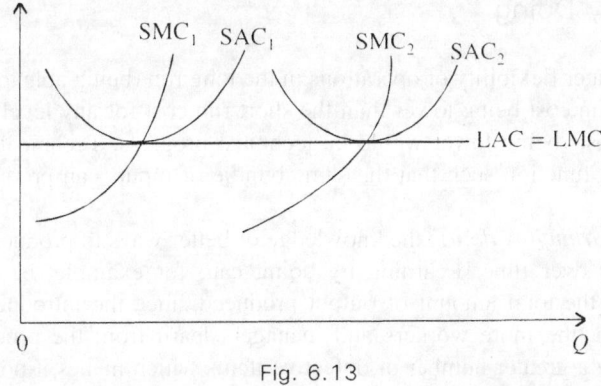

Fig. 6.13

Inkjet printer versus a laser printer: Short-term versus long-term

Suppose that a firm is thinking of buying a printer for one of its employees. It can choose between an inkjet printer which costs Rs 5000 or a laser printer which costs Rs 8000. The per page printing cost for an inkjet is Rs 1.80 and that for a laser printer is Rs 1.50. Which one should the firm buy?

If q denotes the number of pages printed, the total costs will be

$$C_{IJ} = 5000 + 1.8q \text{ and}$$
$$C_L = 8000 + 1.5q$$

The average cost curves are given by

$$AC_{IJ} = 5000/q + 1.8 \text{ and}$$
$$AC_L = 8000/q + 1.5$$

It can be seen that $AC_L - AC_{IJ} = 3000/q - 0.3$ and therefore, for $q > 10,000$, $AC_L < AC_{IJ}$. The average cost curves are drawn in the Fig. 6.14.

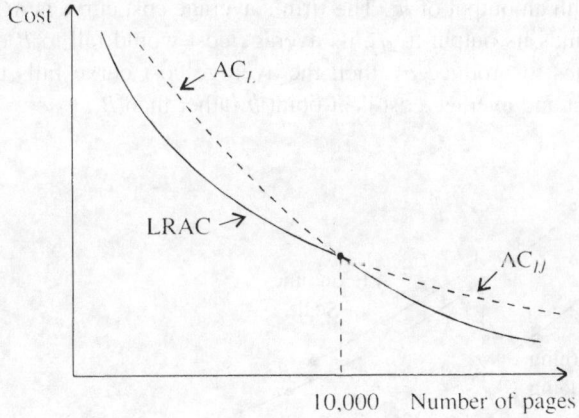

Fig. 6.14

Whether the firm should buy the inkjet printer or the laser printer will then depend on its expected rate of printing of pages. If, for example, only 10 pages are to be printed every day, then it will take 1000 days (almost three years) before the laser printer becomes cost-effective. On the other hand, if the expected rate of usage is (say) 100 pages per day, then the laser printer will become cost-effective after 100 days.

Source: This example is taken from *Microeconomics*, 2nd edn, by J.M. Perloff (Pearson Education).

6.3.1 Learning by Doing

It is now clear that greater flexibility of operations in the long run (being able to suitably vary all the inputs) leads to long run cost being lower than the short run cost for any level of output. A second reason for long run costs being lower would be technical progress. Technical progress refers to a shift in the production function such that the same bundle of inputs can produce a higher level of output after the shift.

A third reason is *learning by doing*: the knowledge of better ways to produce that is the outcome of gain in experience over time. Learning by doing can, for example, be made a function of cumulative output, or the total amount of output produced since the introduction of the product. The more is produced, the more workers and managers learn from the production process. For example, there may be a greater number of defective items which makes it possible to identify the source of a problem and correct it quickly. In particular, this would mean that workers can become more productive if they make more units over a short period than a small number of units over a long period.

The cost of producing computer memory chip falls substantially due to learning by doing. Gruber found that the average cost of erasable programmable read-only memory (EPROM) chips falls with cumulative output but does not fall over time or with the scale of production. With each doubling in the cumulative output of an EPROM chip, its average cost falls by 22 per cent. In contrast, the average cost of a dynamic random-access memory (DRAM) chip does not fall with cumulative output but does fall with time and exhibits economies of scale.

Source: H. Gruber, 'The Learning Curve in the Production of Semi-conductor Memory Chips', *Applied Economics*, 24(8), August 1992: 885–94.

In Fig. 6.15, start with an output of q_1. The firm's average cost curve is AC_1 and the average cost is at point A. If it expands its output to q_2, its average cost would fall to B on the same AC curve. However, if it continues to produce q_2, then the average cost curve falls to AC_2 because of the learning by doing effect and average cost is at point b rather than B.

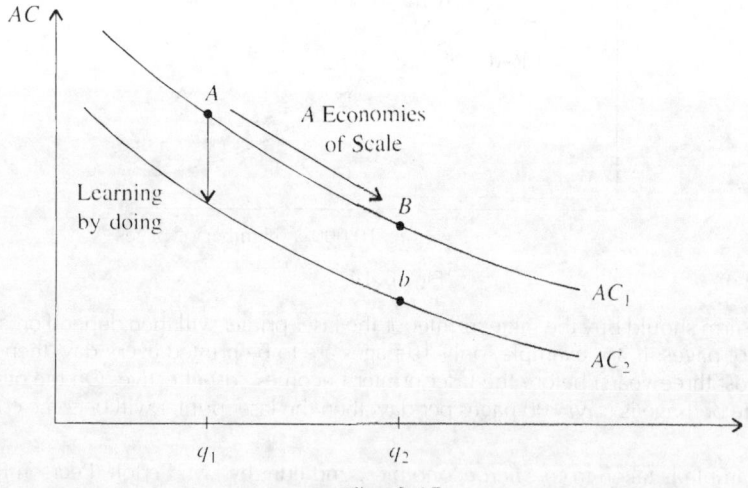

Fig. 6.15

6.3.2 Multi-product Firms

Most of the large corporations today produce a range of products. For such *multi-product firms*, the cost concepts we have developed earlier need to be modified and new concepts developed.

For example, if a firm produces two or more products, it makes no sense to talk about *the* average cost or *the* marginal cost, because output for the firm is a vector. Suppose that a firm produces two goods and has a total cost function $C(q_1, q_2)$, where q_1 and q_2 are the quantities of the two outputs. One can then define the *incremental cost* of increasing Product 2 from 0 to q_2, holding Product 1 constant: $IC_2 = C(q_1, q_2) - C(q_1, 0)$. The *average incremental cost* of increasing Product 2 from 0 to q_2, holding Product 1 constant, is then $AIC_2 = [C(q_1, q_2) - C(q_1, 0)]/q_2$.

With the help of these two concepts, we can then define the *product-specific economies of scale* (PS_i) of q_i holding the other output q_j, constant: $PS_i = AIC_i/MC_i$, where MC_i is just dC/dq_i. Returns to the scale of product i are said to be increasing, decreasing, or constant as PS_i is greater than, less than or equal to unity, respectively.

Another concept that is required in the case of multi-product firms is *economies of scope*. Economies of scope refer to the possibility of achieving lower costs by producing goods jointly rather than separately (sometimes referred to as 'synergy effects'). Such economies exist when $C(q_1, q_2) < C(q_1, 0) + C(0, q_2)$. The degree of economies of scope, SC, is measured as

$$SC = [C(q_1, 0) + C(0, q_2) - C(q_1, q_2)]/C(q_1, q_2).$$

Many possible factors contribute to economies of scope, one of the most important being common inputs. One example of such common input is the use of sheep to produce both wool and mutton. Mutton spoils unless refrigerated. Before refrigeration, it was sometimes more efficient to produce mutton and wool separately. The shearing centre could be so far from population centre that the mutton would spoil by the time it arrived. The alternative of keeping the sheep near the population centre would not be cost-effective.

Topics for Discussion

1. Some of the important components of costs in large Indian firms are materials costs, power and fuel costs, employee costs, overheads, interest on loans outstanding and depreciation. How would you classify these different components of costs in terms of the concepts developed in Chapter 6? Discuss whether the reported costs reflect the opportunity costs. Would your conclusions change if some of the costs are to be attributed to imported inputs?

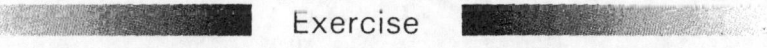

Exercise

1. (a) Complete the following table which shows the amounts of labour inputs applied (L) and the corresponding outputs (Q) in the short run:

L	Q	AP_L	MP_L
0	0	–	
1	15		
2	32		
3	51		
4	66		

5	75
6	84
7	91
8	96
9	99

(b) Suppose that the price of labour is w = Rs 400, the total fixed cost is Rs 10,000 and the total product schedule is the same as in part (a) above. Complete the following table.

Q	TFC	TVC	C	AFC	AVC	AC	MC

etc.

2. A firm's production function is given by $Q = 3K^{0.5} \cdot L^{0.5}$, where K denotes capital and L labour. Capital is fixed at 25 units in the short run, the price of capital is Rs 30 per unit and the price of labour is Rs 5 per unit.
   (a) The fixed cost of production is Rs _____.
   (b) The short run variable cost of producing 45 units of output is Rs _____.
   (c) The short run total cost of producing 45 units is Rs _____.

3. (a) A firm's production function is $Q = K^{0.25} \cdot L^{0.25}$. What type of returns to scale condition does the firm face? Explain your answer.
   (b) If the production function is $Q = K^{0.25} \cdot L^{0.25}$, then derive the expression for the long run total cost function, noting that MRTS at any point of an isoquant is equal to K/L for this production function.
   (c) What are the equations for the long run average and marginal costs?

4. Complete the following table:

Q	TFC	TVC	C	MC	AFC	AVC	AC
0	100	0		–	–	–	–
1		50					
2		95					
3		135					
4			270				
5			300				
6			340				
7				60			
8				80			
9				120			

(Note that the MC figures are being shown against the second of the two numbers involved, rather than in the middle. Thus, if total cost changes from 5 to 7, we write MC = 2 *against* 7 rather than *between* 5 and 7.)

5. In the short run, a firm faces the following input requirements:

Q	L	K
1	25	10
2	40	10
3	60	10
4	85	10
5	125	10

Also, w = Rs 2 and r = Rs 10. On the basis of these figures, complete the following table:
(Again, enter the figures for MC against the second relevant figure)

Q	TFC	TVC	C	MC	AFC	AVC	AC
1							
2							
3							
4							
5							

6. Let $Q = K^{0.5}L^{0.5}$ be the production function so that MRTS = K/L, and let w = Rs 5 and r = Rs 10. What combination of labour and capital will the firms select in the long run if it wants to produce 1000 units at least cost? What is the total cost of producing 1000 units?
7. If w = Rs 50 a day and r = Rs 100 per day, what is the equation of the isocost line if the firm chooses to spend Rs 10,000 a day? If $Q = 2^{0.5}K^{0.5}L^{0.5}$ (that is, MRTS = K/L), what is the minimum average total cost that the firm can achieve with its budget?
8. Suppose that a firm is currently employing 20 workers, the only variable input, at a wage rate of Rs 60. The average product of labour is 30, the last worker added 12 units to total output, and total fixed cost is Rs 3600.

   (a) What is marginal cost?
   (c) What is average variable cost?
   (d) What is average total cost?

9. A multi-product firm produces two commodities whose quantities are denoted by q_1 and q_2. Its total cost function is $C(q_1, q_2) = 100 + q_1^{0.5} + q_2$.
   (a) For each commodity, write down the incremental cost (IC), the average incremental cost (AIC) and the marginal cost (MC).
   (b) What is the degree of economies of scope for this firm?
10. Sunita has collected the following information about Alpha Corporation:

$$MP_L = 10, MP_K = 15, P_L = \text{Rs } 20, P_K = \text{Rs } 15.$$

Explain why these data prove that Alpha Corporation is being run inefficiently. How could Sunita improve efficiency if she is put in charge of Alpha Corporation?

Appendix A

The cost function

We have seen that the firm must minimize the cost of producing any level of output. Keeping input prices fixed, the firm's long run problem can therefore be posed in the following manner:

$$\text{Minimize } wL + rK$$
$$\text{subject to } F(L, K) = Q'$$

In diagrammatic terms, this means that a particular isoquant corresponding to $Q = Q'$ is first fixed. Since $wL + rK = R$ is the equation of a straight line for any R, the 'isocost lines' for the objective function can be represented by means of a family of parallel straight lines. The point at which the lowest such straight line is just tangent to the fixed isoquant Q' provides the best choice input bundle.

It can be readily seen that the solutions are in terms of the three parameters of the problem—the prices and Q':

$$L = L(w, r, Q')$$
$$K = K(w, r, Q')$$

These are called *conditional input demand functions*, because they depend on the level of output Q'.

If we substitute these expressions in the objective function, we obtain the *cost function*:

$$C = wL + rK = wL(w, r, Q') + rK(w, r, Q')$$

You should note the similarity of this function to the expenditure function. In fact, if we consider the problem – min $wL + rK$ subject to $Q' = LK$, then it is obvious that the cost function is going to be:

$$C = 2[(wr)Q']^{0.5}.$$

Shephard's Lemma

Like Roy's Identity, Shephard's Lemma shows us how to recover the conditional input demand functions from the cost function. For example, it can be stated as

$$\partial C/\partial r = K(w, r, Q')$$

Proof: Start with the cost function: $C = wL(w, r, Q') + rK(w, r, Q')$. Then

$$\partial C/\partial r = K + w(\partial L/\partial r) + r(\partial K/\partial r). \text{ (*)}$$

Also $Q(K, L) = Q'$. From this, we get

$$(\partial Q/\partial K)(\partial K/\partial r) + (\partial Q/\partial L)(\partial L/\partial r) = 0$$

And multiplying both sides by the Lagrange multiplier λ, we get

$$\lambda(\partial Q/\partial K)(\partial K/\partial r) + \lambda(\partial Q/\partial L)(\partial L/\partial r) = 0 \Rightarrow r(\partial K/\partial r) + w(\partial L/\partial r) = 0 \text{ (**)}$$
$$\text{(using first order conditions)}$$

From (*) and (**) we obtain $\partial C/\partial r = K(w, r, Q')$

7 Organization and Management of the Firm

7.1 What is a Firm?

So far, we have assumed that a firm is an organization for transforming inputs into outputs. Analytically, the firm is just a production function or a cost function. A firm produces a homogeneous commodity and its technology is represented by a production function (more generally, firms select input and output ratios from their production possibilities set). The *blueprint* of production to the firm is supposed to be provided by engineers. The firm is represented by the cost function which is obtained by solving the problem:

$$\text{minimize } wL + rK$$
$$(L, K)$$
$$\text{subject to } Q = F(L, K).$$

The cost function is written in the form $C = C(Q; w, r)$, or more usually, $C = C(Q)$. It is also assumed that just as the consumers in economic theory have a clearly defined goal of utility maximization, the firm also has an unambiguous objective, that of maximizing its profit.

By identifying the firm as a production process, the issues of organization design and selection of incentives within the firm are completely bypassed. As a result, the economic theory of the firm seems to be totally dissociated from the way managers—those who run real firms—view the workings of the firm. In an earlier chapter, we discussed the complexity of decision-making within a firm. The neoclassical theory of the firm throws little light on these complex issues.

In recent years economists, managers, and legal theorists have been learning from each other and as a result we have a much more rich and insightful view of the firm's working. The important breakthrough in the theory of the firm came when Coase in 1937 asked the question: why do firms exist? Conceptually, all transactions can take place through the market. For example, a car 'manufacturer' can buy all the different parts of a car from different suppliers and only assemble the finished car. In practice, some car manufacturers produce their own gear-boxes or steering wheels, and some choose to buy from others. Almost no big car manufacturing firm produces its own tires. Why do these differences exist? On the other hand, if there are some advantages to organizing activities through firms, then why not have one single giant firm in which all activities are concentrated? Thus, there are clearly demarcated boundaries between activities that take place within firms (relating to the *make* decisions) and those that take place between firms (relating to *buy* decisions).

The answer that Coase provided to this puzzle is that there are costs to using the price system. These costs, which have come to be characterized as *transaction costs* by later writers, may become very large and can be avoided partially or wholly by organizing production activities within firms. Writers like Williamson have pointed out that the firm also faces transaction costs. Economizing on such costs leads to bounds on the activities of firms. Economizing on transaction costs may also explain why certain organizational forms are chosen by firms rather than others.

In this chapter, we take up some of these questions for discussion. We try to evaluate profit-maximization as a reasonably valid behavioural hypothesis. Next, we take a quick look at some of the alternative theories of the firm. No single, coherent, picture emerges from our discussion. But the complexity of operations of a modern corporation are highlighted and some tentative steps taken to model a few aspects of this complexity.

7.2 The Firm's Legal Form

Business firms usually take on one of three legal forms: proprietorship, partnership or limited liability corporation. A proprietorship has a single owner. An example is the owner of the nearby *chai* stall. If the income-tax department can induce him to file returns, his business would be listed as a proprietorship. In a partnership, on the other hand, two or more persons decide to go into business together. Examples are accountancy firms. The third type of organization is the limited liability corporation, where stakes in the ownership are sold as shares. In many corporations, frequently there are lakhs of shareholders, each holding only a few shares in this particular company. The shareholders do not themselves run the company. They elect a Board of Governors which in turn appoints managers to run the firm on a day-to-day basis.

In proprietorships and partnerships, owners are generally the managers and look after the operations of the firm. In contrast, shareholders in large corporations often have neither the willingness nor the ability to manage the firm. The major advantage that the corporation possesses over the other two forms of business is that of *limited liability* of shareholders. If the firm goes bankrupt, the shareholder loses only the face value of the share. Beyond that, she is not liable for the debts of the company. However, in proprietorships or partnerships, the owners are fully liable for the debts of the firm. Suppose that Vijay and Srija have invested, as partners, Rs 25,000 each in a firm, which goes bankrupt, leaving behind Rs 150,000 in debt to creditors. Vijay and Srija will have to sell even other assets (flats, cars, stereo systems, etc.) to repay the debt. But if they had bought stocks worth Rs 25,000 each in a limited liability corporation, they would be liable only for Rs 25,000 each.

7.3 The Profit Maximization Hypothesis

The neoclassical view assumes that a firm tries to maximize profits. The firm is owned by the shareholders. Shareholders get dividends on the shares they hold and these dividends come out of profits. Hence, firms try to maximize profit.

We pose two questions here. First, even on theoretical grounds, are we sure that shareholders try to maximize profits? Second, control in modern corporations rest with managers. What are the managers' goals?

7.3.1 Shareholder Goals

Do the shareholders necessarily want the managers to maximize profits? The answer is no, if the firm has any market power (that is, it can affect prices by its actions) and if the shareholders participate, even indirectly, in the markets that are affected by the operations of the firm. Thus consider four shareholders of RR (Ram-Rahim) Inc., which has market power in both input and output markets.

Shareholder 1 is a consumer of the output of RR. If RR uses its market power to push up its profits, it must do so at the expense of its customers who now have to pay more. If shareholder 1 is a major consumer of RR's products but owns a relatively small fraction of its shares, he can be hurt by RR's attempt to maximize profit more than he is helped by the distribution of the profits to shareholders.

Shareholder 2 sells factor inputs to RR. She may be hurt by receiving less price for her inputs more than she is compensated by the increase in the dividends she receives.

Shareholder 3 has diversified his portfolio and holds shares in many other firms, some of which compete with RR, some of which buy from RR and some of which sell to RR. To the extent RR gains at the expense of any of thse other firms, 3 is made worse off.

Shareholder 4 buys nothing from RR, sells nothing to RR consumes none of the factor inputs of RR and holds only shares of RR. But this shareholder does happen to consume a good that is complementary to one of RR's factor inputs for some consumers. Then as RR holds down the price of its factor inputs, it indirectly increases demand for the factor from other sources, which increases demand for the complementary good, which bids up price of the complementary good, which makes shareholder 4 worse off.

As an example, consider the following quote from *The Economic Times* of 2 March 1998 (FIs in India hold stocks in many firms and the question being debated was whether they should sell out when prices of stocks go up):

'As corporate India wakes up to a dawn of open offers, the role of financial institutions (FIs) is under the microscope. Conventionally perceived as having sided with existing managements, FIs are now hard-pressed to justify whether they are acting in the 'best interests' of their shareholders.

But support to an open offer is not as simple as selling shares and booking profit. FIs are suddenly confronted with a Catch-22 situation: if the offer price is way above the ruling market price, the FIs stand to gain by cashing out; the flip side of the coin is that the offer could place a heavy burden on the balance sheet of the bidding company, in which the FIs might also be the major shareholders.

The India Cements bid for Raasi is a case in point: the FIs hold 35 per cent in India Cements compared to 20 per cent in Raasi'.

We should also note that there might be a potential trade-off between long-term and short-term profitability. A firm can report high profit figures by reducing R&D expenditures. This can have serious implications for long-term profitability, particularly in industries like pharmaceuticals or software where a continuous stream of new and improved products is necessary for the firm to survive. US industries have often been accused of taking such short-term view and thereby losing out to Japanese counterparts over time.

7.3.2 Managerial goals

Berle and Means pointed out in 1932 the rise of the limited liability corporation and the increasing separation of ownership from control in these enterprises. In the modern limited liability corporation, the shareholders elect a Board of Directors, who in turn appoints the managers. The top managers, rather than shareholders, control the firm and look after the day-to-day operations; and their goals can be quite different from that of profit-maximizing. Even if the Board of Directors is perfectly in tune with shareholder goals, it finds it impossible to keep watch on the day-to-day running of the firm.

Alternative goals for managers have been suggested. Some writers have suggested that managers pursue goals like sales maximization subject to a profit constraint, maximization of the rate of growth, etc. Other writers say that the firm is too large, too complex and operates in too uncertain an environment for any kind of optimizing behaviour to make sense. Firms, rather managers, try to attain satisfactory levels of performance for several variables. This is called *satisficing* behaviour.

We now examine briefly the implications of assuming that the firm's objectives reflect that of managers rather than shareholders. In general, let us assume that the manager has an utility function

$U = U(Q, p)$, where Q is the output sold, and p the profit. Higher production and sales of the output means a larger organization which confers on the manager more power and prestige (it can also mean tangible benefits like larger cars or apartments for the manager). Given the demand curve facing the firm, there is a relationship between Q and p that can be represented by $T(Q, p) = 0$, or $p = p(Q)$. Even if the firm is controlled totally by the manager, the manager must maximize utility subject to the constraint T.

For example, suppose that the demand curve facing the firm is $P = a - Q$ (the firm is the only producer of this commodity). There are no costs of production. Then $p = PQ = aQ - Q^2$. When $Q = 0$, or $Q = a$, then $p = 0$. Also, $dp/dQ = a - 2Q$. Hence the slope of the p function is positive when $Q < a/2$, reaches 0 when $Q = a/2$, and becomes negative when $Q > a/2$. This curve is represented in Fig. 7.1.

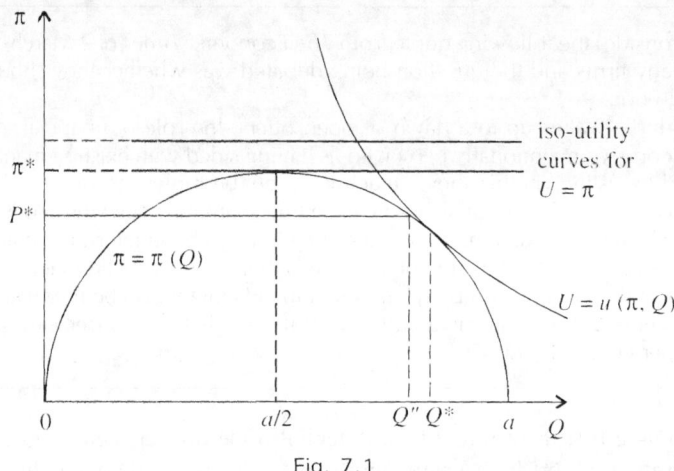

Fig. 7.1

The manager's utility function U can generate a map of indifference or iso-utility curves that show the different combinations of output and profit that can give the manager the same level of utility. Depending on the shape of these curves, the manager will select a point on the profit-output curve. As an extreme case, suppose that $U = p$. Then the indifference curves are horizontal to the Q-axis and the manager chooses $Q = a/2$ that maximizes profit ($p = p^*$). On the other hand, if the indifference curves are convex to the origin, it is easy to see that the manager chooses a point Q^* which is larger than $a/2$, so that profit is not being maximized.

Baumol suggests that the aim of the manager is to maximize Q, but subject to a minimum profit constraint. The manager must keep the shareholders satisfied by making sure that a certain level of profit P^* is being made. This minimum profit constraint is then represented by a horizontal line at the height P^*. The highest output subject to this constraint is Q', which is again higher than $a/2$.

Various arguments have been used to rebut such criticism of the profit-maximization hypothesis. We now try to evaluate these.

7.3.3 The Survival of the Fittest Argument

If, over the long run, a firm does not maximize profits, then it is behaving inefficiently. Either it is incurring unnecessary costs or failing to cash in on revenue opportunities. Other firms will be able to undercut its price or provide better qualities, etc., and erode its market share. In particular, in the long run, product market competition forces firms to minimize costs. As part of this cost minimization process, they have to take actions to raise external capital at the lowest cost. Hence they are forced to adopt corporate governance mechanisms that provide assurance to investors.

This argument is, therefore, based on the disciplining effects of product market competition.

7.3.4 Market for Managers

There is a job market for managers, just as there is one for ordinary workers. A manager, under whom firms perform poorly, will be able to command a lesser value on this market. This argument ignores a number of things. First, even if a firm is performing poorly, it is difficult for outsiders to assess whether the firm is doing poorly because it is being poorly managed or because it is facing adverse market conditions. Second, a firm has a team of managers and it is impossible to evaluate the contribution of each manager to the firm's performance. One can only think of one person in the organization who has to bear the notional responsibility for the firm's performance—the CEO.

7.3.5 Capital Market Controls

It has been argued that if the managers of the firm do not maximize profits, then the firm will be taken over by some corporate raider and the managers will be fired. This threat of capital market disciplining ensures that the managers do try to maximize profits. The argument goes something like this: the inefficient functioning of the firm is reflected in poor share prices since poor dividends are declared. A raider will then buy out the low price shares, gain control over the firm and replace the existing team of managers by a more efficient team. As the performance of the firm improves, so does its share price, and the raider can then make a profit by selling off the shares acquired earlier at the new, higher price.

This argument of course assumes that the existing managers will react passively to the threat of a takeover. Incumbent managers have been known to fight takeover bids tooth and nail if they jeopardized their position. There are now a number of defenses that managers can employ to foil takeover bids.

Takeover Defenses

In the 1980s, North America and the United Kingdom witnessed a spate of hostile takeover attempts. In response, a host of takeover defenses were generated by incumbent management.

White knight: When Mobil Oil attempted a takeover of Marathon Oil, US Steel played the role of a white knight, that is, a friendly acquirer, by making a bid that Marathon's management favoured and finally accepted.

Poison pills: Poison pills are devices aimed at reducing the worth of a company once it has been taken over. One example is a clause requiring that huge dividend payments be made upon take-over—this can significantly raise the cost of acquiring a company.

Scorched earth policies: These policies are those that deliberately reduce the firm's value to the bidder, even if it reduces value to shareholders in the process. One way to do this is to sell off key assets (which are called crown jewels, because they are often the assets that make the company attractive in the first place) at greatly reduced prices.

Golden parachutes: A golden parachute is a clause in the compensation contract providing for very attractive benefits if a manager leaves after a control change. Incumbent managers thereby cushion themselves against the risk of losing their current job should a hostile takeover occur.

Classified or staggered boards: In these boards only a fraction of the members are up for election every year. It then becomes difficult for an outsider to gain quick control over the firm.

Supermajority rules: These require as much as 90 per cent of the votes to effect change and have the same effect as staggered boards.

Greenmail: This commonly consists of an offer by the existing management to buy out the shares acquired by the raider at an attractive premium.

However, there is a much more subtle problem here. Suppose that a firm is being poorly run and that its share price on the market is Rs 10. A raider appears and everybody knows that if the raider succeeds in taking over the firm and making improvements, the share price will go up to Rs 20. To take over the firm, the raider must buy up a majority of the stock. But can he do this successfully? If it is known that the raider will succeed, any individual shareholder knows that the price will rise to Rs 20 and hence will refuse to sell at less than this price. But if the raider must pay this price, he can make nothing for himself by taking over the firm. If, in addition, there are costs to attempting a takeover, the raider will surely back off. This problem of free-riding arises because each shareholder who refuses to sell at or around Rs 10 is trying to free-ride on others: they are hoping that a sufficiently large number of shareholders will sell their shares to the raider, thereby making it possible for the takeover to happen, ultimately pushing up share prices to Rs 20.

The capital market story only makes sense if it can be assumed that the raider has an opportunity to accumulate a number of shares large enough so that the improvements in their value covers the costs of the takeover. But then raids that will result in minor improvements only will not pay for themselves. Therefore while grossly mismanaged firms may be takeover targets, firms that are not so poorly managed will not be targets, and we cannot expect profit-maximization to be achieved by the discipline of takeovers. *This line of reasoning points to the need for internal controls to align management with shareholder interests.*

7.3.6 Takeovers in India

The regulatory mechanism in India had till recently placed several hurdles in the way of takeovers. The Monopolies and Restrictive Trade Practices Act of 1969 had placed various restrictions on mergers, acquisitions and takeovers. Banks could not finance takeovers under the regulations of the Reserve Bank of India. Again, the government financial institutions that control the bulk of shares in many companies had the power to ensure the success of takeover bids to replace inefficient management. But any such move would have invited accusations of political favouritism, so in practice no change in management took place even in grossly mismanaged companies. Moreover, the board of a company had the power to refuse transfers to a particular buyer, thereby making it almost impossible for a takeover to occur without the acquiescence of the existing set of managers. The refusal to transfer the share could be on two grounds: that the transfer was against the interests of the company or against the public interest. Thus the scope for hostile takeovers (as against friendly takeovers) which can be viewed as the capital market's instrument for enforcing efficiency, appeared to be limited. However, in spite of the unfavourable climate, takeovers, mergers and acquisitions continued to take place. During 1988–92, 121 takeovers and mergers occurred.

In 1991, the government omitted the relevant sections and provisions from the MRTP Act by the MRTP (Amendment) Act. The need for prior approval of the Central Government for M&A activities was abolished. The availability of cheap funds through Euro-issues (selling shares in Europe) solved the problem of finance. Starting from 1988, the number of mergers and acquisitions in India seem to be growing at a fast pace. In this context, the SEBI (Substantial Acquisitions of Shares and Takeovers) Regulations, 1994, tried to create a climate in which takeover activities could fulfil the function of effectively disciplining Indian firms.

The main objective of these regulations is to provide greater transparency in the acquisition of shares and the takeover of companies through a system of disclosure of information.

Some of the highlights of the SEBI Takeover Code are:

• Acquirer holding more than 5 per cent of shares in a company must disclose his shareholding to the company and all stock exchanges where the scrip is listed.

- In negotiated takeovers, acquirer cannot acquire more than 10 per cent shares in a company unless she makes a public offer for another 20 per cent of shares at acquisition price or average price of previous six months.
- In open market takeovers, acquirer cannot acquire more than 10 per cent shares unless she makes a public offer at a price not lower than the highest open market price paid by her or average price of previous six months.
- Any person other than the acquirer making a public announcement may within two weeks of such announcement make a competitive bid for acquisition, subject to the same terms and conditions listed above.
- Public offers once made cannot be withdrawn except with the prior approval of the Board under conditions that make it impossible to carry out the offer, for example, in the case of insolvency or death of the acquirer.

The Bhagwati Committee was set up to review the Regulations and recommend changes. The draft takeover code formulated by the Bhagwati Committee was released on 28 August 1996. With the avowed aim of protecting the interests of shareholders, ensuring fairness, transparency and equity, without discouraging the process of takeovers, the Committee sought to provide an orderly framework of regulations in which takeovers can occur.

A number of recommendations of the Bhagwati Committee stand out. Acquirers can take a company private, because it recommends doing away with the existing conditions of 20 per cent public holding after the offer. Acquirers have the option to buy out the remaining shares if the public shareholding were to fall below 10 per cent subsequent to a public offer. Another recommendation was that an acquirer must deposit 10 per cent of total offer amount in an escrow account. The amount will be forfeited in case of default by the acquirer. Also, while retaining the trigger point of 10 per cent for making a public offer, the Committee recommends that consolidation of holdings by existing management be allowed within a specified limit. Persons holding 10–25 per cent of shares may acquire up to 2 per cent shares in any period of 12 months and persons holding 25–50 per cent shares may acquire up to 5 per cent in any 12-month period without attracting the mandatory public offer requirement (this is known as 'creeping acquisition').

7.3.7 Incentives in Organizations

Finally, one can try to align the interests of shareholders and managers by providing the latter with appropriate incentives. For example, the manager can be given a bonus that is a straightforward percentage of sales or profit. However, it has been argued that this promotes a short-term outlook in managers. they try to inflate short term profit figures at the expense of necessary long-term investments.

Another way of reconciling the aims of shareholders and managers is to offer the latter stock option plans. These plans work on the following basis. The manager is given the right to purchase a certain number of shares of the firm at a fixed price p any time within a given period (say, within the next two years). The manager then has an incentive to increase profits and dividends, so that share prices go up within this period. The manager can then buy her shares at price p per share and sell the shares at the higher market price of p^* and pocket the surplus $p^* - p$ per share. Incentives can also be implicit. Poor performance is punished by firing the manager and good performance rewarded by means of promotions and attendant perks.

We now turn to the transactions cost based theories of the firm. We first discuss the contractual theories of the firm and then look at organizational theories.

The use of stock-option schemes has been widespread in the UK and the US. In the US, CEOs have profited hugely from such schemes. In 2001 nine executives cashed in stock options worth more than $100 million, including Larry Ellison, the boss of Oracle (who got the biggest bounty, $706 million), and Lou Gerstner, the boss of IBM. While the evidence on the link between options and performance is thin, options have focused managerial attention on shareholder value. They have encouraged firms to drive down costs, even in the midst of a boom. They have also reduced the costs of starting a business: young and talented employees can be persuaded to join with the mere promise of future growth that stock options represent.

A study by Mercer Human Resource Consulting for the *Wall Street Journal* showed that in 2005 bonuses for the CEOs at 100 large American companies rose by 46.4 per cent. The median bonus was $1.14 million. These are of course large suns of money. Moreover, there are plenty of instances where the rewards seem unreasonable. Michael Eisner, for example, the controversial chief executive of Walt Disney, who was almost booted out of the job by shareholders in 2004, nevertheless received a bonus of $7.25 million. However, the amounts paid as bonuses are still far smaller than those that used to be paid under stock options.

Source: *Economist*, 3 March 2005. 'Fat Cats turn to Low Fat'.

While incentives generally are sought to be provided through monetary rewards, some firms seem to believe that the 'working environment' plays an equally important in aligning management goals with that of the firm's long-term objectives. Companies like HLL, Thermax, Marico and Mahindra & Mahindra do not pay the highest salaries in the market, but still seem to have highly motivated workforces. Some of the ways in which this high level of motivation is sustained and generated are as follows:

- Training and rotation across functional areas—The first provides an incentive to stay on in the job to increase skills while the second prevents boredom.
- Delegation—Giving freedom to employees (often termed 'empowerment') induces innovation and a sense of responsibility.
- Transparency—Transparency relating to sharing of information about the company seems to generate a sense of belonging.
- Trust—The idea is to foster self-accountability among employees, thus lessening the need for monitoring and supervision.

7.4 Contractual Theories of the Firm

There are two main contractual theories of the firm, which may be referred to as the *Coasian* view and the *Knightian* view. The Coasian view stresses the *transaction costs* of using markets versus contracting within organizations, as an explanation for what takes place within the firm. The Knightian view is reflected in work that stresses the importance of *information* and *uncertainty* as explanations for the organization of activities within firms. It is clear that problems stemming from incomplete information can form important components of transaction costs.

The Coasian theory explains the existence of firms on the basis of contractual efficiency. The firm represents a set of contracts that are more efficient than market-mediated contracts either in terms of contract formation or performance. Coase (1937) pointed out that there is a cost of using the price mechanism and this cost includes searching for prices, negotiation of individual transactions, and the cost of specifying contingencies in long-term contracts. The relative costs of markets and of organizations are viewed as the main determinants of the extent of the firm's activities. Thus, for example, a firm trying to decide whether to manufacture a particular component itself or to buy it from the market must consider (a) the production cost of the component in relation to its market price *and* (b) the costs of organizing production in relation to the costs of finding out and bargaining with the suppliers of the component. It is obvious that for standardized parts, the cost of going to the market may be much less than the cost of organizing production.

Production in most firms goes through a number of stages. Raw materials are transformed into inputs which are then transformed into outputs. Vertical integration refers to phenomenon of a firm choosing to carry out these stages itself rather than relying on the market. For example, when a steel plant decides to own the coal-mines, it is integrating backwards. If it decides to sell steel from its own distribution outlets, it is integrating forwards. Transactions cost economics has provided useful insights into the extent of vertical integration within a firm.

Oliver Williamson has extensively analysed transaction costs. He distinguishes between transaction costs of ex ante and ex post types. The first are the costs of drafting, negotiating and safeguarding an agreement. The ex post costs include (1) the maladaptation costs when transactions drift out of alignment in relation to the original agreement, (2) the haggling costs incurred if bilateral efforts are made to correct ex post misalignments, (3) the setup and running costs associated with the governance structures to which disputes are referred, and (4) the bonding costs of securing agreements.

He identifies three major sources of these costs. First, human beings have *bounded rationality*. Bounded rationality refers to human behaviour that is *intendedly rational but only limitedly so*. That is, human beings try to behave rationally (optimize). However, they are faced with both neurophysiological limits as well as language limits. There are limits on the power of individuals to receive, sort, retrieve and process information without error. Language limits refer to the inability of individuals to articulate their knowledge or feelings by the use of words, numbers or graphics in a way that permits them to be understood by others. Bounded rationality is important when the limits of rationality have been reached—that is, under conditions of *uncertainty* and/or *complexity*. The implication is that *comprehensive contracting* is not a realistic organizational alternative: because of the existence of bounded rationality, the parties to a transaction cannot make provision for every possible contingency. That is, the transaction costs of negotiating and enforcing contracts make it prohibitively costly to write long-term contracts which specify all obligations under all contingencies.

Williamson also assumes *opportunism*, by which he means self-seeking with guile. Since contracts cannot be complete, agents will try to behave opportunistically when unanticipated events arise. In such situations, there must be institutions to settle disputes. Such institutions may be external (for example, the legal system) or internal ('governance structures'). The relative efficiency of the different types of institutions determines which one shall be adopted in any particular context.

Williamson identifies the condition of *asset specificity* as a key determinant of in the organization of firms. Asset specificity refers to investments that are specific to transactions in the sense that their values in alternative transactions are significantly lower. An example is a rail line built to carry coal from the pithead to the city. If the coal mine were to close down, the rail line might be useless, that is, there might not be any alternative goods to carry. Asset specific investments often permit significant cost savings to be realized (the cost of transporting coal by trucks will be much higher). But obviously, such investments are risky in that specialized assets cannot be redeployed without sacrifice of value if contracts should be interrupted or prematurely terminated.

Asset specificity creates the possibility of opportunism: once two parties have entered into an agreement and one party (say party A) has made specific investments relying on the initial contract, the other party (say party B) realizes that to some extent A is at its mercy. A is 'locked into' this relationship because of the specific nature of its investment. Hence B will have an incentive to force A to give up more than the originally agreed upon share of gains, threatening otherwise to terminate the relationship. But realizing this possibility ex ante, A might be reluctant to enter into a contract with B. Thus, from society's point of view, some opportunities of welfare-enhancing trade could be forsaken. In our example, the mine owner who invests in the rail line may find herself at the mercy of the electric utility using the coal. The utility may threaten to use the coal only for the backup of its nuclear or hydro-powered plants. On the other hand, the utility might worry that after railroad is built, the mine will try to raise the freight rates, banking on the fact that alternative transportation modes are too expensive. This possibility of opportunistic behaviour is called the *hold-up problem*.

If contracts were complete, the hold-up problems would not arise. The full range of possibilities and safeguards against these would be specified in the contract. Even though complete contracting is not possible, the parties can draw up long term contracts, and try to build into the contract safeguards against such opportunism, for example, through price indexing clauses, cost-plus pricing clauses, liquidated damages and arbitration provisions. *However, when asset specificity is substantial, contractual governance may become very costly. Internal organization of the exchange may then be the more efficient governance structure and this provides the rationale for the existence of firms.*

Williamson complements this analysis of relative governance costs with relative production costs. For example, as the supplier invests in assets more specific to this particular buyer, it loses economies of scale or scope because of its inability to make sales to other buyers. Thus contractual exchange has an additional production cost advantage for a given degree of asset specificity.

It is now obvious to almost everybody that India's infrastructure is in shambles. Unless large investments are soon made in infrastructure development, India cannot hope to have sustainable high rates of growth. However, the challenge of finding the funds to invest in infrastructure projects without jeopardizing the fiscal health of the government remains. Increasingly, cash-strapped governments both at the Centre and the State level are turning to the private sector for investing in such projects. But while infrastructure projects are no doubt socially beneficial, they present certain special risks to the private investor. In particular demand-side risks arise because 'infrastructure is the ultimate non-tradable and is characterized by high asset specificity' (Verma, 2004). Private investors are therefore unwilling to invest in these projects unless they get an adequate risk-premium on their returns from such investment.

Airport privatization, already a contentious issue in India, will face this problem, because airport assets cannot be redeployed for a new use. Unlike an aircraft which can be redeployed on a more profitable route, an airport can only serve the local market. And if the economy faces a recession, demand for airport services may drop, and airport infrastructure will lie idle. After the Asian crisis, for example, investment in airports and mass transit systems that had seemed like risk-free propositions earlier, turned out to be commercially non-viable. There was a slower growth of traffic and reduced willingness of consumers facing economic hardship to pay for convenience. But the specific nature of these assets meant that they could not be harnessed in alternative uses.

Sources: J. Verma, 2004, *Regulatory Dilemmas in Infrastructure Financing*. India Infrastructure Report 2004, 3iNetwork, OUP. *India Infrastructure Report 2006*, 3iNetwork, OUP.

7.5 Organizational Theories of the Firm

Economic entities are created entities within and through which people interact to reach collective and individual goals. The economy is itself an organization, and the issues involved in the alternative ways of organizing the economy get reflected in the lower level organizations like firms.

Ubiquitous specialization leads to the problems of coordination and motivation. The activities of different sets of people must be coordinated and they must also be motivated to take the right decisions. Scattered information must be gathered and utilized properly. These problems may be solved in different ways. At one extreme one can attempt to transmit all the dispersed information to a central computer or planner who is expected to solve the resource allocation problem. One can, on the other hand, have a more decentralized system where agents possessing local information are delegated some decision-making power. The switch from the Unitary form to the Multidivisional form in modern corporations illustrates nicely the relative strengths and weaknesses of these alternative approaches.

7.5.1 The U-form versus the M-form

Alfred Chandler (1966) first drew attention to significant changes occurring in the structure of American industries since the mid-1920s. The multidivisional form (or M-form) gradually came to supplant the unitary form (U-form).

The U-form structure can be represented as follows:

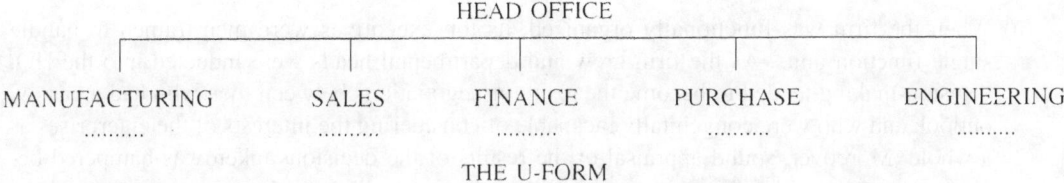

HEAD OFFICE

MANUFACTURING   SALES   FINANCE   PURCHASE   ENGINEERING
....

THE U-FORM

The U-form firm is, therefore, organized along functional lines. Each functional department engages in activities related to a number of products, often in different geographic locations. The U-form therefore has a centralized structure. By contrast, the M-form firm is organized into semi-autonomous divisions:

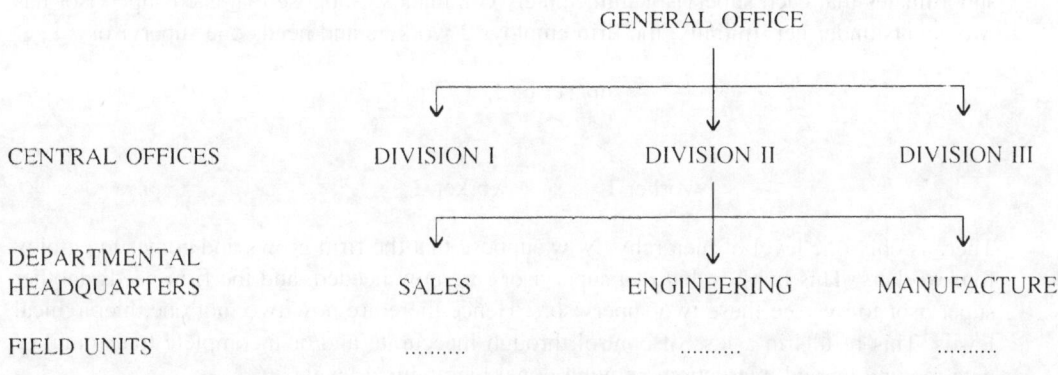

GENERAL OFFICE

CENTRAL OFFICES   DIVISION I   DIVISION II   DIVISION III

DEPARTMENTAL
HEADQUARTERS   SALES   ENGINEERING   MANUFACTURE

FIELD UNITS   ....

THE M-FORM

At the top is a general office; there general executives and staff specialists coordinate, appraise, plan goals and policies and allocate resources for a number of quasi-autonomous, fairly self-contained divisions. Each division handles a major product line or carries on the firm's activities in one large geographic area. Each division's central office, in turn, administers a number of departments each of which is responsible for the performance of a function.

One can also note the existence of various hybrid forms of organization-holding companies, where divisions are affiliated with the parent company through a subsidiary relationship, mixed form, where some divisions will be of a holding company variety, others will be M-form and still others will be functionally organized, etc.

Chandler distinguished between two stages of the development of organizational forms within firms. In stage I, the expansion of an enterprise (in terms of output, capital invested and men employed) led to the emergence and consolidation of the U-form structure. Thus *increase in demand* for a company's products resulted in a strategy of expansion or of combination. Departmental headquarters were developed to administer a number of plants or offices scattered throughout the country. As the enterprise grew, the departmental headquarters in turn came to be administered by a central office. The central office eventually came to have three types of duties:

(i)   coordination and integration of the activities of the various functional departments to meet changing market conditions;
(ii) assisting the functional departments through auxiliary or service departments;
(iii) allocating the resources of the enterprise.

The weakness of the unitary structure stemmed from several factors:

(a) When the firm was functionally organized, its top executives were men trained to handle single function units. As the firm grew and departmental heads were inducted into the HQ, decision-making tended to become the result of negotiations between men who had a narrow outlook and who were congenitally incapable of considering the interests of the enterprises as a whole. Moreover, sound appraisal of the results of the decisions taken was hampered because departmental heads avoided critically evaluating each others' performances.
(b) Objective data on departmental performance proved hard to obtain because of the interdependencies among departments.
(c) Given a certain 'span of control', the growth of the firm necessitates what Williamson calls a 'radial amplification of hierarchical levels'. The span of control refers to the number of subordinates that each supervisor immediately commands. Suppose that each supervisor has two agents under her. Initially, the firm employs 2 workers and needs one supervisor.

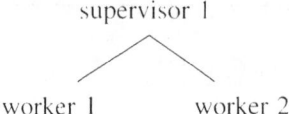

There is only one level of hierarchy. Now suppose that the firm grows and comes to employ four workers. This implies that *two* supervisors are now needed, and the firm needs another supervisor to oversee these two supervisors. Hence there are now two, not one, hierarchical levels. This results in a loss of control through inaccurate and/or incomplete transmittal of data moving up and instructions moving down hierarchical levels.

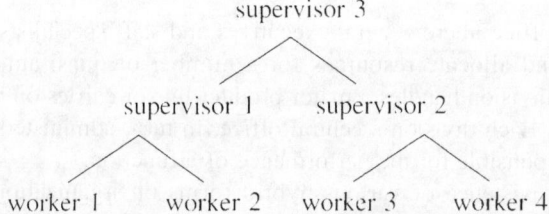

(d) While the lack of product market competition allows for greater scope of discretionary behaviour on the part of managers, one might expect capital market controls to have a disciplinary effect on the operation of the U-form firm. However, as has already been pointed out, capital market controls can only work in a discrete, crude and inefficient fashion: they cannot be expected to fine-tune the operations of the firm precisely because they are *external* to the firm.

These problems became especially acute when diversification took place in response to a falling-off of demand (to utilize existing capacity) and vertical integration continued to take place in widely separated geographical areas. To overcome the control loss problems, the M-form was introduced. The advantages were:

(a) The executives in charge of strategic decisions did not have to worry about the operational aspects.

(b) Operational decisions were left to Heads of multi-function enterprises. Appraisal of divisional performance proved to be more precise than in the U-form because

  (i) divisions *did not* depend closely on each other for their operations, and
  (ii) divisions' performances could be compared either in terms of costs or profits.

  There was interdependence among the semi-autonomous divisions mainly through capital allocation.

(c) It has been claimed that the control loss associated with increasing size is reduced in the M-form because the expansion is achieved by adding divisions rather than deepening hierarchy. It has to be noted, however, that the functional structure reappears in the M-form within each semi-autonomous division.

(d) Williamson has asserted that 'The M-form creates its own internal miniature capital market which replicates external capital market functions and economizes on transaction costs.' Headquarters has access to information on divisions so that it can meter funds swiftly and accurately; it has auditing powers, and, further, it can intervene at low cost when departures from desired behaviour are identified.

But Chandler himself points out certain conditions under which the U-form would remain viable even with expansion: as long as the company's basic activities remain *simple* and *stable*, the impetus to switch to the M-form structure is weakened. Simplicity means that the executives can handle both strategic and operational decisions efficiently. Stability means that over time, the repeated observation of simple processes gives the central office enough information to efficiently monitor the departmental heads.

Examples of industries not accepting the M-form structure in the US were copper, nickel, zinc, steel, and aluminium industries. The copper, nickel, and zinc industries in fact showed a tightening of the U-form structure. Their noteworthy features were, again, of stability and simplicity of operations. In these industries, the same products have been produced in much the same way over a long period of time. Further, they have relatively few and undifferentiated products, relatively few customers, and no vertical integration. As a result, administrative decisions have become almost entirely operational ones; strategic decisions are few and simple. Similar considerations apply to the steel industry where the market has not been differentiated enough to permit the growth of autonomous, integrated organizations. In the aluminium industry, close connection between the marketing and production activities provides an impetus for continued centralization.

The exclusive focus on the American experience of organizational changes tends to the viewing of the M-form as a logical and inevitable progression from the U-form. One tends to lose sight of the basic question of transaction costs and other ways of organizing firms to economize on transaction costs. We now briefly contrast the German and Japanese experiences with the American one.

As Cable and Dirrheimer (1983) report, in West Germany divisionalization typically followed an earlier phase of diversification, though often with a long lag. What is more interesting is that two major companies *reverted* from M-form to other organizational forms after 1975.

The possible gains to adoption of M-form would appear to be small in Germany, because there seems to be less scope for managerialism as well as the existence of an adequate substitute for the

> The Indian Aluminium Company Ltd. (Indal) was established in 1938. It started its manufacture with a 2500 tonnes per year aluminium sheet rolling factory in 1941. Later it engaged in bauxite mining, foil-rolling and converting, production of wire rods, and production of extruded products. In 1989 Indal diversified into the electronics industry. The company underwent several changes in its organizational structure. Before 1976, it had a functional setup. Under the MD, there were General Managers in charge of Production, Commerce, Engineering and Projects, Personnel, etc. After the reorganization in 1976, the MD had under him GMs in charge of Smelter and Chemicals, Fabrication, in addition to GMs in charge of Commerce, Engineering and Projects, Personnel, etc.
>
> The divisionalization was carried forward further in 1990, when the MD had under him a Management Committee, monitoring Divisional Managers in charge of Metal & Carbon products, Chemicals, Rolled Products, Extrusions and Foils.
>
> *Source*: S.B. Budhiraja and M.B. Athreya, 1996, *Cases in Strategic Management*. New Delhi: Tata McGraw-Hill.

external capital market. First, firms are required to have a *dual board system* by law: there must be a non-executive supervisory board in addition to the executive board, that has access to internal company information and powers of appointment to and dismissal from the the executive board. Ownership is concentrated and there is a system of bank control of shareholders' proxy voting rights. Second, in Germany the stock market is a relatively unimportant source of corporate funds. Bank borrowing is an important source, especially for financing inventories and long-term investment. Bank finance is provided by a small number of banks which usually have a strong representation on the supervisory boards of leading firms. Thus banks would seem to perform the duties of the Head Office in M-form enterprises in respect of internal capital market functions.

The role of banks is also quite important in Japan. Cable and Yasuki (1985) draw attention to the existence of loosely knit large business groups in Japan that (a) do not have a hierarachical, parent-subsidiary relationship and (b) do not possess a central organization corresponding to the general office of the M-form firms. These business groups function in a manner that significantly reduces transaction costs:

(i) Information exchange—the groups have regular meetings both at the top and intermediate management levels; it is believed that information is exchanged mainly on topics that are of a broad strategic nature.
(ii) Mutual shareholding amongst group members probably increases the incentive towards co-ordination of group activities.
(iii) Trading relationships between members of the same group, consequently, would be subject to less risk and uncertainty than with outsiders. It would also reduce incentives for pursuing vertical integration strategies.
(iv) Finance is supplied primarily by banks because there is no adequate external capital market. Each group contains a number of different types of financial institutions, meeting the differing financial needs of members of the group. Further, the group bank typically acts as both lender and financial advisor to the group. It can do this efficiently as it has extensive knowledge of company affairs as a result of the information exchange process within the group.

The Japanese and German experiences lend substance to Williamson's assertion that external capital market controls do not work to discipline firms. However, the M-form does not emerge as the natural alternative to the U-form: the multidivisional structure may be rendered redundant when possible gains from a switch to this form are small (as in West Germany), or when a different set of arrangements can achieve reduction in transaction costs (as in Japan).

Topics for Discussion

1. Would you expect the strategic environment of a firm to shape its organizational structure? Explain your answer (the subsequent chapters in this book consider the different types of market structures or strategic environments).
2. In India, financial institutions invest in equity and play a critical role in providing funds for investment. Should these institutions behave like ordinary shareholders? Should they shoulder additional responsibilities?

Exercise

Assume that the manager has a utility function $U = Q\pi$ where Q is the output sold, and π the profit. The demand curve facing the monopoly firm is $P = 90 - Q$ and the cost function is $C = 10Q$.

(a) How much would the manager produce and what will be the profit of the firm?
(b) If instead, the manager's utility function is $U = \pi$, how much will be produced and what will be the firm's profit?

8 | The Firm in a Perfectly Competitive Market

8.1 Perfect Competition

The theory of consumer behaviour enabled us to derive the market demand curve starting from the tastes and preferences of the consumer. The second set of participants in the market is the firms and we want to derive the supply curve by analysing their behaviour in markets.

We call the collection of the firms in the market for a particular commodity an *industry*. The definition of an industry in practice can be ambiguous. Take two firms that produce glass containers and plastic containers, respectively. Should they be considered to belong to the same 'container industry'? Or should they be considered to be parts of the glass products industry and the plastic products industry respectively?

The industry structure that we consider is an idealized market structure called *perfect competition*, which acts as a benchmark for comparing what happens in other market structures. A perfectly competitively industry is characterized by the following features:

1. All firms sell a *homogeneous product*, that is, the outputs of all firms are identical from the viewpoint of buyers. This implies that there is no problem in defining the industry.

   Gold mined in one part of the world is perfect substitute for gold from another part of the world. On the other hand, mineral water is not homogeneous since waters bottled from different sources have different chemical composition and different tastes.

2. There is unrestricted mobility of resources in the long run. In particular, firms can enter and exit from the market freely.

   In particular, this means that no technological, legal or regulatory barriers constrain entry or exit. Governments sometimes issue a limited number of licenses in certain industries and may require payment of compensatory fees if a firm owning such a licence wishes to exit from the industry.

3. The number of buyers and sellers in the market is 'large'. This means that each agent in the market believes that her actions will have negligible effect on the market price. Therefore, all agents in the market act as if the market price is fixed independently of their own actions, that is, everyone in the market is a 'price-taker'.

   Consider the effect of having a small number of 'large' buyers. A market demand curve shows, for every possible price, the quantity that all the buyers will demand collectively. This obviously means that given any price, buyers determine their actions, assuming that they cannot influence the price. However, if some buyers are large, they can influence the price and it is quite possible that different buyers will pay different prices.

   In the market for gold, there are numerous buyers located all over the world. Compared to the total volume of transactions in gold in any given day, each buyer demands only a very small quantity of gold. But the market for uranium consists of a few large buyers, such as defence organizations of the nuclear powers, each of whom can obviously influence market conditions, including price.

4. Finally, we assume that all agents possess perfect information.
   (i) All firms have the same production function and the same cost function.
   (ii) All firms are aware of the prices of inputs and opportunities available in other industries.
   (iii) All buyers are instantaneously aware of all the prices charged by all the sellers.

Example 8.1: It is hard to think of an industry that fits the definition of perfect competition. The two markets that are commonly believed to be perfectly competitive are agriculture and the stock markets. Both these markets are characterized by the existence of a very large number of buyers and sellers. In the agricultural sector, different commodities are produced, but within each category, product differentiation tends to be small. Techniques of production are well-known. Moreover, entry into and exit from the sector is relatively easy. Similar observations can be made about a stock market. All the instruments traded on the stock market are paper instruments of various types, differentiated only by their face value and yields. The information about these is constantly upgraded and available.

The implication of all these assumptions taken together is that a uniform price is established throughout the market and all firms/sellers behave as if they are unable to affect this price by their own individual actions.

8.2 Economic Profit vs Accounting Profit

We assume as a behavioural rule that the objective of the firm is to maximize profit. However, in keeping with the practice of considering only opportunity costs, we assume that the firm tries to maximize economic profit rather than accounting profit.

Accounting profit is equal to total revenue minus explicit costs, while economic profit is equal to total revenue minus all opportunity costs. We know that opportunity costs consist of both explicit costs and implicit costs. Therefore,

Economic profit = Accounting profit − Implicit costs
          = Accounting profit − (opportunity costs of resources not otherwise
                  accounted for)
          = Accounting profit − 'normal profit'

We use the term normal profit to indicate that the resources used in the firm that have no explicit costs attached to them could have been used elsewhere and earned returns in such alternative uses. If a firm is to stay on in an industry, economic rationale demands that it make profit at least sufficient to cover the returns from alternative uses. This is its *normal profit*. If economic profit is greater than zero, then the firm is making *supernormal profits*, and resources are attracted into the industry. If it is less than zero, the firm can earn more elsewhere, and it would want to exit from the industry. Therefore, in economics, if we say that a firm is earning zero or negative profits, this does not mean that its accounting profit is zero or negative. The point is that even a positive accounting profit may hide the true cost of resources being used by the firm.

Example 8.2: Consider a firm with a owner-manager. Suppose that the owner has invested Rs 100,000 in the firm. This could have been put into a fixed deposit account and earned interest at 10 per cent. The owner could have worked elsewhere and earned Rs 50,000 every year. Then the total implicit cost of resources employed in the firm is Rs 60,000. This will be the normal profit for the firm. If the accounting profit is equal to this amount, the owner will be indifferent between remaining in the business and working elsewhere; the economic profit in this case is zero.

We assumed that there are only two inputs, capital and labour services, which are bought at given market prices. Any labour input from the owners or any capital services provided by the owners must be included in the total costs that are calculated to ensure that there are no implicit costs that are unaccounted for. Then, if we define profit as revenue minus costs, the concept of profit will be that of economic profit.

8.3 Short-run Profit Maximization

The consequence of the assumptions made about perfect competition is that any firm in a perfectly competitive market takes the output price to be fixed: $p = p^*$. The firm tries to maximize economic profit

$$\pi = p^* \cdot q - C(q) = \text{TR} - C(q),$$

where q is the output of any firm (we will reserve Q to denote industry output) and TR denotes the total revenue.

The first order condition is $dp/dq = 0$, and the second order condition is $d^2p/dq^2 < 0$. From the former, we get the condition for profit-maximization as

$$p^* - dC/dq = 0,$$
$$\text{that is, } p^* = \text{MC}.$$

The firm should choose that level of output q^* which equates price with marginal cost. What about the second order condition? This reduces to $d^2p/dq^2 = -d^2C/dq^2 < 0$, that is, $d\text{MC}/dq > 0$. In other words, the MC curve should be upward sloping at q^*.

In Fig. 8.1, p^* is a horizontal straight line because from the firm's viewpoint, market price is given independently of its own output. Both q' and q^* are characterized by the equality of the market price with marginal cost. However, only at q^* is the second order condition satisfied, that is, the MC curve is upward sloping. Accordingly, it is the output at which profit is maximized.

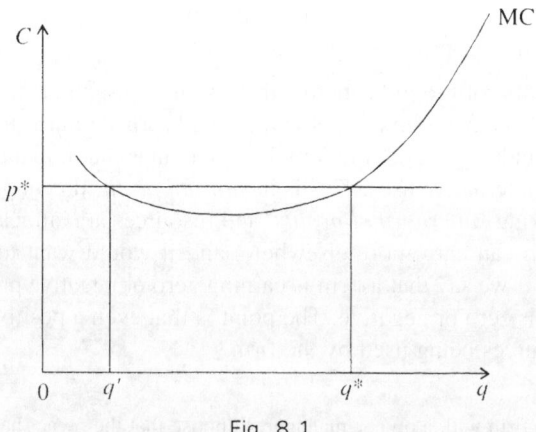

Fig. 8.1

What is the intuition behind the price = marginal cost condition? Starting from any level of production let the firm consider the effect on profit of producing an additional unit. This additional unit will add $p^*\Delta q$ to revenue and ΔC to total costs. If $p^*\Delta q > \Delta C$, the extra unit adds more to revenue than to cost, and should be produced. If $p^*\Delta q < \Delta C$, the extra unit adds more to costs than to revenue, and the firm would be better off by producing a lesser amount: this way, it can increase profit by cutting down on costs. The profit-maximizing point is reached when $p^*\Delta q = \Delta C$, which means that $p^* = \Delta C/\Delta q$. It should be remembered that this discussion is subject to the fulfilment of the second order condition.

Instead of using the diagram to represent price and marginal cost, we could have worked with total revenue and total cost directly. From the firm's point of view, p^* is a fixed number. Hence $TR = p^*q$ represents a straight line through origin, with slope p^*. Profit is maximized when the vertical distance between the total revenue and total cost curves in Fig. 8.2 is maximized. This occurs when the slopes of the two curves are the same at q^*. Alternatively, the slope of the profit curve is zero at q^*.

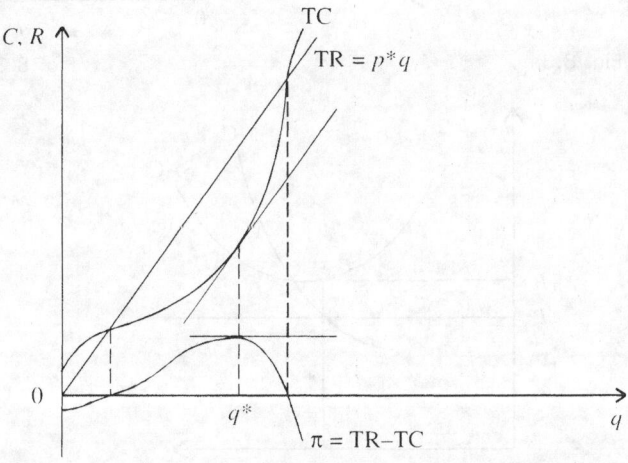

Fig. 8.2

Example 8.3:

q	p^*	$TR = p^*q$	C	$p = TR - C$	$MR = DTR$	$MC = DC$
0	10	0	12	−12	–	–
1	10	10	14	−4	10	2
2	10	20	15	5	10	1
3	10	30	17	13	10	2
4	10	40	20	20	10	3
5	10	50	25	25	10	5
6	10	60	35	25	10	10
7	10	70	50	20	10	15
8	10	80	81	−1	10	31

These numbers are only illustrative. Note that profit is maximized at output levels 5 and 6. Price is equated to MC only at output level 6, however. The second order condition is also satisfied since MC is increasing at $q = 6$.

The economic profit is easy to represent graphically. Note that $p = p^*q - C = q(p^* - C/q) = q(p^* - SAC)$. Profit is measured by the area of the rectangle p^*E^*AB. Then $p =$ or $<$ or > 0 according as $p^* =$ or $<$ or $>$ SAC. The three possibilities are shown in Fig. 8.3.

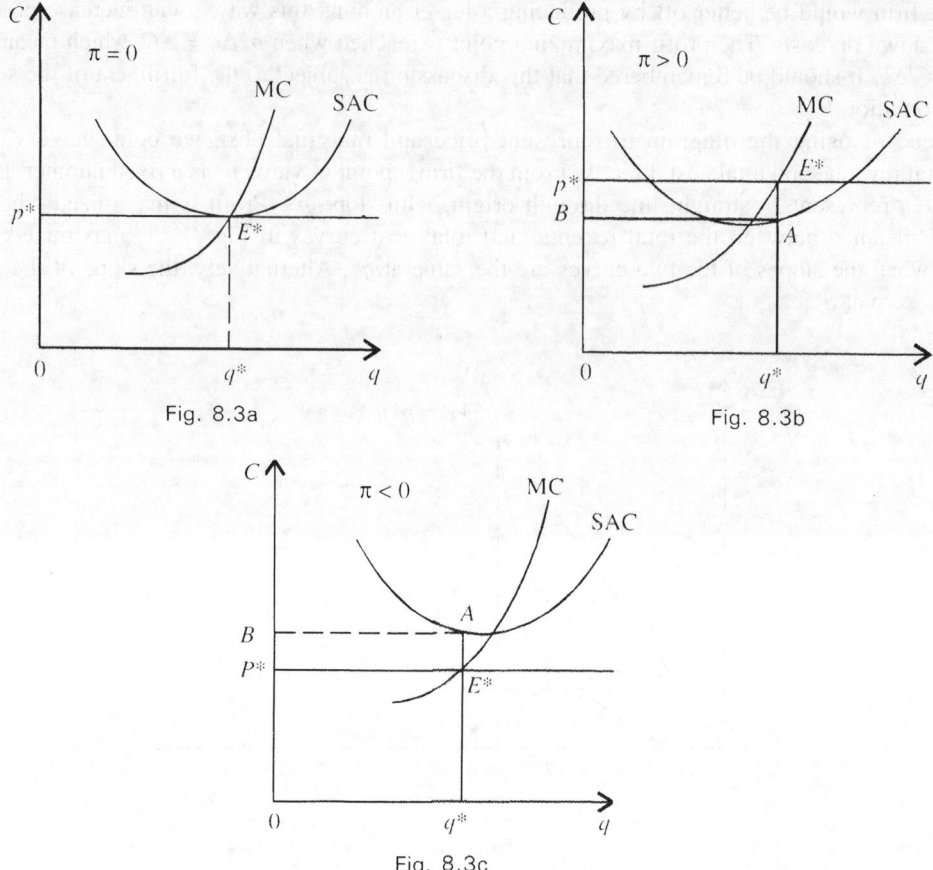

Fig. 8.3a

Fig. 8.3b

Fig. 8.3c

We can throw further light on the firm's problem by writing out the profit function fully:

$$\Pi = pF(L, K) - wL - rK$$

As in Chapter 5, $Q = F(L, K)$, where F is the production function. In the short run, we have assumed that K is a fixed input; thus $K = K^*$(say). The firm therefore chooses L to maximize its profit. The first order condition then is $pdF/dL = w$. This expression can be interpreted in a number of ways:

1. $pdF/dL = w$ means that the *value of marginal product* pdF/dL is equated to the wage rate. Employing one more unit of labour costs the firm w. On the other hand, this extra unit of labour increases output (dF/dL) which can be sold at the fixed price p—this is the addition to revenue. The firm will continue to employ labour so long as the addition to revenue exceeds the additional wage cost.
2. $dF/dL = w/p$ means that the marginal product of labour is equated to the real wage rate. The interpretation is the same as earlier, only difference being that the trade-off is posed in real terms.
3. $p = w/(dF/dL)$ is just the price equals marginal cost condition. To see this, note that total cost is $C(Q) = wL + rK$ where rK is fixed in the short run. Then $MC = dC/dQ = w(dL/dQ) = w/(dQ/dL) = w/(dF/dL)$.

8.3.1 The Shutdown Point

If the firm is making a loss in the short run, should it stop production? (As the firm must continue to pay for the fixed input in the short run, it cannot exit from the industry in the short run.) The firm must balance the loss from shutting down production with the loss from continuing to produce, and choose the action that minimizes the loss.

If the firm continues production, it makes a loss = TR – (TFC + TVC). If it shuts down, then it does not earn any revenue. It avoids the variable costs, but must continue to pay the fixed costs, i.e. the loss is equal to the fixed cost. The firm will then decide to continue even when it is making a loss if – |TR – (TFC + TVC)| < TFC (the minus sign is used to convert the loss to a positive number so that we can compare it with the size of the fixed cost).

This condition, after some manipulation, reduces to TR > TVC, that is, $p^* > $ AVC. The reason for this should be easy to see. The firm incurs fixed cost in any case. If by continuing to produce, *it can cover all its variable costs and have something left over to cover its fixed cost*, it should do so. If it is unable to do this, then it is incurring some variable costs over and above its fixed cost and should shut down operations. The two situations are shown in Fig. 8.4.

The market price p^* is given to the firm. Then the condition for continuing to produce becomes $p^* > $ min AVC, that is, the line representing market price should be above the minimum point of the AVC curve. If $p^* = $ AVC, the firm is indifferent between shutting down and continuing to produce.

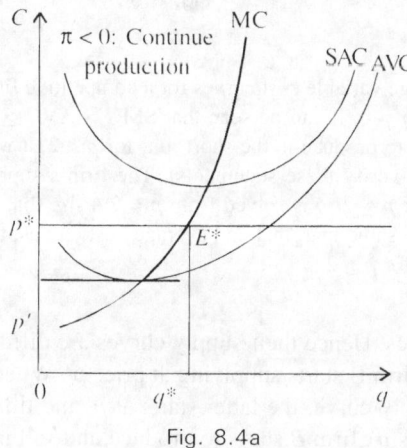
Fig. 8.4a

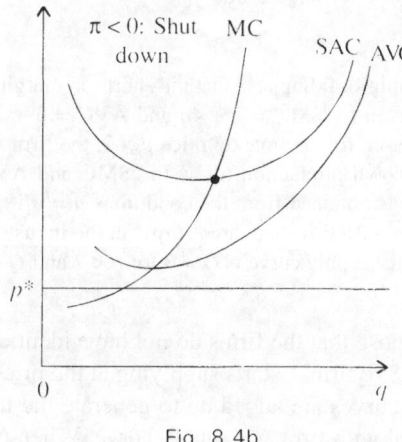
Fig. 8.4b

8.4 The Short-run Supply Curve

To summarize, in the short-run the firm's decisions should be conditioned on the relationship between the market price and various costs.

If $p^* < $ min AVC, then discontinue production.
If $p^* \geq $ min AVC, then choose q^* such that $p^* = $ MC and dMC/$dq > 0$.

These two conditions enable us to derive the firm's short-run supply curve, which shows *the amount the firm will supply at any given market price*. For $p^* < $ min AVC, $q = 0$, which means that the supply curve is the y-axis for such p. For $p^* \geq $ min AVC, the firm is going to choose an output such that $p^* = $ MC (the second order condition is automatically satisfied because for outputs lying beyond the minimum point of AVC, MC curve must be rising). Hence for $p^* \geq $ min AVC, the supply curve at each price is the corresponding point on the MC curve. In other words, the MC curve above the minimum point of the AVC curve is the short-run supply curve of the firm. For $p^* < $ min AVC, supply is zero. In Fig. 8.4a, the supply curve coincides with the vertical axis for $p \leq p'$, and is the thickly marked portion of the MC curve for $p > p'$.

The industry supply curve is then obtained from the supply curves of the firms in exactly the same way as the industry demand curve. At each price, the MC curves are added horizontally. In fact, we have assumed that the firms have the same technologies, and hence the same MC curves. The industry supply curve will then be nMC, where n is the number of firms in the industry in the short run. The derivation of the industry supply curve if only two firms are in the market is shown in Fig. 8.5.

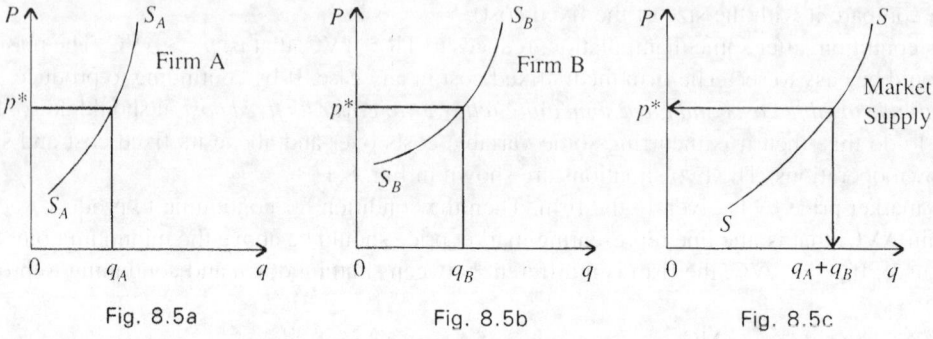

Fig. 8.5a   Fig. 8.5b   Fig. 8.5c

Example 8.4: Suppose that the short run marginal and average variable cost curves for a competitive firm are given by SMC = $2 + 4q$ and AVC = $2 + 2q$. For any $q \geq 0$, it can be seen that SMC $\geq$ AVC ≥ 2. Therefore for any market price $p \geq 2$, the firm will continue to produce in the short run; for $p < 2$, it will shut down production (draw the SMC and AVC curves to verify these statements). The firm's supply curve is obtained from the conditions $q = 0$ if $p < 2$ and for $p \geq 2$, q is solved from $p = 2 + 4q$, that is, $q = (p - 2)/4$. If there are n firms in the industry all with the same marginal and average cost curves, the industry supply curve is $Q = 0$ for $p < 2$ and $Q = n(p - 2)/4$ for $p \geq 2$.

Suppose that the firms do not have identical MC curves. Hence their supply curves are different. In Fig. 8.6, firm A starts supplying at the price p', while firm B starts supplying at price p'. When the supply curves are added up to generate the industry supply curve, the latter starts at p' and till p' is identical with firm A's supply curve. When price exceeds p', firm B starts to produce and sell in the market and its supply curve is added to A's.

We can now bring the industry demand and supply curves together to determine the short run equilibrium market price p^* and the quantity Q^* (see Fig. 8.7b). Given p^*, we can also immediately find out the level of output produced by each firm from Fig. 8.7a. Given our strong assumptions, $q^* = Q^*/n$. In the short run, the firm can make either an economic profit or loss. Even if it is making a loss, it can continue to produce if the market price is above the AVC.

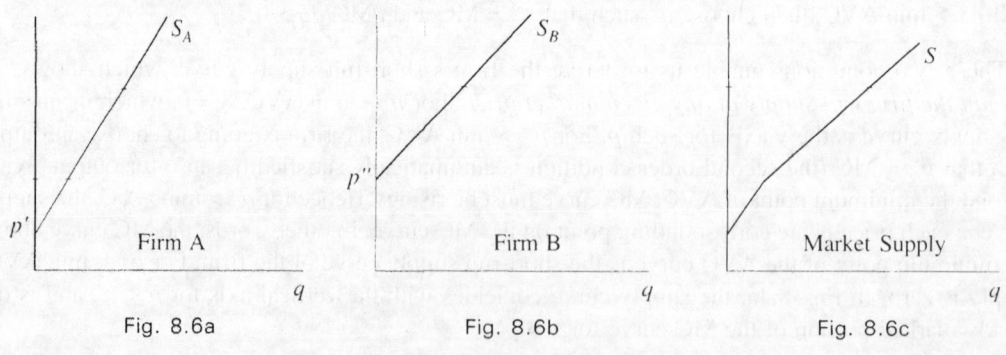

Fig. 8.6a   Fig. 8.6b   Fig. 8.6c

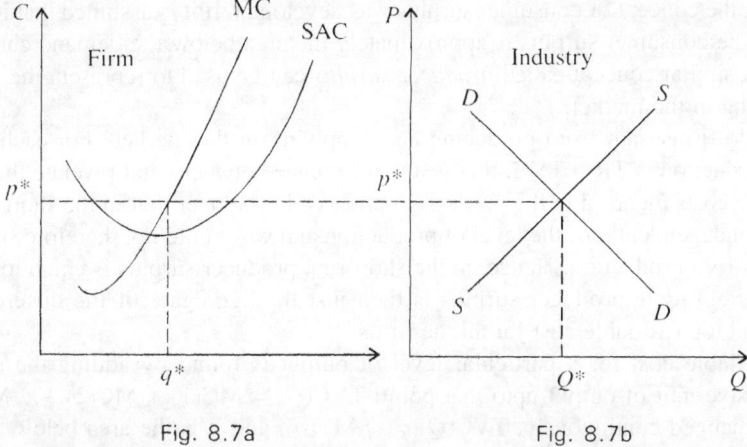

Fig. 8.7a   Fig. 8.7b

In addition to satisfying the two conditions to determine the profit-maximizing output of the firm, the short-run competitive equilibrium is also characterized by the condition that market demand must equal market supply.

One important point to remember about the industry equilibrium is that it is contingent on an unchanging supply curve. As we have seen, the industry supply curve is aggregated from the firm supply curves, which are nothing but the MC curves above the minimum point of the AVC curves. The marginal cost for each firm depends on the input prices, r and w and therefore, so does the position and shape of the industry supply curve. In the short run, each firm has a fixed amount of K and this does not change when the firm's output changes. But a firm's demand for L definitely increases when it tries to produce more. Along the industry supply curve, the industry output changes and therefore the industry's demand for L also changes. If the industry is a 'significant' purchaser in the labour market, this should affect the aggregate demand for labour and lead to a change in w. But then the industry supply curve will shift. Hence we are implicitly assuming that the particular industry under consideration is too small a customer in the labour market to affect w through changes in its demand for L. This assumption allows us to work with an unchanged industry supply curve.

In more compact notation, $MC_i = MC_i(q_i, Q)$; that is, the marginal cost of the ith firm depends on its own output as well as the industry output, since the latter affects the input prices. One can then derive a 'quasi-supply curve' in the following manner. Consider any Q. This will determine a set of marginal cost curves, one for each firm. Summing these curves horizontally, we get the SMC_i curve. Draw a vertical line at Q and mark the point of intersection of this vertical curve with the SMC_i curve by S. This is the only point on the SMC_i curve consistent with an industry output of Q. Next take some Q' and repeat the process. Label the new point of intersection S'. The curve SS' generated in this way is the so-called quasi-supply curve.

8.5 Welfare Property of the Market Equilibrium Revisited

Suppose that the industry is perfectly competitive and we are able to derive a market supply curve. The price-quantity pair at the intersection of the market demand and supply curves constitutes an equilibrium. In Chapter 2 we noted that the market equilibrium will be Pareto optimum, that is, it will have the desirable property that no reallocation of the commodity can improve some agent's position without harming at least one other agent. We now take a look at the welfare property of the market equilibrium once again.

In Chapter 4, the concept of consumer surplus was developed. If it is assumed that income effects are small, then the consumer surplus is approximately the area below the demand curve and above the price line. A similar concept called *producer surplus* can be used to represent the gains to firms from participating in the market.

How much do firms gain from producing and supplying in the market? For each firm, the net benefit from production is TR – TVC, that is, the difference between total revenue that it earns and the total variable costs incurred in the production process. Remember that in the short run, the fixed cost is incurred independently of the level of production and we should not therefore subtract it from the net benefits from production. Hence, in the short run, producer surplus is equal to TR – TVC = P + TFC. The *aggregate* producer surplus is then just the aggregate of the difference between total revenue and total variable cost for all the firms.

The total variable cost for a particular level of output is found by adding the marginal cost for each successive unit of output upto that point: $TVC(Q) = MC(1) + MC(2) + \ldots MC(Q)$. When output can be changed continuously, $TVC(Q) = \int_0^Q MC(q)$, and it is the area below the MC curve for the firm. The industry supply curve is obtained by horizontally summing all the firms' MC curves. Therefore the aggregate producer surplus is represented by the rectangle p^*OQ^*E (which is total revenue) minus the area under the supply curve $OSEQ^*$ in Fig. 8.8. It is then the area p^*ES.

The sum of consumer and producer surplus in equilibrium, representing the *total gains from trade to the participants in the market*, is the area DES. We can show that this is the maximum gain possible, that is, for any other output and price, the joint gains to trade will be lower. We call this result the achievement of *static efficiency* under perfect competition.

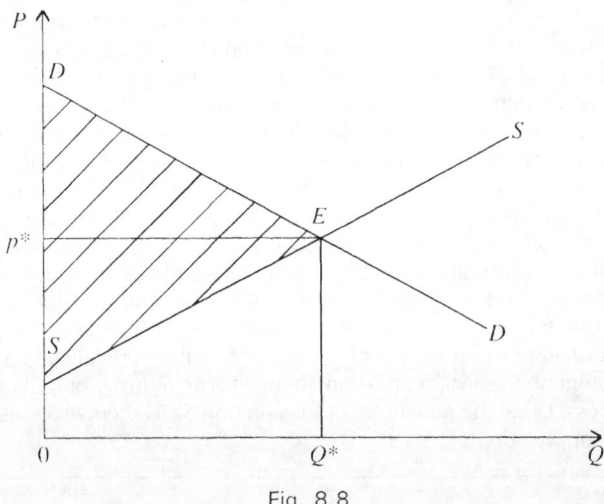

Fig. 8.8

In Fig. 8.9a, we consider a situation where the market price p' is above p^* and in Fig. 8.9b, a situation where the market price p' is below the equilibrium price. We assume that the 'short side of the market' rules, that is, if quantity demanded (supplied) > quantity supplied (demanded), then quantity supplied (demanded) will be transacted. In both cases, consumer surplus plus producer surplus (the shaded areas) is less than DES. The difference, which is the area ABE, is known as the 'deadweight loss'. It is a deadweight loss in the sense that it represents potential gains from trade that is realized by neither the buyers nor the sellers in the market.

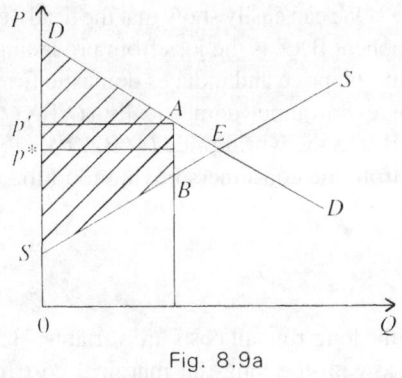

Fig. 8.9a

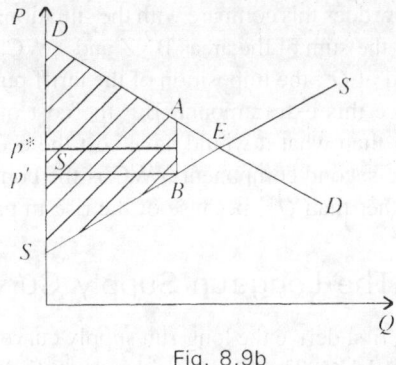

Fig. 8.9b

8.5.1 International Trade: Free Trade and Tariffs

We can use these concepts to look at some important questions in international trade. Consider the demand and supply of commodity X in a country. Suppose first that the country is a closed economy which does not allow any import of the commodity X. If the market for this commodity is perfectly competitive, then the equilibrium price P^a and quantity Q^a are determined at the intersection of the domestic demand and supply curves. In Fig. 8.10, the consumer surplus is measured by the area DEP^a and the producer surplus by the area $P^a ES$.

Next, suppose that the country allows X to be freely imported. Let us assume that the country is 'small' in the sense that the supply curve of imports is horizontal at the world price P^*. Now the supply curve becomes $OSBCS_{III}$. The price is P^* and the quantity is Q^*. The consumer surplus is DP^*C and the producer surplus is SP^*B. The producer surplus has shrunk, but the increase in consumer surplus more than makes up for the fall in producer surplus.

But since domestic producers are hurt by free trade, they lobby for protection and suppose that they persuade the government to impose a quantity tariff of t per unit. The tariff creates a wedge between the world price and the price at which X can be sold in the domestic market. The total supply curve shifts to $OSXYS_t$. The domestic price becomes $P_t = P^* + t$ and quantity transacted is Q_t. The consumer surplus is DP_tY and producer surplus is SP_tX.

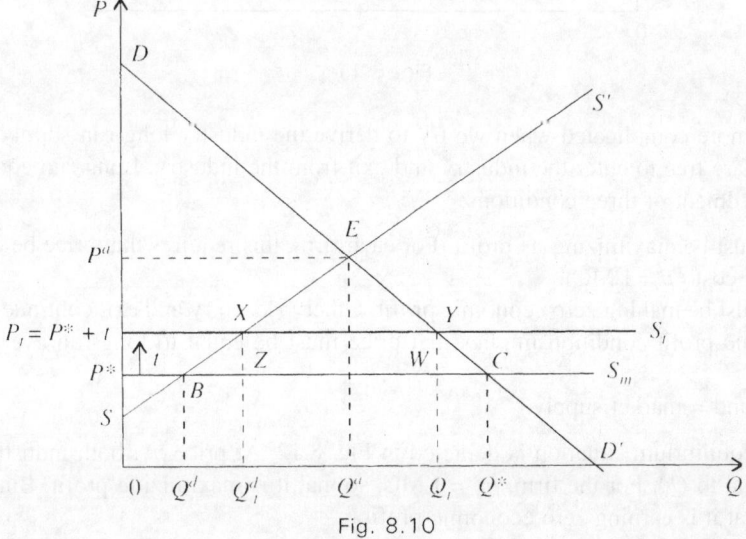

Fig. 8.10

How does this compare with the situation under free trade? One can easily show that the deadweight loss is the sum of the areas BXZ and YWC. The first component BXZ is the loss from producing Q_t^d instead of Q^d: the imposition of the tariff pushes up the domestic price and induces domestic firms to produce this extra amount. But the cost of producing this extra output domestically (Q^dBXQ_t^d) is higher than what it would have cost the economy to import it at the world price (Q^dBZQ_t^d).

The second component YWC is the consumption loss from the consumers buying too little of X (Q^t rather than Q^*) because of the rise in price from P^* to P^t.

8.6 The Long-run Supply Curve

Let us first derive the long-run supply curve of the firm. In the long-run, all costs are variable. Hence, LTC = LVC. The firm maximizes profit by equating price with the long-run marginal cost: $p^* =$ LMC. The second order condition is that the LMC curve is upward sloping at the point of equilibrium.

In contrast to the short-run situation, the firm shuts down production and *exits from the industry* if it makes less than a normal profit. Therefore, its long run supply curve is given by the portion of LMC that lies above the LATC curve.

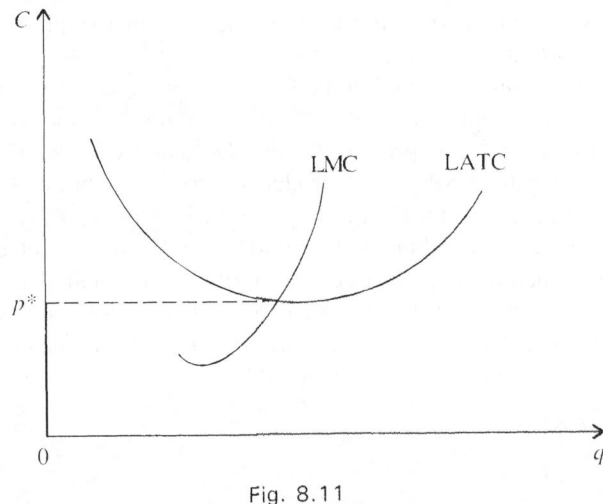

Fig. 8.11

Matters are more complicated when we try to derive the industry long-run supply curve. In the long-run, firms are free to enter the industry and exit from the industry. Long-run equilibrium then requires the fulfilment of three conditions:

1. Each firm must be maximizing its profit. For each firm, this requires that price be equal to long-run marginal cost (p = LMC).
2. Each firm must be making zero economic profit. Otherwise, entry and exit continue to occur. The zero economic profit condition implies that price must be equal to long-run average total cost (p = LATC).
3. Market demand = market supply.

A long-run equilibrium situation is depicted in Fig. 8.12. At price p^*, both industry supply and demand are equal to Q^*. For the firm, p^* = LMC, so that it is maximizing profit. But p^* = LATC, which means that it is earning zero economic profit.

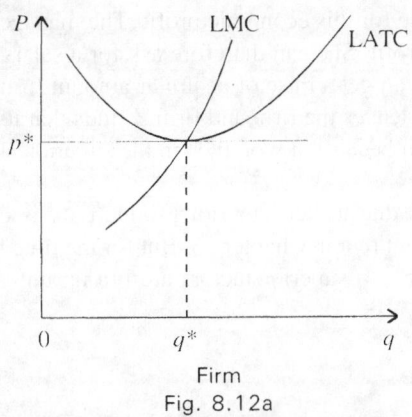

Firm
Fig. 8.12a

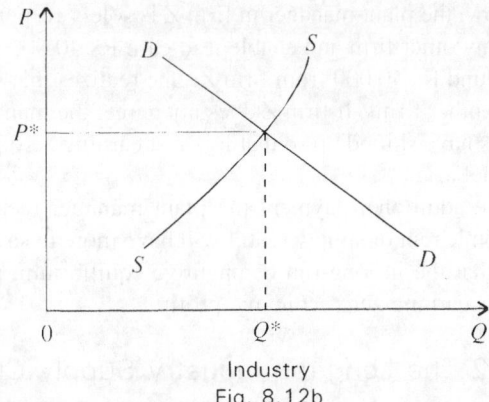

Industry
Fig. 8.12b

Thus there are some remarkably attractive features of competitive long-run equilibrium. Price is equal to marginal cost, which means that all possibilities for mutually beneficial trades have been exhausted. Price is equal to the minimum point of the LAC curve (zero super-normal profits are being earned), implying that unit cost is minimum. Finally, all producers earn only the opportunity cost of the resources they are using in the firms.

8.6.1 Rent and Long-run Competitive Equilibrium

We have been assuming so far that all firms in a competitive industry have identical cost curves (in other words, they are just clones of each other) because there is perfect information. Now suppose that one of the firms has lower cost curves than the other firm. When can this happen and what happens to the zero-profit result?

The lower cost curves cannot come from superior technology because in the long-run all firms should have access to the same technology. It is, however, possible that the firm has a superior resource which enables it to have lower costs. Suppose that a firm Z employs a very dynamic and efficient plant manager who can enthuse the workers to work hard and hence lower the costs for the firm. No other firm has such a manager.

In panel a of Fig. 8.13, any of the other firms is just breaking even at the going market price of Rs 100 and producing 3000 units. However, the firm with the cost advantage, that is, firm Z, equates LMC with this price and produces 4000 units. Its long-run average cost at this output is Rs 90, so that it earns an economic profit of Rs 40,000. This is shown in panel b.

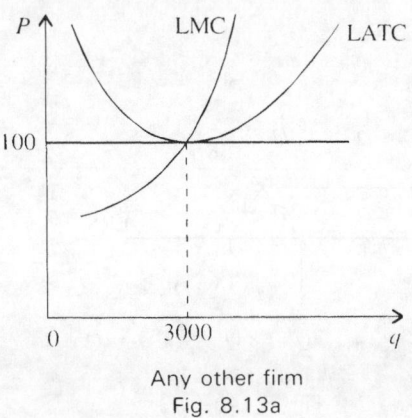

Any other firm
Fig. 8.13a

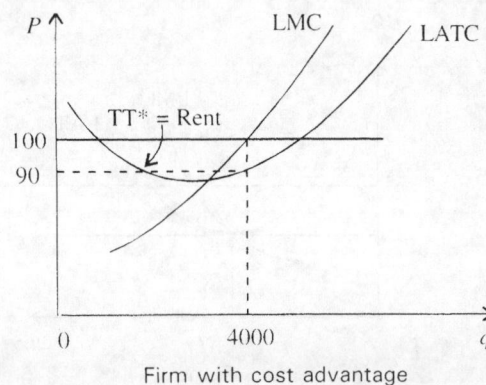

Firm with cost advantage
Fig. 8.13b

Now, the plant manager in firm Z is solely responsible for this economic profit. The manager can join any other firm and enable it to earn Rs 40,000 as profit. She can therefore ask for a salary hike of around Rs 40,000 from firm Z. She realizes that she can get a raise of a similar amount from any of the other firms. If firm Z does not agree, the manager leaves the firm and firm Z finds that its cost curves have shifted up so that it is just earning zero profit because it would be in the situation shown in panel a.

The additional payment the plant manager receives due to her superior productivity is called economic rent or simply rent. I will have more to say about rent in Chapter 13. But for the time being note that the in long-run competitive equilibrium, returns to superior factors are bid up until each firm is earning zero economic profit.

8.6.2 The Long-run Industry Supply Curve

We now examine the derivation of the long-run industry supply curve. In the short-run, the number of firms is fixed and K for each firm is fixed. In the long-run, the number of firms can change and firms can change quantities of both K and L. To characterize the long-run industry supply curve, we must take note of the effect of changing industry production on the industry's demand for L and K and the resultant changes in w and r. For example, if the output of the car industry is sought to be increased, then the car industry's demand for both L and K will increase. This leads to a shift in the demand curves in both the markets for K and L and hence increases in the input prices. These changes in w and r will affect cost curves in the car industry.

8.6.3 Constant Cost Industry

The simplest situation one can think of is one where the changes in demand for L and K from car-makers are too insignificant to affect prices in the markets for L and K. Since neither w and r will be affected, we call this a *constant cost industry*. The cost curves of the firms in the car industry do not shift.

Start with a long-run equilibrium situation in this industry. The market price is p^* and each firm is producing q^*. Now suppose that the industry demand curve shifts to $D'D'$. In the short run, the number of firms does not change. The existing firms take advantage of the rise in price to p' to make supernormal profits. Each firm moves up its SMC curve to maximize profit. This is represented by the movement from A to B.

Over time, the supernormal profits earned by existing firms attract new firms. As they enter the industry and increase supply, the market price starts to fall. This process continues until each firm is earning just normal profit. This is represented by the movement from B to C.

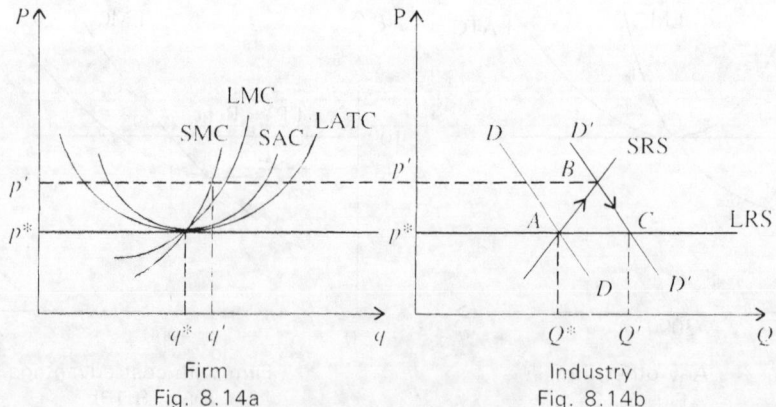

Firm
Fig. 8.14a

Industry
Fig. 8.14b

Finally, equilibrium is restored at point C. At point C, price is once again p^* and each firm produces q^*. However, the industry output has increased from Q^* to Q' because the number of firms is higher. The long-run supply curve for the industry is the horizontal line LRS at the price p^*.

8.6.4 Increasing Cost Industry

In an *increasing cost industry*, the attempt to increase industry output leads to an increase in w and r and this shifts up the cost curves of the firm. The firm is said to suffer from *pecuniary diseconomies*. Consider again an initial equilibrium situation and a subsequent shift in the demand curve from DD to $D'D'$. We can make a couple of statements about the new equilibrium. First, a higher price will be associated with a higher industry output. It is the higher industry output that leads to increase in input prices, hence to higher cost curves and necessitates the establishment of a higher price at equilibrium (to satisfy the zero profit condition). Second, without knowing how the cost curves shift, we cannot say anything about what happens to the output of each firm or the number of firms in the new equilibrium. The industry output is higher, but this may imply the same or a smaller number of firms, each producing more in equilibrium. The long-run supply curve, LRS, is upward sloping, in contrast to the constant cost case.

8.6.5 Decreasing Cost Industry

There are certain cases when the prices of inputs fall with an increase in industry output. This might happen if the inputs are manufactured using technologies enjoying substantial economies of scale. The firms enjoy the benefits of *pecuniary economies*. We call such industries *decreasing cost industries*. In these situations, the industry long run supply curve must be downward sloping. An increase in industry output lowers cost and therefore must be associated with a lower price by the zero-profit condition.

To conclude this discussion, three features of long run industry supply curves are noted:

1. In contrast to the short run industry supply curve, the long run industry supply curve is not obtained by horizontally summing firms' marginal cost curves for a fixed number of firms. The reason this cannot be done is that the number of firms is *not* fixed in the long run.
2. At each point on the LRS curve, each firm is earning only normal profit. Hence there is no incentive for firms to enter the industry or exit from the industry.
3. The LRS curve takes into account changes in input prices. But it is still being assumed that (a) technology is fixed and (b) input supply curves remain fixed. In some industries, over time price declines and quantity increases. An example is the VCR industry. This does not necessarily mean that the LRS curve is downward sloping. It may simply be the result of the LRS curve shifting to the right over time due to technological improvements, as in Fig. 8.15.

In long run equilibrium, because of the zero profit condition, consumers receive the entire surplus because producers earn zero profits. However, we must remember that zero economic profits means that the firm is earning just enough to keep it in the industry; it would not be better off by shifting to a different industry. The sum of consumer surplus and producer surplus becomes equal to consumer surplus. Producer surplus is zero, because profits are zero and there are no fixed costs in the long run.

In general, it is clear that short-run and long-run effects of shifts in demand are different. If there is an increase in demand, the market price will increase more in the short run than in the long run. If the demand curve shifts to the left, the price will fall more in the short run than in the long run. On the other hand, there is a greater change in the market quantity in the long run than in the short run.

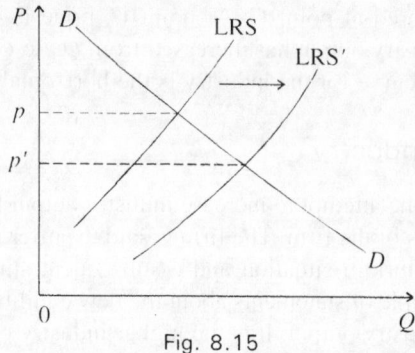

Fig. 8.15

8.7 Elasticity of Supply

We have already defined the price-elasticity of demand. Similarly, the responsiveness of supply to price changes can be measured by

$$e_s = (\partial Q/\partial p)(p/Q).$$

at a point (Q, p) on the supply curve. For upward sloping supply curves, this will be positive. For discrete changes, we can again use

$$e_s = (\Delta Q/\Delta p)(p/Q).$$

The price-elasticity is a positive number (the supply curve has a positive slope) and ranges from zero to infinity. If it is greater than one, supply is said to be relatively elastic. If it is less than one, it is said to be relatively inelastic.

The price elasticity of supply depends on the extent of capacity available relative to current production. A seller who has considerable excess capacity can step up production with respect to even a small increase in price. Its supply curve will be relatively elastic. On the other hand, if capacity is tight, the firm may not increase production very much even if price increase substantially.

The elasticity of supply also depends on time. In the short run, as we know, some inputs may be costly or impossible to change. Moreover, over time, there may be technical progress or learning by doing. For all these reasons, the long run supply curve will tend to be flatter than any short run supply curve.

8.7.1 Using Demand and Supply Elasticities Together

We can use the demand and supply elasticities together to predict the price change resulting from shifts in the demand and supply curves. To simplify things, assume that the demand for a product depends only on its own-price and income while supply depends only on own-price:

$$Q_d = Q_d(P, I), Q_s = Q_s(P)$$

We will analyse a shift in the demand curve caused by an increase in I. We compare the two equilibrium positions, which means that the percentage change in quantity demanded between the two situations is equal to the percentage change in quantity supplied (in equilibrium, quantity supplied is equal to quantity demanded).

Taking total differentials, we get

$$dQ_d = (\partial Q_d/\partial P)dP + (\partial Q_d/\partial I)dI = -(-\partial Q_d/\partial P)(P/Q_d)(Q_d/P)dP + (\partial Q_d/\partial I)(P/I)(I/P)dI$$
$$\Rightarrow dQ_d/Q_d = e_d(dP/P) + e_I(dI/I)$$

where the e's are the elasticities.

Similarly, considering the supply curve, we get

$$dQ_s/Q_s = e_s(dP/P)$$

Since we know that the percentage changes in quantity must be the same,

$$dQ_d/Q_d = dQ_s/Q_s$$

Then

$$-e_d(dP/P) + e_I(dI/I) = e_s(dP/P)$$

which enables us to solve for the percentage change in price in terms of the percentage change in income:

$$dP/P = [e_I/(e_s + e_d)](dI/I)$$

Another example relates to taxation. Go back to the discussion in section 2.6.3. Notice that the relative elasticities of the demand and supply curves determine to what extent the burden of a tax is distributed between two sides of the market. We can very easily show how the elasticities of supply and demand determine the effects of a specific tax on the equilibrium price and quantity. Start from a situation with no tax and next consider what happens when the government imposes a per unit tax of t on the sellers. In the new equilibrium, P^d is going to be determined from $f(P^d) - g(P^d - t) = 0$. Totally differentiating this equation with respect to P^d and t, we get:

$$(df/dP^d)dP^d - (dg/dP^d)dP^d + (dg/dt)dt = 0.$$

Rearranging terms, we find that

$$dP^d/dt = (dg/dP^d)/[(dg/dP^d) - (df/dP^d)]$$

By multiplying both the numerator and denominator of the right hand side of this expression by (P^d/Q), we can express the effect of t on P^d as:

$$dP^d/dt = \frac{(dg/dP^d)\,(P^d/Q)}{[(dg/dP^d)\,(P^d/Q) - (df/dP^d)\,(P^d/Q)]} = \frac{s}{s - e}$$

where s is the supply elasticity and e is the price-elasticity of demand. Note that when $t = 0$, consumer and producer prices are identical. Since we are considering a discrete change in the tax rate — from 0 to t — we can write

$$\Delta P^d = \{s/(s - e)\}\Delta t$$

One can thus see that when $s = 0$, that is, the supply curve is totally inelastic or when $e \Rightarrow \infty$, that is, the demand curve is perfectly elastic, there will be no effect on P^d. The tax will be fully borne by the seller.

Contestable Markets

In a perfectly competitive market, competition is intense, with many firms competing with each other to serve the market. In the long run, competition drives down the market price to a level that just covers the cost of production, allowing the firms in the industry to make only normal profits.

Even without a large number of firms in the market, the predictions of the competitive model can still hold. The competitive pressure is then provided by potential entrants. If the existing firms make supernormal profits, it might be possible for new firms to enter the market quickly, capture the market from the existing producers by charging lower prices, garner profits and then exit before the existing firms can retaliate by dropping their prices. The threat of potential entry can then force the existing firms, even if they are few in number, to behave competitively.

(contd)

(contd)

What then matters is the ease of entry into the market. The ease of entry depends on the extent of sunk costs of entry. Remember that sunk costs are those that cannot be recovered if the firm decides to exit from the industry. Advertising, for example, is a sunk cost. If a firm has spent large amounts on advertising to build up its brand image in the market, and then exits from the industry, these costs cannot be recovered. Fixed costs may not be sunk costs. If a firm has purchased an office building, then the forgone interest on the money used to buy the building is a fixed cost. It will be part of the costs even if the firm stops production. However, if the firm exits from the industry, it can sell off the building and recover at least a part of the cost of the building.

It is important to realize that sunk costs are avoidable costs if a firm chooses *not to enter* a market. Until it enters a market, a firm has an advantage: it has not incurred the sunk cost. Once it enters a market, it incurs the sunk costs.

If there are large sunk costs of entry, then potential entrants worry that after entry competition might get fierce. The firm might start making losses, but if it tries to leave the industry, it would be unable to recover the sunk costs. The firm will then be reluctant to enter the market. This gives the incumbent firms the ability to exercise market power without fear of 'hit-and-run-entry'. On the other hand, markets with low sunk costs of entry will be contestable markets, where competitive results will hold even if there are a small number of firms.

Topics for Discussion

1. The perfectly competitive market structure acts as benchmark against which the performance of other types of market structures can be evaluated. Discuss whether perfect competition is useless as a benchmark because its assumptions are unlikely to be satisfied in any industry.
2. Suppose that in a constant cost industry, each firm's LAC curve is horizontal. Discuss how this case differs from the one in which each LAC curve is U-shaped.
3. Does the fact that a business manager may not know the definition of marginal cost contradict the theory developed in this chapter?

 Exercise

1. *True* or *false*: In a constant cost industry, a tax of a constant, fixed amount on each unit of output sold will not affect the amount of output sold by a perfectly competitive firm in the long run. Explain.
2. (a) The market price facing a perfectly competitive firm in the short run is Rs 25. Complete the following table (write down the MC figures against the second of the two relevant figures):

Q	TR = PQ	P	STC	MC	Profit
0		–	25	–	
1			49		
2			69		
3			86		
4			100		
5			114		
6			128		
7			144		
8			163		
9			185		
10			212		
11			246		
12			300		

(b) Identify the profit-maximizing output level for the firm.

(c) Complete the following table based on the table in 1(a).

Q	TVC	AVC
0		
1		
2		
3		
4		
5		
6		
7		
8		
9		
10		
11		
12		

(d) If the market price drops to Rs 16, what should be the firm's output and why?

3. The equation of the total cost curve facing a perfectly competitive firm in the short run is $TC = 50 + 2q^2$.

(a) For this firm, what are the equations of the ATC and AVC curves?

(b) Explain why this firm will never shut down its production in the short run.

(c) Prove that the ATC curve reaches its lowest point when $q = 5$.

(d) If the firm faces a market price of Rs 100 per unit, what will be its profit-maximizing level of output?

4. In a competitive industry, there are 500 firms each with the cost function $C = q^2/2 - 1/8$.

(a) Obtain the equation of the supply curve for each of these firms.

(b) Obtain the equation of the market supply curve.

(c) If the equation of the market demand curve is $Q^d = 1000(1 - p)$, what is the equilibrium price and equilibrium (market) quantity? How much will each firm produce at this price? What will be the profit/loss of each firm?

5. A competitive firm has the average variable cost function $AVC = 10 - 0.03q + 0.00005q^2$. The total fixed cost for this firm is Rs 600. The market price is Rs 10 per unit.

(a) What is the marginal cost function for this firm?

(b) How much output will the firm produce in the short run?

(c) How much profit/loss will the firm earn?

(d) What will be the answers to (b) and (c) if the market price is Rs 5 per unit?

6. The equation of the demand curve facing a competitive industry is $Q = 5 - P/2$ and the equation of the long run supply curve is $P = Rs 2$. What will be the industry price and output in the long run equilibrium? What will be consumer surplus?

7. All firms in a competitive industry have long run total cost curves given by

$$LTC = q^3 - 10q^2 + 36q.$$

where q is the firm's level of output. What will be this industry's long run equilibrium price?

8. A competitive industry faces a demand $Q = 800 - 8p$. Each firm faces identical cost conditions

$$C_i = 200 + 10q_i + 2q_i^2$$

where q_i is the output of the ith firm. There is free entry and an unlimited number of potential entrants. What are the equilibrium output and price? How many firms produce in equilibrium?

9 | Monopoly

A perfectly competitive industry can be viewed as one with the most intense competition among the sellers in the market. At the other extreme, we can think of a situation where there is only one firm facing no immediate competition. Such an industry is called a monopoly. In other words, *a monopoly is the sole producer of a commodity that has no close substitutes*. The firm and the industry are identical. The demand curve faced by the firm is the downward-sloping industry demand curve. In contrast to a perfectly competitive firm that behaves as a price-taker so that the demand curve facing it is horizontal, a monopoly acts as a price-maker. It knows it can set its own price.

Of course, the existence of the downward-sloping demand curve sets a constraint on the monopolist's actions. The monopolist can either set the price and then sell the quantity indicated by the demand curve. Or it can choose which quantity to sell and then set the maximum price indicated again by the demand curve. The monopolist cannot set both the price and the quantity at her will.

It is sometimes difficult to decide whether a firm is a monopoly or not. For example, suppose that there is only one firm producing plastic containers. Is this a monopoly? The answer will depend upon whether other types of containers are close substitutes of plastic containers. If they are (the cross-price elasticities are high), then one must consider the firm's position in the market for all types of containers and the firm may very well not be a monopoly in the market for containers.

In the real world, there are few pure monopolies. However, it is still worth considering the monopoly market structure in some detail, because when there are a few firms in the market, they exercise some market power (that is, act as price-setters), and we can get an insight into their strategies by analysing the monopoly case. Further, in India, the public sector has enjoyed monopoly or near-monopoly positions in electricity, postal services and airlines.

9.1 Sources of Monopoly Power

How does a firm come to be the only one to serve a market? We can identify five factors in general, any one or combinations of which can enable a firm to become a monopoly.

1. *Control over critical inputs.* If in an industry, an input is critical in the production process, and one firm controls the supply of the input, then that firm can become a monopoly. Other firms cannot enter the industry because they do not have access to the critical input.

The criticality of an input can be the result of technical requirements as well as the firm's success in establishing the uniqueness of a certain component in the eyes of the customers. An example of the former was the monopoly of the Aluminum Company of America (Alcoa) in the production of aluminum (aluminium) through its control over the supply of bauxite in the early part of the twentieth century. It signed long-term contracts with companies supplying bauxite and these contracts specified that the bauxite could not be sold to anyone else. An example of the latter is the almost sole control over most of the world's supply of raw diamonds exercised by De Beers for a long time. Even though synthetic diamonds are now produced in large quantities and sometimes can fool even experienced jewellers, the public's preference for 'the real thing' enabled De Beers to exercise monopoly power in the diamond industry.

2. *Economies of scale and scope.* In the long run, the existence of economies of scale implies that the firm has a downward-sloping average cost curve. The more the firm produces, the lower its unit cost of production. This makes it difficult for newcomers to compete with the existing low-cost producer. Further, in such situations, the least costly way of serving the market is to have a single producer serve the market. In Fig. 9.1, if the entire output OQ' is produced by one firm, the average cost is AC. If, on the other hand, there are two firms each producing half the amount, the average cost for each is AC', which is higher than AC.

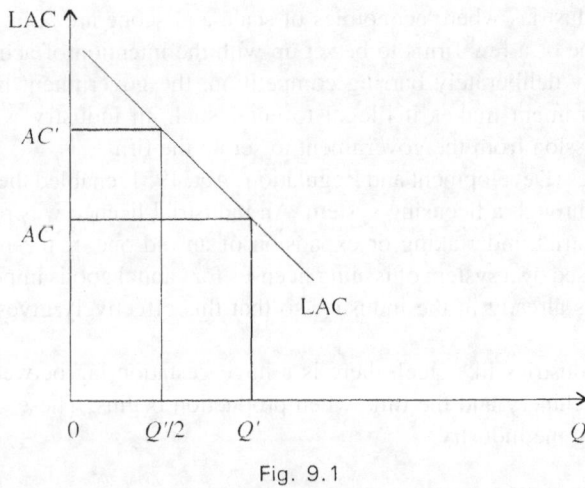

Fig. 9.1

Cable television and local telephone service illustrate economies of scope. Both services can be reached to individual subscribers through a network of cables laid down by the service provider. The existence of economies of scope means that a combined provider of cable television and telephone service can achieve lower average costs than providers specializing in either television or telephone services.

3. *Intellectual property rights.* To encourage innovation, most countries give an inventor sole control over the use of an invention for a certain number of years. These are called patents. In India, a patent is granted for seven years. Patents create monopolies, and as we shall see later on, monopolies lead to inefficiencies and deadweight losses. This static inefficiency is supposed to be balanced by gains to *dynamic efficiency*: it is argued that unless inventors and innovators are rewarded in this manner by creating time-bound monopolies, less effort would be put into invention and innovation and society would lose out on the technological progress front.

To take the case of Alcoa again, the monopoly position of the firm was maintained initially by the many patents that it had obtained for the different phases of the aluminium ingot production process. However, while giant firms like Alcoa can utilize the patent process to their own advantage, individual innovators often find it impossible to keep track of the many infringements of their patent rights and obtain legal redress.

A copyright establishes intellectual property in published expressions, including literary works, computer software and engineering drawings. A developer of a new software can acquire monopoly rights over its use by getting it copyrighted.

Baumol provides a number of examples of innovators/inventors who were unable to profit from their technological contributions to mankind. Eli Whitney, who invented the cotton gin, earned virtually no reward from his invention because his 1794 patent was infringed almost immediately and Whitney spent his time thereafter fighting such infringements in courts. He did not obtain a favourable verdict until 1807. Samuel F.B. Morse, who invented the Morse code and transformed it into a very practical device, suffered the harassments of almost continuous litigation and detraction. Alexander Graham Bell's name is almost synonymous with telephone, yet patent litigation to establish the true author-ship of the telephone dragged on for almost 18 years.

Source: William J. Baumol, 1993, 'Enterprising litigation and entrepreneurs enmeshed in law', in *Entrepreneurship, Management, and the Structure of Payoffs.* The MIT Press.

4. *Regulation.* In industries where economies of scale and scope are strong, a government may decide to allow only one or a few firms to be set up with the intention of achieving lower average cost in the industry. By deliberately barring competition, the government hopes to avoid costly duplication. The government makes it illegal to enter such an industry without a government licence, that is, a permission from the government to set up the firm.

In India, the Industries (Development and Regulation) Act, 1951, enabled the government to direct industrial investments through a licensing system. An industrial licence was required for setting up a new large-scale industrial undertaking or expansion of an old one or the manufacture of a new article. This was buttressed by a system of issuing licenses for capital goods imports. Usually, licenses are issued only to firms already in the industry, so that this effectively gives monopoly power to incumbent firms.

5. *Entry Lags.* In industries like steel, there is a huge gestation lag between the time the work starts on plants and machinery and the time when production begins. These gestation lags prevent new firms from entering the industry.

9.2 The Profit-maximizing Monopolist

As in the case of a perfectly competitive firm, we continue to assume that the monopoly tries to maximize profit. But unlike the perfectly competitive firm, the monopolist faces the downward-sloping industry demand curve. Let the equation of the (inverse) demand curve facing the monopolist be $P = P(Q)$, where $dP/dQ < 0$. The total cost function is $C = C(Q)$.

The monopolist tries to maximize $\Pi = \text{TR} - C$, where $\text{TR} = P(Q) \cdot Q$ and $TC = C(Q)$. The first order condition is

$$d\Pi/dQ = d\text{TR}/dQ - dC/dQ = 0, \text{ that is, } d\text{TR}/dQ = dC/dQ.$$

The expression on the left hand side is the *marginal revenue* (MR), that is, the change in total revenue per unit of change in output. The expression on the right hand side is just the marginal cost (MC). Hence the first order condition for profit-maximization can be written succinctly as MR = MC. Once the monopoly selects its output the market price is determined at the corresponding point on the demand curve. Fig. 9.2 shows two (equivalent) ways of looking at the profit-maximizing monopolist's output. One can either draw the TR and C curves and then the resultant profit curve. The profit-maximizing output is reached at the peak of the profit curve, where the slope of the profit curve is zero. Otherwise, one can directly work with the MR and MC curves.

The second order condition is that $d\text{MR}/dQ - d\text{MC}/dQ < 0$, or $d\text{MR}/dQ < d\text{MC}/dQ$: at the profit-maximizing level of output, the slope of the MR curve must be less than the slope of the MC curve. If we assume that the MC curve is upward sloping, then the second order condition is satisfied either

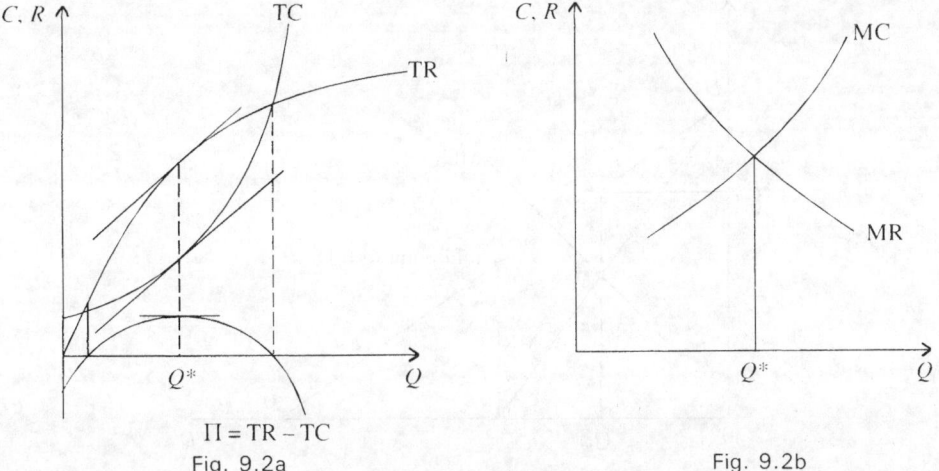

Fig. 9.2a

$\Pi = TR - TC$

Fig. 9.2b

if the MR curve is downward sloping, or if the MR curve is upward sloping but cuts the MC curve from the left to the right.

We should note here that the equality of marginal revenue with marginal cost is a quite general condition for profit-maximization. The same condition is being used in the case of a perfectly competitive firm to derive the profit-maximizing output. However, since the demand curve facing a perfectly competitive firm is horizontal, TR = $p^* \cdot Q$, and hence MR = p^*.

The intuition behind the MR = MC condition is the same as before. The firm has to examine whether an extra unit of output adds more to cost or to revenue. If it adds more to cost, that provides a signal to cut down on output. If it adds more to revenue, output should be expanded.

Example 9.1: Linear demand and cost curves. Let the equation of the inverse demand curve faced by the monopoly be $P = a - Q$, and let the cost function be $C = cQ$. Then total revenue is TR = PQ = $aQ - Q^2$. Then MR = dTR$/dQ = a - 2Q$. The MR curve will be a straight line, having the same P-intercept as the inverse demand curve and intersecting the Q-axis at the mid-point of the inverse demand curve's intercept. MC = $dC/dQ = c$. Equating the two, we get $a - 2Q = c$, or $Q^* = (a - c)/2$. Note that we need the condition that $a > c$ for $Q^* > 0$, that is, the inverse demand curve must have an intercept that is higher than the marginal cost. From the equation of the inverse demand curve, $P^* = a - (a - c)/2 = (a + c)/2$. Note that $P^* - c = (a - c)/2 > 0$ if $a > c$. So price is higher than marginal cost.

9.2.1 Marginal Revenue and Elasticity

The MR = MC condition can be written in a slightly different way. We note that MR = dTR$/dQ = d(P(Q) \cdot Q)/dQ = P + Q(dP/dQ) = P\{1 + (Q/P)(dP/dQ)\} = P(1 - 1/e)$, where $e = -(dQ/dP)(P/Q)$ is the price-elasticity of demand.

Two things follow.

- First, the MR = MC condition can be written as $P(1 - 1/e) = $ MC which means that $P - $ MC = $P/e > 0$. Therefore, the monopolist sets price above marginal cost. This is to be contrasted with the perfectly competitive result that $P = $ MC.
- Second, since we are implicitly assuming that MC > 0 at the monopolist's profit-maximizing output, this tells us that $1 - 1/e > 0$, or $e > 1$. *The monopoly will always maximize profit on the elastic portion of the demand curve.* This is demonstrated in Fig. 9.3 for the linear demand curve case.

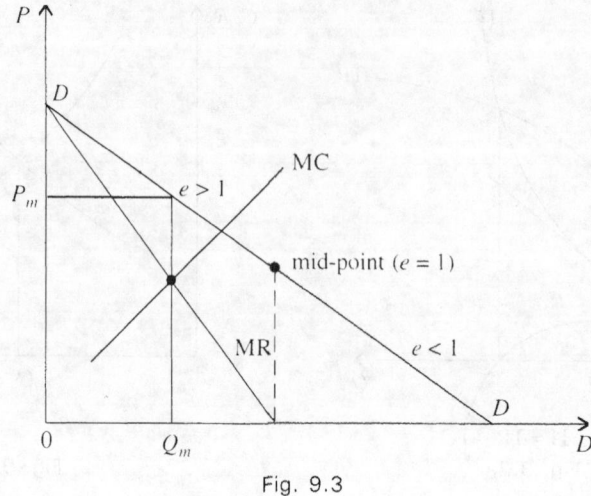

Fig. 9.3

We can also see that $(P - MC)/P = 1/e$. Then $1/e$ is the *profit-maximizing markup* over price for the monopoly. The markup of price over marginal cost divided by price is called the *Lerner index* of monopoly power. This is a measure of the monopolist's ability to set price above marginal cost. In general, we note that higher e, smaller is the markup. The monopolist's ability to charge a price above the marginal cost is lower, the higher is e, that is, the more elastic the demand. Under perfect competition, e goes to plus infinity, which shows (i) again that MR = P and that (ii) $P - MC = 0$, that is, profit-maximizing markup is zero.

> **Example 9.2:** Linear demand and cost curves again. Let the equation of the inverse demand curve faced by the monopoly be $P = a - Q$, and let the cost function be $C = cQ$. The price-elasticity of demand $e = -(-1)$ $(P/Q) = (a - Q)/Q$. Then $e = 1$ for $Q = a/2$, $e > 1$ for $Q < a/2$ and $e > 1$ for $Q > a/2$. So long as $c > 0$, $Q^* = (a - c)/2 < a/2$, which means that the profit-maximizing output is obtained at the elastic segment of the (inverse) demand curve.

9.2.2 The Shutdown Condition

In the short run, the perfectly competitive firm should shut down production if $p <$ SAVC. Under perfect competition, the demand curve facing the firm is a straight line at $p = p^*$ and therefore the shutdown condition is $p^* <$ SAVC. The monopolist will similarly shut down production if the demand curve everywhere lies below the short run average cost curve. Then price will be always below average cost and the monopolist will sustain losses on account of variable cost in addition to the fixed cost if she continues to produce. So she will stop producing.

9.2.3 The Monopolist does not Face a Supply Curve

One important difference between the competitive market and monopoly is that no supply curve exists in the latter case. Equilibrium in the competitive market is established at the intersection of the industry demand and supply curves. The monopolist, on the other hand, either chooses the price or the output and the corresponding output or price is determined on the demand curve simultaneously. It makes no sense to ask: given some price P, how much will the monopoly supply in the market? Therefore no supply curve can be derived.

9.2.4 Taxation of a Monopolist

What happens if a tax is imposed on a monopolist? If the tax is a lump-sum tax T, it is clear that there will be no effect on either monopoly price or quantity, because the monopolist will now be maximizing $\pi - T$.

Suppose that a specific tax of t per unit is imposed. To simplify matters, let us again consider linear demand and cost curves: $P = a - Q$, $C = cQ$, $a > c$. Then $Q^* = (a - c)/2$ and $P^* = (a + c)/2$. Next, let the tax be imposed on quantity at the rate t, $a > (c + t)$. The total cost curve facing the monopolist becomes $C = (c + t)Q$. Quantity is now $Q^{**} = (a - c - t)/2$ and price $P^{**} = (a + c + t)/2$. Hence, $P^{**} - P^* = t/2$, which shows that price has increased by only half the amount of the tax per unit.

However, it is not generally true that the price increases by less than the tax. Suppose that the demand curve is a constant-elasticity demand curve. We know that MR $= P(1 - 1/e)$. Equating this to MC $= c$ and solving, we get $P' = c/(1 - 1/e)$. After the tax is imposed, price is $P' = (c + t)/(1 - 1/e)$. It can be seen that the change in price is $t/(1 - 1/e)$. Since $e > 1$ (the monopolist must be operating in the elastic segment of the demand curve, so that $e > 1$ for a constant elasticity demand curve), $1 - 1/e$ is a fraction and therefore the increase in price exceeds t.

9.3 Perfect Competition versus Monopoly

In this section, we compare the performance of monopoly and perfectly competitive markets from the social welfare point of view. We will find that static efficiency considerations seem to indicate that perfect competition is a more preferred form of the market. However, dynamic considerations might give an edge to monopoly.

We have seen that perfect competition leads to a situation where the potential gains from trade between buyers and sellers are fully realized. The market price reflects what the buyers want to pay, while the marginal cost reflects the additional cost to sellers of supplying output. Any gap between the two means that further gains from trade can be made. Under perfect competition, $p = $ MC, and all gains are fully realized. Aggregate social welfare, measured by consumer surplus plus producer surplus, is maximized. In contrast, the monopoly charges a price that is higher than marginal cost and there is a 'deadweight loss' under monopoly.

To show this, assume that conditions of constant cost prevail. The competitive industry long run supply curve is a horizontal straight line. The long run competitive industry equilibrium is established in Fig. 9.4 at E^* with price $= p^*$ and quantity $= Q^*$, where $p^* = $ LMC. Consumer surplus is equal to the triangle Dp^*E^*. Producer surplus is zero. Now, consider a monopoly with the same long run demand curve and marginal cost curve equal to LRS. The monopoly will select price and output using the MR = MC condition. Hence it will produce Q_m amount of output and charge a price p_m. Consumer surplus is then the area DAp_m while producer surplus is equal to p_mABp^*. Comparing with the aggregate social welfare under perfect competition, we find that there is a deadweight loss under monopoly equal to the area ABE^*.[1] Note that under monopoly, consumer surplus is lower while producer surplus is higher than under perfect competition.

To see more clearly what is the source of the deadweight loss, consider a situation where the marginal cost curve is upward sloping, as in Fig. 9.5

In Fig. 9.5, the deadweight loss is the area $B + C$. When output is restricted to the monopoly level Q_m, then people who actually buy the product suffer a loss of consumer surplus equal to the area A because they are now paying a price P_m that is higher than the competitive price P_c. But there is a further loss in consumer surplus equal to the area B: some of the consumers now do not buy the

[1] Note that in this case, the deadweight loss is equal to $0.5(p_m - p^*)(Q^* - Q_m)$.

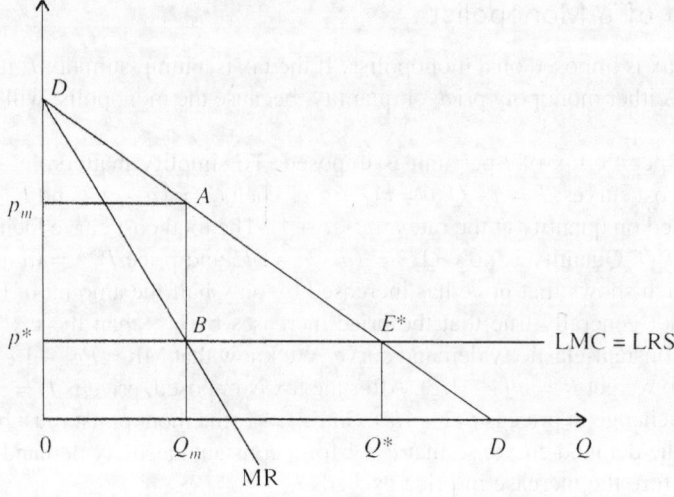

Fig. 9.4

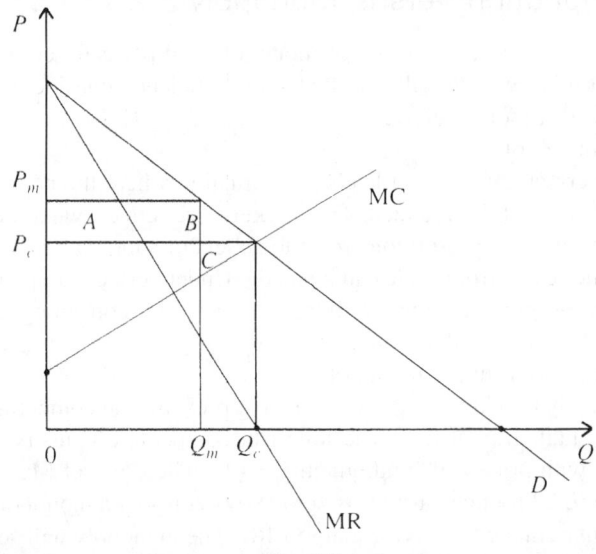

Fig. 9.5

product because the price is too high for them. Part of the lost consumer surplus (area A) is captured by the monopolist as producer surplus. But there is also a loss of producer surplus equal to the area C because output is restricted to be Q_m under monopoly rather than Q_c. Between Q_m and Q_c, the competitive price would still have been higher than MC at every level of production.

Posner has argued that the producer surplus under monopoly may also represent a deadweight loss. This is because the possibility of earning monopoly profits can lead a firm to spend real resources to earn monopoly power. For example, a firm can hire lobbyists, lawyers and economists in an attempt to persuade legislators to restrict entry into the industry. Such behaviour is called 'rent-seeking behaviour'. If there are a number of firms competing to become the monopoly in a market, they might spend as much as the producer surplus on such activities. So the deadweight loss under monopoly can be higher than the area $ABE*$.

Another criticism of monopoly is that the monopolist can 'take it easy'. In the absence of competition, it has no special incentives to lower costs.

Public Sector Monopoly in Gas Transmission and Distribution

Gas Authority of India (Gail India Ltd.) has a monopoly in the wholesale supply and transport of natural gas. It is the owner and operator of India's largest Gas Transmission Networks (4600 km pipelines), the world's longest exclusive LPG pipeline (1269 km) and seven Gas Processing Facilities with an aggregate capacity of 1.3 MMTPA of LPG, Propane, Pentane, and SBP.

Building pipelines is a high-entry barrier business, so even if there is competition, it will take a while to match the entrenched Gail with its ability to supply West and North India via the Hazira-Bijapur-Jagdishpur pipeline.

GAIL was rated among the top 10 Indian companies in terms of profits and revenue according to October 2003 ET 500, a list of top 500 companies in India compiled by the *Economic Times* daily. Its profit after tax figures for the recent years show that its monopoly status has enabled it to garner large profits:

			PAT			(in Rs Cr)
1999–2000	2000–2001	2001–2	2002–3	2003–4		2004–5
861	1126	1185	1639	1869		1954

The calculation of static costs and benefits fails to highlight some of the potential dynamic gains from monopoly. The prospect of earning monopoly profits may motivate firms to innovate—develop new products, improve products or find lower cost methods of production. The grant of patent protection is necessary to induce research and development. Further, as we have already noted, the existence of increasing returns to scale leads to downward sloping average cost curves and in such a situation, the lowest per unit cost is achieved only if there is a single firm in the market.

9.4 The Cartel and the Multiplant Monopoly

A cartel is an agreement to restrain competition. It can be an organization of producers who jointly decide how much to produce and how the total production is to be allocated between the different firms in the cartel. The joint decision means that the cartel can act like a monopoly, if it comprises all the firms in the industry, and if it can prevent non-members from entering the industry. A classic example of a cartel is the Organization of Petroleum Exporting Countries (OPEC) which tries to decide the total amount of petroleum to be produced and exported by member countries. It can also be a cartel of buyers formed to restrain competition in demand and ensure that buyers do not raise prices by bidding against each other.

Let us consider a seller cartel. Such a cartel is like a monopoly which has a number of plants. The difference is that, in the case of a multiplant monopoly, all the plants are under single ownership and if necessary some of the plants can be shut down. In the case of a cartel, the plants are produced by different firms and it is difficult, if not impossible, for the cartel to order that some of the member firms stop production.

Let us first consider the decision-making by a cartel. The cartel faces a linear (inverse) demand curve $P = a - Q$, where $Q = \Sigma q_i$ is the aggregate output of the cartel. Let there be n firms in the cartel, each with the cost function $C_i = F + cq_i^2$, F, $c > 0$. Then the maginal cost function for each firm is $MC_i = 2cq_i$, and the average cost function is $AC_i = F/q_i + cq_i$.

The cartel's problem is to maximize the profit from the operation of all its members. It therefore must choose q_i, $i = 1, 2, \ldots n$, to maximize

$$\Pi(q_1, q_2, \ldots q_n) = PQ - \Sigma\{F + c(q_i^2)\}.$$

The first order conditions are $\delta\Pi/\delta q_i = 0$, $i = 1, 2, \ldots n$. In terms of marginal revenues and costs, $MR = MC_i$, $i = 1, 2, \ldots n$. These yield us the n conditions $a - 2\Sigma q_i - 2cq_i = 0$ for all i.

Since all firms have identical cost functions, we know that all firms will produce the same amount of output. That is, $q_i = q$ for all i. This tells us that $a - 2nq - 2cq = 0$, that is,

$$q^* = a/2[n + c].$$

From the inverse demand curve,

$$P^* = a(n + 2c)/2(n + c).$$

It can be seen that an increase in n or c reduces each firm's output in equilibrium. What happens to total output $Q^* = nq^*$? $Q^* = na/2[n + c] = a/2[1 + c/n]$. As n increases, c/n falls and hence Q^* increases. This means that P^* falls, because the demand curve is downward sloping. The profit of each member of the cartel will fall as n increases: $\Pi_i = P^*q^* - (F + cq^{*2}) = a^2/4(n + c) - F$, which falls as n increases. Thus members of a cartel have an interest in keeping the number of firms in the cartel as small as possible and discouraging new members from joining the cartel.

A multiplant monopolist's problem will be very similar to that of a cartel, except for the fact that the multiplant monopolist can choose n, that is, the number of operational plants. Let there be n plants, each with the same cost function as above. For the plants that are operational, the monopolist will again choose q^* and P^* as before. The number of plants will be chosen to ensure that at q^*, average cost is minimum for each operational plant. But $AC_i = F/q_i + cq_i$ and is minimized when $dAC_i/dq_i = -F/q_i^2 + c = 0$, that is, $q_i = (F/c)^{1/2}$. Now set $q_i = q^*$ and solve for n. Overlooking the fact that n should be an integer, we get $n^* = (a/2)(\ (c/F)^{1/2} - c$. Note that the number of plants increases with an increase in a as well as a decrease in fixed cost F.

9.5 Public Policy towards Monopoly

Since monopoly leads to a higher price and a lower output than a comparable competitive industry, governments try to restrict monopoly power in various ways. One type of public policy is directed towards increasing competition in the industry and such a policy is part of a *competition or antitrust policy*. This can aim at the prevention of the formation of monopolies or even at the break-up of existing monopolies. For example, if two firms in the industry are proposing to merge and form a new firm, the government will sometimes allow the merger to proceed only if it is satisfied that the merger will not, by creating a large firm, have an adverse effect on the competition in the industry. Or, as in the case of AT&T (called Ma Bell) in USA, the government may force the company to break up into smaller, independent firms (the 'progenies' of AT&T came to be known as Baby Bells) to create competitive conditions in the industry. The government can also try to prevent firms in an industry forming a cartel and acting like a monopoly by coordinating their strategies.

In November of 2001, the European Union imposed record fines against drug companies for colluding to fix the price of vitamins. Eight companies were fined 855.2 million euros (£529.5 million) for what the EU antitrust chief, Mario Monti, described as the 'most damaging series of cartels the commission has ever investigated'. Hoffman-La Roche of Switzerland received the largest fine, 462 million euros, for being the 'prime mover and main beneficiary' of the cartel. The second-largest fine—296 million euros—was levied against Germany's BASF, the world's second-biggest maker of vitamins.

(contd)

(contd)

The EU said that the eight had been under investigation since 1999 for collusion to eliminate fair competition for vitamin pills and to overcharge consumers. The companies fixed prices in the European market through a cartel that had a 'formal structure and hierarchy', including a regular exchange of sales figures and pricing data. The cartels were established in products covering vitamins A, E, B1, B2, B5, B6, C, D3, Biotin (H), Folic acid (M), Beta Carotene, and carotinoids.

In addition to Hoffmann-La Roche and BASF, the EC also fined Aventis SA (France), Solvay Pharmaceuticals (the Netherlands), Merck (Germany) as well as Daiichi Pharmaceutical, Esai and Takeda Chemical Industries, all of Japan. The EU said La Roche and BASF formed a 'common front' to enlist Japanese rivals to their cartel. It said that the involvement of La Roche's most senior executives suggested 'the arrangements were part of a strategic plan conceived at the highest levels to control the world market in vitamins by illegal means'.

Under EU law, companies found guilty of antitrust practices can be fined up to 10 per cent of their total annual sales.

Source: 'Vitamin cartel fined for price fixing', *The Guardian*, Wednesday, 21 November 2001.

One of the key questions here relates to the definition of the industry. The firms trying to merge with each other will use a broader definition of industry to project their combined marketshare as 'small', while government prosecutors will operate on the basis of a narrower definition. Moreover, to the extent an industry is dynamic and technical knowledge constantly changing, even an initial high level of marketshare will not enable a firm to retain its monopoly status for long.

The MRTP Act and the Competition Act

In India, the Monopolies and Restrictive Trade Practices (MRTP) Act came into effect from 1970. Chapter III of this Act regulated the expansion of large industrial houses with gross assets exceeding Rs 20 crore, or of 'dominant' firms (defined by market shares in excess of 33.33 per cent) with assets over Rs 1 crore. Such firms had to seek special approval to expand their capacity by more than 25 per cent of existing levels. Mergers and amalgamations that resulted in the creation of firms satisfying the above definitions also required clearance from the commission set up by the Act. These provisions had two important effects. One was that the combination of market share and asset classification, together with the system of industrial licensing and product reservation, prevented Indian private sector firms from attaining globally competitive scales of operation. Second, because the MRTP prevented growth in certain areas, it forced large firms to diversify into activities in which they had no comparative advantage. This Chapter III was eliminated by the Narasimha Rao government in 1991.

Some other provisions of the MRTP Act remain. Companies sometimes bring charges against each other for indulging in 'unfair practices'. An example was the charge of false and misleading advertisement by one leading toothpaste manufacturer against another. A second example is also interesting. Two advertising and media companies—Hindustan Thompson Associates (HTA) and Business India (BI) Group—own respectively the TV rating agencies IMRB and MARG. An advertising company filed a complaint against these firms and the MRTP Commission's preliminary investigation on the basis of this complaint seemed to show that the rating agencies manipulate data to give a misleading picture of viewership, and force advertisers to pay higher rates to the advertising agencies.

On the other hand, the Commission allowed a firm called Exim Oil India Ltd., to continue with certain restrictive trade practices, on the basis of the argument that these practices were of a marginal degree, and hence unlikely to affect competitiveness in the market significantly.

Source: *The Economic Times*, 18 June 1998.

The Competition Act, 2002 was enacted on 13 January 2003. But provision relating to repeal of MRTP Act has not yet been notified. The Competition Commission of India (CCI) has been established by the Central Government with effect from 14 October 2003.

(contd)

(contd)

The three main elements of the Competition Act are:

1. Enterprises cannot come together (enter into an agreement) for anti-competitive purposes
2. Abuse of dominant position will not be allowed
3. Mergers/combinations may be investigated

An agreement includes any arrangement, understanding or concerted action entered into between parties. *It need not be in writing or formal or intended to be enforceable in law.*
Anti-competitive agreements include: Agreement to limit production and supply, agreement to allocate markets, agreement to fix price, bid rigging or collusive bidding, c conditional purchase/sale (tie-in arrangement), exclusive supply/distribution, resale price maintenance, refusal to deal, etc.

Abuse of dominant position includes:

- Imposing unfair conditions or price
- Predatory pricing
- Limiting production/market
- Creating barriers to entry
- Applying dissimilar conditions to similar transactions

Combinations
If the CCI is of the opinion that a combination is likely to cause or has caused adverse effect on competition, it shall issue a notice to show cause the parties as to why investigation in respect of such combination should not be conducted. CCI can investigate combinations that exceed a threshold limit in terms of assets or turnover (not that exceed some predetermined market share).

For anti-competitive agreements and abuse of dominance

- The Commission can grant interim relief
- Can impose a penalty of not more than 10 per cent of turnover and in case of cartel three times the amount of profit made out of the cartel
- After enquiry, can issue cease and desist order
- Can award compensation
- Can modify agreement
- Can recommend to the Central Government for division of enterprise in case it enjoys dominant position

Source: The Competition Act, 2002, No. 12 of 2003. Competition Commission of India.

9.6 Regulation

A second type of public policy deals with monopolies already in existence and we analyse this type of policy in the present section. Such policy is more commonly known as *regulation*.

First consider a monopolist with the long run marginal cost curve LMC. The price under monopoly, p_m, is higher than the competitive price p^* and the quantity, Q_m, is lower. This results in a deadweight loss. To eliminate the deadweight loss, the government may impose a price ceiling of p^* on the monopolist. The demand curve facing the monopolist then becomes p^*E^*D; the MR curve is p^*E^*MN and the monopolist produces the competitive level of output (Fig. 9.6).

Such an approach will be feasible if the regulating agency is fully aware of the costs of the monopoly. In practice, the regulator may have only an imperfect idea of the nature of the monopolist's cost curves and therefore impose a 'wrong' price which will lead to a deadweight loss (you can check this by assuming, for example, that the regulator estimates the marginal cost curve to be higher than what it actually is and therefore sets the price too high). Second, when the monopolist's price is lowered, the monopolist can try to bypass the regulation in other ways, for example, by producing goods of lower quality.

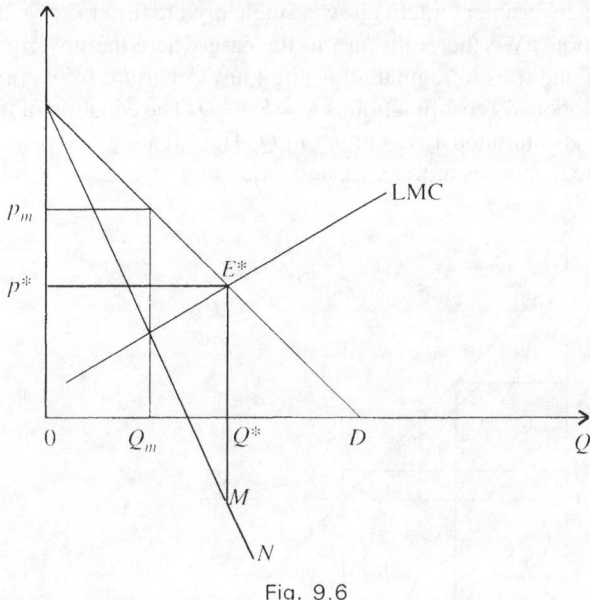

Fig. 9.6

9.6.1 Natural Monopolies

Government regulators face a more difficult situation when the monopoly is a natural monopoly, that is, if one firm can produce the total output at a lower cost than several firms could. Consider the situation where the long run average cost curve of the monopoly is continuously declining over the entire range of market demand.[2] In this case, the goal of minimization of per unit cost dictates that only one firm serve the market.

Example 9.3: The condition for natural monopoly is

$C(Q) < C(q_1) + C(q_2) + C(q_3) + \ldots + C(q_n)$, where $Q = q_1 + q_2 + \ldots + q_n$.

Suppose that the total cost function is $C = 50 + 10Q$. If output per day is 25, one firm can produce this amount at an average cost of Rs 12 and total cost of Rs 300. On the other hand, if there are two firms and one produces 12 units while the other produces 13 units, the total cost of production is $170 + 180 =$ Rs 350 which is greater than the cost of production of a single firm.

Governments have often used the argument of natural monopoly to debar private firms from operating in markets, and taken over the industry. State ownership, over time, has proved to be an unsatisfactory instrument, mainly because state-run enterprises have been perceived to be much more inefficient than private enterprises. There are many reasons for this, including the lack of proper incentive systems and multiple control (by different government departments).

[2] A firm may be a natural monopoly even if its cost curve does not always keep on falling. If a U-shaped average cost curve reaches its minimum at 200 units of output, it may be less costly for only one firm to produce an output of 201 units even though the average cost is rising at that output. A cost function with economies of scale everywhere (declining AC curve) is therefore a sufficient but not a necessary condition for a natural monopoly.

For these reasons, the government might allow a single private firm to serve the market, but would try to regulate its operations. We therefore turn to the case where the government allows a private firm to serve the market and tries to regulate it to limit any departure from competitive norms.

Suppose that the monopolist's cost function is $C = F + cQ$. The equation of the average cost curve is $AC = F/Q + c$, which is continuously declining in Q. The situation is represented in Fig. 9.7. The monopolist, if unregulated, chooses a price p_m, and a quantity Q_m.

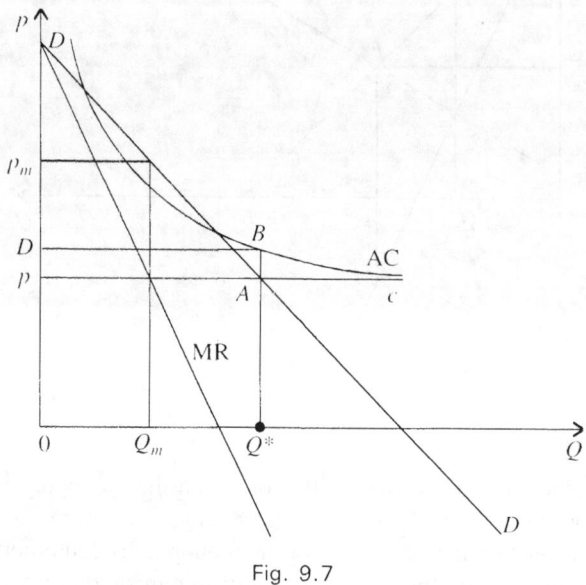

Fig. 9.7

First, let us analyse a situation where the regulator has full knowledge of the firm's demand and cost curves. Then it has two options:

Marginal cost-pricing. The government chooses a price such that $p = MC$. The monopolist is then required to charge a price $p = c$. At this price, the monopolist produces Q^* and the deadweight loss is eliminated. However, because the average cost curve is everywhere declining, the firm will make a loss under this pricing scheme, equal to the area pABD. Since we are considering a long run situation, the firm must be given a subsidy to cover its losses, otherwise it will exit from the industry. But giving a subsidy means that funds have to be diverted from other items in the budget. Otherwise, the subsidy will add to the fiscal deficit and have adverse macroeconomic consequences.

Average cost-pricing. To avoid this problem, the regulator might set price = average cost. Then $p = p''$ is chosen. At this price, the monopolist breaks even (makes only normal profits) and does not need to be subsidized. However, a deadweight loss, equal to the area LMN, remains (Fig. 9.8).

Example 9.4: Suppose that the equation of the total cost curve for a natural monopoly is $LTC = 20Q - (1/8)Q^2$ and the demand function is $P = 50 - Q$. Then $LMC = 20 - (1/4)Q$, $LATC = 20 - (1/8)Q$, and both are declining in Q.

If regulators force the monopolist to follow the marginal-cost pricing rule, she sets $P = 50 - Q = LMC = 20 - (1/4)Q$. Then $Q = 40$, $P = 10$ and $LAC = 20 - (1/8)Q = 15$. This shows that the monopolist will incur a loss of 5 on every unit produced and that the total loss will be 200.

If she is forced to follow the average-cost pricing rule, she sets $20 - (1/8)Q = 50 - Q$, and produces $Q = 240/7$, just breaking even.

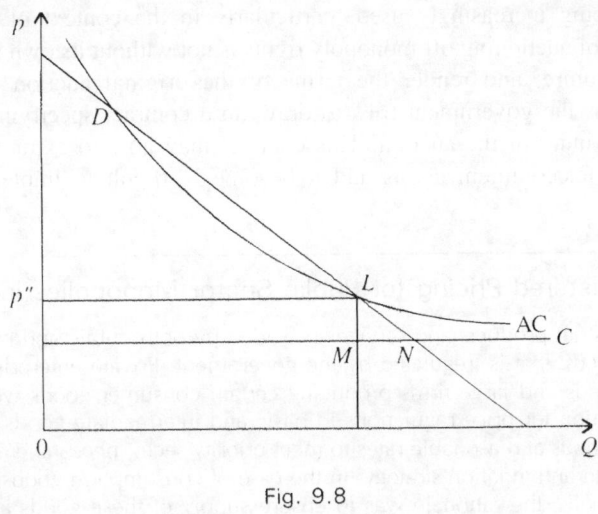

Fig. 9.8

In practice, as regulators possess only imperfect knowledge of cost and demand conditions, they often adopt a simple criterion: the rate of return.

Rate of return regulation. The firm is allowed to set a price that enables it to earn a predetermined rate of return on its investment. If this rate is the competitive rate of return, there is no problem. However, determining the competitive rate of return might be difficult, particularly if the industry was never competitive (benchmarking by international standards may not help, because in other countries cost and demand conditions may be quite different). If the regulators cannot estimate the correct competitive rate of return and by mistake set the rate below the competitive rate, the firm will produce goods and service of lower quality and in the end, go out of business. If the rate is set higher than the competitive rate of return, the firm will earn supernormal profits.

In practice, regulators seem to err on the side of setting rates of return higher than the competitive rate. Averch and Johnson (1962) showed that this has some unintended and unwelcome consequences. The first is the *gold-plated water cooler effect.* The firm has an incentive to purchase more capital equipment than is necessary, because every extra rupee of investment earns more than the competitive rate of return. This tendency will be more pronounced if the allowed rate of return exceeds the actual cost at which the firm can borrow additional funds. Instead of ordinary water coolers, we expect to find the firm purchasing gold-plated water coolers to boost its investment figures. The second is a *cross-subsidy effect.* Suppose that the monopolist is serving two markets. The monopolist will try to increase the *total quantity* sold in the two markets, because this will increase its use of capital. It can do this by setting MR = MC in one market, earning a profit, and using the profit to charge a much lower price in the second market, so that volumes are larger there.

Auctioning of monopoly rights. Demsetz has pointed out that even if unit costs are lowest when the market is served by a single supplier, there can be intense competition to determine who that supplier will be. The government can take advantage of this by auctioning off the rights to serve a market with a natural monopoly. If there is competition among potential suppliers, bids will be driven up to (or near to) the point of the discounted stream of future monopoly rents. The government can then expect to collect partly or wholly the potential gains to the monopolist.

This method is being increasingly used, particularly in the context of telecommunications. However, the process of auctioning off monopoly rights is not without its own problems. Conditions may change in the future, and render the terms of the original auction contract obsolete or undesirable. Moreover, the government tries to draw up a contract specifying how the market is to be served by the winner of the auction. This contract may go into extraordinary details in the case of services like telecommunications and it becomes difficult to implement the contract in practice.

Administered Pricing for Public Sector Monopolies in India

Prices of many industrial products and services provided by both public and private enterprises in India are 'administered', that is, regulated by the government. Private enterprises producing basic and intermediate goods and large firms producing certain consumer goods were subject to price controls. The motivation for price regulations in basic and intermediate goods has been to ensure the supply of these goods at reasonable rates to meet priority sector needs and/or to moderate price increases as part of an anti-inflation strategy. In the case of consumption goods like cotton textiles, sugar and vegetable oils, the rationale was to ensure supply of these goods at low rates through ration shops.

The Planning Commission recommends a 12 per cent return on capital, but the practices vary. Consider first the public monopolies producing non-traded goods, like railways, power, posts and telegraphs, etc. Here the pricing problem is generally considered in three stages. (1) An estimate of overall revenue requirement is made on the basis of a test-period cost data, demand forecasts, and input norms. (2) The joint and common costs are allocated on one of the FDC norms. (3) A rate structure is arrived at, giving due consideration to social goals and political compulsions. For enterprises selling their commodities to other public sector units and/or governments, the markup pricing rule is followed.

For monopolies selling traded goods, the relevant border prices are taken into consideration. For example, the imported price of crude and the domestic costs of crude oil are pooled together to arrive at uniform price of crude oil for each refinery. Retention prices are established for each refinery, assuming norms about capacity utilization and 15 per cent return on capital employed. The government has been slowly moving away from this system towards one based more directly on international crude prices.

As Sankar notes, the administered pricing mechanism in India lacks transparency. Prices are announced, but the precise reasons for fixing the prices is never spelt out. As a result, it is difficult, if not impossible to find out the extent of tax/subsidy implicit in the prices. Moreover, there is very little coordination among the different agencies responsible for fixing the prices.

For a long time, the administered pricing mechanism suppressed the market mechanism and relied excessively on physical rationing—power cuts, waiting lists, etc.—for the allocation of resources.

Source: U. Sankar (1998), 'Pricing Policies', in D. Mookherjee (ed.) *Indian Industry*. New Delhi: Oxford University Press.

Topics for Discussion

Collect information about the market shares of some large Indian firms in the private sector in different industries, paying particular attention to the definition of the industry in each case. [The Markets and Market Shares reports of the Centre for Monitoring the Indian Economy (CMIE) provide easy access to such information.] Discuss whether any of these fit into the definition of a monopoly. Identify the sources of monopoly power, if any, with special reference to government policies.

Carry out the same exercise for some public sector firms (for example, Indian Airlines).

Exercise

1. A monopolist faces the following demand and cost schedules:

Price (Rs)	Quantity	Total Cost (Rs)
20	7	36
19	8	45
18	9	54
17	10	63
16	11	72
15	12	81

(a) How much output should the monopolist produce?
(b) What price should the firm charge?

2. A monopolist's demand function is of the form $P = 100 - Q$, and she faces a total cost function $C = 4Q^2$. The monopolist charges a single price to all her customers and tries to maximize profit.

(a) How much will the monopolist produce and what price will she charge?
(b) What is the deadweight loss under monopoly?
(c) Now suppose that a quantity tax of Rs 10 per unit is imposed on the monopolist's product. Her total and marginal cost functions will now be

$$C =$$
$$MC =$$

(d) What will be the output of the monopolist after tax and what price will she charge?
(e) What fraction of the tax does the monopolist bear?

3. A monopolist firm faces a demand with a constant price-elasticity of 3. It has a constant marginal cost of Rs 40. If marginal cost should increase by 25 per cent, would the price charged by the monopolist also increase by 25 per cent?

4. A monopolist has a cost function given by $C(Q) = Q^2$ and faces a demand curve given by

$$P = 120 - Q.$$

(a) What is the profit-maximizing monopolist's output and price?
(b) What is the consumer surplus? monopoly profit?
(c) Now suppose that the monopolist has to follow a marginal-cost pricing policy. What is her output and price?
(d) What is now the consumer surplus? monopoly profit? How does this case differ from (b) above? Represent the two situations in a diagram.

5. A monopoly firm has two factories for which the costs are given by $C_1(Q_1) = 10Q_1^2$ and $C_2(Q_2) = 20Q_2^2$. The firm faces the demand curve $P = 700 - 5Q$ where $Q = Q_1 + Q_2$. Calculate the profit-maximizing values of Q_1, Q_2 and P.

6. The equation of the total cost curve for a natural monopoly is $LTC = 20Q - (1/8)Q^2$ and the demand function is $P = 50 - Q$.

(a) If regulators force the monopolist to follow the marginal-cost pricing rule, how much will she produce and what price will she charge? What will be her profit/loss?
(b) If she is forced to follow the average-cost pricing rule, how much will she produce and what price will she charge?

7. A natural monopolist has the total cost function $TC = 350 + 2q$. The demand function for the monopolist's product is $q = 41 - P/2$. If government regulations prohibit this firm from making any positive profits, show that there are two possible levels of production at which the monopolist can meet the regulation and still survive.

If instead the monopolist is required to follow the marginal cost-pricing rule, how much subsidy must be paid to the monopoly to cover its loss?

10 Pricing Strategies with Market Power

A monopolist faces a downward sloping demand curve and can set its price, unlike a competitive firm that takes the market price as given. In our discussion of monopoly pricing so far, we have assumed that the monopolist selects, for every good that it sells, the price that maximizes its profit from that good, and charges the *same* price to all buyers for every unit sold of that good. In practice, firms with market power employ a variety of pricing strategies to try to extract more of the consumer surplus. In this chapter, we analyse the phenomenon of price discrimination, both at a point of time and over time, as well as tying and bundling, and auctions.

10.1 Price Discrimination

We have been assuming that the monopolist sets MR = MC and charges the same price to all customers. If the monopolist can set different prices for different customers, it can be immediately shown that this enables her to increase her profit. Consider the profit-maximizing output for the single-price monopolist. At this output level, price p_m is greater than marginal cost. Thus, an extra unit sold can generate more revenues for the monopolist, if *only the last customer* can be charged a price slightly lower than p_m. Thus, while all other customers are charged a price of p_m, the monopolist gains by charging p' for the extra unit that is sold and making additional profit of AB. Therefore charging different prices to different customers can increase profit.

For a single-price monopolist, this course of action is unattractive, because the lower price has to be charged to *all* customers and the consequent loss in revenue outweighs the gain from the last customer.

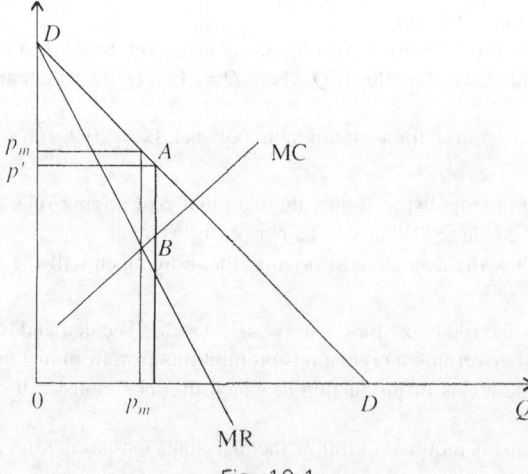

Fig. 10.1

In the real world, different groups of buyers are often charged different prices for similar products. Sometimes such non-uniform pricing simply represents quality differences or transport costs. At other times, the same price charged to different buyers represents non-uniform pricing, for example, if the buyers are located in different areas. The buyers who are located farther away are in effect having to pay less if the final price, including delivery charges, is the same for all buyers. To bypass such problems, we follow Stigler's (1987) definition: there is *price discrimination*, when different buyers are charged different unit prices for similar goods, and the prices are in different ratios to marginal costs.

Price discrimination seems to be all pervasive. Some common examples of price discrimination are given below:

- Pricing of cinema hall tickets by *time of day or day of the week*—usually matinee shows are priced lower than evening shows, while weekend shows are priced higher than shows on weekdays.
- Pricing of transport services by *age*—children and senior citizens typically are charged at lower rates for riding on buses or trains.
- Pricing of professional services by *income categories*—doctors often charge relatively wealthier patients more than poorer patients, sometimes even foregoing fees for the latter.

The Government of India sets prices of motor spirit, high speed diesel and aviation turbine fuel, which are used for 'luxury' purposes, above their respective costs, and prices of kerosene and LPG below their costs.

- Pricing of goods by *different degrees of recognition or frequency of purchase*—the neighbourhood grocer charges lower prices to nearby residents who purchase frequently and refuse to lower prices for casual customers; airlines offer frequent flier incentives.
- Pricing of books by different *editions*—differences between the prices of hardback editions that come out earlier and paperback editions that come out later generally seem to be too large to be explained by the relative costs of binding.
- Pricing by *region*—prices for local telephone services can be significantly different from long-distance rates for calls made abroad.

10.2 Conditions for Successful Price Discrimination

Even though all firms would like to price discriminate, many are not able to do so. There are three conditions that must be satisfied for price discrimination to take place successfully.

1. The firm must have some degree of market power, that is, the ability to set prices because it faces a downward sloping demand curve. A perfectly competitive firm can never price discriminate.
2. The firm must be able to separate customers into two or more groups. Sometimes, the customers can be easily separated, for example, they may be buyers living in different regions, or they may be distinguished by physical characteristics like age or sex. Sometimes the firm may try to induce buyers to reveal their types through their purchases, for example, matinee shows will be attended by people who are not working fulltime.
3. The firm must be able to prevent arbitrage by buyers, that is, resale by buyers who paid the lower prices to buyers who are willing to pay higher prices.

The requirement that resale should not be possible can be satisfied for a number of reasons:

- Services—Most services, like doctors' services, once purchased, cannot be resold. The commodity is consumed in the act of purchase.
- Warranties—The firm can void a warranty if the object is resold. Warranties can often be used only by the original purchasers.

(contd)

(contd)

- Adulteration—Suppose that alcohol can be used for drinking purposes and for medicinal purposes. To prevent buyers for medicinal purposes from reselling alcohol to drinkers, the firm can adulterate the alcohol sold to the former to make it unfit for human consumption
- Transaction cost—If consumers incur large transaction costs to resell the product, then resale is unlikely. Tariffs and transportation costs are examples of transaction costs that prevent resale at a profit. Sometimes, the firm can design a method of price discrimination that makes the transaction cost of resale prohibitively high. Suppose Pepsi places coupons in certain copies of a newspaper and these coupons can be used to get discounts from retailers. The buyers who get the coupons will have to find out buyers who did not get the coupons and bargain with them for resale. This process will generally be considered prohibitively costly in relation to the size of the discount available.
- Contractual remedies—As a part of the sale contract, the firm may prohibit the buyer from reselling the product. Companies sometimes provide low-rent housing to some of their workers. Tenants are prohibited from subletting their apartments, at the risk of being thrown out if they violate the contract.
- Vertical integration—A firm that produces more than one stage of production is said to be vertically integrated. Suppose that a steel producer sells steel parts at a higher price to car manufacturers than it sells to furniture manufacturers and these parts are easily interchangeable. There is then an incentive for furniture manufacturers to resell the parts to car producers. To prevent this, the steel manufacturer can decide to produce furniture itself, that is, integrate forward into furniture production.
- Government intervention—The government can enact laws that prevent resale. Or it might raise the transaction costs of resale by requiring resales to be registered and hefty fees to be paid.

Source: D.W. Carlton and J.M. Perloff, 1994, *Modern Industrial Organization*, 2nd edn HarperCollins.

10.3 Different Degrees of Price Discrimination

The traditional classification of the different types of price discrimination is due to Pigou (1920), who distinguished between first, second and third degree price discrimination. The basis for this classification is the amount of information available to a seller about potential buyers. First degree price discrimination takes place when the seller has complete information about each buyer's demand curve. The seller resorts to second degree price discrimination when she knows the distribution of buyer types, but cannot recognize the type of any individual. Finally, third-degree price discrimination occurs when the seller can classify buyers into different observable categories and relevant information about each category is available. We will first consider the three types of price discrimination and then analyse other practices like tying and bundling that facilitate price discrimination.

10.3.1 First-degree or Perfect Price Discrimination

The seller has perfect information about the demand curves of buyers and for each unit sold, charges the buyer an amount equal to the maximum willingness to pay for that unit.

Consider a case where there are five buyers, each demanding one unit of the commodity. The maximum prices they are willing to pay are given below. Let MC = 8.

Buyer	Maximum price buyer is willing to pay	Total market demand
A	10	1
B	9	2
C	8	3
D	7	4
E	6	5

The monopolist will go on selling as long as price > MC. Therefore, she will sell one unit each to buyers A, B, and C, charging them respectively 10, 9, and 8. In this way, the perfectly discriminating monopolist captures the entire consumer surplus (remember that the consumer surplus for any unit is the maximum price the buyer is willing to pay for that unit, less the price the buyer actually pays).

Next, suppose that each consumer wants one unit of a product, but consumers are willing to pay different amounts. By ranking the consumers according to their maximum willingness to pay and plotting the aggregate demands, we get a downward sloping aggregate demand curve. The firm then charges each consumer the maximum that the person is willing to pay and sells to any customer whose maximum willingness to pay exceeds or is equal to the marginal cost.

This is shown in Fig. 10.2. Assume that MC = m, a constant. In a perfectly competitive industry, the quantity produced would have been Q^* and each buyer would have been charged $p^* = m$. A perfectly price discriminating monopolist also produces Q^*. However, only the last (marginal) buyer is charged p^*. Everyone else is charged the price on the demand curve. The first unit is sold at the price p_1, the second at the price p_2, and so on. The demand curve facing the monopolist then becomes the *marginal revenue curve*: each extra unit is sold at the price on the demand curve. In this way, the monopolist appropriates the entire consumer surplus (equal to the area Dp^*A).

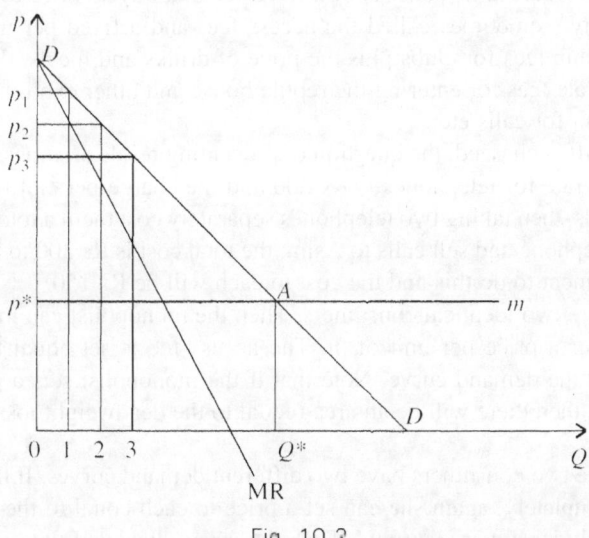

Fig. 10.2

The results from the efficiency standpoint are the same for perfect competition and perfect price discrimination. Neither gives rise to any deadweight loss. However, the distributional implications are quite different since under perfect competition, consumer surplus is positive and under perfect price discrimination, consumer surplus is zero and the entire surplus is captured by the monopolist.

Similar arguments apply when there are different buyers in the market with different individual demand curves.

Although all firms would like to attain the holy grail of perfect price discrimination, the costs of gathering information about each consumer's preferences generally makes it difficult to perfectly discriminate. Recent advances in computer technology are making it possible for firms to gather more information about their customers cheaply and practice finer price discrimination.

Why do corporations want personal data? The simple answer, according to Andrew Odlyzko, the director of the University of Minnesota's Digital Technology Center, is that such information is the key to discriminatory pricing.

In a paper entitled 'Privacy, Economics and Price Discrimination on the Internet', Odlyzko focuses on how technology can bring price discrimination to new levels of sophistication and prevalence. In 2000, Coca-Cola tested a vending machine that would raise prices on a hot, humid day and lower them when temperatures fell. Today, Amazon.com knows what, when, and how often customers buy and is experimenting with offering personalized bundles—buy two books and get a discount, for example—to induce people to buy more. Twenty years ago, neither experiment would have been possible.

According to Odlyzko, managers who invest in privacy-eroding data-collection technology are not always conscious that they are moving toward a world of widespread discriminatory pricing. Rather, they are trying out ways to use information to increase profits. But as corporations become more sophisticated in collecting and parsing consumers' personal information, success will lead them to more pervasive price discrimination.

Source: http://www.businessweek.com/technology/content/jul2003/tc20030731_6139_tc073.htm

A commonly encountered method for the achievement of perfect price discrimination is the use of *two-part tariffs*. A two-part tariff consists of a fixed fee that buyers have to pay to be allowed to purchase the commodity (sometimes called the access fee) and a fixed per unit charge thereafter. Examples are membership fees for clubs plus the price of drinks and meals, the entrance fee to the zoo together with separate fees for entering the reptile house and other exhibits, monthly rentals for telephones plus payment for calls etc.

When a two-part tariff is charged, the question of preventing resale assumes importance. Suppose that the monthly rental rate for telephones is Rs 200 and the charge per call is Re 1. If Seema and Asim each make 50 calls, then taking two telephones separately cost them a total of Rs 500. If Seema can subscribe to the telephone and sell calls to Asim, the total cost is Rs 300 to her. Seema and Asim can enter into an agreement to do this and the cost to each will be Rs 150.

Suppose that there are two identical consumers. Then the monopolist can maximize her gains by charging each consumer a price per unit of m. The access fee is set equal to the corresponding consumer surplus from the demand curve. Note that if the monopolist sets a price that is different from the marginal cost, then there will be an area (equal to the deadweight loss) that she will not be able to capture.

Now suppose that the two consumers have two different demand curves. If the monopolist knows each demand curve completely, again she can set a price to each equal to the MC and then set the access fee equal to each consumer's surplus. Thus the access fees and the prices differ from consumer to consumer (the prices will not differ when the MC is constant). In Fig. 10.3, consumer 1 is charged an access fee of CS_1 and consumer 2 is charged an access fee of CS_2. The per unit charge for each is m.

But if the monopolist has no way of distinguishing between different consumers, she must charge the same access fee and the same price per unit to all of them. The access fee she charges cannot exceed the minimum consumer surplus, if she is to sell to both the consumers. The firm then faces a dilemma. If she charges a low per unit price, she sells more of the product and can charge a higher access fee from each consumer. But her ability to charge a high access fee from the second consumer is constrained by the low willingness-to-pay of the first consumer. In some cases, the firm may make greater profits by concentrating on the second consumer and charging an access fee so high that the first consumer is priced out of the market and only the second consumer buys the product.

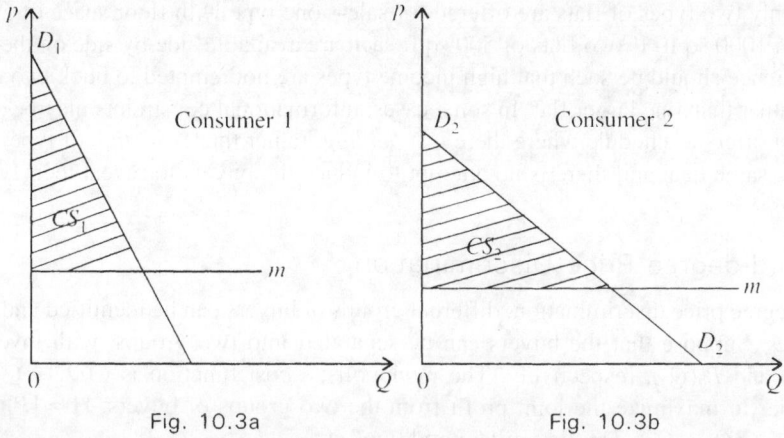

Fig. 10.3a   Fig. 10.3b

Two-part and multi-part tariffs are common in many public utilities and transportation services in India. For electricity supply, a household has to pay a lump-sum connection charge, and monthly rental and power consumption charges based on a declining block schedule. To get a telephone, one has to deposit a sum at the time of application, pay installation charges, and pay bimonthly rental and call charges.

10.3.2 Second-degree Price Discrimination

Second-degree or nonlinear pricing occurs when buyers face nonlinear price schedules, that is, the price paid depends on the quantity or quality bought. An example is quantity discount. An individual who purchases one 500 gm pack of butter pays Rs 50 for the pack, while the individual who buys 5 packs of 100 gm pays Rs 12 per pack. Sometimes differences in quality, too, get reflected in a nonlinear manner in prices. The price difference between a high quality and a low quality good is more than that can be explained by differences in quality alone.

Given that the demand curves are downward sloping, customers are willing to pay more for the first unit than for the successive units. Then the firm can price discriminate by letting the price a customer pays depend on the number of units a customer buys. Moreover, a customer who makes a bulk purchase is more price-sensitive than a customer who buys a small amount for another reason: she is going to spend more and even a small increase in price will make it worth her while to search for substitutes. Hence by providing quantity discounts, the seller is discriminating between different types having different price elasticities of demand. The seller is, however unable to identify a priori the type of a buyer. Only the amount of purchase by a buyer reveals a buyer's type.

Thus, we are considering a situation where the monopolist will not be able to identify the type of a particular buyer, though she may have a good idea about the distribution of buyer types. That is, the monopolist may know that 60 per cent of the buyers in the neighbourhood will be middle-income, 30 per cent low-income and 10 per cent high-income types. But the income group to which a particular buyer belongs may be difficult to establish. The monopolist then constructs a price schedule in such a way that buyers reveal their types by choosing points on the schedule. For example, high income buyers choose flats with three bedrooms, middle income buyers choose flats with two bedrooms, and so on.

It is important for the monopolist to ensure that buyers of a certain type do not find attractive a package that has been designed for a lower type. For example, suppose that all buyers are only interested in the floor space of the flats they buy and high income types want to buy flats with larger floor space. Only two types of flats are offered for sale—one type with floor space of 500 sq ft and the others with 1000 sq ft. If two flats of 500 sq ft each are available side by side on the same floor, the price difference should be such that high income types are not tempted to book two smaller flats side by side rather than one larger flat. In some cases, informational constraints may be so acute that the monopolist offers a schedule where there is a *pooling*, rather than a *sorting* of types. All buyers are offered the same deal and there is no attempt to induce the buyers to reveal their types through their purchases.

10.3.3 Third-degree Price Discrimination

Under third-degree price discrimination, different groups of buyers can be identified and are charged different prices. Suppose that the buyers can be separated into two groups, with inverse demand curves $P_1(Q_1)$ and $P_2(Q_2)$, respectively. The monopolist's cost function is $C(Q_1 + Q_2)$. Then the monopolist tries to maximize the joint profit from the two groups of buyers: $\Pi = [P_1(Q_1)] (Q_1) + [P_2(Q_2)] (Q_2) - C(Q_1 + Q_2)$. The first order conditions are

$$\partial\Pi/\partial Q_1 = \partial\Pi/\partial Q_2 = 0.$$

These yield the conditions $MR_i(Q_i) - MC(Q_1 + Q_2) = 0$, $i = 1, 2$. The conditions can then be written alternatively as $MR_1(Q_1) = MR_2(Q_2) = MC(Q_1 + Q_2)$. So long as any one of these equalities is violated, the monopolist is not maximizing profit. For example, if the MR from group 1 is higher than that from group 2, the monopolist can gain more by selling extra units to group 1. And if MR in any market is different from the MC of selling to that market, the monopolist can increase profit by increasing or decreasing production in that market.

This case is intermediate between the two cases we have already discussed. The monopolist cannot perfectly identify a buyer, but she can place a buyer in a certain group whose characteristic is known to her. Thus she has too little information to allow her to practice first degree price discrimination, but more information than a seller forced to practice second degree price discrimination.

The condition that the marginal revenues in the two markets should be equal to each other gives us one more piece of information. Remember that $MR_i = P_i(1 - 1/e_i)$, where e_i is the price-elasticity of demand in the ith market. Then $MR_1(Q_1) = MR_2(Q_2)$ implies that $P_1/P_2 = (1 - 1/e_2)/(1 - 1/e_1) = (e_1e_2 - e_1)/ (e_1e_2 - e_2)$. This shows that prices charged to the two groups of buyers are equal if the price elasticities are equal. Otherwise, $P_1 >$ or $< P_2$ according as $e_1 <$ or $> e_2$. That is, the higher price will be charged to that group of buyer which has a more inelastic demand.

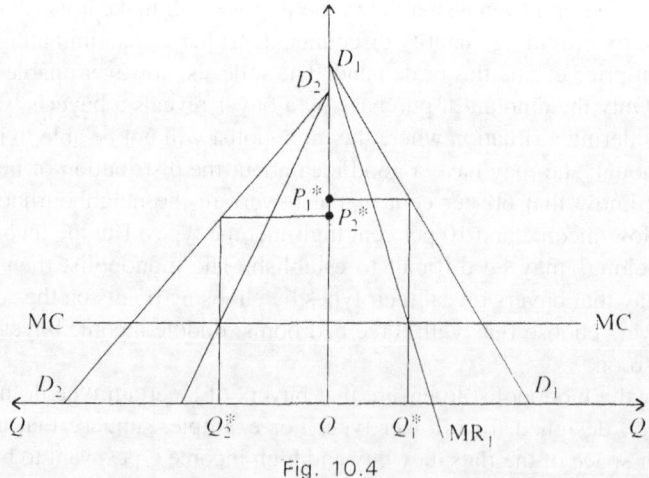

Fig. 10.4

The situation is graphically represented in Fig. 10.4 for linear demand curves (and hence linear MR curves). The MC curve is horizontal. The monopolist equates MC with MR in each market and produces Q_{1*} and Q_{2*} respectively for the two groups. Note that the higher price is set in the market with the steeper demand curve.

Example 10.1: Let $P_1 = 80 - 5Q_1$, $P_2 = 170 - 20Q_2$, and MC = 10. Then $MR_1 = 80 - 10Q_1$ and $MR_2 = 170 - 40Q_2$. Setting $MR_1 = MC$ and $MR_2 = MC$, we get $Q_1^* = 7$ and $Q_2^* = 4$. Then, from the inverse demand equations, $P_1^* = 45$ and $P_2^* = 90$.

10.4 Durable Goods Monopolies: Price Discrimination over Time

Till now, we have been discussing the pricing of goods that are perishable through usage and that must be bought repeatedly. In contrast, durable goods do not perish even after repeated usage. Examples are 'white goods' like refrigerators that can be used for a long time. It follows that units of durable goods at different points of time tend to be substitutes. If I buy a TV this year, it is highly unlikely that I will buy a TV next year.

This raises an interesting possibility. If the monopolist seller charges the price that maximizes today's profit then a certain number of people buy TV today. Tomorrow's demand curve then lies below today's demand curve (with an unchanged or slowly growing number of consumers). The monopolist is tempted to charge a lower price tomorrow.

In Fig. 10.5, the monopolist faces the demand curve DD in period 1. To simplify, assume that the marginal cost is a constant c. She equates MR_1 with the horizontal MC curve and sells Q_1 amount at a price P_1. In the second period, the demand curve facing her is AD, since people who have already purchased the durable good will not return to the market in this period. Corresponding to AD, the marginal revenue curve is MR_2. Therefore, the monopolist would like to set a price of P_2 in period 2 and sell an amount $Q_2 - Q_1$. This process continues till the price drops to the level of marginal cost. It is clear that in this scenario, the monopolist is tempted to keep on lowering her prices in successive periods.

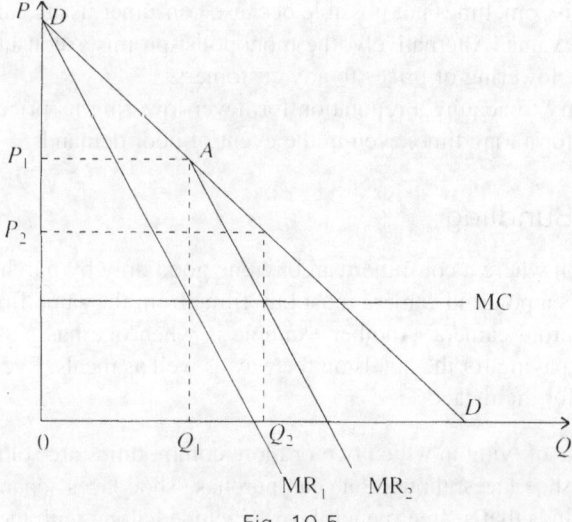

Fig. 10.5

But if buyers can correctly anticipate this, then they will postpone their purchases today. The problem then is to work out the equilibrium time path of prices, given the expectations of the buyers about future price changes. Coase (1972) had conjectured that if the time periods are short enough and the consumers can rationally anticipate buyer's actions, then the price might immediately drop down to the level of marginal cost and the monopolist forfeit all market power. Thus, in the case of a durable goods monopoly, paradoxically the power to lower prices in the future hurts the monopolist. One useful way to think about this is to consider the monopolist is any period as a different firm. Then a monopolist of today is competing with many monopolists of tomorrow and this competition drives the price quickly to the competitive level of marginal costs.

The monopolist has the option of either *renting* out the product or *selling* it. By renting the product to a consumer for a price p_r, the monopolist maintains ownership of the product, but contracts with the consumer to let the consumer enjoy the services from the product for the period specified under the contract. The seller of a product, on the other hand, will transfer the ownership rights to the consumer for price. Renting out the product avoids the Coasian problem because in each period, the people who have rented the product must come back to the monopolist for a renewal of the rental contract. The monopolist who sells has an incentive to cut the price in the future, whereas such behaviour does not occur if the good is rented out. However, in certain instances, renting is not feasible. Then the monopolist must sell the product and intertemporal price discrimination can take place.

How can a durable-goods monopolist escape this predicament? The monopolist's task is to influence consumers' expectations by credibly committing to not lowering prices in the future. This can be done in a number of ways:

1. The monopolist can refuse to sell her product and only rent or lease it. However, for goods like cars, this is infeasible. Cars can be rented for short periods, but not on a regular basis because the consumer renting the car is unlikely to be as careful in driving a rented car as he would be in driving his own car.
2. The monopolist can produce less durable goods, thereby limiting her ability to lower the price in the future.
3. The monopolist can ensure that future production is prohibitively costly, for example, via capacity constraints that she sets herself. An artist can destroy the plates used to make lithographs.
4. The monopoly can guarantee to buy back the good in the future from any consumer at the price they paid for it. This is sometimes not possible because consumer usage can change the nature of the good or lower its value. Alternatively, the monopolist promises consumers to give them the benefits of any future lowering of prices to any customers.
5. The monopolist can try to acquire a reputation for never lowering its prices. This she can do by sticking to its prices for a long time, even in the event of poor demand.

10.5 Tying and Bundling

Tying refers to a situation where a consumer can buy one good only by purchasing another good as well. Someone who buys a polaroid camera must buy films from the same firm because other films cannot be used in a polaroid camera. Another example is when one has purchased a 'pilgrimage' package which involves paying for the hotels on the way as well as meals. Even if one chooses to eat outside, one has to pay for the meals.

Bundling is a special case of tying in which two or more commodities are sold only in fixed proportions. Shoes come with shoe laces, though one can purchase shoe laces separately, too. One buys a health food packet and finds that a 'free' pencil-box is included along with the packet. Another type of tying occurs through *requirements tie-in sales*, when buyers are required to purchase a minimum quantity of a second commodity, B, from the same seller, if they purchase a commodity A from him. *Exclusive dealing* is a special form of a requirements contract in which customers are required to buy all of a product or service from a firm. Exclusive dealing is not always a case of tying, since buyers may be required to purchase all of a commodity from a firm independently of the purchases of any other commodity.

We first discuss some of the reasons why tying might occur. Then we examine bundling in more detail.

10.5.1 Reasons for Tie-in Sales

Efficiency. In some cases, tying increases efficiency by lowering transaction costs. A radio consists of many individual components. It would be inefficient to sell these separately and then provide the buyer with a manual to help put the components together (some people like to do things themselves and might prefer to assemble the radio themselves, but for most people a completely assembled radio is better).

Evasion of regulations. Suppose that there is a Rent Control Act that does not allow a landlord to charge more than Rs 2000 per month for a flat. The landlord thinks that the correct rent would be Rs 2500. The building has a garage which is otherwise unused. The landlord can then rent the flat only if the tenant agrees to rent the garage, too, for a rent of Rs 500 per month. In this way, tying helps a firm to evade regulations.

Secret price discounts. A firm may want to gain higher market share by cutting its price, but fears that this will invite retaliatory price-cutting by its competitors if they come to know about it. The firm can then use a tie-in to provide price discounts secretly. A bowl worth Rs 5 is provided along with each packet of cornflakes if the firm producing the cornflakes wants to give a price discount of Rs 5. A related reason may be that the firm wants to give a price discount without appearing to do so. Why? Because it thinks that the higher price on the packet signals higher quality to customers and any overt lowering of price will bring it directly into competition with a lower price, lower quality customer.

Quality assurance. A firm can claim that it alone can assure the quality of certain accessories that consumers are required to buy from it. For example, Kodak claimed that it tied the development of its films to its film sales because it did not believe that independent developers could develop its films as well as it (Kodak) could.

Price discrimination. Tie-in sales can also be used for purposes of price discrimination, where price discrimination can be defined more broadly as a pricing strategy that enables a firm to capture a part of the consumer surplus and increase profit.

10.5.2 Requirements Tie-in Sales

A simple example will show how the requirements tie-in sales can be used to price-discriminate between consumers.

Suppose that a firm has a machine that automatically stamps a person's name and other details on stick-on labels. Some people need lots of such labels, say 10,000 per year. Another type needs only 1000 labels a year. The machine works for one year and then has to be replaced. Before the machine came on the market, labels had to be manually stamped and the cost was 10 paise per label. The price for the label paper in the competitive market was 50 paise per label paper. The first type of customer would therefore be saving Rs 1000 per year with the machine while the second type would be saving Rs 100 only.

Now suppose that the monopolist manufacturing the machine decides to give away the machine for free to a consumer provided that the latter buys all the stick-on label paper from it. It prices the paper at 60–10 paise above the competitive price.

As a result, the type one consumers who accept the firm's offer effectively pay a higher price of Rs 1000 for the machine, while type 2 consumers pay Rs 100. The tie-in therefore allows the monopolist to charge buyers effectively different prices for the machine. Buyers who value the machine more pay more. The monopolist captures all the consumer surplus in this case.

10.5.3 Bundling

Bundling may be either *pure* or *mixed*. Pure bundling occurs when a firm sells two or more products only in a bundle and not individually. Mixed bundling occurs when the commodities are made available both in bundles and individually. We first show how and under what circumstances pure bundling can add to a firm's profits.

Suppose that there is a monopoly selling shaving cream and toothpaste as a bundle. There are two types of customers, one type concerned more with presenting before the world a dazzling set of teeth, the other a clean-shaven look. Their reservation prices (that is, the maximum amounts they are willing to pay for shaving creams and toothpastes) are given below in rupees per tube. It can be seen that there is a negative relationship between the reservation prices of the two types. Type 1 values toothpaste more and type 2 values shaving cream more. There are 100 consumers of each type. Cost of production is assumed to be zero to simplify the calculations. The firm therefore is concerned with total revenues only.

	Shaving Cream	Toothpaste	Total
Type 1	12	30	42
Type 2	13	25	38

If the firm were selling the commodities separately, and wanted to ensure that all customers bought both commodities, then it must price a tube of shaving cream at Rs 12 and a tube of toothpaste at Rs 25. Its total revenues will be Rs 7400 (Rs 12 × 200 + Rs 25 × 200).

However, suppose instead that the two commodities are always sold as a bundle. Type 1 consumers are willing to pay upto Rs 42 for a bundle and type 2 Rs 38. The firm charges Rs 38 for a bundle, thereby ensuring that both types buy the bundle. In this case, the total revenue is Rs 7600. The firm adds to its profit by selling the bundle rather than the commodities separately. However, even the bundling strategy fails to capture all of consumer surplus, which in this case happens to be Rs 4200 + Rs 3800 = Rs 8000.

Bundling will not work if the reservation prices are positively correlated, that is, both types of consumers have similar preferences. An example is given below.

	Shaving Cream	Toothpaste	Total
Type 1	13	30	43
Type 2	12	25	37

It can be easily demonstrated that both the pure bundling strategy and the separate pricing strategy generate the same total revenue of Rs 7400.

Let us now consider mixed bundling. The firm offers the commodities for sale as a bundle as well as individually. Many restaurants arrange their menus with *prix fixe* and *a la carte* selections.

Patrons can buy items as a bundle in the prix fixe section. These are also available separately in the a la carte section, although the total price is higher.

Suppose that 'puri-bhaji' is available as a bundle in a restaurant, and puris and bhajis can also be purchased separately. There are 4 types of customers, A, B, C, and D. There are 100 customers of each type. Their reservation prices (in paise) for each puri and helping of bhaji are $A = (5, 90)$, $B = (60, 50)$, $C = (70, 10)$, and $D = (75, 5)$ respectively. Each customer buys only one puri and one helping of bhaji. To keep things simple, again assume that there are no production costs.

The restaurant has to determine prices for the three options: separate pricing, pure bundling and mixed bundling (which involves pricing puri-bhaji as a bundle as well as pricing puri and bhaji separately).

For the separate pricing strategy, puri sells for 60 paise and bhaji sells for 50 paise. At this price, types B, C, and D purchase puris and types A and B purchase bhajis. The total revenue is Rs 180 + Rs 100 = Rs 280.

If a pure bundling strategy is used, the optimal price is 80 paise a bundle. All types buy the bundle and total revenue is Rs 320.

Finally, consider a mixed bundling strategy. The firm is trying to gain a part of the consumer surplus that could not be extracted by the separate pricing and pure bundling strategies. It tries to separate customers with marked preference for puris from customers with more preference for bhajis. The prices are now 70 paise for puris, 90 paise for bhajis and Rs 1.10 for a bundle. (You can play around with these numbers to convince yourself that these are the best prices from the restaurant's point of view.) The bundle price is such that only type B customers purchase the bundle (for type B customers, the bundle price is lower than the total of the separate prices). C and D buy puris separately, while A types buy only bhajis. the total revenue now is Rs 110 + Rs 140 + Rs 90 = Rs 340. The mixed bundling strategy has enabled the restaurant to increase profit by extracting some part of the consumer surplus.

However, even the mixed bundling strategy does not extract all of consumer surplus. It still leaves Rs 25 in consumer surplus. The sum of the reservation prices for all the consumers is Rs 95 + Rs 110 + Rs 80 + Rs 80 = Rs 365. Under the mixed bundling strategy, the consumers pay Rs 340, which is still less than the maximum amount they are willing to pay.

Auctions

Auctions have been used as a method of selling goods far back in history. One of the earliest references to a regularly organized auction deals with the Babylonian marriage market, where brides were auctioned to Babylonian men. Since then auctions have been used to sell a variety of 'commodities', ranging from slaves to famous pictures to perishable goods like fresh fishes and cut flowers. Auctions have gained increasing favour as a means of extracting some of the consumer surplus from the buyers.

There are four basic types of auctions:

English auction. In an English auction, bidders announce or otherwise indicate their bids in an open manner. Each successive bid must be higher than the previous one, so this is an increasing-price auction. The bids are known to everyone participating in the auction; the auctioneer repeats the last bid a number of times to make sure that everyone is aware of the price that must be beat. The process of bidding continues until only one bidder is left. The English type of auction is used when a unique object is being sold.

Dutch auction. In a Dutch auction, the auctioneer starts with a high price. The price is then systematically lowered until one bidder accepts the bid, usually by pressing a buzzer. Most Dutch auctions are run automatically. They use a clock-like device that ticks down every few seconds to a

(contd)

(contd)

lower bid. Dutch auctions are used for selling perishable goods like fishes. In a Dutch auction, participants are faced with a trade-off between waiting to get a lower price and running the risk of losing out to somebody who decides to accept a higher price.

First-price sealed bid auction. Each bidder submits a bid in a sealed envelope. The envelopes are opened at the same time and the highest bidder selected. The method is generally used by governments and firms for selling items that have become redundant, old or damaged, like old cars or computers. (It is not necessary that the bids be opened at the same time; the bidders must submit their bids without knowing what the other bids are.)

Sometimes the time of receiving the bids is stamped on the bids. If there is a tie between the highest bidders, the one who submitted the bid earlier is chosen.

Second-price sealed bid auction. This is similar to the first-price sealed bid auction, except that *the winner pays the amount bid by the second-highest bidder.*

Topics for Discussion

1. The government uses the process of inviting 'tenders', which is essentially a first-price, sealed-bid auction, to allocate licenses. The right of private firms to provide cellular phones and pagers in certain cities was decided through a process of tendering. Discuss the pros and cons of this method.
2. Do you think that price discrimination is undesirable? Should price discrimination be banned?

Exercise

1. Banana Computer Co. sells Banana computers both in the domestic and foreign markets. Because of differences in the power supplies, a Banana purchased in one market can not be used in the other market. The demand curves associated with the two markets are as follows:

$$P_d = 20,000 - 20Q_d, \ P_f = 25,000 - 50Q_f$$

Banana's production process exhibits constant return to scale and it takes Rs 1,000,000 to produce 100 computers.

(a) What are the equations for Banana's long run average and marginal cost functions?
(b) If Banana can charge different prices in the two markets, what will be its output and price in the two markets?

2. A monopolist faces the demand curve $Q = 10 - P$ and has total cost function $TC = 2Q$. If the monopolist is able to practice perfect price discrimination, how much profit will the monopolist earn?

3. S. Tendulkar and B. Bhutia have the same sports agent to market their sponsoring services. Disregard the agent's costs. Perfect price discrimination is not possible.

(a) Suppose that the agent faces a cricket-product firm and a football-product firm that are willing to pay the following amounts for sponsorship by the two players:

	S. Tendulkar	B. Bhutia	Together
Cricket-prod. firm	Rs 470,000	Rs 90,000	Rs 560,000
Football-prod. firm	Rs 500,000	Rs 50,000	Rs 550,000

Is it more profitable for the agent to sell the services of the two players as a 'bundle' or separately? What should be the prices charged for their services?

(b) Suppose, instead that the figures are as follows:

	S. Tendulkar	B. Bhutia	Together
Cricket-prod. firm	Rs 490,000	Rs 80,000	Rs 580,000
Football-prod. firm	Rs 470,000	Rs 30,000	Rs 500,000

Is it more profitable for the agent to sell the services of the two athletes as a 'bundle' or separately? What should be the prices charged for their services?

4. A firm faces a single buyer with an inverse demand curve given by $P = 1,000 - Q$ and its marginal cost is $MC = 200$. If the firm uses a two-part tariff to achieve the same profit as perfect price discrimination, what will be its access price and the per unit price?

5. Why does a two-part tariff cause customers who purchase few units to pay more *per unit* than customers who buy more units?

6. A monopolist selling in two markets faces the demand curves $P_1 = 164 - 2q_1$ and $P_2 = 108 - 5q_2$ in the two markets. Her marginal cost function is $MC = 8$. She has no fixed costs. If the monopolist can charge different prices in the two markets, what prices will she charge in the two markets?

7. A discriminating monopolist sells in two markets with elasticities equal to 4 and 2 at the optimum. The prices charged will be in the ratio _____.

11 Theories of Oligopolistic Competition

In a perfectly competitive market, each firm can sell as much as it wants to at the ruling market price. It believes that it cannot affect this price and since it can sell as much as it wants to at this price, it is not bothered about what other firms in the market are doing. The monopolist, on the other hand, faces no close substitutes for its products. Except when sunk costs of entry are low and threat of potential entry is high, it also does not take into account what other firms are doing.

In most markets, firms have to take into account the actual and potential responses from rival firms. We call these oligopolistic markets. An oligopoly is characterized by the presence of 'few' sellers in the market. The word 'few' does not refer to any number or range of numbers. We say that there are few firms in the industry if each firm must take explicitly into account reactions from rival firms.

Example 11.1: Consider the Mopeds segment of the auto industry and the market shares of some of the major firms in India. These firms have to anticipate closely each others' actions in formulating their strategies.

Mopeds segment: Market shares

Market Shares	2001	2002	2003	2004	2005
TVS Motor Co.	38.98	46.2	48.75	57.44	59.13
Kinetic Engg.	25.03	36.81	31.54	34.17	32.28
Majestic Auto	16.01	16.98	19.59	6.97	7.25

Source: CMIE.

Since firms can react in many ways and since in anticipating reactions, the beliefs, perceptions and calculations become important, there is no single theory of oligopoly. We can, however, present a series of models that capture some of the main issues in the theory of oligopolistic behaviour.

11.1 Nash Equilibrium

The basic concept of equilibrium employed in oligopolistic models is that of *Nash equilibrium*. Since oligopoly involves strategic interactions, it is helpful to present such models in game-theoretic frameworks, as game theory has been specifically developed to analyse situations in which 'players' or agents interact strategically.

Games can be represented either in normal form or extensive form. We start with normal form games. A *normal form game* consists of n players, indexed by $i = 1, 2, \ldots n$, their strategies s_i, and their payoffs π_i. The payoff to each player will, in general, depend on the set of strategies chosen by all the players: $\pi_i = \pi_i (s_1, s_2, \ldots s_n)$. Each player is free to choose strategies from some set S_i. Such a strategy might refer to the price level chosen by the firm or the quantity produced, or advertising expenditure, etc. Players choose their strategies *simultaneously* and the game is played only once. Players are 'rational' in the sense that their choices of strategies are dictated only by the payoffs consequent upon such choices..

For any vector $y = (y_1, y_2, \ldots y_n)$, denote by y_{-1} the vector $(y_1, y_2, \ldots y_{i-1}, y_{i+1} \ldots y_n)$, which is the vector excluding the i-th player.

Definition: A Nash equilibrium is a strategy vector $s^* = (s_1^*, s_2^*, \ldots s_n^*)$, such that

$$\pi_i (s_i^*, s_{-i}^*) \geq \pi_i (s_i, s_{-i}^*), \text{ for all } i \text{ and for all } s_i.$$

This definition simply means that a set of strategies forms a Nash equilibrium if deviation by any one player from the set fails to improve the payoff for that player. In other words, the strategy s_i^* maximizes the payoff for player i, given that all other players are also choosing strategies from the Nash equilibrium set of strategies. In a Nash equilibrium, the strategies are *optimal against each other*.

We can note two points about this definition. First, players have the option of randomly choosing their strategies, that is, playing a strategy not for sure, but with some given probability. We abstract from such *mixed strategies* and confine our discussion to *pure strategies*, that is, strategies that are played for sure. Second, the Nash equilibrium is a very weak concept of equilibrium. It is easier to understand it from a negative viewpoint; if a player's strategy is not the best she can play given the choices of other players, the situation cannot be stable. She will have an incentive to choose some other strategy.

Example 11.2: Consider the Battle of the Sexes game. A husband and a wife are planning to spend the evening together. They can either go shopping or stay at home, watching TV. Spending the evening together is preferable for each to doing things separately. However, the players have somewhat different preferences. The husband would rather stay at home while the wife would rather go shopping. The payoffs are given below (the first number in each cell conventionally refers to the 'row' player's payoff).

		Wife	
		Go Shopping	Watch TV
Husband	Go Shopping	(1, 2)	(0, 0)
	Watch TV	(0, 0)	(2, 1)

There are two Nash equilibria in this game: (go shopping, go shopping) and (watch TV, watch TV). If the wife wants to go shopping, the husband's best strategy is to choose to go shopping and get a payoff of 1, rather than watch TV alone and get a payoff of 0. If the husband wants to go shopping, it is also the best strategy for the wife. Similarly for the other Nash equilibrium.

Since there are two Nash equilibria, this raises the question which equilibrium do we expect to observe in practice? Game theorists have tried to strengthen the concept of Nash equilibrium to rule out some strategies and try to get a unique equilibrium.

Example 11.3: We can also have games in which there exists no Nash equilibrium at all. An example is given below. Munna and Munni are playing a game. If Munna hides upstairs and Munni searches there, he gets 0 and Munni gets 1. If Munna hides upstairs and Munni searches downstairs, Munna gets 1 and Munni gets 0. And so on.

		Munni	
		Upstairs	Downstairs
Munna	Upstairs	(1, 0)	(0, 1)
	Downstairs	(0, 1)	(1, 0)

It can be easily checked that there is no Nash equilibrium in pure strategies in this game.

Example 11.4: To sharpen our idea of Nash equilibrium, we can consider a game where each of two firms A and B has three advertising strategies—low, medium, and high budgets. The payoffs are in Rs crores per year:[1]

		B		
		Low budget	Medium budget	High budget
A	Low budget	(60, 45)	(55, 50)	(45, 35)
	Medium budget	(50, 35)	(65, 30)	(30, 25)
	High budget	(45, 10)	(60, 20)	(50, 40)

For A's choices of low, medium, and high budget, the optimal strategies for B are medium, low, and high budget respectively. For B's choice of low, medium, and high budget, the optimal strategies for B are low, medium, and high budget respectively. One can easily check that the only Nash equilibrium in this game is the pair (high, high). Both players could have done better if both had chosen 'low'. But this is not a Nash equilibrium: for example, when A chooses 'low', B's best choice is not 'low', but 'medium', which means that B has an incentive to deviate from (low, low).

Firms can use many instruments to compete in the marketplace. These can be roughly classified according to the speed at which they can be altered.

Short Term	Medium Term	Long Term
Price	Technology	Research & Development
	Capacity	
	Product Characteristics	

We begin with price competition and then consider models of quantity competition.

11.2 Bertrand Competition in Prices

The Bertrand model focuses on price competition, that is, situations where firms try to gain market shares by undercutting each others' prices. In the basic model, the surprising result that emerges is that even with a few firms in the market price competition can lead to a duplication of perfectly competitive results.

[1] This example is taken from C.R. Thomas and S.C. Maurice, *Managerial Economics*, 8th edition, Tata McGraw-Hill.

Suppose that there are only two firms in the industry (so that the industry is a 'duopoly') that produce an identical commodity at a constant per unit cost of c. There is no fixed cost. Then $AC = MC = c$. The industry demand function is $q = D(p)$. The firms are denoted by subscripts 1 and 2.

The profit of the i-th firm is $\pi_i(p_i, p_j) = (p_i - c)D_i(p_i, p_j)$, where

$$D_i(p_i, p_j) = \begin{cases} D(p_i) & \text{if } p_i < p_j \\ \frac{1}{2} D(p_i) & \text{if } p_i = p_j \qquad i \neq j, i, j = 1, 2. \\ 0 & \text{if } p_i > p_j \end{cases}$$

In other words, the firm charging the lower price captures the entire market. If both firms charge the same price, then the market is divided up equally between the two firms.

We now investigate the properties of the Nash equilibrium in prices. A Nash equilibrium is a pair of prices (p_i^*, p_j^*) such that

$$\pi_i(p_i^*, p_j^*) \geq \pi_i(p_i, p_j^*), \qquad i \neq j, i, j = 1, 2.$$

The Bertrand Paradox states that in equilibrium, firms will charge equal, competitive prices, and therefore make zero profits:

$$p_1^* = p_2^* = c.$$

It is quite easy to understand the proof of this result. The proof consists in showing that neither unequal prices nor prices that are equal, but not equal to c can form a Nash equilibrium. In either case, at least one of the firms will have an incentive to change its price, more specifically, to undercut the other. Moreover, if the prices are equal to each other and to c, such a pair *will* form a Nash equilibrium.

Consider the situation where $p_1^* > p_2^* > c$. Then firm 1 makes zero profit. But it can do better by charging a price $p_2^* - \varepsilon$, where $p_2^* - \varepsilon > c$. It then captures the entire market and makes a positive profit $(p_2^* - \varepsilon - c)D(p_2^* - \varepsilon)$.

If $p_1^* = p_2^* > c$, then firm 1 (say) is making a profit $(p_1^* - c)D(p_1^*)/2$. Can it do better than this? If it charges a slightly lower price $p_1^* - \varepsilon$, such that $p_1^* - \varepsilon > c$, it captures the entire market and makes a profit $(p_1^* - \varepsilon - c) D(p_1^* - \varepsilon)$. This will be higher than before because for small ε, the fall in profit margin is negligible, but the firm more than doubles its volume.

If $p_1^* > p_2^* = c$, then firm 2 is making zero profit, even though it serves the entire market. By charging a price $p_1^* - \varepsilon$, such that $p_1^* - \varepsilon > c$, it can still have the entire market, but make higher profit.

In all these three cases, it is in the interest of either one or both firms to charge a different set of prices. Now consider what happens when the prices are equal to each other and also to c. If a firm charges a lower price, it will capture the entire market. But its price will not cover cost and it will make a loss, which will be worse than the zero profit it was earning earlier. If it charges a higher price, it cannot sell anything and makes zero profit. Therefore a pair of prices that are equal to one another and to the constant MC, constitute a Nash equilibrium. The Nash equilibrium in prices mimics the perfectly competitive outcome, even though there are only two firms in the industry.

In 1997, SAIL (Steel Authority of India Limited) resorted to heavy discounted sales of its products, forcing other steel makers to sell their products at a loss. In 1998, RINL (Rashtriya Ispat Nigam Ltd.) started offering large discounts on 'long' products, trying to get rid of its year-old stock. The market leaders like SAIL and TISCO were planning to raise their prices taking advantage of the higher import duty announced in the budget and a depreciation of the rupee. The price cuts by RINL forced these firms to hold back on price hikes in the high value long products and concentrate on price increases in the flat products category.

What happens if one firm is more efficient than another? Suppose that $c_1 > c_2$. Then firm 2 can exploit its cost advantage by charging a price of $c_1 - \varepsilon$, thus preventing firm 1 from being able to operate at a profit, and at the same time making a positive profit itself.

While the Bertrand Paradox highlights the competition engendered through price-cutting, it seems to be an extreme result. Even when firms compete via prices, they make profits. There are various ways of resolving the Bertrand Paradox and we discuss them briefly next.

1. The Edgeworth solution. Edgeworth pointed out that the introduction of a capacity constraint can solve the Bertrand Paradox. Suppose that firm 1 has a productive capacity K such that $D(c) > K$. That is, even if the firm prices at marginal cost, it cannot meet the entire market demand. Then $p^*_1 = p^*_2 = c$ cannot be an equilibrium. At $p^*_1 = p^*_2 = c$, both firms make zero profit. Suppose that firm 2 raises its price slightly. Then all customers try to buy from firm 1, but it cannot meet the entire demand because of the capacity constraint. Then some customers are forced to buy from firm 2 which makes a positive profit. Therefore (p^*_1, p^*_2) such that $p^*_1 = p^*_2 = c$ is no longer a Nash equilibrium in prices.

2. The temporal dimension. In the Bertrand model, firms move simultaneously, and they make a move only once. In real life, firms interact repeatedly. If a firm tries to undercut another's price, it can get locked in a price war and suffer losses. A firm must weigh the short-term gains from price-cutting with the long-term losses from a continued price war before it takes the decision to cut its price.

3. Product differentiation. It will be shown in the next chapter that if products are not identical, then a Nash equilibrium in prices may involve firms charging different prices and making positive profits.

11.3 Cournot Competition in Quantities

Consider now a duopoly where firms choose quantities rather than prices. Given the quantity choices q_1 and q_2, the market price adjusts to the level $p(q_1 + q_2)$ that clears the market; $p(q_1 + q_2)$ is the inverse demand function. We assume that $p'(q)$ (that is, dp/dq) < 0 at all $q \geq 0$.

The Cournot-Nash equilibrium for this model consists of a pair of quantity choices (q^*_1, q^*_2) such that

$$\pi_i(q^*_i, q^*_j) \geq \pi_i(q_i, q^*_j),\ i \neq j,\ i, j = 1, 2.$$

We can solve for the equilibrium quantities by looking at the best response functions or the 'reaction functions' of the two firms. Firm 1's reaction function shows the quantities that firm 1 should produce to maximize its profit, for any level of output produced by firm 2. It can be obtained from the equation $\partial p_1/\partial q_1 = 0$, which yields the best output of firm 1 as a function of firm 2's output: $q_1 = R_1(q_2)$. Similarly, we can use the equation $\partial p_2/\partial q_2 = 0$ to get the reaction function for firm 2, $q_2 = R_2(q_1)$.

The Cournot-Nash equilibrium quantities are obtained by solving the two reaction functions together (why?). Graphically, the Cournot-Nash equilibrium is represented by the point of intersection of the reaction curves. Of course, further assumptions are needed to ensure that at least one Cournot-Nash equilibrium exists. Fig. 11.1 shows a situation where more than one Cournot-Nash equilibrium exist.

It will be instructive to analyse the Cournot-Nash equilibrium for the case where both demand and cost functions are linear. Suppose that the inverse demand function is

$$p = a - (q_1 + q_2),$$

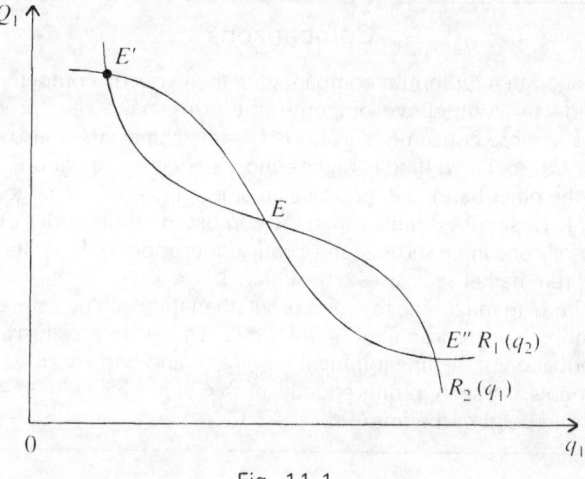

Fig. 11.1

the cost functions are $C_i = cq_i$, $i = 1, 2$, and $a > c$. Then $p_i = [a - (q_1 + q_2) - c]q_i$, $i = 1, 2$.

The reaction function for firm 1 is obtained from $\partial p_1 / \partial q_1 = 0$. This yields $a - c - 2q_1 - q_2 = 0$, or $q_1 = (a - c - q_2)/2 = R_1(q_2)$. Similarly, $q_2 = (a - c - q_1)/2 = R_2(q_1)$.

These two reaction functions are downward sloping straight lines. The point of intersection is the quantity pair that constitutes the Cournot-Nash equilibrium.

In equilibrium, $q^*_1 = R_1(q^*_2)$ and $q^*_2 = R_2(q^*_1)$. Solving, we get

$$q^*_1 = q^*_2 = (a - c)/3.$$

The market-clearing price is $p^* = a - (q^*_1 + q^*_2) = (a + 2c)/3$ and each firm earns a profit $p_i(q^*_1, q^*_2) = (a - c)^2/9$. It is also easy to calculate the consumer surplus. The total quantity produced is $2(a - c)/3$ and the price charged is $(a + 2c)/3$. The consumer surplus is just the area of the triangle bounded by the inverse demand curve and the price line $p = (a + 2c)/3$, and it is $2(a - c)^2/9$. Then consumer surplus plus producer surplus is $4(a - c)^2/9$.

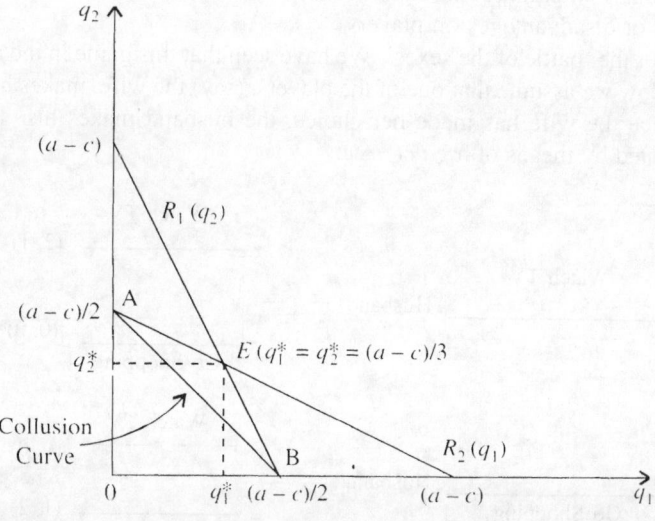

Fig. 11.2

Comparisons

How does the Cournot-Nash equilibrium compare with the perfectly competitive and the monopoly outcomes? In the perfectly competitive outcome, the firms make zero profits. Price is equal to the marginal cost c. Therefore consumer surplus is $(a - c)^2/2$ and this is also the measure of social welfare. Since $1/2 > 4/9$, social welfare is higher under perfect competition.

A monopolist, on the other hand, will produce an amount $(a - c)/2$, charge a price $(a + c)/2$, and make a profit $(a - c)^2/4$. This profit is higher than the combined profits under Cournot duopoly, since $1/4 > 2/9$. The sum of consumer surplus and profit under monopoly is $3(a - c)^2/8$, which is the smallest among the three market structures (check that $3/8 < 4/9$).

If the two firms collude to maximize the joint profit, then they will be acting like a monopoly. We have seen that a monopolist will produce $Q = (a - c)/2$. That is, in a collusive outcome $q_1 + q_2 = (a - c)/2$. This is the equation of the line joining the points A and B in Fig. 11.2. If the two firms agree to produce equal amounts and share profits equally, each will produce $q = (a - c)/4$ and the collusive outcome will be the mid-point of the line AB.

If there are n identical firms, $n > 1$, then the reaction function for firm i will be

$$(a - c) - [2q_i + \Sigma q_{-i}] = 0,$$

where q_{-i} refers to outputs of all firms other than the i-th firm. Since the firms are identical, we can consider the symmetric Cournot-Nash equilibrium in which all outputs are equal to q^*. Substituting in the expression for the reaction function, and solving, we get $q^* = (a - c)/(n + 1)$, and $p^* = a - nq^* = (a + nc)/(n + 1)$. As n becomes large, it is obvious that the output of each firm becomes negligible, and the industry output nq^* approaches $(a - c)$, the competitive level of output. Also, p^* tends to c, the marginal cost. Hence the Cournot-Nash equilibrium tends to the perfectly competitive equilibrium as the number of firms tends to infinity.

11.4 Extensive Games and Subgame Perfect Equilibrium

Until now, we have restricted our attention to games in which all players make their moves simultaneously. However, in many situations, choices are made *sequentially* and this sequencing of choices can confer advantages or disadvantages on players.

Let us again consider the 'battle of the sexes'. We have seen that this game in the normal form has two Nash equilibria. Now we assume that one of the players, (say) the wife, makes her choice before the husband does. Once the wife has made her choice, the husband makes his. The sequence of moves can be represented by means of a *game tree*:

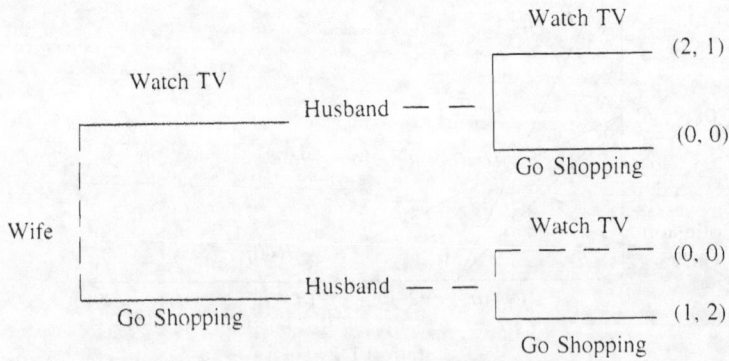

A 'node' in the game tree is a point at which a player chooses a strategy. A 'branch' stands for a particular choice by a player. Once a player makes a choice, the players are in a 'sub-game' consisting of the strategies and payoffs available to them from that point on. Thus if the wife chooses to watch TV, there is a subgame in which the husband can choose to watch TV or go shopping, and the associated payoffs are determined by the husband's choice conditional on the wife's choice. There are three subgames in this example: (a) the entire game, (b) the subgame when the wife chooses to watch TV, and (c) the subgame when the wife chooses to go shopping.

We now strengthen the requirement of equilibrium: a combination of strategies must be a Nash equilibrium not only for the entire game, but also in each of the subgames. Such a combination of strategies is called a *subgame-perfect equilibrium.*

In the original normal form game, one Nash equilibrium consisted of both players watching TV. Is this also a subgame-perfect equilibrium? Suppose that the husband threatens to 'always watch TV'. If the wife takes this threat seriously, she should choose to watch TV and get a payoff of 1. If she chooses to go shopping and he watches TV, her payoff will be 0.

But is this a *credible threat*? If the wife does go shopping, it is in the husband's best interest not to watch TV and get 0, but go shopping and get 1. The wife will realize this and call the husband's bluff. The husband being a rational player who always takes decisions on the basis of the payoffs, will follow suit. Why? Because in the subgame following the wife's decision to go shopping, the best strategy for him is to go shopping and get 1, rather than carry out the threat and get 0. Therefore the only subgame perfect equilibrium consists of both players choosing to go shopping.

In the simple game considered here, it is easy to work out the subgame-perfect equilibrium by *backward induction.* Start with the last stage of the game and find out the husband's optimal choices in each subgame. The optimal choice for him is watching TV if wife watches TV and going shopping if wife goes shopping. The associated payoffs are (1, 2) and (2, 1). The wife then compares her payoffs from these two choices and decides to go shopping because then her payoff is 2 rather than 1.

The logic is that the first mover can anticipate the optimal strategies of the other player contingent on her own strategy. If the wife goes shopping, the husband's optimal strategy is to go shopping. The payoffs will then be 2 for the wife and 1 for the husband. If the wife watches TV, the husband's optimal strategy is to watch TV. In this case, the payoffs will then be 1 for the wife and 2 for the husband. The wife can then predict what her payoffs will be for each of her decisions and therefore take the best decision for herself.

In the subgame-perfect equilibrium, the wife is better off because both players go shopping and her payoff is 2. You should be able to figure out quickly that this happens because the wife is a first-mover in this game; in other words, she enjoys a *first-mover advantage.* If, instead, the husband had moved first, the subgame-perfect equilibrium would be one in which both players watch TV and the husband gets 2.

We next turn to a couple of models in which choices are made by firms sequentially and the concept of subgame-perfect equilibrium must be employed.

11.5a The Stackelberg Leader-follower Model

In the Stackelberg model, one firm (the 'leader') gets to choose the quantity first and then the other firm (the 'follower') selects the level of its output. The leader then enjoys a *first-mover advantage* in that it can anticipate the actions of the follower and make its optimal choice accordingly.

The subgame-perfect equilibrium is obtained by solving the problem backwards. We again consider the linear demand and cost function case. Let firm 2 be the follower. First, we derive firm 2's reaction function which is $q_2 = (a - c - q_1)/2$. Firm 1 realizes that for any q_1 it selects, firm 2's output will be chosen from the reaction function and the profit for the associated quantities will be realized. Therefore, firm 1 maximizes its profit given the constraint $q_2 = (a - c - q_1)/2$. Given this constraint,

$$\pi_1 = [a - (q_1 + q_2) - c]q_1 = \tfrac{1}{2}(a - c - q_1)q_1.$$

The first order condition $dp_1/dq_1 = 0$ yields $q_1^S = (a - c)/2$ and $q_2^S = (a - c)/4$. The leader now produces more than the follower, unlike in the Cournot model, where both produced the same quantity in equilibrium. Next calculate the profits:

$$\pi_1 = (a - c)^2/8, \text{ while } p_2 = (a - c)^2/16.$$

The leader's profit is higher than the profit earned in the Cournot model and also higher than the follower's. The follower is worse off than in the Cournot model.

The Stackelberg solution can be derived in the following way. The reaction function of the follower is the constraint facing the leader. Given this constraint, the leader tries to maximize profit by finding out the highest *iso-profit curve* that just touches the constraint. The iso-profit curves are the loci of those combinations of q_1 and q_2 for which the firm earns a constant amount of profit. Let $\pi_1 = [a - (q_1 + q_2) - c]q_1 = K$, a constant. Setting, $d\pi_1 = 0$, we can solve for the equation of the slope of an iso-profit curve: $dq_2/dq_1 = (a - c - 2q_1 - q_2)/q_1$. The slope of the reaction function for firm 2 is $-(\tfrac{1}{2})$. Setting $(a - c - 2q_1 - q_2)/q_1 = -\tfrac{1}{2}$ and employing the equation of the reaction function for firm 2, we find again that $q_1^S = (a - c)/2$ and $q_2^S = (a - c)/4$.

Diagrammatically, the Cournot-Nash solution is obtained at the intersection of the two reaction functions. But in the Stackelberg model, we have seen that the leader takes as given the follower's reaction function, and chooses to produce at the point where one of its iso-profit curves is tangential to the reaction function of the follower.

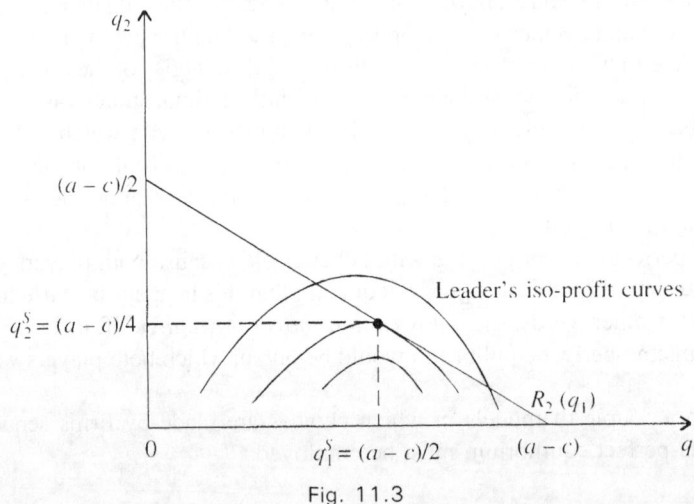

Fig. 11.3

11.5b Dominant Firm with a Competitive Fringe

While it is difficult to find pure monopolies, examples of 'dominant' firms are easy to come across. In India, for a long time, Indian Airlines was the dominant airlines serving domestic routes, with 85–90 per cent of the market share. In the car market, Maruti Udyog Ltd. had a market share between 75 per cent and 80 per cent. Pricing decisions of such dominant firms often seem to be accepted and closely followed by other firms in the market. For example, when Indian Airlines used to increase its fares, the smaller firms seemed to immediately follow suit.

We now consider a model where there is a dominant firm in the market, as well as a competitive 'fringe', that is, a number of small firms that act like price-takers, accepting the price set by the dominant firm as the market price. In this model, we again have a leader-follower type of situation. The dominant firm sets its price, fully anticipating the response from the fringe firms. While the dominant firm obviously is in a better position than the fringe firms, the existence of the fringe firms sets checks on its exercise of monopoly power.

11.5b.1 No Entry

First, let us analyse the case where there is a fixed number n of identical fringe firms. Their supply curve is just the sum of the marginal cost curves. Let this be denoted by $S(p) = nq_f$. The demand curve facing the industry is $D(p)$. Then $D(p) - S(p)$ is the *residual demand curve* faced by the dominant firm. The latter sets a price; fringe firms meet a certain part of market demand given this price, and the dominant firm supplies the rest.

The situation is depicted below. The residual demand curve in the right hand side is derived by horizontally subtracting $S(p)$ from the $D(p)$ curve. Note that this is a kinked curve. If the market price is set below p', the fringe firms do not supply anything and the residual demand curve becomes the market demand curve. The MR curve has two segments, each related to the corresponding segment of the residual demand curve. The dominant firm equates MR with MC, and sets the price p^*. At this price, the fringe firms supply an amount Q_f^* while the dominant firm supplies Q_d^*.

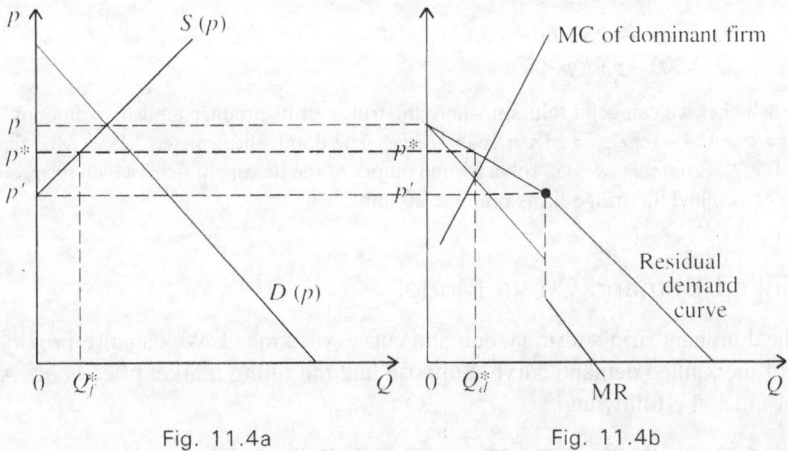

Fig. 11.4a   Fig. 11.4b

Several things can be noted here. First, unless the dominant firm enjoys a significant cost advantage over the fringe firms (its MC curve is much lower than the $S(p)$ curve), it loses some of its market share to the fringe firms. Second, it has to choose a lower price than a pure monopoly. Third, if the dominat firm cuts its price, it is reflected throughout the industry.

11.5b.2 Free Entry by Fringe Firms

Let us consider an extreme case where new fringe firms can instantaneously enter the industry. Therefore, the $S(p)$ curve is horizontal. Whenever profits are made by existing fringe firms, entry takes place until profits are driven down to zero. The residual demand curve facing the dominant firm has a horizontal segment and this sets a ceiling on the price that the dominant firm can charge.

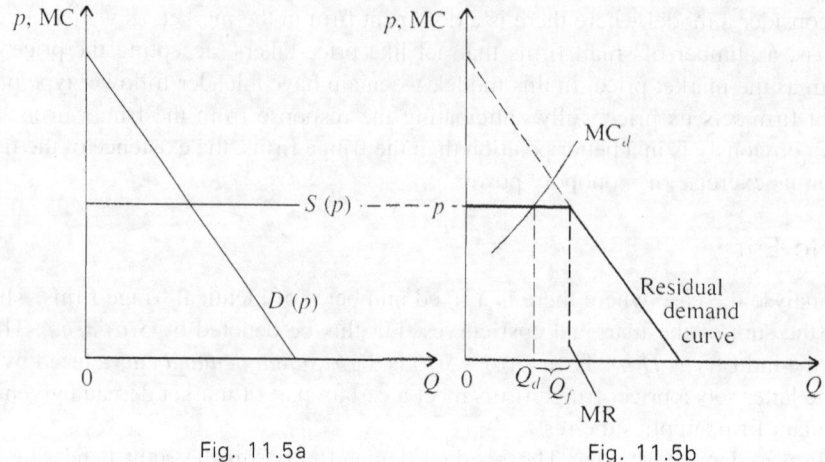

Fig. 11.5a   Fig. 11.5b

Example 11.5: Let the equation of the market inverse demand curve be $p = 200 - Q_d - Q_f$, where Q_d is the amount produced by the dominant firm and Q_f is the amount produced by the fringe firms. The equation of the MC curve for the dominant firm is $MC = 20 + 0.2Q_d$. The fringe supply curve is given by $p = 20 + 4Q_f$. Then $Q_f = (p - 20)/4 \geq 0$ for $p \geq 20$.

The equation of the residual demand curve facing the dominant firm is

$$Q_d = 200 - p - Q_f = 200 - p - (p - 20)/4$$

$$= \begin{cases} 205 - 1.25p & \text{for } p \geq 20 \\ 200 - p & \text{for } p < 20. \end{cases}$$

Let us see whether we can get a solution where the fringe firms produce a positive amount. Then $Q_d = 205 - 1.25p \Rightarrow p = 164 - 0.8Q_d \Rightarrow MR = 164 - 1.6Q_d$. The dominant firm sets MR = MC, that is, $164 - 1.6Q_d = 20 + 0.2Q_d$. From this, we can solve for the output of the dominant firm, which turns out to be 80. It sets a price of 100 and the fringe firms produce 20 units.

11.5b.3 Kinked Demand Curve Model

We saw that the dominant firm's residual demand curve was kinked. We can also provide a different interpretation of the kinked demand curve. Suppose that the ruling market price is p^*. A firm in the market then assumes the following:

1. If it raises its price above p^*, other firms in the market will not change their prices, and hence it will lose a lot of customers. Thus, for prices above p^*, its demand curve will be quite elastic.
2. On the other hand, if it lowers its price below p^*, other firms will do the same as a defensive measure. Hence it will not be able to get many more customers through price cuts. The demand curve below p^* will be rather inelastic.

Given a kinked demand curve, the MR curve facing the firm will have two segments, with a vertical segment in between. If the firm's MR curve is cut by the MC curve in this vertical segment, then the firm charges p^* to its customers. Moreover, even if the cost conditions change and the MC curve shifts a bit, it is possible that the same price will be charged. So this model seems to explain why observed prices remain sticky even under changing cost conditions. Obviously, a major shortcoming of this model is that it leaves unexplained how p^* was determined in the first place.

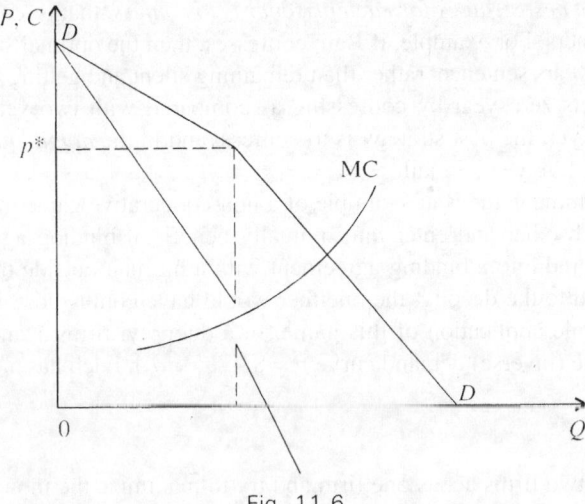

Fig. 11.6

11.6 Collusion versus Cheating

In this section and the next, we try to see how firms can try to actively change the environment in their own favour. First, we explore the question of collusion. Next, we will discuss strategic moves by firms.

In any market, monopoly profits represent the highest aggregate profits attainable. If more than one firm compete in the market, their output will be higher than monopoly output and their joint profit is bound to fall short of the monopoly profit. It then makes sense for the firms to enter a collusive agreement and restrict aggregate output to the monopoly level to earn monopoly profits, which can then be shared appropriately amongst themselves. One would then expect to come across many instances of collusion (cooperative behaviour). However, collusion is usually very difficult to sustain. The classic case of collusion is the OPEC oil price cartel. This cartel had some initial successes in raising oil prices by enforcing production quotas amongst member countries, but in recent years has been relatively ineffective.

A normal form game, called the 'Prisoners' Dilemma Game', can be used to throw light on the difficulty of sustaining cooperation or collusion. Ram and Rahim have been caught while trying to burgle a flat. The OC of the thana in which they are jailed knows that they had earlier been involved in a train dacoity, but has no proof of this. The OC has the two prisoners put in separate cells. He visits them in turn and says to each: 'If you confess to the dacoity, but the other doesn't, then you will get no jail sentence, while the other prisoner will be jailed for 10 years. If neither confesses, then we can only jail you for burglary, and each will get a sentence of 2 years. If both confess, then each will be jailed for 5 years.'

The payoff matrix, as the prisoners see it, will appear as follows:

		Ram	
		Confess	Not confess
Rahim	Confess	(5, 5)	(0, 10)
	Not Confess	(10, 0)	(2, 2)

The aim of each prisoner is to minimize the number of years spent in jail. Obviously, if both keep quiet, they each spend only 2 years in jail. However, it can be checked that *regardless of what the other prisoner does, the best strategy for each prisoner is to confess,* that is, confessing is a *dominant strategy* for both prisoners. For example, if Ram confesses, then the optimal strategy for Rahim is to confess and get a five years sentence, rather than remaining silent and getting ten years. If Ram does not confess, Rahim gets zero year by confessing as compared with two years by not confessing. Therefore, for each player, the best strategy is to confess, and in the *dominant strategy equilibrium,* each ends up spending five years in jail.

The Prisoners' Dilemma game is an example of a non-cooperative game in which players cannot communicate with each other and enter into mutually beneficial binding agreements. If Ram and Rahim could have entered into a binding agreement with a hit man outside the jail to eliminate the prisoner who confessed to the dacoity, then neither would have confessed.

Consider an economic application of this game. In a duopoly, firms 1 and 2 produce the same commodity and face the (inverse) demand curve $p = 8 - (q_1 + q_2)$. Each has a cost function given by $C_i = 4q_i$.

1. Monopoly

   In a monopoly, the two firms act as one firm and try to maximize the monopoly profit $\pi_m = pq - cq = (8 - q)q - 4q = 4q - 2q^2$. The monopoly output then should be $q = 2$ and $p =$ Rs 6. Total profit is 4. Since the firms are duplicates of each other, it makes sense to assume that they will agree to produce half the monopoly output each and earn half the profit, that is, 2. Each agrees to charge a price of Rs 6 in the market.

2. Suppose firm 1 charges 6 in the market, as per the agreement. If firm 2 charges 5, it can grab all the customers. Since $q_1 = 0$, $q_2 = 8 - 5$. Firm 1's profit is 0, while firm 2's profit is $5 \times 3 - 4 \times 3 = 3$.

3. If firm 2 keeps to the agreement and firm 1 cheats, by a similar argument 2 earns 0 while 1 earns 3.

4. If both firms break the agreement and charge 5, total output has to be 3. Again, assuming that each firm gets half the customers at this price, each produces 1.5 units and earns profit of $5 \times 0.15 - 4 \times 1.5 = 1.5$.

These payoffs are summarized in the payoff matrix below:

		Firm 2	
		Charge Rs 6 (cooperate)	Charge Rs 5 (cheat)
Firm 1	Charge Rs 6	(2, 2)	(0, 3)
	Charge Rs 5	(3, 0)	(1.5, 1.5)

It is clear that for both firms cheating is the dominant strategy and the proposed cartel breaks down. Each firm charges Rs 5 and earns a profit of 1.5. Both would have been better off if both had charged the high price. This is of course a happy situation from the point of view of customers who end up paying a lower price. The market output (3) is also higher than the monopoly outcome (2). The dominant strategy equilibrium is not Pareto optimal, since both firms could have earned more if they had not cheated.

The 'cheat, cheat' outcome occurs because each firm has to guard against opportunistic behaviour by the other. One cannot trust the other. If A tries to be 'nice' and charge a high price, B will always find it advantageous to cheat and vice-versa. However, both firms are fully aware of the payoffs involved and of the virtues of cooperation. But they do not have any way of entering into an agreement that will be respected by both parties.

This can also be shown in the following way. Suppose that there are two firms in the industry with cost functions $C_i(q_i)$, $i = 1, 2$. They face an inverse demand curve $p(q_1 + q_2)$, where $p' < 0$. If they want to maximize joint profits, then their problem is

$$\max_{q_1, q_2} p(q_1 + q_2)(q_1 + q_2) - C_1(q_1) - C_2(q_2),$$

and the first order conditions yield

$$p(q_1^* + q_2^*) + p'(q_1^* + q_2^*)(q_1^* + q_2^*) = C_i'(q_i^*), \; i = 1, 2.$$

Note that these two conditions imply that $C_1'(q_1^*) = C_2'(q_2^*)$, so that the two firms work together as a multi-plant monopolist.

In this situation, if one firm sticks to the agreed-upon output, then there is always an incentive for the other firm to cheat, that is, produce a little bit more. Suppose that firm 1 believes that firm 2 will produce q_2^*. Then it examines $dp_1(q_1^*, q_2^*)/dq_1$.

$$\begin{aligned} d\pi_1(q_1^*, q_2^*)/dq_1 &= p'(q_1^* + q_2^*)q_1^* + p(q_1^* + q_2^*) - C_1'(q_1^*) \\ &= -p'(q_1^* + q_2^*)q_2^* \text{ by the first order condition (since we are considering} \\ &\quad \text{the effect at the joint-profit-maximizing point)} \\ &> 0. \end{aligned}$$

A small increase in output from the agreed-upon level, given that firm 2 does not deviate from its quota, improves firm 1's profit.

11.6.1 Achieving Cooperation

Can cooperation then emerge in a world where everyone is trying to do the best for herself (pursuing a self-interest standard of rationality)? The players who get locked in a prisoners' dilemma type situation will want to escape and achieve the joint-payoff-maximizing outcome. Others may like to see them remain trapped in the dilemma (for example, the consumers in the duopoly situation). Whatever be the point of view, we want to understand the ways in which prisoners' dilemma can be averted. Then we can try to facilitate or block these ways, depending on our preferences.

The central questions are:

- Can an agreement be reached?
- How can cheating be detected ?
- What prospect of punishment will deter cheating?

Reaching an agreement may not be a simple matter. In brief, the more *heterogeneous* the industry and larger the number of firms, the more difficult is it to reach an agreement. If, for example, cost conditions differ and product differentiation exists to a significant degree, different firms will have different expectations and it will not be easy to reach an agreement. Also, the *larger the number of items* on which firms have to agree, the greater the hurdles in the way of concluding successful negotiations. If conditions in the market are *uncertain*, agreements must be reached more often, thereby increasing negotiation costs. In addition, divergence of opinion about future conditions becomes likely.

Detection of cheating can be difficult because of the following reasons:

1. It may be difficult to disentangle random factors from deliberate cheating. For example, a fall in prices may be due either to cheating, that is, one agent producing more than the agreed upon quota, or simply to a fall in demand.

2. In real life, there are many dimensions of choice. Producers not only select prices, they also have to decide on product quality, services etc. It is often well-nigh impossible to reach an agreement on all these dimensions. Even if agreement can be reached, it adds to the difficulty of detecting cheating because cheating can take place in various ways. In fact, the chances are that collusion will focus on the more transparent dimensions of choice while competition shifts to the less observable ones.

3. Identifying the cheater may be even more difficult than detecting cheating when there are several players. In this case, punishment cannot be selective, but will affect the innocent and guilty alike.

Who punishes?

Another example of a Prisoners' Dilemma game comes from the world of advertising. Suppose that there are two firms who have the choices of either raising their ad spending or leave spending at the same level. The payoff matrix is given below, with the numbers representing profits in Rs crores:

		Firm 2	
		Leave spending the same (cooperate)	Raise ad spending (cheat)
Firm 1	Leave spending the same	(6, 6)	(2, 8)
	Raise ad spending	(8, 2)	(5.5, 5.5)

In this game, the dominant strategy for both firms is to increase ad spending. Hence they both increase spending and make lower profits, even though both would have made more by not changing the level of spending. If one firm refrains from increasing ad spending, what assures it that the other firm will not take advantage of the situation?

In the USA, tobacco manufacturers were spending heavily on advertising in the late 1960s. In 1970, the US Congress enacted a law which made it illegal to carry cigarette advertising on television. This might have led to a fall in the numbers of Americans who smoked, but it also had the unintended consequence of increasing the profits of cigarette manufacturers. The government in effect implemented and policed a set of strategies that benefited all the cigarette makers.

The willingness and ability to punish cheating have to be present. Moreover, the existence of a suitable punishment plan is vital. 'Punishment' in this context does not necessarily refer to physical punishment, though the Iraq-Kuwait war was an example of one. More generally, the possibility of punishment arises from the fact of repeated interactions between players. Thus consider the following hypothetical game.[2] Iraq and Iran have the choices of either restricting production to 2 million barrels of crude per day, or produce a larger amount of 4 million barrels per day.

		Iraq's Output (millions of barrels per day)	
		2	4
Iran's Output	2	(46, 42)	(26, 44)
	4	(52, 22)	(32, 24)

[2] This example is from Dixit and Nalebuff (1991). Check that the dominant strategy of each firm is to produce 4 million barrels per day.

The payoffs can be interpreted as profits per day in millions of dollars. Suppose Iran cheats for a day successfully, while Iraq stays honest, Iran gains US$ 6 million. When Iraq finds out Iran has cheated, the mutual trust breaks down. The two settle down to a regime of high outputs. Relative to cooperation, Iran now loses US$ 14 million a day. Even if it takes Iraq a while to detect the cheating, Iran loses in the long run. For example, if it takes Iraq a month to detect the cheating, Iran's gain is US$ 180 million. Once cheating is detected, it takes only 13 days ($13 \times 14 = 182$) to wipe out Iran's gain from cheating. Punishment, in its broader sense, means a refusal to cooperate. The result of punishment is that the cheater forgoes the higher payoffs that accrue from cooperation.

11.6.2 Repeated Games

The Prisoners' Dilemma type of situation can therefore be avoided when players interact repeatedly, and have to balance the short-term gains with the long-term losses. The simplest way of introducing repeated interactions is to consider *repeated games*. Repeated games have the following features:

- The one-stage game is repeated again and again.
- Stationary environment—the past has no tangible effect on the present and the future.
- Any effect arises only because the players remember what has happened and condition their actions on that history.

However, a repeated game does not by itself generate cooperation. Suppose that the Prisoners' Dilemma game is repeated a *finite number of times* and each player knows exactly when the game will end. Selten has demonstrated that the only subgame-perfect equilibrium in this game is where each player cheats in every round of the game. Why? Consider the last or the n-th round. Everyone knows that the game will end after this round is played, so this is like a one-round Prisoners' Dilemma game, and both players will cheat. Next consider the last-but-one round, that is $(n-1)$th round. Since players will cheat in the last round regardless of what went on before, they will consider this round again independently of other rounds, and cheat. And so on.

So to induce cooperation, we require either that the game be played an infinite number of rounds or that players be uncertain about the exact date of termination of the game.

When repeated interaction is possible, the players have to compare the short-term gains from cheating with the possible long-term losses from cheating. These losses are generated by the possibility of detection of cheating and consequent non-cooperation by other players. Non-cooperation can take various forms. For example, in the Cournot Quantity-setting game, each firm might play its static Cournot output following any deviation.

One can characterize a player's decision in the following way. A player will refrain from cheating if

$$G < pLT/d$$

where G represents the gain from cheating, p the probability of being detected and punished, L the one period loss from cheating, T a multiple to capture the length of the punishment period and d the discount rate. Thus, there will be a tendency for players to cheat when (i) it is difficult to detect and punish cheating (p is low), (ii) the loss from punishment is small (L and/or T are small), (iii) the future is not important (d is large), and (iv) the gain from cheating is significant (G is high).

11.6.3 Choice of Punishment

What characteristics should punishments have to deter cheating? How severe should they be?

To take the second question first, one might think that the punishment should be as severe as possible. Then the mere threat of punishment will deter cheating and the punishment need never be employed at all. The problem with this line of thinking is that it ignores the possibility of mistakes. The detection process may fail, indicating cheating where there is none. If punishment is too big, such mistakes will be very costly.

An answer to the first question emerged from a computer tournament conducted by Robert Axelrod of University of Michigan, Ann Arbor. In 1979, Axelrod invited a number of professional game theorists to submit strategies to be used in a series of prisoners' dilemma games. He asked for strategies to be encoded as computer programmes that could respond to a 'C' (cooperate) or 'D' (defect, cheat) of another player, taking into account the remembered history of previous interactions with that same player. A programme should always reply with a 'C' or 'D', but its choice could be random. Fifteen strategies were entered, and each was made to play with every other programme and itself 200 times. The overall goal was to amass as many points as possible.

The programme that won is called TIT FOR TAT and its strategy is cooperate on move 1; thereafter, do whatever the other player did the previous move.

A second and larger tournament was held later. Altogether 62 entries were received, including TIT FOR TAT. The result of the tournament surprised everybody: TIT FOR TAT was again the winner.

How did TIT FOR TAT manage to win? One can use a mini-tournament to explore this question. Suppose that there are only two strategies: TIT FOR TAT and ALWAYS DEFECT. They play against themselves and each other 200 times. The payoff matrix is the following:

		Player B	
		C	D
Player A	C	(2, 2)	(0, 3)
	D	(3, 0)	(1.5, 1.5)

The results of head on collisions are as follows:

ALWAYS DEFECT vs ALWAYS DEFECT

	Strategies		Payoffs	
Move	A	B	A	B
1–200	D	D	1.5	1.5
Total			300	300

TIT FOR TAT vs ALWAYS DEFECT

	Strategies		Payoffs	
Move	A	B	A	B
1	C	D	0	3
2–200	D	D	1.5	1.5
Total			298.5	321.5

TIT FOR TAT vs TIT FOR TAT

	Strategies		Payoffs	
Move	A	B	A	B
1–200	C	C	2	2
Total			400	400

The total payoffs are then:
TIT FOR TAT: Rs 400 + Rs 298.5 = Rs 698.5
ALWAYS DEFECT: Rs 300 + Rs 321.5 = Rs 621.5

Thus TIT FOR TAT wins this mini-tournament, even though it *never wins* in head-to-head competition (it defects only after the other player defects). If there is any prospect that an opposing strategy permits some degree of cooperation, playing TIT FOR TAT will yield a higher payoff than ALWAYS DEFECT.

Axelrod argues that TIT FOR TAT embodies four principles that should be evident in any effective strategy: clarity, niceness, provocability and forgiveness. TIT FOR TAT is as clear and simple as it is possible to get. It is nice in that it never initiates cheating. It is provocable, that is, it never lets cheating go unpunished. On the other hand, it is forgiving, because it does not hold a grudge and is willing to restore cooperation.

Dixit and Nalebuff, however, argue in their book 'Thinking Strategically' that TIT FOR TAT is a flawed strategy because it does not allow for the possibility of misperceptions. The moment the player with the TIT FOR TAT strategy thinks that the opponent has cheated, he immediately switches to cheating, making no allowance for the possibility of a mistake being made. Moreover, it lacks a way of saying 'enough is enough', that is, it never initiates a move towards cooperation. One should be more forgiving when a defection seems to be a mistake rather than the rule. Even if the defection was intentional, after a long-enough period of punishments it may still be time to call it quits and try reestablishing cooperation.

11.7 Entry Deterrence

Economists have long been preoccupied with the question of entry in a market, since the ease of entry in a market plays a significant role in maintaining competitive conditions in the market. At one extreme, the contestable markets theory (discussed earlier), shows that the mere threat of entry can be a sufficient check on the exercise of market power by the existing firms in a market. On the other hand, economists also worry whether incumbent firms can prevent new firms from entering the market.

Bain distinguished between three types of situations with regard to the ease of entry in a market. These are:

1. Blockaded entry. The existing firms do not have to take any special actions to deter entry into the market. The 'primitive' conditions of demand, technology etc. are such as to prevent entry.
2. Ineffectively impeded entry (also referred to as accommodated entry). The existing firms find it more profitable to allow entry rather than try to prevent entry.
3. Effectively impeded entry. The existing firms find it more profitable to deter entry.

A simple model can be used to clarify the different types of entry situations. Suppose that there are two firms—the incumbent firm denoted by the subscript 1 and an entrant denoted by 2. The entrant will have to bear a fixed cost of entry F if it decides to enter the market. The incumbent first selects the output level q_1. The entrant then decides whether to enter or not, and also the output q_2 if it decides to enter. Firm 1 is therefore a Stackelberg quantity leader while firm 2 is a follower. The market demand curve is $P = a - q_1 - q_2$. Each firm has a cost function $C_i = cq_i$.

We know that the reaction function of the entrant is $q_2 = (a - c - q_1)/2$. At this output level, its profit will be $p_2 = [(a - c - q_1)/2]^2 - F^2$. If $F = 0$, then $p_2 = 0$ when $q_1 = (a - c)$. If $F > 0$, then $p_2 = 0$ when $q_1 = (a - c) - 2F$.

In Fig. 11.7, M_2Q_1 is firm 2's reaction curve. If firm 1 produces nothing, then firm 2 will produce the monopoly level of output and this is represented by the point M_2. Given this reaction curve, firm 1's Stackelberg leadership point is S_1, where a iso-profit curve for firm 1 is tangential to M_2Q_1. Z_1 is the point where this iso-profit line meets the q_1 axis. The point A_1 is of special interest to us. It is the point at which firm 2's profit becomes zero, so that for higher output levels by the leader, firm 2's profit is negative. It will not enter for $q_1 > B_1$, and the reaction curve to the right of this point

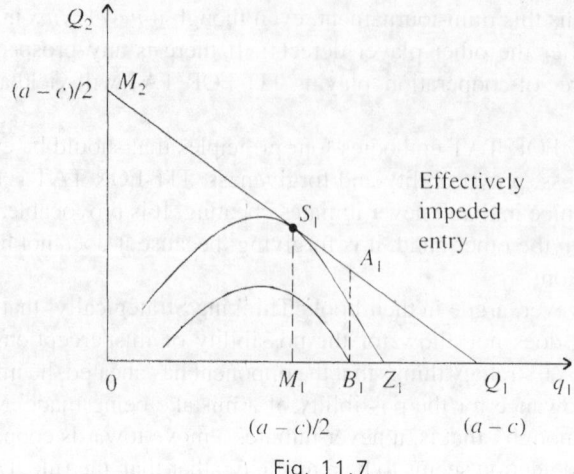

Fig. 11.7

essentially becomes the q_1 axis. We have already noted that if $F = 0$, that is there is no fixed cost of entry, then the point A_1 coincides with the point Q_1.

We can now illustrate Bain's classification.

Case 1. $F = 0$. The reaction function for firm 2 is $M_2 Q_1$. Firm 1 acts as the Stackelberg leader and selects S_1, where firm 2 also produces a positive amount. Entry is *accommodated*.

Case 2. $F > 0$. Firm 2's reaction function is discontinuous and is represented by $M_2 A_1 B_1 Q_1$.

(a) F is small and B_1 lies to the right of Z_1. Then S_1 remains the optimal point for firm 1 and again, entry is accommodated.

(b) On the other hand, if F is so large that B_1 lie to the left of M_1, then firm 1 selects M_1 in order to make monopoly profit. Entry is *blockaded* because the fixed cost of entry is so high that firm 2 stays out of the market.

(c) $M_1 < B_1 < Z_1$. The iso-profit curve passing thorugh B_1 is lower (indicates a higher profit level) than the one through S_1. Hence firm 1 will produce slightly more than B_1. Firm 2 stays out and firm 1 makes higher profits than at S_1. Entry is *effectively impeded*, or deterred.

11.7.1 Strategic Decisions

In the model we analysed, firm 1 enjoyed a first-mover advantage and under certain circumstances could effectively utilize this advantage to deter entry. We can distinguish between two types of decisions by firms (1) strategic decisions designed to alter the environment in which firms operate and (2) quantity (or price) decisions taken in the context of a given environment. We now consider strategic decisions that enable existing firms to prevent others from entering the market.

Consider the following game in a normal form. Firm 1 is a monopoly and firm 2 is a potential entrant. If firm 2 does enter the market, firm 1 has the option of 'fighting' (for example, by flooding the market and hence lowering prices) or 'sharing' the market. The hypothetical payoffs are shown below (the second number in each pair gives the entrant's payoff):

		Firm 2	
		Not Enter	Enter
Firm 1	Fight	(100, 0)	(30, –50)
	Share	(100, 0)	(40, 60)

At first sight, it seems that there are two Nash equilibria in this game—(Not Enter, Fight), (Enter, Share). If firm 1 'fights', it is best for firm 2 to not enter. If firm 2 does not enter, firm 1 is indifferent between fighting and sharing, so we can say that 'fight' is the best strategy for firm 1. Similarly for the other pair of strategies.

However, let us assume that firm 2 gets to move first, that is, it gets to decide whether to enter or not. Then firm 1 decides whether to fight or share. This sequence of moves can be represented in a extensive form game by means of a game tree:

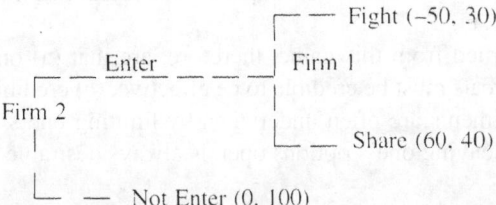

We know that the way to analyse this game is to go to the end and work backward. Suppose firm 2 has already made a choice and firm 1 is sitting on one branch of the game tree. If firm 2 has chosen to stay away, firm 1 will earn 100. But if firm 2 has entered, then the sensible ('rational') thing for firm 1 to do is to 'share' and the payoffs are (60, 40). Firm 2 will therefore enter and earn 60.

Firm 1 can of course threaten to fight if firm 2 enters. If this threat is taken seriously, it will be better for firm 2 not to enter, since firm 2 will get −50 if it enters and 0 if it does not. However, firm 2 realizes that this threat is an empty threat given that firm 1 is a rational player: if it does enter, given the payoffs, firm 1 will find it optimal to share in the event of entry (and get 40 instead of 30). Knowing this, firm 2 will enter and earn 60. The subgame-perfect equilibrium is one in which entry is accommodated.

Now consider a strategic decision that the incumbent can take. Suppose that the incumbent can purchase some extra productive capacity that will allow it to produce more at a lower marginal cost. For the sake of concreteness, assume that buying the extra capacity adds 10 to the fixed cost of the firm and lowers variable cost by 20 if extra output is produced (this also includes the effect of a fall in the price). The payoffs are now given in the figure below:

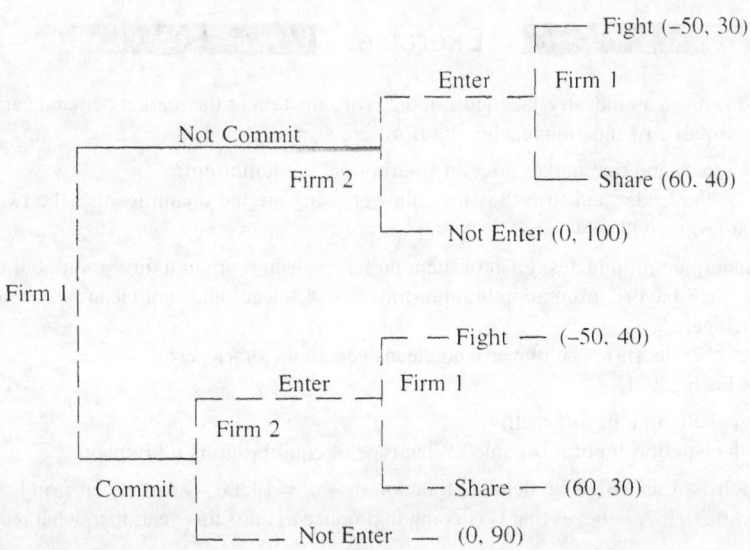

Building the extra capacity dramatically changes the complexion of the game. If firm 1 commits by purchasing the extra capacity, it becomes rational for firm 1 to fight rather than share, and this makes its threat to fight *credible*. Recognizing this, firm 2 will decide not to enter, and firm 1 will earn a monopoly profit of 90. On the other hand, in the absence of any commitment, firm 1 will accommodate entery and earn 40. Therefore, by backward induction, firm 1 should invest in the excess capacity and earn monopoly profit of 90. Note that firm 1 does not need to actually use the excess capacity. The presence of the excess capacity represents a *commitment* to fight on the part of firm 1, because by incurring the expenditure on the excess capacity, the incumbent has denied itself the (rational) option of sharing the market.

The important lessons we have learned from this game, therefore, are that (a) one can gain by making appropriate threats, (b) such threats must be credible to be effective, (c) credibility is ensured through commitments, and (d) commitments are often undertaken by limiting one's options. Thus, in strategic contexts, it is not true that leaving one's options open is always desirable. One's lack of freedom can have strategic value.

Topics for Discussion

1. Look at the recent trends in world petroleum prices. Do you think that the OPEC has been successful in maintaining high petroleum prices? How do energy conservation measures in various countries affect OPEC's efforts?
2. Treat the government and 'the union' as two players in a static game. The union cares for nominal wages and the inflation rate. The government cares for the employment level as well as the rate of inflation. Try to build models to predict different outcomes in different equilibria (Cournot-Nash vs Stackelberg). A paper you can use as a reference is Gylfason and Lindbeck (1994).
3. Try to identify some dominant firms in Indian industries (in terms of market shares) and examine whether there is reason to believe that other firms in the industry treat them as dominant firms.
4. The Golden Rule says, 'Do unto others as you would have them do unto you'. The Silver Rule says, 'Do not do unto others what you would not have them do unto you'. The Brazen Rule says, 'Do unto others as they do unto you'. Which rule is closest to the Tit-for-Tat rule? Which rule would you base your behaviour on and why? Which rule do you think is most likely to promote cooperation in society?

Exercise

1. There are only two firms in an industry-labelled 1 and 2. The equation of the market demand curve is $P = 12 - (q_1 + q_2)$ and the (total) cost functions facing the firms are $C_i = 4q_i$, $i = 1, 2$.

   (a) What will be outputs and the market price in Cournot-Nash equilibrium?
   (b) If firm 1 acts as the leader and firm 2 as the follower, what are the quantities that the two firms will produce? What profits will they earn?

2. Karishma and Madhuri are roommates. Each of them prefers a clean room to a dirty room, but neither likes to clean the room. Their payoffs from adopting the strategies of 'clean' and 'not clean' are as follows:
   Both clean: Each gets 5.
   One cleans, the other doesn't: The player who cleans gets 0, the other gets 8,
   Neither cleans: Each gets 1.

   (a) Represent the payoffs in a payoff matrix.
   (b) What will be the equilibrium of this game? What type of equilibrium is it? Explain.

3. Suppose that duopolists A and B face a demand function $q_a + q_b = 13200 - 800P$. Each firm has a constant marginal cost of Rs 0.50. If A believes that B is going to produce q_b units this year, then what is A's reaction function?

4. The demand function facing the firms in a duopoly is $P = 16 - Q$, where Q is the industry output. Each firm's total cost function is $TC_i = 4q_i$, $i = 1, 2$. What will be the price and consumer surplus in a Bertrand equilibrium?

5. In a Cournot oligopoly, there are 20 identical firms, with cost functions $C_i = 3q_i$, $i = 1, 2, \ldots, 20$. The (inverse) market demand function is $P = 150 - Q$, where Q is the aggregate output. In a Cournot-Nash equilibrium how much will each firm produce and what will be the price?

6. In the matrix below, the first payoff in each pair goes to Player A and the second to Player B. Let a, b, c, and d be positive constants. If Player A chooses bottom and Player B chooses right in a Nash equilibrium, then we know that:

		Player B	
		Left	Right
Player A	Top	$(1, a)$	$(c, 1)$
	Bottom	$(1, b)$	$(d, 1)$

(a) $b > 1$ and $d > 1$.
(b) $c < 1$ and $b < 1$.
(c) $b < c$ and $d < 1$.
(d) $b < 1$ and $c < d$.

7 The demand function in a duopoly market is $Q = 20 - P$, where Q is the total output sold by the two firms 1 and 2. The firms have total cost functions $TC_i = 8q_i$, $i = 1, 2$.

(a) If the firms collude to act as a monopoly, what will be the industry output and profit?
(b) What will be the price and the outputs in a Cournot equilibrium ? What will be the profits?
(c) If firm 1 acts as a Stackelberg leader and firm 2 as a Stackelberg follower, what will be the leader's output and profit in equilibrium?

8 Tarun and Aruna live in adjoining apartments. Tarun plays the dholak and this disturbs Aruna at her studies. Aruna wants to install sound-proofing (the noise of installation will irritate Tarun). Their payoffs are given below (the first payoff in each pair refers to Aruna):

		Tarun	
		Be Noisy	Be Quiet
Aruna	Install Soundproofing	$(2, 2)$	$(-1, 1)$
	Not install	$(1, 3)$	$(4, 4)$

(i) What are the two Nash equilibria of this game?
(ii) If Tarun gets to move first, what will be the subgame-perfect equilibrium?

9 Establish that the following game has no Nash equilibrium in pure strategies.

		Player 2	
		L	R
Player 1	T	$(0, 3)$	$(3, 0)$
	B	$(2, 1)$	$(1, 2)$

10. Consider a Stackelberg model where $p = 80 - Q$, $(Q = q_1 + q_2)$, $C_1 = 10q_1$, and $C_2 = 10q_2 + 100$. If firm 1 acts as the Stackelberg leader, what is the minimum amount it must produce to drive down firm 2's profit to zero?

11. In a certain industry, there is one dominant firm that sets the price and 25 identical competitive fringe firms that act as price-takers. The equation of the market demand curve is given by the equation $16Q = 480,000 - 15P$, where $Q = Q_D + Q_F$, Q_F being the total production of the fringe firms. The equation of the marginal cost curve for the dominant firm is $MC = 2Q_D$ and the fringe supply curve is given by $P = 16Q_F$.

   (i) Find the equilibrium values for Q_D and P.
   (ii) How much does each fringe firm produce in equilibrium?

12. (a) An incumbent monopoly firm faces the inverse demand curve $P = 100 - Q$. It has no fixed cost and its marginal cost is 40. Calculate the profit-maximizing monopolist's profit.
   (b) Suppose that a second firm is contemplating entering the industry. The entrant's $MC = 40$, but there is a fixed cost of entry of 100. If a Cournot game in quantities is played after entry, calculate the profits of the incumbent firm and the entrant in the Cournot-Nash equilibrium.
   (c) Now, suppose that the incumbent firm can purchase a machine for 1804. If the machine is used, its MC becomes 4. The purchase of the machine represents a commitment on the part of the incumbent. Calculate the incumbent's profit if the second firm does not enter (the entrant makes 0 profit if it does not enter).
   (d) Assuming that the incumbent has made the commitment and that a Cournot quantity-setting game is played after entry, calculate the incumbent's and entrant's profit if entry takes place(note that the marginal costs are different for the two firms in this case).
   (e) Represent in the form of a game tree the sequential moves game where the incumbent first decides to commit or not and then the entrant decides whether to enter or not. What is the subgame-perfect equilibrium of this game?

12 Product Differentiation

In the model of perfect competition, all the firms in an industry produce a homogeneous output. In this chapter we explore models in which firms try to differentiate their products from one another. Products within an industry are said to be differentiated if consumers treat the different products as close but imperfect substitutes. It is important to understand that even physically identical goods will be treated as different commodities if the buyers view them as such. The same drug paracetamol for paediatric use is sold as different brands, for example, Crocin syrup, Metacin syrup, Zupar syrup, etc. They will be considered as different products since consumers perceive them as such. On the other hand, product heterogeneity, per se, does not ensure product differentiation. Consumers might treat even heterogeneous products as identical products.

Porter identifies 'differentiation' as one of the three generic strategies a firm can adopt to secure its competitive advantage in an industry (the other two are 'cost leadership' and 'focus'). He points out that approaches to differentiation can take many forms: design or brand image (Pepe jeans vs Ruf 'n Tuf jeans), technology, features, customer service, dealer network, or other dimensions. He also points out that typically the firm differentiates its products in a number of dimensions. According to Porter, 'Differentiation provides insulation against competitive rivalry because of brand loyalty by customers and resulting lower sensitivity to price'.

When products are differentiated, it becomes a difficult task to define the industry. Demand elasticities are usually employed to characterize differentiated product industries. When the industry is perfectly competitive, we know that goods within the industry are perfect substitutes of each other, and the cross-price elasticities vis-à-vis other industry products are weak. The existence of product differentiation makes firms' own demand curves less elastic and decreases inter-market cross elasticities.

There are a number of observed facts about product differentiation that economic models must try to explain.

- Many industries produce a large number of similar but differentiated goods. For example, a number of toothpastes are available in the market.
- Firms in the same industry produce differentiated products. The outputs of two competing firms in the same industry are rarely, if ever, identical.
- The set of products made by the firms in any industry is but a small subset of all the products that are possible. Toothpastes, for example, come only in packs weighing 50 gm, 100 gm, 200 gm, etc. The colour of the paste is usually restricted to white, red, and blue.
- In most industries, firms produce a range of differentiated products. Bicycle firms producing for the 'special' segment produce Mountain Terrain Bikes (MTBs), children's bikes in different colours, bikes for women, etc.
- Any one consumer purchases only a small subset of the products that are available in any industry. Even when there are many family members, a family will buy (say) only three types of laundry detergents, one for ordinary washing, one for high quality clothes and one for woolens.

• Different consumers buy different bundles, thus showing that tastes and preferences vary from consumer to consumer.

Models of product differentiation tend to be of two types. In the *address-type* models, goods are characterized by their attributes. For example, one might say that different toffees are characterized only by their sweetness. Consumers (in this case, children), have different tastes regarding sweetness, some prefer their toffees to be very sweet and some their toffees to be not so sweet. This provides the rationale for different firms to produce toffees with different degrees of sweetness, aimed at different segments of consumers. Address-type models try to characterize the degree of product differentiation in equilibrium, that is, whether firms decide to produce goods that are close substitutes or that have attributes far apart in the space of attributes (that is, whether the toffees that are produced will have more or less the same degree of sweetness, or whether they will have very different degrees of sweetness).

In the *non-address type* models, there is a set of goods that can be produced and consumers have tastes over these goods. Consumers like variety. A subset of the available range of goods will be produced in equilibrium. There is a trade-off between producing large amounts of a small variety of goods and small amounts of a large variety of goods.

It is clear that not all the models can explain all the observed facts. We therefore consider samples of both types of models.

12.1 Non-address Type Models: Fixed Number of Products

12.1.1 Two Differentiated Products: Quantity Competition

Consider a duopoly producing two differentiated products indexed by $i = 1, 2$. There is no cost of production. Each firm produces a single commodity. Following Dixit (1979), we assume that the inverse demand functions for the two products are

$$p_1 = \alpha - \beta q_1 - \gamma q_2 \text{ and } p_2 = \alpha - \gamma q_1 - \beta q_2, \text{ where } b > 0, \beta^2 > \gamma^2.$$

The assumption $\beta^2 > \gamma^2$ implies that the price of a brand is more sensitive to a change in the quantity of this brand rather than to a change in the quantity of the rival brand.

A measure of differentiation will tell us how differentiated the two commodities are in the eyes of the consumers. If the commodities are close substitutes, then the own-price and cross-price effects will be almost the same, that is, β^2 will be almost equal to γ^2. We can then use as a measure of differentiation the variable $\delta = \gamma^2/\beta^2$. The products are highly differentiated when δ is close to 0, that is, γ^2 is close to 0. If it is equal to 0, then the price of each product depends only on the quantity of that product, and not on the quantity of the rival product: $p_i = \alpha - \beta q_i$, $i = 1, 2$. On the other hand, when δ is close to 1, the goods are close substitutes. If it is equal to 1, there is only one inverse demand function, with the price depending on the total quantity of the two commodities: $p = \alpha - \beta q_1 - \beta q_2$.

Let us now examine the Nash equilibrium in the output levels. The i-th firm tries to maximize

$$\pi_i(q_1, q_2) = (\alpha - \beta q_i - \gamma q_j)q_i, \, i, j = 1, 2, \, i \neq j,$$

with respect to q_i, treating q_j as fixed. The reaction functions are given by

$$q_i = R_i(q_j) = (\alpha - \gamma q_j)/2\beta, \, i, j = 1, 2, \, i \neq j.$$

The reaction functions are downward sloping straight lines, and they are represented in Fig. 12.1. Note that as γ increases and approaches β, that is, the products become more homogeneous, the reaction functions become steeper. If γ tends towards 0, the reaction functions tend to become vertical to the respective axes.

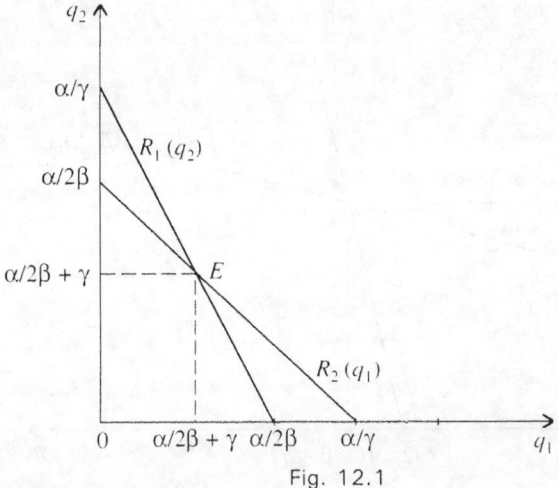

Fig. 12.1

From the two reaction functions, we can solve for the equilibrium quantities, prices and profits. These are (by symmetry) $q_i^* = \alpha/(2\beta + \gamma)$, $p_i^* = \alpha\beta/(2\beta + \gamma)$ and $\pi_i^* = \alpha^2\beta/(2\beta + \gamma)^2$, $i = 1, 2$. We note an important result here: As γ falls and tends towards zero, the profit of each firm increases. That is, *as the products become more and more differentiated, the profits of both firms increase.* This explains why firms try their best to convince consumers that their products are unique. If products are highly differentiated, then each firm in effect becomes a monopoly and enjoys monopoly profits.

12.1.2 Two Differentiated Products: Price Competition

The Bertrand model of price competition with homogeneous products yielded the surprising result that firms in even a duopoly acted competitively. The introduction of product differentiation leads to a less surprising result in a model with price competition.

Let us again consider the inverse demand functions $p_1 = \alpha - \beta q_1 - \gamma q_2$ and $p_2 = \alpha - \gamma q_1 - \beta q_2$. We can invert this system to solve for the demand functions (we express the quantities as functions of prices, using Cramer's rule). The demand functions are

$$q_1 = a - bp_1 + cp_2 \text{ and } q_2 = a + cp_1 - bp_2,$$

where $a \equiv \alpha(\beta - \gamma)/(\beta^2 - \gamma^2)$, $b \equiv \beta/(\beta^2 - \gamma^2) > 0$, $c \equiv \gamma/(\beta^2 - \gamma^2) > 0$, by the earlier assumptions.

We solve for the Nash equilibrium in prices. Each firm takes the other's price to be given and tries to maximize $\pi_i(p_1, p_2) = (a - bp_i + cp_j)p_i$, $i, j = 1, 2$, $i \neq j$. The reaction functions are given by $p_i = R_i(p_j) = (a + cp_j)/2b$, $i, j = 1, 2$, $i \neq j$.

The reaction functions in prices are represented below. Note that the reaction functions are now upward sloping.

Finally, from the reaction functions in prices, we solve for prices, quantities and profits:

$$p_i^* = a/(2b - c) = \alpha(\beta - \gamma)/(2\beta - \gamma), \quad q_i^* = ab/(2b - c) = \alpha\beta/(\beta + \gamma)(2\beta - \gamma),$$
$$\text{and } \pi_i^* = a^2b/(2b - c)^2 = \alpha^2(\beta - \gamma)^2\beta/(2\beta - \gamma)^2.$$

How does a change in the degree of product differentiation affect profits? The profit for each firm can be written as $\pi_i^* = (\alpha^2\beta)[(\beta - \gamma)^2/(2\beta - \gamma)^2] = (\alpha^2\beta)[(\beta - \gamma)/(2\beta - \gamma)]^2$. It is easy to show that as γ increases, that is, the products become less differentiated, the term $(\beta - \gamma)/(2\beta - \gamma)$ falls, so that profits decrease.[1] In the limit, when γ increases to the level of β, and the products become homogeneous, profits fall to zero and we get back the Bertrand result.

---

[1] Let $z = (\beta - \gamma)/(2\beta - \gamma)$ and show that $dz/d\gamma < 0$.

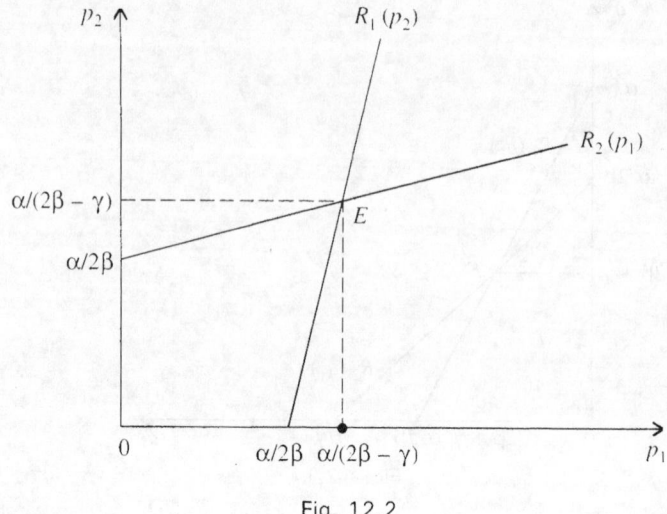

Fig. 12.2

Therefore, whether there is quantity competition or price competition, increasing product hetero-geneity increases the level of profit for both firms. This explains why firms try to differentiate their products from each other. Note that the degree of product differentiation is exogenous to these models. In the address-type models, we will discuss what happens when firms are allowed to choose the degree of differentiation strategically.

Example 12.1: Suppose that the demand functions for the two brands are $q_1 = 168 - 2p_1 + p_2$ and $q_2 = 168 + p_1 - 2p_2$. Both brands can be produced free of cost. The two firms try to choose prices to maximize

$$\Pi_1 = p_1 q_1 = 168p_1 - 2p_1^2 + p_1p_2$$
$$\Pi_2 = p_2 q_2 = 168p_2 - 2p_2^2 + p_1p_2$$

The equations of the reaction functions or the best response functions are

$$168 - 4p_1 + p_2 = 0$$
$$168 - 4p_2 + p_1 = 0$$

Note that these are upward sloping. Solving the two equations, we get $p_1 = p_2 = 56$ and therefore $q_1 = q_2 = 224$. The profits of the two firms are then 12,544 each. Even though marginal costs are zero, both firms choose to set positive prices and earn positive profits in Nash equilibrium.

12.2 Non-address Type Models: Chamberlinian Models

In Chamberlin's model of monopolistic competition there is a clearly defined 'industrial group' which consists of a large number of producers of goods that are close but imperfect substitutes of each other. Chamberlin's model stands midway between models of perfect competition and monopoly. Since there are many small producers and free entry and exit in the long run, this makes the model akin to perfect competition. Firms do not believe that they can influence market conditions nor do they react to each others' actions. However, firms produce goods that are imperfect substitutes for each other. Hence, each firm has a market niche, where it can act as a monopoly. In other words, the demand curve facing each firm is downward sloping. This market power lessens as more and more firms enter the industry, since more and more substitute products are thereby made available to consumers.

A fundamental feature of Chamberlin's model is the perfect symmetry in the position of all individual firms in the industry. Each firm believes that other firms will not respond in any way to its price and quantity decisions. Yet, when one firm finds it optimal to alter its price, others also do so by symmetry. This changes the demand conditions facing the firm. In other words, each firm confronts two different demand curves: there is a *dd* curve that describes what happens when it alone changes its price and there is a *DD* curve that describes what happens when all the firms change prices together. Obviously, the *dd* curve is more elastic (flatter) than the *DD* curve. The firm makes its decisions on the basis of the *dd* curve, rather than the *DD* curve, because, as we have already noted, each firm believes that other firms will not respond in any way to its price and quantity decisions.

The long run monopolistic competition equilibrium, as envisaged by Chamberlin, involves two important components. First, each firm, acting as a monopoly, must be maximizing profit by equating MR with MC. Second, free entry and exit leads to a situation where each firm earns zero profit. If profit is negative, some firms leave the industry while if it is positive, firms continue to enter the industry. This requires $p = AC$ in equilibrium. The Chamberlinian equilibrium, with price p^* and quantity q^*, is shown in Fig. 12.3.

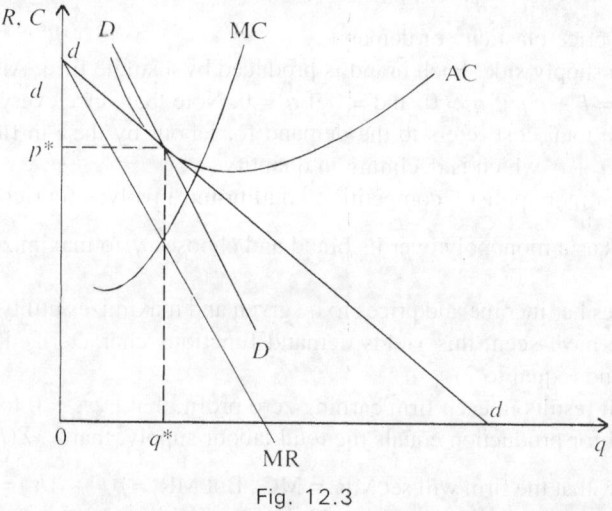

Fig. 12.3

Note that because the demand curve *dd* is downward sloping, the Chamberlinian equilibrium, which takes place at a point of tangency of the AC curve with the demand curve, occurs at a point to the left of the minimum point of the AC curve. Under perfect competition, the long run equilibrium takes place at the minimum point of the AC curve. Therefore, compared with perfect competition, it seems that monopolistic competition leads to higher per unit production costs. However, consumers now have more variety and the higher average cost can be thought of as the price they pay for this variety.

We now develop a model of monopolistic competition to analyse the trade-off between variety and volume. Suppose that there is an industry producing N differentiated brands indexed by $i = 1$, $2,...N$. N is not fixed but is endogenously determined in this model by the free entry and exit condition. The quantity produced of the i-th brand is denoted by q_i while p_i is the unit price. There is only one consumer in this economy and this consumer loves variety. The consumer's preferences are represented by the utility function $u(q_1, q_2,...) = \Sigma(q_i)^{1/2}$. The indifference curves are then convex to the origin, showing that the consumer likes to mix the brands in the consumption bundle. (Suppose that there are only two brands. Then MRS = $(q_2/q_1)^{0.5}$, which is strictly diminishing in q_1.)

The individual sells labour to the firms and gets wages. She also gets profits, if any. Her total income is I. The wage rate is normalized to be equal to 1, so that all 'monetary' values (p_i, π_i, I) are denominated in units of labour. The consumer treats her income to be given and faces the budget constraint

$$\Sigma p_i q_i \leq I = L + \Sigma \pi_i.$$

The consumer maximizes utility subject to her budget constraint. To solve this problem, form the Lagrangean

$$\Lambda = \Sigma (q_i)^{1/2} - \lambda (I - \Sigma p_i q_i).$$

The first order condition for every brand i is

$$\tfrac{1}{2}(q_i)^{1/2} - \lambda p_i = 0, \, i = 1, 2, \ldots N.$$

Inverting, we get the demand functions:

$$q_i(p_i) = 1/[4\lambda^2 p_i^2], \text{ or } p_i(q_i) = 1/[4\lambda q_i^{0.5}] \Rightarrow \varepsilon = -(\delta q_i/\delta p_i) \, (p_i/q_i) = 2.$$

Here e is the own price-elasticity of demand.

Next, consider the supply side. Each brand is produced by a single firm. All firms have identical cost structure: $C_i(q_i) = F + cq_i$ if $q_i > 0$, and $= 0$ if $q_i = 0$. Note that since everything is denominated in units of labour, the total cost refers to the demand for labour by the i-th firm. The average cost curve is $AC_i(q_i) = F/q_i + c$, which is declining in quantity.

The Chamberlinian monopolistic competition equilibrium involves four conditions:

1. Each firm behaves as a monopoly over its brand and chooses q_i to maximize profit $\pi_i = p_i(q_i)q_i - (F + cq_i)$.
2. The consumer takes her income and prices to be given and maximizes utility subject to the budget constraint. As we have seen, this yields demand functions characterized by a constant price-elasticity of demand (equal to 2).
3. Free entry and exit results in each firm earning zero profit, that is, $\pi_i = 0$ for all i.
4. Labour demanded for production equals the total labour supply, that is, $\Sigma (F + cq_i) = L$.

From (1), we know that the firm will set $MR_i = MC_i$. But $MR_i = p_i(1 - 1/\varepsilon) = p_i(1 - 1/2) = p_i/2$ and $MC = c$. Hence $p_i = 2c$ is the equilibrium price. Next, by condition (3), $\pi_i = \{p_i(q_i) - c\}q_i - F = cq_i - F = 0$. The equilibrium quantities are then $q_i = F/c$.

Finally, we want to see how many brands are produced in this industry. Condition (4) tells us that $N\{F + cx(F/c)\} = L$. Hence, $N = L/2F$.

In this model, then, only a finite number of brands will be produced. Moreover, when the fixed cost is large, N is small and q_i is large. When the fixed cost is low, the number of brands is larger, but a smaller quantity of each brand will be produced.

12.3a Address-type Models: The Hotelling Model

Suppose that there are two stores in a town located at two different points on the main street. Their different locations can be interpreted as product differentiation in the sense that customers prefer to buy from the nearby store because of lower transportation costs. This confers a degree of monopoly power on the two stores and they can charge different prices.

This model is equivalent to a model in which products are defined by their characteristics and consumers have preferences over these characteristics or attributes. An example is the ranking of chocolates by their 'sweetness':

Chocolates------A-----------------------------------

Less sweet-------------------------- > More sweet

Some consumers like chocolates that are less sweet while others like chocolates that are more sweet. By deciding to produce a chocolate with the level of sweetness given by A (that is, deciding to locate at A), a firm gains an advantageous position vis-à-vis consumers who prefer chocolates with degrees of sweetness close to A.

Another example comes from the field of politics. There is a political spectrum ranging from the left (communists) to the right (conservatives). Parties have to decide where to locate themselves on this spectrum, given that voters have preferences distributed in a certain manner along the spectrum.

To present Hotelling's model, we make the following assumptions:

1. There are two firms. They locate along a straight line (road) which is of length L. The location decisions are treated as exogenous in this model. They produce and sell commodities that are identical in all respects except for the location at which they are sold.
2. Consumers are distributed uniformly over the line and each has a unit demand. Demands are therefore perfectly inelastic. The only decision a buyer takes is which firm to patronize and this decision is based on the minimum price (including the transportation cost) at which the commodity is available.
3. To go to a store/firm, a consumer has to pay a transportation cost of t per unit of distance.
4. Cost of production is zero for both goods.
5. Finally, to present the model in a simple form, we assume that an equilibrium in which firms charge strictly positive prices, always exists.

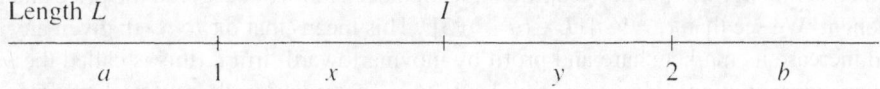

The firms are located at points 1 and 2 respectively. The distances from the end-points are a and b. Note that firm 1 has an intrinsic advantage vis-à-vis the consumer who are located to the left of 1; unless firm 2's prices are significantly lower, these consumers will prefer to buy from firm 1. Similarly for consumers who are located to the right of the point 2 for firm 2.

I is the point where the consumer is exactly indifferent between 1 and 2. Therefore, for the consumer at I, $p_1 + tx = p_2 + ty$. Since we also know that $a + x + y + b = L$, we can solve for both x and y (and hence the point I), *given the prices*:

$$x = \tfrac{1}{2} [(L - a - b) + (p_2 - p_1)/t], \; y = \tfrac{1}{2} [(L - a - b) - (p_2 - p_1)/t].$$

Therefore, the market for 1 (the quantity firm 1 can sell) is

$$q_1 = a + x = a + \tfrac{1}{2} [(L - a - b) + (p_2 - p_1)/t],$$

and that for firm 2 is

$$q_2 = b + y = b + \tfrac{1}{2} [(L - a - b) - (p_2 - p_1)/t].$$

We now consider the Nash equilibrium in prices. The profit equations are

$$\pi_1 = p_1 q_1 = p_1[a + \tfrac{1}{2} \{(L - a - b) + (p_2 - p_1)/t\}],$$

and

$$\pi_2 = p_2 q_2 = p_2[a + \tfrac{1}{2}\{(L - a - b) - (p_2 - p_1)/t\}],$$

Setting the first partial derivatives equal to 0, we get

$$\partial\pi_1/\partial p_1 = a + \tfrac{1}{2}(L - a - b) + p_2/t - 2p_1/t = 0,$$
$$\partial\pi_2/\partial p_2 = a + \tfrac{1}{2}(L - a - b) - 2p_2/t + p_1/t = 0.$$

Solving from these two equations of reaction functions in prices, we finally obtain

$$p_1^* = t\{L + (a - b)/3\} \text{ and } p_2^* = t\{L - (a - b)/3\},$$

from which we can solve for the quantities:

$$q_1^* = \tfrac{1}{2}\{L + (a - b)/3\} \text{ and } q_2^* = \tfrac{1}{2}\{L - (a - b)/3\}.$$

If the firms are located symmetrically from the two end-points, then $a = b$, and the firms charge the same prices and produce the same quantities: $p_1^* = p_2^* = tL$ and $q_1^* = q_2^* = \tfrac{1}{2}L$. However, in general, the firms charge different prices. For example, if $a > b$, we can see that firm 1 has a larger set of 'captive' customers and we expect it to exploit this advantage by charging a higher price. Since $a > b \Rightarrow a - b > 0$, we can see that $p_1^* > p_2^*$ and $q_1^* > q_2^*$. Firm 1's locational advantage allows it to charge a higher price and also sell more than firm 2.

To get the result that a unique equilibrium of the above type exists, we need to assume that the firms are not located too close to each other. It can also be shown that if the firms are located at the same point, then the unique equilibrium is where both prices are zero, that is, we are back to Bertrand equilibrium.

So far, it has been assumed that the locations are exogenously given. That is, the degree of product differentiation is fixed. What happens if the firms are allowed to choose both prices and locations simultaneously? Unfortunately, there will be no Nash equilibrium in this two-dimensional game. To show this, let us find out what firm 1's optimal location decision will be, given the price and location of its opponent. We see that $\pi_1 = \tfrac{1}{2}t[\{L + (a - b)/3\}]^2$. This means that $\delta\pi_1/\delta a > 0$: given any a and b, firm 1 can increase its market share and profit by moving toward firm 2 (this is called the *principle of minimum differentiation*). However, this leads to a contradiction, because when firms get too close to each other, an equilibrium will not exist.

d'Aspremont and others (1979) have shown that if we introduce quadratic transportation costs and consider a two-stage game where firms first decide where to locate and then choose prices, then a subgame-perfect equilibrium involves *maximum differentiation*: $a = b = 0$ and the firms locate at the end-points.

12.3b Address-type Models: The Circular Location Model

Instead of a linear location model, we can analyse a circular location model, where firms are located on the circumference of a circle. An analogy is the distribution of departures for a particular airlines during a 24-hour period. The airlines can have infrequent departures (for example, twice a day, once at 6 am and once at 6 pm) or frequent departures (say, every half an hour). Customers have preferences over timings, characterized by their distribution along the circumference. It is usual to find airlines opting for infrequent departures to a certain location while long distance bus services between the same locations tend to be quite frequent.

Suppose that restaurants locate along the circumference of a circle and the length of the circumference is 1 mile. (We can think of bhelpuri sellers located along the bank of a circular lake.) There

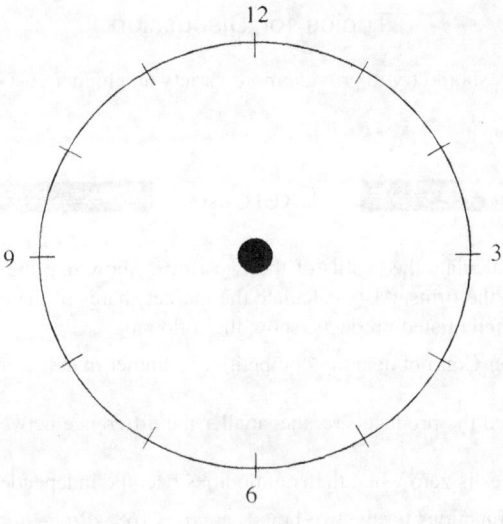

Fig. 12.4

are L consumers distributed uniformly on the circumference. Each consumer demands only one meal during the day. The bhelpuri sellers offer exactly the same product. There is a transportation cost of Rs t per unit of distance travelled. We try to find out the number of sellers that minimizes the total cost of providing bhelpuris.

There are two components of production costs. First, the start-up cost for each bhelpuri seller is Rs F. Second, each meal costs Rs m, that is, the marginal cost of providing a helping of bhelpuri is Rs m.

Suppose that there are N sellers located evenly on the circumference. The distance between any two adjacent sellers is $1/N$ mile. A consumer has to make a round-trip to the nearest seller to get a meal. The maximum one way distance is $1/2N$ (for the consumer located exactly midway between two sellers) while the minimum is 0. Therefore, the average distance one way is $\{1/(2N) + 0\}/2 = 1/(4N)$ and the average roundtrip distance is twice this, that is, $1/(2N)$. The *total* transportation cost then is $tL\{1/(2N)\}$: this is the transportation cost per unit multiplied by the total number of consumers times the average distance travelled.

The production cost is, first, FN, which is the total of start-up costs for the N sellers. Second, the total cost of meals is mL. Hence total production cost is equal to $mL + FN$.

We wish to find out the number of sellers N that minimizes the sum of total transportation costs and total production costs: $C = tL\{1/(2N)) + (mL + FN)$. Differentiating C with respect to N, we get

$$(tL/2)(-N)^{-2} + F = 0,$$

which gives us

$$N^* = \sqrt{(tL/2F)}.$$

This expression for the optimal number of sellers has a very intuitive economic interpretation. If the transportation cost t goes up, then N^* increases. The whole point about having additional outlets is to economize on transportation costs. N^* also increases with L. The more people there are who live in each segment of the circumference, the more people there are who will benefit from a reduction in average transportation costs. Finally, N^* is lower when F is higher, that is, higher the set-up costs, as expected.

Topics for Discussion

Do you think that an economy should try to provide more variety at a higher cost or less variety at a lower cost to consumers?

Exercise

1. In the Hotelling Model, calculate the profits of the two firms. Show that the profit of each firm increases with the distance between the firms. Also, calculate the market shares of the two firms.

2. In the model with two differentiated products, show the following:

   (i) The market price under Cournot quantity competition is higher than it is under Bertrand price competition.

   (ii) The more differentiated the products are, the smaller the difference between the Cournot and Bertrand prices.

   (iii) The difference in prices is zero when the commodities become independent.

3. Suppose that the demand functions for the two brands are $q_1 = 168 - 2p_1 + p_2$ and $q_2 = 168 + p_1 - 2p_2$. Both brands can be produced free of cost.

   (i) If both firms set their prices simultaneously, solve for the Nash equilibrium of the game.

   (ii) Suppose that firm 1 sets its price before firm 2. Solve for the subgame-perfect equilibrium prices.

   (iii) Show that both firms collect a higher profit under a sequential moves game than under a simultaneous moves game, and the firm that sets its price first makes a smaller profit than the firm that sets its price later.

4. Two firms selling identical products are located on a straight road 15 km long. They do not have any cost of production. Consumers are distributed evenly on the road. Each consumer demands one unit. There is a transportation cost of Rs 0.50 per km. The firms are located 9 km and 3 km respectively from either end of the road.

   What will be the equations of the demand functions for the products of the two firms?

13 Factor Markets

The firm uses various types of inputs or factors in its production process. Traditionally, factors of production have been divided into four categories—labour, capital, land (natural resources) and entrepreneurship. This division is not always watertight. Capital refers to produced means of production like plants and machinery, while natural resources refer to the original or primary means of production like minerals. However, some natural resources can be produced, for example, agricultural crops like cotton. Even the supply of land can be increased by means of reclamation. Again, nowadays a lot of attention is paid to the question of investing in 'human capital', that is, the process of adding to and upgrading skills and knowledge of workers. Entrepreneurship can be viewed as a special type of labour which is used to build up and run organizations. In this chapter, we examine how markets for the various factors operate.

13.1 Labour

In this section, we first analyse how wage rates are determined in the labour markets. Next, we discuss the concept of efficiency wages. In the next section, we turn to the phenomenon of collective bargaining between unions and management.

13.1.1 Labour Demand and Supply: Competitive Labour Market

In the market for labour, the roles of firms and consumers are reversed. Firms demand labour and consumers supply labour. The demand for labour is a *derived* demand, since firms demand labour on the basis of the demand for their final outputs. Note also that workers cannot be bought or sold (slavery is usually prohibited by law), but labour services can be.

To simplify matters, we assume that there is only one type of labour in the economy, so that there is a single wage rate. The firm acts as price-taker in the labour market and takes the wage rate w to be given.

In the *short run*, the firm's capital is fixed and output is solely a function of labour: $Q = Q(L)$. The firm tries to maximize $\pi = pQ - wL$. The first order condition is $d(pQ)/dL = w$. We can distinguish between two cases:

1. If the firm operates in a perfectly competitive output market, then the first order condition becomes $p(dQ/dL) = w$. That is, $p.\,\mathrm{MP}_L = w$, where MP_L is the marginal product of labour. The expression on the left hand side is known as the 'value of marginal product of labour' and we can write it as VMP_L. The VMP_L measures the addition to total revenue from the employment of one more unit of L while w measures the cost of employing an extra unit of L. The second order condition is $p.d\mathrm{MP}_L/dL \leq 0$, that is, $d\mathrm{MP}_L/dL \leq 0$.

The solution is shown in Fig. 13.1a. We know that the firm will equate the wage rate to the value of marginal product of labour at a point where the marginal product of labour curve is downward sloping. In Fig. 13.1a, the VMP_L curve is inverse U-shaped and therefore w^* is equal to VMP_L at two levels of L, L', and L^*. But only at L^* is the VMP_L curve downward sloping and hence the second order condition is satisfied. Therefore, the downward sloping portion of the VMP_L curve can be viewed as the inverse demand for labour curve.

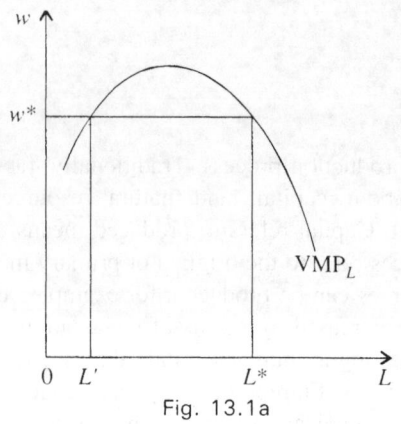

Fig. 13.1a

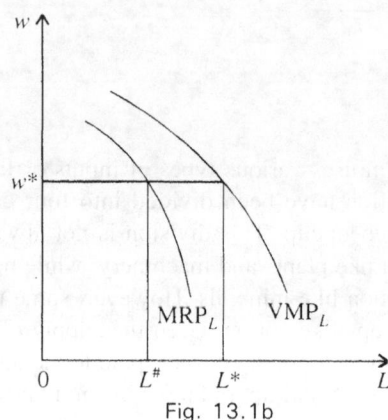

Fig. 13.1b

2. If the firm has some market power, then $p = p(Q)$, and the first order condition becomes $d(pQ)/dL = w$. Remembering that $Q = Q(L)$, we can write this as $[d(pQ)/dQ][dQ/dL] = w$, by the Chain Rule. The first term within the brackets on the left hand side is nothing but the marginal revenue. Hence the condition for profit maximization becomes $MR \cdot MP_L = w$. The term on the left hand side is called the marginal revenue product of labour and denoted by MRP_L. Hence the condition can be written more compactly as $MRP_L = w$. We know that the MR curve always lies below the demand curve. Hence the MRP_L curve will always lie below the VMP_L curve and for any wage rate w^*, the demand for labour from a firm with market power ($L^\#$ in Fig. 13.1b) will be less than the demand from a firm which is a price-taker in the product market.

In the *long run*, all inputs are variable. A fall in w will directly lead to a substitution of L for K, reducing costs and increasing the output of the firm. This will further add to the demand for labour. Hence the long run demand curve for labour will be flatter than the short run curve.

After obtaining the demand curves for labour for the individual firms, we can ask how the market demand curve for labour could be derived. The market demand curve for an output is derived by horizontally summing the individual demand curves.[1] We cannot do this for labour. Suppose that the output price is p^* to begin with and that this gives rise to a set of value of marginal product curves. When the wage rate is lower, all firms try to expand output and consequently, L. However, the increased output can only be sold at a lower price p' in the product market, and in consequence each VMP_L curve (and hence the ΣVMP_L curve) shifts to the left. The market demand for labour is lower than if the product price had not changed. In other words, the market demand curve for labour is less elastic than the curve we would generate if the output price were fixed and we summed the VMP_L curves across all firms.

[1] Market demand curves for final goods usually refer to a single market. But inputs such as labour and capital are used in many output markets. Thus, to derive the labour demand curve, we must first determine the labour demand curve for each individual output market and then sum across output markets.

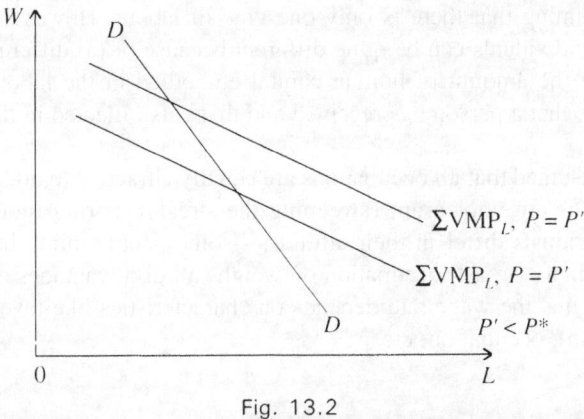

Fig. 13.2

In practice, there are many different types of labour and each type of labour will be demanded by different industries. For example, electricians are employed in residential construction, automobile industry, commercial office building, computer industry, etc. In many of these industries, the wages paid to electricians account for a very small fraction of the total costs. A small change in the wages of electricians will affect the total costs of these industries by a negligible amount and will have no perceptible effect on their product prices. For such industries whose product prices are affected imperceptibly, we can derive the market demand for labour curve by horizontally summing the VMP_L curves.

On the supply side, we have seen in Chapter 4 how the supply curve for labour can be derived by considering the labour-leisure choice of consumers. Such supply curves can be backward-bending: when the wage rate is sufficiently high, a further increase in the wage rate can lead to workers reducing their labour supply to enjoy more leisure.

The market supply curve for labour can be obtained by horizontally summing the individual labour supply curves. Even if some of these are backward-bending, we expect the market supply curve to be upward sloping. An increase of wages leads to a change in the number of hours worked by existing workers. But this also attracts workers from other categories of labour where wages have not increased.

Finally, the market demand and supply curves for labour together will determine the wage rate and the total employment of labour (Fig. 13.3).

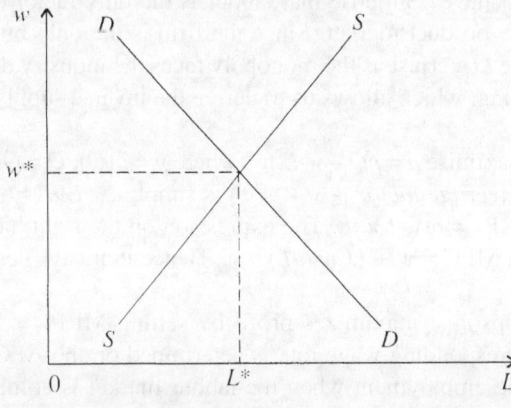

Fig. 13.3

We have been assuming that there is only one type of labour. However, the quality of labour supplied by different individuals can be quite different because of (a) differences in innate abilities and (b) differences in the amount of human capital embodied in the labour. The latter refers to education, training etc. that a person has received and that gets reflected in the quality of labour the person can provide.

Second, we have assumed that all occupations are equally attractive to all labourers. But we know that certain occupations are unpleasant (sweeping the streets), boring (counting out money?) or risky. Moreover, individuals differ in their attitudes—some people think that the job security and lack of responsibility in a 'sarkari' occupation outweighs all disadvantages of such jobs.

Therefore, we find that the wage rate depends on characteristics like level of education, gender, location (rural vs urban), occupation, etc.

Example 13.1: Take the agricultural sector in India and consider the average wages for employees between ages 15–59, in rupees per day.

Urban Males				Rural Males			
Not literate	Literate up to middle	Secondary	Graduation and above	Not literate	Literate up to middle	Secondary	Graduation and above
32.44	39.83	87.55	122.32	21.57	26.62	57.66	76.00

Source: NSSO Report No. 409.

Further, workers and firms confront different types of market structure in different industries. We next consider how the wage rates are determined when the labour market is not perfectly competitive.

13.1.2 Monopsony

Consider a market where one firm acts as the sole employer. Such a sole employer is called a monoposonist. (In general, the term monoposonist refers to a single buyer.) The classic example of a monopsonist is a 'company town' where the entire town is built up around a single company. All activities are controlled by the firm in question.

How will such a firm behave? Suppose that labour is the only factor of production and that the firm is a monopolist in the product market. Since the firm is the only buyer of labour, it faces the market labour supply curve $L(w)$ (just as the monopoly faces the industry demand curve). The supply curve $L(w)$ is upward sloping, which allows us to derive the inverse supply curve $w(L)$ which is also upward sloping.

The firm then tries to maximise $p = pQ - w \cdot L(w)$, where $p = p(Q)$, $Q = Q(L)$. The term $w \cdot L$ is called the *total factor cost*. The *average factor cost* (AFC) is simply $(w \cdot L)/L = w(L)$. The firm then maximizes profit by setting $MRP_L = d(w \cdot L)/dL$. The expression on the right hand side is called the *marginal factor cost*, or MFC: $MFC = w + L(dw/dL) > w$. Hence it always lies above the average factor cost curve.

In Fig. 13.4, the monopsonist maximizes profit by setting $MRP_L = MFC$, and demanding L^* amount of labour. The corresponding wage rate is determined on the AFC curve and it is w^*. How does this compare with the employment when the labour market is competitive? Suppose that the same MRP_L curve is obtained from the demand curves of numerous firms who act as price-takers in

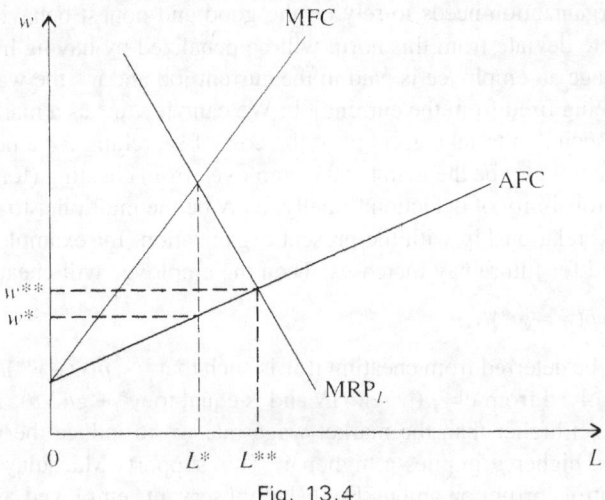

Fig. 13.4

the labour market. Then the equilibrium would have been reached at the intersection of the MRP_L curve and the AFC curve. The wage rate would have been higher (w^{**}) and the employment (L^{**}) also larger.

Example 13.2: Suppose that $MRP_L = 12 - L$, and $AFC = 2 + 2L$. Then total factor cost $= AFC \cdot L = 2L + 2L^2$. $MFC = d(TFC)/dL = 2 + 4L$. The monopsonist sets $MRP_L = MFC$, that is, $12 - L = 2 + 4L$. Solving, we get $5L = 10 \Rightarrow L^* = 2$. The corresponding wage is $AFC = 2 + 2.2 = 6$.

13.1.3 Efficiency Wages: The Shapiro-Stiglitz Model

In an influential book first published in 1971, Peter Doeringer and Michael Piore argued that there is a sharp distinction between internal and external labour market arrangements. External market arrangements refer to the labour markets where wages are determined by the forces of supply and demand. *Internal labour markets* refer to the arrangements within modern enterprises. Entry into such markets is limited to the so-called 'ports of entry'. The pricing of labour, and its allocation from the point of entry to other work positions, is governed by administrative rules and customs. These rules and customs accord the members of the internal labour market rights and privileges not available to workers participating in external labour markets, such as guarantees of job security, opportunities for career mobility, etc. Nowhere are wages within internal labour markets free to vary as would wages in competitive markets. Wages here may be tied to the nature of the job performed, or to levels of skill or seniority, or to the performance of the firm or even the performance of an industry.

Why do internal labour markets work this way? The market system attempts to solve the problems of controlling and coordinating the actions of agents through the price system. But the firm, which is a complex organization within which many agents with different informations, different motivations and different skills and abilities work together, must rely on a system of proper incentives and communication channels to solve these problems. The wage structure within a firm reflects these requirements. We present below a simple model to illustrate the incentive problem in a firm and why the wage rate in the internal labour market can differ from the market wage rate.

Suppose that an organization needs to rely on the good and honest behaviour of its employees. Any employee found to deviate from this norm will be penalized by having his employment terminated. Let w be the wage an employee is paid in the current job and w^* the wage he could get in an alternative job after being fired from the current job. We can view w^* as a market-determined wage; it is assumed to be discounted to take account of the cost of searching for a new job, including any period of unemployment. Let g be the gain for the employee from cheating (for example from taking bribes) and p be the probability of detection. Finally, let N be the multiplier to express the long-term value of the continued relationship with the present organization, for example the number of years left on the job adjusted for future pay increases. Then the employee will cheat if and only if

$$g > p(w - w^*)N.$$

The employee will be deterred from cheating if w is such that $g < p(w - w^*)N$. The smallest w that can deter cheating is solved from $g = p(w - w^*)N$ and is equal to $w^* + g/(Np)$. This wage is called an *efficiency wage*: it is set higher than the market wage rate w^* to induce the worker to work more efficiently. Note that a higher g implies a higher w. This supports Macaulay's observation on the efforts of Clive to control corruption among English civil servants employed by the East India Company in India around 1765: 'Clive saw clearly that it was absurd to give men power and to require them to live in penury. He justly concluded that no reform could be effectual which should not be coupled with a plan for liberally remunerating the civil servants of the company'.

Clive did not merely rely on higher pay to deter cheating: he also brought in outsiders to audit and inspect local practices. Let $M(p)$ be the monitoring cost involved in every accounting period when the probability of detection is p: $M'(p) > 0$ and $M'(p) > 0$. If the company wants to deter cheating, it can minimize its total cost in each period by choosing w and p to solve the following problem:

$$\text{minimize } M(p) + w$$
$$p, w$$
$$\text{subject to } p(w - w^*)N \geq g$$

It is clear that the company will not pay a wage rate higher than that necessary to satisfy the constraint. Hence $w = w^* + g/(Np)$. The problem then reduces to minimizing $M(p) + w^* + g/(Np)$ with respect to p only. The first order condition gives

$$M'(p) - g/(Np^2) = 0$$

(The second order condition is satisfied since $M'(p) + g/(Np^3) > 0$.)

Let us carry out a couple of comparative static exercises. First, suppose that only N changes. Differentiating both sides of the first order condition, we get

$$M'(p)dp - (g/N)(-2)p^{-3}dp - (g/p^2)(-1)N^{-2}dN = 0,$$

which, after some manipulations, yields

$$dp/dN = -[g/N^2p^3]/[M'(p) + 2g/(Np^3)] < 0.$$

Thus if in the absence of cheating, the relationship is a long-term one, then the employee has more to lose from cheating and less monitoring is needed. We can also show that $dp/dg > 0$: if the gain from cheating is larger, it pays to step up the monitoring activities.

13.2 Unions and Collective Bargaining

Another feature of internal labour markets is that in many firms, wages are determined through a process of bargaining between the management and the union. A labour union is a group of workers who bargain collectively with employers regarding the terms and conditions of employment. Usually the workers elect union representatives who bargain with the management.

The assumption that there is only one union is obviously a simplification. Sometimes, an union subscribes to the ideology of a particular political party. One can then find several unions in the same firm, each union owning affiliation to a different political party. Again, different levels of hierarchy can have different unions. Thus 'officers'can have an union different from the union of clerical workers. Firm level unions can also be members of national level unions. Then bargaining first takes place between an association of firms and the union at the national level. Once this settlement takes place, unions at the firm level bargain on the basis of the agreement reached at the national level.

We abstract from these complexities and assume that a firm's workers are employed in only one union. Trade unions are concerned with a number of issues, ranging from the basic aim of increasing wages to broader political issues concerned with the labour movement as a whole. Moreover, there might be conflicts between the interests of the workers and their union representatives. We assume that the union is concerned only with the economic issues of wage and employment and further, that there is a clearly defined union utility function.

The union has a fixed number of identical workers and cares for the utility of only the workers in the unionized sector. Let $u = u(w)$ be the utility of any of the union members. The union's objective function is $U(w, n) = nu(w) + (t - n)u(b)$, where n denotes the employment in the unionized sector, t is the total number of union workers and b is the reservation wage rate. This reservation wage can be interpreted as unemployment welfare, that is, all the benefits the worker would get if he were not employed by the firm. It therefore consists of several elements—unemployment benefits, the value of leisure, the value of working around the house, etc.

We assume that $u'(w) \equiv du/dw > 0$ (marginal utility is positive), $u''(w) \equiv d^2u/dw^2 < 0$ (marginal utility is declining with w), $w > b$, and $0 < n \leq t$. Note that $U(w, n) = n\{u(w) - u(b)\} + tu(b)$, and the term $tu(b)$, being a constant, can be neglected.

The union's indifference curves can be obtained by setting $U = U^*$, where U^* is a constant. Then $dU = nu'(w)dw + \{u(w) - u(b)\}dn = 0$ on an indifference curve, which shows that $dw/dn = -\{u(w) - u(b)\}/nu'(w) < 0$ because $u(w) > u(b)$ by $w > b$ and $u'(w) > 0$. It can also be shown that the indifference curves are convex to the origin.

We will discuss two types of models: in one type of models, the union determines the wage rate, leaving the employer to determine the level of employment, and in the other type, the union and the employer bargain over the wage rate and/or the employment.

13.2.1 The Monopoly Union Model

Consider the first type of model. The firm tries to maximize profit $\pi = pq(n) - wn$, $q'(n) > 0$ and $q'(n) < 0$. Suppose that the product market is competitive and the firm believes that w is given. Then the first order condition for profit-maximization leads to the familiar condition $pq'(n) = w$, or value of marginal product is equated to the wage rate. (Assume that the second order condition is satisfied.) This, we know, makes value of marginal product curve the demand curve for labour. The union next chooses the best w at the point of tangency of the labour demand curve with the highest indifference curve. The union has monopoly power in the sense that it can unilaterally set the wage rate.

The union in this situation is trying to maximize $U = n\{u(w) - u(b)\} + tu(b)$ subject to $pq'(n) = w$. Now, $dU/dw = nu'(w) + \{u(w) - u(b)\}(dn/dw)$. From the labour demand function, $pq'(n)(dn/dw) = 1$, that is, $dn/dw = 1/pq'(n)$. Using this result, we see that the union maximizes utility by setting $dU/dw = nu'(w) + \{u(w) - u(b)\}\{1/pq'(n)\} = 0$.

The condition $dU/dw = nu'(w) + \{u(w) - u(b)\}(dn/dw) = 0$ can be written as

$$\varepsilon = wu'(w)/[u(w) - u(b)],$$

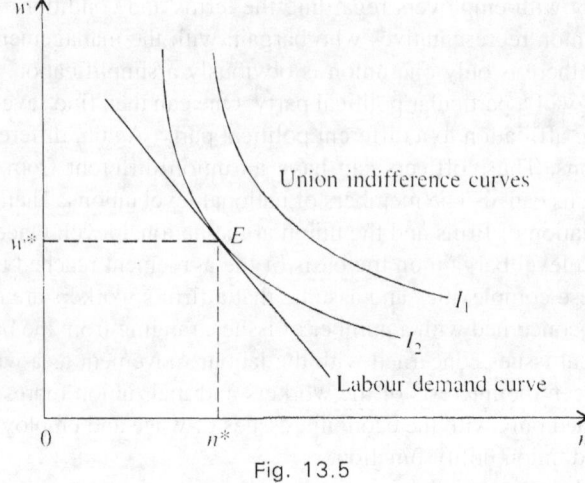

Fig. 13.5

where $\varepsilon = -(dn/dw)(w/n)$, that is, the elasticity of labour demand. We can then conclude that the wage will be set by the union at a level such that the percentage increase in a member's utility due to a percentage increase in wages is exactly equal to the elasticity of labour demand.

The intuition behind this result is that an increase in wages reduces employment in the union sector, so that some workers (the employed) gain while others (the unemployed) lose. The precentage increase in utility due to the wage rise must be offset against the precentage loss in employment and consequent reduction in utility.

A final observation is that the solution we have derived is a subgame-perfect equilibrium. The model can be viewed as a two-stage model. In the first stage, the union chooses w. In the second stage, the firm, taking w as given, chooses n. To obtain the subgame-perfect equilibrium, we need to solve the problem backwards. First, the firm's response function is obtained in the form of the labour demand curve, for any given w. Next, the union selects the best w on the response curve (acting like a Stackelberg leader).

Example 13.3: Suppose that labour is the only input and that the firm enjoys constant returns to scale. Hence we can write the production function as $q = n$. The product market is perfectly competitive so that p is given. Let the utility function of any union member be $u(w) = w$.

The first task is to derive the firm's demand curve for labour. $\pi = (p - w)n$, and the first order condition yields $n = (a - w)/2$. We then see that $p = [(a - w)/2]^2$.

The union tries to maximize $U = n(w - b) + tb$, subject to $n = (a - w)/2$. Therefore $U = [(a - w)/2](w - b) + tb$. Maximization of U with respect to w leads to $w = (a + b)/2$, which we can write as $w = b + (a - b)/2$ which shows that the union manages to set wage at a level higher than the reservation wage rate b.

13.2.2 Bargaining Models

In the monopoly union model, the union imposes its wage decision on the firm. While this might be true in a few industries, casual observation suggests that wages are more likely to be the outcome of a bargaining process between the union and the management. When the firm and the union are bargaining over wages, they are in a *bilateral monopoly* situation, in which a single seller of labour confronts a single buyer. The union emerges as the single seller of labour, because nonunion workers cannot be easily or costlessly substituted for union workers by the firm. There is a cost of training new workers. Moreover, union members can even prevent physically nonunion members from joining work. The firm emerges as the sole buyer of labour, because workers face costs of relocating to other jobs, perhaps even of becoming unemployed.

The two parties can bargain over many issues which can again be conveniently summarized under the headings of wage and employment. There are two broad approaches to modelling bargaining behaviour—the axiomatic approach and the non-cooperative game-theoretic approach. The former is a static approach and focuses on the *outcome* of the bargaining process. The latter tries to model the *process* of bargaining. Here, we shall discuss only the former approach.

The axiomatic approach can be interpreted in the following way. Suppose that the union and the firm are bargaining with each other. They appoint an arbitrator to determine an acceptable outcome. The arbitrator formulates a set of axioms that any reasonable and acceptable bargaining outcome must satisfy and tries to search out such an outcome. This solution is accepted by the two bargainers.

Within the axiomatic approach, we can distinguish between *right-to-manage* models and *efficient bargaining models*. In a right to manage model, the union and the firm first bargain over the wage rate and then the firm decides on the employment. In an *efficient bargaining model* the union and the firm simultaneously bargain for both w and n. In contrast to the right to manage model, the efficient bargaining model yields an effcient solution, in the sense that no one can be made better off without making the other bargainer worse off.

Strikes and Lockouts

An union can achieve a wage rate greater than the competitive wage rate if (a) there is some surplus to be shared between the firm and the union and (b) the union has some bargaining power. The union will possess some bargaining power if it is costly to replace the members of the union with nonunion workers. An union's threat to strike enhances its bargaining power if the firm cannot quickly and easily replace the striking workforce.

A paradox posed by Hicks in this context is that if there is perfect information and rational economic agents, then we will never see any strike in equilibrium. A strike imposes costs in terms of a reduced surplus to be shared between the union and the firm, since some output is forgone during the period of the strike. The owners lose profits while the workers lose wages and salaries. If agents can fully anticipate this, they may as well reach an agreement without a strike, because then they will have a larger pie to bargain over. Hence, there will be no strikes.

The strike literature has subsequently developed in three directions. The first is to relax the assumption of rationality, the second is to reject the theoretical approach in favour of ad hoc empiricism and the third is to drop the assumption of perfect information. Thus if the union acts irrationally and holds out for a wage rate that is above the maximum that the management is prepared to concede, then the negotiations break down. Or, if management is unaware of the range of wages acceptable to the union, it can hold out for a wage below the minimum labour is willing to accept.

A lockout describes a situation in which the employer closes down production to enhance bargaining power vis-à-vis the union. The Hicksian paradox would appear to apply equally well to lockouts.

Strikes and Lockouts in India

Year	Public Sector	Private Sector	Strikes	Lockouts	Total
1991	653	1157	1278	532	1810
1992	617	1097	1011	703	1714
1993	359	1034	914	479	1393
1994	316	885	808	393	1201
1995	343	723	732	334	1066

Source: The Indian Journal of Labour Economics, April–June 1997.

13.3 Capital

The term capital refers to all the instruments of production that are deliberately made by man to carry on production in the future. Examples of capital assets are machines, aircraft, trains, etc. They are long-lived and provide services over a number of periods. Durable consumer goods like refrigerators look very much like capital assets. However, capital goods are used to produce consumer goods or capital goods that can produce consumer goods. A consumer durable good provides services that can be directly consumed. Unlike labour and output which are measured as *flows*, we measure capital as a *stock*. If a firm owns a factory with equipment worth Rs 50 lakh, we say that it has a capital stock worth Rs 50 lakh. On the other hand, we will say that so many labour-hours has been used each day/month/year to produce so much of output in the corresponding period.

The firm hires labour services on a period-by-period basis. But capital equipment can be rented as well as owned. Moreover, the markets for both real capital, that is, productive equipment, and financial capital, that is, paper assets, are interrelated. We will consider these issues in turn.

13.3.1 The Demand for Rented Capital

Consider first the firm's decision to *rent* capital. If r is the rental rate in a perfectly competitive rental market for capital, then the firm will rent capital up to the point at which its marginal revenue product of capital is equal to the rental rate:

$$MR \cdot MP_K = r,$$

where MP_K is the marginal product of capital. If the product market is perfectly competitive, then $P \cdot MP_K = r$, that is, the value of marginal product of capital is equated to the rental rate.

Deriving the market demand curve for capital involves complications similar to that were discussed for the market demand curve for labour.

13.3.2 The Rental Rate and the Interest Rate

The rental price of a piece of real capital equipment is intimately related to the interest rate at which money can be borrowed. Suppose that a firm is in the business of renting machines and that it has purchased a new equipment worth Rs 1000. At what rate should it rent out the machine?

If the going interest rate is 10 per cent per year, then the yearly rental rate should be at least Rs 100. Otherwise, it would be better for the firm to put its money in the bank rather than be in the business of renting machines. Next, the machine may need Rs 50 worth of maintenance per year. But even the best maintenance cannot prevent a degree of wear and tear. Moreover, over time, as new machines come into the market, the economic value of machines goes down. Suppose, that every year the value of the machine goes down by Rs 50 (it can be sold on the market at a price that is Rs 50 less than the orginal purchase price). Let us club the depreciation and economic obsolescence factors together and price them at Rs 100. Then the firm needs to earn a rental of at least Rs 250 per year to make it worth its while to be in the renting business.

Our discussion can be summarized as follows. Let m stand for the annual maintenance expenses, expressed as a fraction of the price of the capital good and let d stand for the physical and technological depreciation, similarly expressed. If i denotes the market rate of interest, then the annual rental rate r must be the sum of i, m and d in a perfectly competitive market:

$$r = i + m + d.$$

If, for example, $r > i + m + d$, then capital will be hired until r is again equated to $i + m + d$. Note that the higher the interest rate is, higher the rental rate, other things remaining the same. Hence a higher interest rate leads to a lower rental demand for capital.

13.3.3 Purchase of Capital Goods

Labourers cannot be bought or sold. But firms have the option of purchasing capital equipment. In fact, the supply of capital goods on a rental basis may not exist. The reason is that the rental rate must be renegotiated from year to year. A second reason is that the firm renting a capital good may not be careful in using it, and the actual wear and tear may be more than what is covered by the rental rate agreed upon. So far as such goods are concerned, the firm must purchase them.

How will the firm decide whether to buy a piece of capital equipment or not? The firm will wish to balance the benefits of owning the machine against the costs. On the benefit side, the capital equipment will make it possible to produce more output each year over a number (say, N) of years, starting next year. This will increase total revenue by Rs R per year for N years. At the end of N years, the machine can be sold for scrap for Rs S. On the other hand, the machine costs Rs M every year to maintain.

We know that Re 1 this year is worth Rs $(1 + i)$ the next year, Rs $(1 + i)^2$ the year after, and so on. This is because the money can be put in a bank and made to earn interest at the rate i per year. Therefore, Re 1 next year is worth Rs $1/(1 + i)$ this year, Re 1 the year after is worth Rs $1/(1 + i)^2$ this year, and so on. Therefore, the stream of returns the firm earns over N years must be converted into an equivalent *present discounted value*.

The net present discounted value of the stream of returns produced by the machine, including the scrap value, can be written as

$$PV = (R - M)/(1 + i) + (R - M)/(1 + i)^2 + \ldots + (R - M)/(1 + i)^N + S/(1 + i)^N.$$

The cost of the machine is its purchase price P_K. The machine will be purchased if and only if PV is greater than or equal to P_K.

It is easy to see that the higher the interest rate, the lower the present discounted value of the stream of returns. We can view the decision to invest in the capital good in a slightly different way. Suppose, we ask the question: what is the discount rate such that $PV - P_K = 0$, when this rate is applied to discount the stream of returns? This discount rate is called the *internal rate of return*. Thus, the internal rate of return g is such that

$$PV = (R - M)/(1 + g) + (R - M)/(1 + g)^2 + \ldots + (R - M)/(1 + g)^N + S/(1 + g)^N - P_K = 0.$$

Consider a simple example. A machine yields Rs 1100 for one year, then becomes unusable, without any scrap value. The purchase price of the machine is Rs 1000. Obviously, the internal rate of return is 10 per cent. Now, if the internal rate of return is higher than the rate of interest, the capital asset should be purchased, because it provides a return higher than the opportunity cost of the funds employed.

An inverse demand curve for the capital asset can now be constructed. This plots the internal rate of return against the number of assets. As more and more capital assets are demanded, the internal rate of return falls since more assets means more supply of the products of the capital goods in the future and hence lower future returns. Equilibrium in the market is reached when the internal rate of return becomes equal to the interest rate. If the interest rate rises, note that less of the capital good will be purchased in equilibrium. In Fig. 13.6, when the rate of interest is i, M^* amount of capital assets will be demanded.

We also note that the purchase price of capital is usually certain, since it is in the present. However, the revenues from capital accrue over a period of time and can often be highly uncertain. The person who buys the capital equipment must work on the basis of some estimates of these revenues and maintenance costs rather than any predetermined numbers.

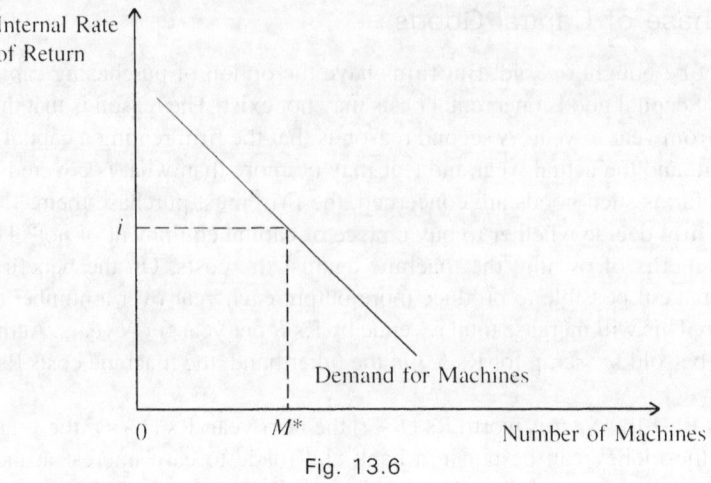

Fig. 13.6

13.3.4 Interest Rate Determination

Interest rates are determined in the market for loanable funds. The *demand* for loanable funds depends, among other things, on the demand for capital. In any period, a firm will own a certain amount of capital stock, K. This may be different from the amount of capital the firm would like to have, K^*. In the given period, the firm wishes to bridge a fraction, say z, of the gap between K and K^*. Then $z(K^* - K)$ is the firm's demand for loanable funds. The total demand for loanable funds will therefore partly depend on the firms' demand for loanable funds in different industries. In addition, consumers also borrow to finance the purchase of houses, cars, and other goods. Governments borrow to build roads and bridges and schools and also to finance the budget deficits. The aggregate demand for loanable funds is the horizontal summation of the demand curves for all these sectors.

There are multiple suppliers of loanable funds. Consumer savings (chanelled through banks, non-banking financial intermediaries, mutual funds, etc.) supplement savings made by firms out of profits. Foreign lenders can also play an important role. Adding all the sources of supply horizontally, we get the aggregate supply curve.

The intersection of the demand and supply curves for loanable funds determines the rate of interest, i.

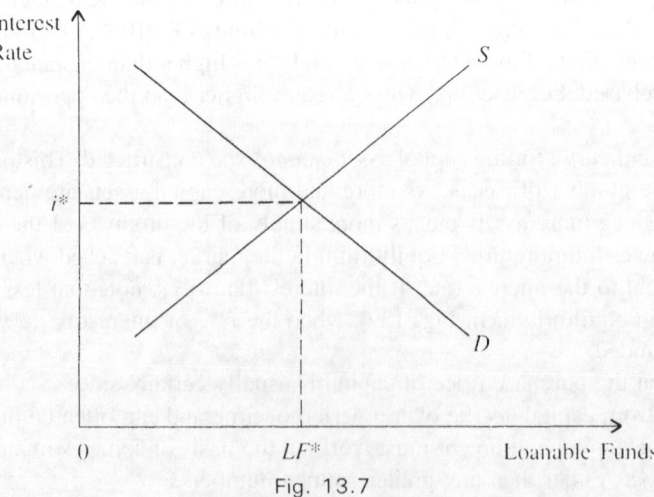

Fig. 13.7

13.3.5 Nominal and Real Rates of Interest

Suppose that you borrow Rs 1000 from a bank which you agree to repay in a year's time at 5 per cent interest. Also suppose that all prices in the economy rise by 10 per cent at the end of the year. Then the annual rate of inflation is 10 per cent. What is then the real cost of the loan?

Suppose that at the beginning of the year, rice cost Rs 10 a kg, and you used your borrowing to buy 100 kgs of rice. At the end of the year, this rice can be sold off for Rs 1100. Only Rs 1050 is needed to repay the loan. Therefore, the real cost of the loan, measured in rupees on the due date, is—Rs 50. While you came out ahead by Rs 50, the bank that loaned you the funds came out Rs 50 behind.

When banks expect the rate of inflation to be positive, they charge an interest premium to counteract the erosion in the real purchasing power of future loan repayments. The actual number that appears on the bank contracts is the *nominal rate of interest*. In our example it is 5 per cent. The real rate of interest is the nominal rate of interest adjusted for the change in purchasing power due to inflation. If n is the annual rate of interest expressed as a fraction, and q is the annual rate of inflation similarly expressed, then the real rate of interest i is

$$i = (n - q)/(1 + q).$$

For small q, i is almost equal to $n - q$.

It should be noted that in our previous discussions, we have implicitly assumed that the interest rate is the real interest rate, since the firm will be comparing the real costs of investment with the real benefits.

13.3.6 The Market for Bonds

When a firm tries to raise money for new investments, it can do so by issuing either bonds or stocks. We now consider these financial instruments in turn.

A firm can directly borrow funds by issuing bonds. Suppose I lend Rs 100 to a firm. The firm issues me a certificate, called a bond, which promises to pay me a fixed rate of interest on this Rs 100 for a number of years n, and then to pay me back the Rs 100 at the end of n years. I am then a creditor of the firm. The sum of Rs 100 which I lend to the firm, and which is mentioned on the certificate, is called the face value of the bond.

Once bought, a bond can be traded in the open market. The market value of the bond can be considerably different from the face value of the bond. Why is this so?

Suppose that the market rate of interest is 5 per cent and the face value of a bond is Rs 1000. The bond promises to pay back the Rs 1000 after 10 years and in the meanwhile pay Rs 50 every year to the holder of the bond. Then one finds it worthwhile to invest in the bond, because the Rs 1000 invested in the bond fetches the same interest as an equivalent amount kept in a bank.

Now, suppose that the rate of interest goes up to 10 per cent. Then the bond will be worth only Rs 500 because one can earn Rs 50 every year by keeping Rs 500 in a bank. So no one will be willing to pay more than Rs 500 for the bond.

The price of the bond will not fall all the way to Rs 500 because the buyer knows that the bond will pay Rs 1000 on maturity. If the maturity date is imminent, the value of the bond will be Rs 1000, no matter what the market rate of interest is. The face value of the bond and the market value will almost coincide. But the further away the maturity period is, the less will the face value affect the market value of the bond. In the limit, if the bond (called a *consol*) promises to pay a certain amount for ever, the face value will not matter at all. Suppose that a bond promises to pay Rs 100 for ever, and the rate of interest is 5 per cent. Then the value of the bond will be Rs 2000, the sum of money that will pay Rs 100 at 5 per cent interest rate.

Generally, if I is the consol's annual payment and i the interest rate, then the value of the bond will be Rs (I/i).

13.3.7 The Market for Stocks

A bondholder does not have an ownership share in the firm issuing the bond. An alternative way for a firm to raise funds is to sell ownership shares. The firm hires a broker to arrange a new issue of stock certificates. The broker prepares a description of the firm's investment proposal, including the return prospects and attendant risks and offers the stock for sale to the public.

If a firm has sold a total of 1,000,000 shares of stock, each stock constitutes a claim against $1/(1,000,000)$ of the firm's current and future profits. Profits may either be distributed to stockholders as dividends, or reinvested in the company.

A stockholder can gain or lose in either of two ways. First, she is entitled to a share of the dividends declared by the firm every year. Second, she can sell the stocks and make capital gains or losses. If a firm performs poorly in the sense that it does not make profits, then there is poor prospect of dividends being declared in the future and the stock values in the open market will be low.

A bondholder's risks are limited, so long as there is low probability of default. The stockholder, on the other hand, directly participates in the risks of running the firm, by sharing in the uncertain returns of the firm.

Industrial Securities in India

In India, firms raise funds through (a) ordinary shares, (b) preference shares, and (c) debentures or bonds. Ordinary and preference shares are also known as stocks or equities. We have already discussed ordinary shares. A preference share carries a fixed rate of dividend like a debenture. The holders of preference shares are entitled to be paid after the claims of the creditors have been met but before ordinary shareholders receive any income. Preference shares, again can be of different types:

1. Cumulative and non-cumulative—On cumulative preference shares, if dividend is skipped in any period(s), it has to be paid subsequently.
2. Convertible and non-convertible—Convertible preference shares can be converted into ordinary shares subsequently.
3. Redeemable and non-redeemable—A redeemable preference share matures in a fixed period of time. Therefore, for all practical purposes, this type of share can be viewed as a debenture.
4. Participating and non-participating—Participating preference shareholders can earn a higher dividend than the fixed one if the company makes good profits.

It is clear, then, that certain types of shares are very similar to bonds. Certain types of bonds, again, are similar to stocks. For example, convertible debentures can be converted at the option of the holder into ordinary shares of the company. The other type of debenture that has attracted a lot of attention is the rights debentures. Such debentures are not issued to the public, but to the existing shareholders in a certain ratio to the ordinary shares held by them. They are subscribed mainly by financial institutions and various trusts rather than by small investors, because of their low interest rates and lack of liquidity.

Source: L.M. Bhole, 1992, *Financial Institutions and Markets: Structure, Growth and Innovations,* 2nd edition.Tata McGraw-Hill.

13.4 Natural Resources

In addition to labour and capital, natural resources are often important inputs in the production process. There is now growing concern that the fast expanding global economy is in danger of outstripping the capacity of earth and its resources. As a result, attention has been focused on the rate at which such resources should be depleted.

Earlier economists used the word 'land' to refer to natural resources. A key concern was why owners of land earned a return on land, called *rent*. In common usage, rent refers to periodic payments made regularly for the hire of a good, say a house. Now, the rent for a house includes a payment for the use of the land on which the house is situated, but it also includes the return on the investment made on the house. To abstract from these other components and focus on rent for the hire of land only, we consider a landlord renting out his land to a tenant. The landowner does not have to do anything to earn a return on the land. He earns a rent just because he happens to own the land. Then why does rent exist?

The answer that was given was that land earned a rent because it was scarce. In fact, it was viewed to be in fixed supply, that is, the supply of land was perfectly inelastic. The addition to the existing amount of land was too small to have any discernible effect on the supply of land.

Let there be perfect competition in the land market: there are many landowners who want to rent their land. All land is homogeneous. Tenants can sell the product from land and therefore they demand land. First, suppose that the demand curve is DD. The available supply is not exhausted. Competition among the landowners drives the rent to zero. Next, suppose that the demand curve shifts to $D'D'$. Since land is in inelastic supply, a positive rent (equal to r^*) emerges. In the Fig. 13.8, the rent is equal to the area $OSAr^*$. It is clear that this concept of rent can also be used to characterize the earnings of any factor of production that is in perfectly inelastic supply.

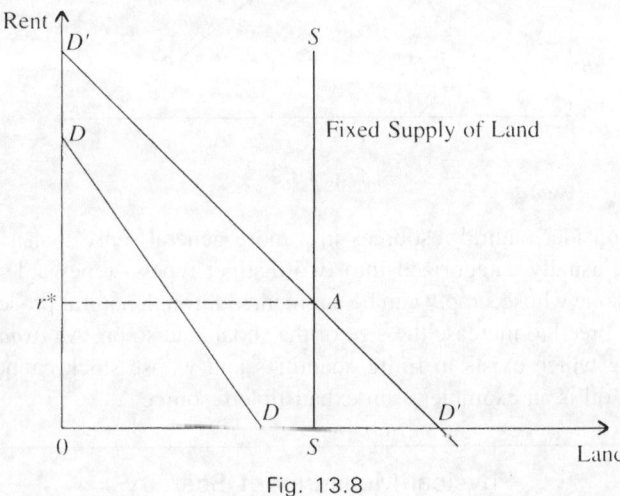

Fig. 13.8

The characteristic feature of *pure scarcity rent* just now described is that while a rise in the prices of other factors generally causes an increase in their supply (at least in the long run), a rise in rent cannot increase the supply of land. Even with competitive markets, higher earnings for land can persist in the long run.

The concept of rent has been extended to that of quasi-rent. A *quasi-rent* is earned by a factor that is in perfectly inelastic supply in the short run, but in elastic supply in the long run. In our earlier discussion, capital K has been taken to be fixed in the short run. Hence quasi-rent in the short run accrues because of K. We know that $\pi = TR - TVC - TFC$, which means that the quasi-rent is $TR - TVC = \pi + TFC$. If, for example, the short-run price is high, then $\pi > 0$, and the quasi-rent exceeds the rental on the machine (= $TFC = rK$). If short-run $\pi < 0$, the quasi-rent falls below the rental on the machine.

More generally, *economic rent* can be defined as the difference between the payments made to a factor of production and the minimum amount that must be spent to obtain the use of that factor. Fig. 13.9 illustrates the concept of economic rent as applied to a competitive labour market. In equilibrium, the wage rate is w^* and the quantity of labour is L^*. All workers are paid w^*. However, except for the last 'marginal' worker, this wage rate is above the minimum amount required for the other workers. Remember that the supply curve can be interpreted as showing the minimum prices needed to induce supply of any amount. Hence economic rent is the area w^*EL^*0 – the area BEL^*0 = the area w^*EB.

If the supply curve had been perfectly inelastic, then the minimum amount needed to get L^* is 0 and we are back to the case of pure scarcity rent. If the supply curve is perfectly elastic, the rent is zero.

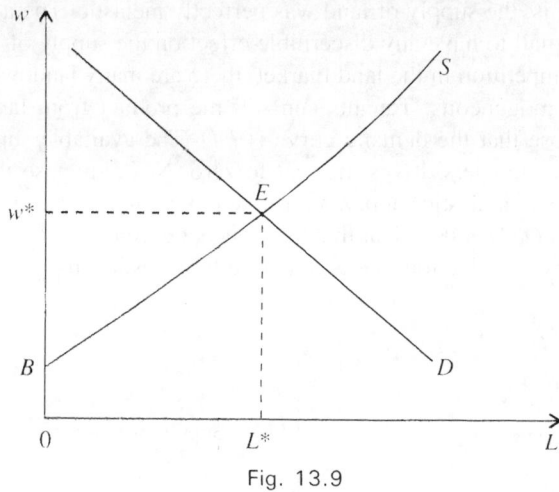

Fig. 13.9

We now turn to consider natural resources in a more general sense than land resources alone. Natural resources are usually categorized into two distinct types—renewable and exhaustible. A *renewable* resource is one whose supply can be augmented through natural processes. Thus trees can be planted, fishes can breed to increase the size of the shoal, and so on. An *exhaustible* resource, on the other hand, is one which exists in finite quantities and whose stock cannot be replaced once exhausted. Petroleum oil is an example of an exhaustible resource.

Physical Measures of Scarcity

One physical measure of scarcity of extractive resources like oil that is often used is the estimated reserves. Dividing the estimated reserves by some measure of depletion like annual production or consumption of the resource in question, we can predict the number of years for which the reserves will last. However, over time, the estimated reserves figure changes for several reasons. New reserves are discovered. Processes for extracting or converting the reserves more cheaply are developed. Economic conditions can also affect the estimates. If reserves are defined as the known amounts of the resources that can be *profitably* produced at current prices using current technologies, then a fall in the price of the resource can increase the amount of the reserves that can be used profitably.

Another measure is *crustal abundance*. This refers to the material that exists in minute concentrations on the 'average rock' on the earth's crust. The crustal abundance measure gives a much rosier picture of the availability of resources than the reserves measure. However, cost barriers will often make it prohibitive to extract resources from the rocks.

Considerable attention has been paid to the question of the *optimal depletion* of natural resources. We will next examine some of the basic conclusions that have emerged.

13.4.1 Renewable Resources

Renewable resources are different from exhaustible resources by virtue of the fact that they are naturally regenerated within a time period relevant to human exploitation. Catching a fish or cutting a tree does reduce the population of fish or trees immediately, but this effect may be temporary if the natural growth is permitted unhindered for a few periods. Thus renewable resources can be exhausted, but need not be.

Renewable resources are often assumed to follow a 'natural growth law'. The growth rate is assumed to be simply a function of the size of the resource stock. Moreover, the relationship is not monotonic, but inverse U-shaped. The growth rate at first rises with the size of the stock, and then falls. The reason is that the natural environment has a 'carrying capacity' for the resource, a maximum population that it can sustain.

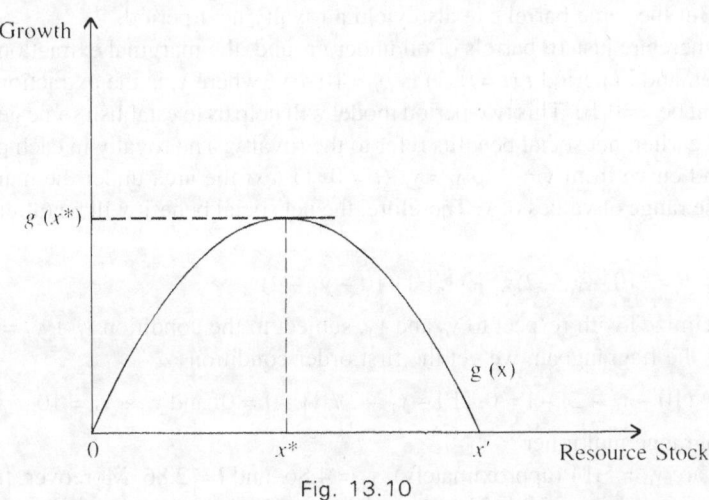

Fig. 13.10

The natural growth law is represented by the growth curve $g(x)$ in Fig. 13.10. The carrying capacity is $x = x'$, the largest stock that the environment can sustain. There is zero growth for this size of the stock. One can then ask: what is the stock corresponding to the maximum amount that can be harvested each period indefinitely? As can be seen from the figure, the *maximum sustainable yield* is $g(x^*)$, and the corresponding stock is x^*. If the stock is allowed to grow to x^*, then each period the addition to the stock will be $g(x^*)$, and this can be harvested without depleting the stock x^*.

What should be the optimal depletion of the resource if it is owned by an individual? Let us consider a simple two-period situation. The stock in the first period is x_0 and g is the growth rate. The owner has the option of letting the stock grow and then sell it in period 1 at the known price p per unit. For one unit of the stock that is left to grow, the revenue in period 1 will be $p(1 + g)$. On the other hand, she can harvest this unit in period 0 and invest the proceeds at the market rate of interest i per period. Then she will get $p(1 + i)$ in the next period. She will go on harvesting as long as $p(1 + g) > p(1 + i)$ and stop when these two are equal. Hence the optimal depletion rule is $g = i$, that is, the growth rate should be equated to the interest rate.

13.4.2 Exhaustible Resources

The stock of an exhaustible resource cannot be replenished. Once the earth's stocks of oil, gold, iron etc. run out, we will have to do without them. In this section we look at the rule for optimal depletion of an exhaustible resource.

The owner of an exhaustible resource also has to decide between selling it in the current period or holding it. However, unlike renewable resources, the stock of an exhaustible resource cannot grow. Hence the only reason for holding an exhaustible resource and not selling it immediately is the expectation of a future rise in its price.

The difference between the price and marginal extraction cost of an exhaustible resource may be called the royalty. The royalty must be taken into account in determining how to allocate the resource over time. Instead of the usual price = marginal (extraction/production) cost condition for efficiency, we now have price = marginal extraction cost + royalty. We wish to find out the behaviour of the royalty over time, given that the aim is to maximize net benefit to society.

Consider a barrel of oil. The net social benefit from extracting the barrel today is clearly the royalty, the difference between the amount consumers are willing to pay (price) and the marginal extraction cost. But the same barrel can also yield a royalty next period.

Suppose that there are just 10 barrels of oil under ground, the marginal extraction cost is Rs 2 per barrel, and the demand in period t $(t = 0, 1)$ is $p_t = 10 - y_t$, where y_t is the extraction in period t. Let the rate of discount be $r = 0.10$. This two period model will help us to establish some general principles.

As mentioned earlier, net social benefits refer to the royalty. The royalty in each period is the area below the demand curve from $y = 0$ to $y = y_t$, $(t = 0, 1)$ *less* the area under the marginal extraction curve for the same range of values of y. Therefore, the net social benefit will be (after discounting the term in period 1)

$$B = (10 - y_0 - 2)y_0 + (1/1.1)(10 - y_1 - 2)y_1$$

This is to be maximized with respect to y_0 and y_1, subject to the condition $y_0 + y_1 = 10$.

After forming the Lagrangean, we get the first order conditions

$$(10 - y_0 - 2) - 1 = 0, (10 - y_1 - 2)/1.1 - 1 = 0, \text{ and } y_0 + y_1 = 10,$$

where 1 is the Lagrange multiplier.

The solutions are $y_0 = 5.14$ (approximately), $y_1 = 4.86$, and $1 = 2.86$. Moreover, from the demand equations, $p_0 = 4.86$ and $p_1 = 5.14$. These numbers can be interpreted as follows. The royalty in period 0 is $p - MC = 4.86 - 2.00 = 2.86$. The royalty in period 1 is 3.14, but notice that when discounted, it comes to just 2.86 (3.14/1.1). Therefore, the present value of the royalty is the same in both periods. The undiscounted royalty has grown precisely by 10 per cent, the discount rate. Our first result then is: *the present value of the royalty must be the same in all periods*, or, equivalently, *the undiscounted royalty must rise at the rate of discount.*

The intuition is that efficiency requires that the marginal gains from current extraction must be equal to the marginal gains from the rise in the value of the asset in the future. The latter is just the difference between price and marginal cost. Hence extraction is apportioned in such a way that the royalty rises at the common rate of interest. If the resource is extracted and sold today, the seller gets $(p_0 - MC)$. This amount can be put in a bank and by the second period it would have grown to $(p_0 - MC)(1 + r)$. If the oil is sold tomorrow, then the seller will obtain $p_1 - MC$. The oil is sold in both the periods only if $(p_1 - MC) = (p_0 - MC)(1 + r)$.

Our result shows that $(p_1 - MC) = (p_0 - MC)(1 + r)$. More generally, we will have $(p_t - MC) = (p_0 - MC)(1 + r)^t$, which can be written as $p_t = MC + (p_0 - MC)(1 + r)^t$. *Price draws away from the marginal extraction cost, rising at a rate that approaches the rate of interest.* In the simple case where $MC = 0$, price rises at the rate of interest.

This rise in prices will have two consequences. First, since the demand curve for the exhaustible resource is downward sloping, the rise in price will cause a gradual reduction in the quantity demanded. The initial stock will be used up gradually, not precipitously. Second, the effect of rising prices will encourage the search for substitutes.

13.5 Entrepreneurship

In the nineteenth century as well as the early twentieth century, one-man enterprises were quite common. One person hired the other factors of production like labour, capital and raw materials and organized the productive activity in a firm. Such a person was the entrepreneur and her rewards were the profits from the operations of the firm.

Profit was therefore the reward for the use of some input in the production process. What was the nature of the input provided by the entrepreneur? According to F.H. Knight, the entrepreneur's role was to bear the *non-insurable risks* and *uncertainties* associated with the production process. The difference between insurable and non-insurable risks is that the probability that some events will occur can be predicted statistically, while the probability that others will occur cannot be so predicted. For example, it is possible for an insurance company to predict that (say) 1 per cent of the factories in a given region will catch fire in a year. The company can then offer an insurance against the fire hazard which can be bought by the entrepreneur. But it is impossible for insurance companies to predict what percentage of firms will make losses and what percentage will make profits. The entrepreneur in a particular firm has to use her own judgement about whether a particular product will sell on the market, whether an advertising campaign will be successful, whether a lowering of price will provoke similar price-cuts from rivals, etc. Wrong estimates on any of these events will hurt profits, but there is no insurance available to guard against the effects of misjudgements.

Entrepreneurs usually worked for their own firms and sometimes invested capital in the firm. The total income of the entrepreneur therefore could have a wage component and an interest component in addition to the profit component.

The rapid expansion of the joint-stock form of organization in the twentieth century has led to a separation of ownership from control. Profits are distributed to shareholders, but many small shareholders do not take any part in running the firm. The top managers of a firm like the CEOs usually take entrepreneurial decisions, but their rewards come not from the uncertain stream of profits, but rather from fixed salaries. We have already seen that shareholder and managerial goals may not coincide and shareholders may try to devise incentive schemes that align their goals more closely with the goals of managers.

Topics for Discussion

1. Individuals are often very reluctant to discuss their wages or salary with their coworkers. What economic motives do they have to keep such information secret? When workers are unionized, wage information is often revealed in the form of salary schedules. Why do unions prefer to reveal wage information?
2. In India, new stocks are issued in roughly two ways: issue to the public and right issue. The right issue is made only to existing shareholders. But even in a public issue like that through prospectus, there is a practice of prior allotment of securities to certain categories of investors like directors, promoters, friends of promoters, etc. Do you think that rights issues are desirable from the point of view of the efficient governance of a firm?

Exercise

1. A competitive firm faces a price of Rs 10 for its product in the output market. Some figures relating to its operations are given below:

Number of workers	Output	Marginal product of labour	Value of marginal product of labour	Wage rate (Rs)
0				
1	300			2000
2	700			2000
3	1200			2000
4	1800			2000
5	2300			2000
6	2700			2000
7	3000			2000
8	3200			2000
9	3300			2000
10	3300			2000

Fill the blanks with appropriate numbers. How many workers would the profit-maximizing firm employ and why?

2. Suppose that a perfectly competitive firm has a production function $Q = L^{0.5}$. What is the equation of the firm's labour demand curve? If the firm is a monopolist and the equation of the inverse demand curve facing the firm is $p = a - Q$, what is the equation of the labour demand curve?

3. Suppose a monopsonist's inverse demand curve for labour is given by $w = 80 - L$.

   If the supply curve of labour is $w = 4L$ and the MFC curve is $w = 8L$, what is the optimal amount of labour and what is the wage paid? How would the answer change if the firm is perfectly competitive?

4. Suppose that the purchase price of a machine is Rs 10,000. If the annual interest rate is 0.08, the maintenance rate is 0.02 and the rate of depreciation is 0.10, how much will be the machine's annual rental fee?

5. If you buy a transistor for Rs 100 down and Rs 100 a year for two more years, what is the present value of these payments at a 5 per cent rate of interest?

6. A machine that costs Rs 100 will yield returns of 30 at the end of each of the next three years, at which time it will be sold as scrap for Rs 30. If the interest rate is 10 per cent, should the firm purchase the machine?

7. Suppose Shyam has an utility function $u = M + 2T^{0.5}$, where M is income and T leisure.

   (i) Derive his labour supply function.
   (ii) What is the minimum wage at which he is willing to work at all?
   (iii) Will the curve be backward-bending?

14 Externalities and Public Goods

If markets always functioned efficiently when left to themselves, there would be no need for government intervention. But markets sometimes fail to achieve efficient allocation of resources. One reason might be the presence of imperfect competition. Other reasons for *market failure* can be the presence of externalities and public goods and we now turn to a discussion of these.

We have been assuming till now that actions or decisions by one individual agent do not directly affect anybody else. If I go to the market and buy a pair of shoes, this is entirely a personal decision and has no direct effect on anyone. However, there are other types of actions that directly affect others. If you are driving past a hospital and blow your horn loudly, this can seriously affect the condition of a heart patient admitted to the hospital. On the other hand, when a parent inoculates her children against small pox, this has beneficial effects on other children who come in contact with them.

An *externality* is defined as an action by one individual agent that provides benefits or costs affecting another individual agent. The externality is *negative* when the action has negative effects on the second agent. For example, if my neighbour plays loud music at 3 am in the morning and I lose my sleep, then this is an example of a negative externality. The externality is *positive* if the effect is beneficial, as when one man's flower garden gives enjoyment to another.

We can also distinguish between consumption externalities and production externalities. A *consumption externality* occurs when one person is affected directly by another person's production or consumption. An example is when somebody starts smoking and sets another person coughing. A *production externality* occurs when the production possibilities of one firm are affected by the activities of other firms or consumers. Thus if a large firm in the industry demands more labour and sets off a wage increase, this creates a negative production externality on a smaller firm employing labour.

14.1 Externalities: The Problem

When an externality exists, efficient allocation of resources may not take place because agents often do not take the externality into consideration.

We can show this with the help of an example of a negative externality. Suppose that there is a chemical dyes industry that is perfectly competitive. Firms in the industry face a constant MC curve and hence the industry supply curve is horizontal. The industry discharges pollutants in a lake which kill off the fish in the lake. Each unit of output therefore generates pollution and the harm done by each additional unit of pollution (killing off the fishes in the lake) is represented by the *marginal externality cost* (MEC) curve.

In this industry, the MC curve represents the *marginal private cost* (MPC) curve. If unregulated, firms in the industry consider only these costs in deciding on the optimal output, because the effects on fishing do not concern them. The competitive output is obtained at the intersection of the industry supply and demand curves, and this is Q_P.

However, society consists of both the firms in the chemical dyes industry and the fishermen dependent on the lake for their livelihood. The *marginal social cost* (MSC) is therefore the sum of MPC and MEC and is obtained in Fig. 14.1 by vertically adding the two curves. From society's point of view, both the direct production cost as well as the negative cost of pollution must be taken into account. The MSC curve will obviously lie above the MPC curve and the resultant output, that is socially optimal, will be Q_C, which is less than Q_P. Thus, if a negative externality is present, the level of production determined in the market by considerations of private cost will be *higher* than the socially optimal level of output. Similarly, it can be shown that if a positive externality is present, the level of production that is determined by considerations of private cost will be lower than the socially optimal level of output.

Note, however, that the socially optimal output in the presence of a negative externality *is not* zero. Achieving a zero pollution level would require shutting down the chemical dyes industry, not an attractive option from the society's point of view. In some other cases, the MEC may in fact be so high that the socially optimal level of output will be zero. Thus to save the Taj Mahal, courts may order all polluting industries in the vicinity of Taj Mahal to shut down.

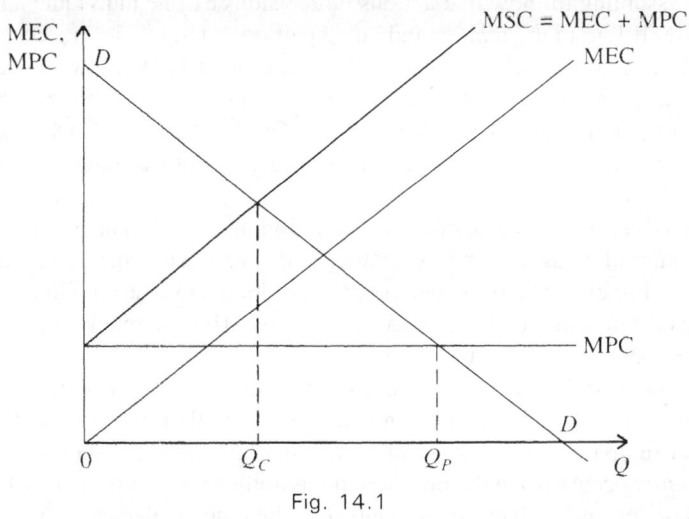

Fig. 14.1

Example 14.1: Let the equation of the inverse demand curve be $p = 20 - Q$, let the MC curve be given by MC = 2 and let MEC = 2Q. The market solution will be found from $20 - Q = 2$, that is, $Q_P = 18$, $P = $ MC = 2. To get the socially optimal solution, we note that MSC = MC + MEC = $2 + 2Q$. Setting $2 + 2Q = 20 - Q$, we get the socially optimal solution $Q_C = 6$, $P = 14$.

14.2 Solutions to the Externality Problem

Four types of solutions have been proposed to deal with externalities. As before, we keep on considering a negative externality.

1. Standard setting. If the government knew the effects of the externality exactly, then it can simply ask the polluting industry to produce the correct amount of output. Otherwise, it can mandate legal levels of pollution. An emissions standard is a legal limit on how much pollutant a firm can emit. If the firm exceeds this limit, it can face monetary or even criminal penalties. In the example considered, a ceiling of 12 may be put on the industry pollution level.

The problem with this solution is two-fold. The government or the regulatory agency often does not possess enough information and second, the costs of enforcing limits are ignored. If an industry emits smoke and the firms have to cut down on smoke emission by putting filters on chimneys, then this cost should be taken into account.

2. Pigovian tax. A second solution is to levy a tax on the output so that the price rises to reflect the cost of pollution. To do this, we must look at the *MEC at the optimal level of output*. At the socially optimal output level of 6, MEC = 12. Suppose that the government levies an excise tax of Rs 12 per unit on producers. Then MC = 2 + 12 = 14. We see that $20 - Q = 14$ implies that $Q = 6$, that is, the socially optimal level of pollution is reached in the marketplace.

It should be obvious that in the case of a positive externality, the remedy is an appropriate subsidy rather than a tax.

An example of a Pigovian tax is an effluent fee that can be levied on motorists. All vehicles would be annually inspected along with an odometer reading and tests to estimate the likely emissions of the vehicle during the past year. Different municipalities can then levy fees based on the estimated amount of pollution that had actually been generated by the operation of the vehicle. Under this system, people would face the true cost of generating pollution. Second, they can try to find out low-cost ways of reducing their emissions—investing in pollution control equipment, changing their driving habits, etc.

3. Missing markets. The problem with externalities is that there is no property right and no market for certain 'goods'. Take pollution. It may be considered to be an output of the production process, since both chemical dyes and pollution are the results of production. However, there is no market for pollution (a 'bad') and no price for it. The firms are the suppliers of pollution. The consumers are the potential 'buyers', and since pollution is a bad, we can anticipate that consumers will buy this good *only if they are paid to buy it*: the price of a 'bad' will be negative.

Suppose that there are two firms. Firm 1 operates in a perfectly competitive market and produces an output x which imposes a cost $e(x)$ on firm 2. The profits of the two firms are then:

$$\pi_1 = px - c(x) \text{ and } \pi_2 = -e(x).$$

We assume that $dc/dx > 0$ and $de/dx > 0$. Also, $c'(x) > 0$ and $e'(x) > 0$. Private profitability considerations will lead firm 1 to produce x such that $p = c'(x)$. From the social point of view, the externality costs must be taken into account and the socially optimal level of output will be obtained by maximizing $S = px - c(x) - e(x)$. The condition for this is $p = c'(x) + e'(x)$, where the expression on the right hand side represents marginal social cost.

Now suppose that there is a market for pollution. Let the price per unit of pollution be r. Denote by x_1 the amount of pollution firm 1 wants to sell and by x_2 the amount of pollution firm 2 wants to buy. The profits are then

$$\pi_1 = px_1 + rx_1 - c(x_1) \text{ and } \pi_2 = -rx_2 - e(x_2).$$

The first order conditions are

$$p + r - c'(x_1) = 0 \text{ and } -r - e'(x_2) = 0.$$

When demand for pollution equals the supply of pollution, $x_1 = x_2 = x$, and we are back to the social optimality condition $p = c'(x) + e'(x)$.

There are a number of things to be noticed about this solution. Since $e'(x) > 0$, $r < 0$: the price of pollution is negative. Second, for a market for pollution to exist, there must be property rights in pollution. Either the polluting firm should have the right to pollute or the polluted firm should have the right to clean air/water, that is, should 'own' clean air/water. The third thing is that markets for certain types of pollution can be quite 'thin'. There may be very few agents in the market. When I am disturbed by a neighbour playing loud music, the market, if it exists, will consist of only two agents. In this case, one expects bargaining to take place between the agents.

How does one create markets for externalities? One way is to allocate trading permits in pollution. The largest polluters are assigned a quota for their emission of polluting substances. If they exactly meet their quota, no fines or penalties will be levied. On the other hand, if they emit pollution below their quotas, they will be free to sell the difference to others on open market. Thus, for example, if the firm's quota is 86 tonnes of nitrogen oxide emission a year, and it actually emits only 80 tonnes, it will be free to sell the right to emit 6 tonnes to nitrogen oxide to other firms. Firms can then compare the open market price of emission credit to the cost of reducing emissions and decide what to do. The firms who can reduce emissions more cheaply will sell credits to firms that cannot do so.

The same type of mechanism is sought to be evolved for nations. Different nations will be given quotas which can either be utilized or sold to other nations. The contentious issue is who should take the lead. Under the Berlin (1995) mandate, the specific commitments will concern industrialized countries only. Many in the US argue that this is unfair and inefficient, because the most rapid emissions growth is in developing countries. Developing countries question this finding. Moreover, industrialized countries, comprising just 30 per cent of the world's population, are responsible for over 85 per cent of the greenhouse gases accumulated in the atmosphere so far. Many developing countries are still struggling to provide adequate food, shelter, health and education to their people. Developing countries find it immoral that they should take action that might jeopardize their growth prospects before the industrialized world has even stabilized its own emissions.

---

4. Internalization. Suppose that the chemical dyes industry is a monopoly and that the monopoly also owns the lake which is polluted by the discharge of industrial effluents. Then there is no externality; the externality has been *internalized* in the sense that the polluting firm must take into account the cost of pollution. The firm will select x to maximize profit which now becomes $px - c(x) - e(x)$, and the efficient level of output will be produced.

14.2.1 The Coase Theorem

Suppose that parties affected by an externality can negotiate costlessly with each other. Coase pointed out that in this case, an efficient outcome will result, no matter how the initial property rights to the externality-creating variables are assigned.

Coase's idea is quite simple. Suppose that the polluting firm is given the right to pollute. Then the polluted agent will have an incentive to pay the former to restrict pollution. The firm will accept this offer so long as the gain from this outweighs the loss in profit from cutting down production. The polluting firm's loss in profit is given by the marginal profit schedule: $p - c'(x)$. The polluted firm's gain from restricting pollution comes from the MEC schedule: $e'(x)$. The polluted firm can go on paying the polluter to restrict production as long as $e'(x) > p - c'(x)$. The firms will stop at the point where $e'(x) = p - c'(x)$. But this is precisely the condition for socially optimal amount of pollution to take place.

Suppose on the other hand, that the polluted agent is given the right to clean air. Then rather than producing nothing, it is in the interest of the polluting firm to offer the polluted agent a sum of money in return for the right to pollute (or to prevent the latter from going to court). For every extra unit of pollution, the firm will weigh the marginal gain in profit it can make and be prepared to offer a maximum amount based on this. The polluted agent will go on accepting so long as this payment adequately compensates it for the extra cost of pollution. The end-result will be the socially optimal level of pollution.

Example 14.2: Suppose that firm 1 is a monopoly and faces an inverse demand curve $p = 11 - x$. Total cost is $C = 2x$ and MEC $= 2x$.

x	Profit $= px - 2x$	Marginal Profit	MEC
1	8		
		6	2
2	14		
		4	4
3	18		
		2	6
4	20		
		0	8
5	20		

The marginal figures are given between two x figures to emphasize their marginal nature. Suppose that the monopolist is given the right to pollute. The monopoly, from profit-maximizing consideration, will produce 5 units (or 4). If the polluted agent wants it to reduce output (and pollution) by one unit, it will be prepared to pay up to 8, whereas the loss in profit will be 0. Hence, the firm and the agent should be able to reach agreement over this reduction. This process continues until $x = 3$. For a further one unit reduction in x, the maximum the polluted can pay is 4, which is exactly equal to the marginal loss in profit for firm 1. We can expect bargaining to stop here, and the socially optimal amount of x to be produced.

Of course, while the efficiency result is the same in both cases, the distributional implications are quite different. In one instance, the polluted agent has to pay the polluter, in the other the polluter has to pay. The Coase theorem also depends crucially on the absence of any transaction cost, that is, any cost of bargaining. If bargaining costs are substantial, then the gains from negotiation may be neutralized entirely by such costs, and the socially optimal outcome will not be reached.

Identification of transaction costs can alert us to situations where in the absence of government intervention, the market will not be able to reach the desired outcome, even if property rights are established. These costs include, among other things, (a) costs of discovering who is it one must deal with, (b) forming associations of affected agents to conduct bargaining, (c) conducting negotiations, (d) drawing up the contract, and (e) undertaking inspection to ensure that the conditions of the contract are being made, and so on.

The Coase theorem has an interesting implication. When there is a negative externality, we have seen that the socially optimal output x_s is less than the privately optimal output x_p. This means that when output is reduced from x_p to x_s, the gain to the agent that is suffering from pollution must be greater than the loss to the polluting party. Hence there will be a tendency for the agents to merge, internalize the externality and share appropriately the increase in the *total gain*.

Suppose that there is a chemical dyes firm and a fishing firm that is affected adversely by the operations of the former. Let m be the output of the chemical dyes firm which (for simplicity) sells its output in a perfectly competitive market at the price of Rs 5. Its cost function is $C(m) = m^2$. The chemical dyes firm maximizes profit $p_m = 5m - m^2$, by setting $5 = 2m$, so that $m^* = 5/2$. Its profit then is Rs 25/4.

Now suppose that the fishing firm is also perfectly competitive and faces a price of Rs 4. Its cost function is $C(f) = f^2 + mf$. Since $m = m^* = 5/2$, the fishing firm's profit function is $p_f = 4f - f^2 - 2.5f$. It maximizes profit by setting $f = 3/4$. Its profit is then 9/16.

Instead, if both firms were jointly owned, then the owner would be interested in maximizing the joint profit

$$\pi = \pi_m + \pi_f = 5m + 4f - m^2 - f^2 - mf.$$

The first order conditions are $\partial p/\partial m = \partial p/\partial f = 0$ and the solutions then are $f = 1$ and $m = 2$. We can see that the joint profit $p = 7$. This is higher than the aggregate profit of $25/4 + 9/16 = 6.8$ that the firms make when they take decisions independently. Hence, if the firms merge, total profit will increase and the extra profit can be shared between them. *Therefore, when a negative externality exists, the goal of profit-maximization itself will encourage firms to internalize the externalities.*

14.3 The Tragedy of the Commons

The 'tragedy of the commons' highlights what happens when property rights are not well-defined. Suppose that a village has a field in which all villagers graze their cows. The cost of purchasing a cow is Rs a. The number of cows is c and $f(c)$ is the total yield of milk from the cows when c cows graze on the field. We assume that $f'(c) > 0$, but $f''(c) < 0$, that is, the milk production function is concave. Each extra cow reduces the grass available for the other cows and therefore the average milk yield. In other words, $f(c)/c$ diminishes as c increases.

14.3.1 Private ownership

If the field is owned by only one villager, this person will buy cows to maximize profit $S = f(c) - ac$. The first order condition is $f'(c) = a$. The value of marginal product is equated to the input cost. Let the solution be $\hat{c}$.

14.3.2 Common ownership

Now suppose that the field is held in common and no villager can be prevented from grazing cows on the field. Given any c, the value of the yield of milk per cow is $f(c)/c$. Each villager will compare this return with the price of cows, a. Suppose that there are c cows in the field. The villager contemplating grazing an additional cow will compare $f(c + 1)/(c + 1)$ with a, and graze the cow if $f(c + 1)/(c + 1) > a$. Thus cows will be added to the stock grazing on the field until $f(c^*)/c^* = a$. This may also be interpreted as the free-entry, zero-profit condition: $f(c^*) - ac^* = 0$.

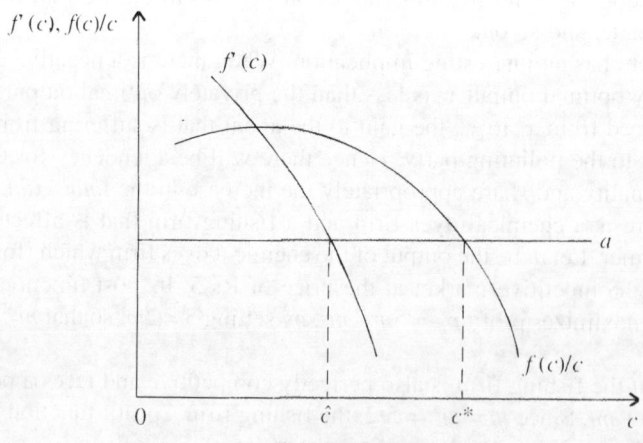

Fig. 14.2

How does this solution compare with the solution when the grazing area has a single owner? We assumed that $d[f(c)/c]/dc < 0$, so that $[f'(c) - \{f(c)/c\}]/c < 0$. This shows that $f'(c) < f(c)/c$. Hence $c^* > \hat{c}$. There will be *too many* cows grazing on the field. Adding cows to the number already grazing has a negative externality effect on milk production. However, when the land is owned in common, villagers will not take into account this negative externality, and too many cows will be grazed.

Similar tendencies are observed with respect to the use of all common property resources. Overfishing is a prime example. In the seasons when fishes breed, uncontrolled fishing may have a particularly disastrous effect on the catch of fish in the rest of the year. For sustainability, fishing must be restricted. However, each individual fisherman neglects this effect. While each fisherman has a negligible effect on the total stock of fish, the accumulated effects of thousands of fishermen result in a serious depletion of fish resources over time.

This can be depicted by a Prisoners' Dilemma Game:

		Others	
		Restraint	No restraint
Individual	Exercise restraint	(8, 8)	(2, 10)
	Don't exercise restraint	(10, 2)	(5, 5)

An individual fisherman's profits depend partly on the actions of other fishermen. If others exercise restraint, one individual's dominant strategy is not to exercise restraint, because the individual catch is too small to have any effect on sustainability of the yield. And if others do not exercise restraint, the individual has no incentive to do so.

Other examples include the use of common forest lands and use of groundwater resources in large metropolitan cities.

Does the preceding discussion imply that property rights to all common property resources (CPRs) should be handed over to individuals? The existence of CPRs in developing countries like India introduce a measure of equity in income distribution. Dependence on common property is greatest among the poor because they do not possess income-generating private property assets. Therefore they depend on CPRs for fuelwood, crop wastes, cow dung, weeds, fodder, organic manure like dry leaves and forest litter, etc. CPRs also support a variety of income-producing activities like milk production or fishing. The support provided to the poorest sections by the common pooling of resources sometimes serves to redress the bias in favour of larger and richer farmers that most technological advances in agriculture seem to have.

14.4 Public Goods

Suppose that there is a room full of people and one person starts smoking. The non-smokers all have to endure the smoke from the cigarette in equal degree, even though they may have very different preferences and resources. Similarly, when the street lamps are lighted, the benefit accrues in equal measure to all pedestrians and motorists.

When a private good like bread is consumed, the consumption of a particular piece of bread by one individual excludes another individual from consuming the same piece of bread. Moreover, different individuals can consume different amounts of bread. We say that a good is *excludable* if people can be excluded from consuming it. A good is *nonrival* in consumption if additional units can be provided to another consumer at zero marginal cost (one person's consumption does not reduce the amount left for others, that is, everyone can consume the same amount). Goods that are both non-excludable and non-rival are called *pure public goods*. More generally, goods that are non-excludable are called *public goods*.

There are many commodities that have features of either excludability or non-rivalry or none or both. The next table provides some examples of each.

	Exclusive	Nonexclusive
Rival	Most goods	Online computer services
	Clothes	Fishing
	Shoes	Congested highways
	Food	
Non-rival	When not at capacity:	*Pure public goods*
	Airline seats	National defence
	Horse racing	Streetlights

Most of the goods we consume are private goods, which are both rival and exclusive. When I buy a piece of clothing, I prevent others from buying it, and my purchase affects the cost of producing an additional garment. Note that when a particular flight is taking off and some seats are empty, the marginal costs of filling up these seats will be zero. Seating some people there will not affect the availability of seats to others. So we classify this good as non-rival in consumption. A congested highway provides an example of a good that is rival in consumption but nonexclusive. No one can be prevented from driving on the highway. Yet every extra car on the highway diminishes the space left for other cars to drive on and makes driving more difficult (reduces the consumption of service from the highway). Similarly, additional subscribers to an on-line computer service can slow down the access time of existing subscribers.

14.5 Optimal Provision of a Public Good

In this section, we discuss the optimal level of a public good whose amount can be varied continuously. Consider an economy with only two goods, one private and the other public. Suppose that there are two agents, whose initial wealth levels are given by w_1 and w_2. Their respective contributions to the public good are given by g_1 and g_2, and let x_1 and x_2 denote the consumption of the private good of each person. Let G measure the amount of the public good (in rupees) and $c(G)$ be its cost. If G amount of the public good is provided, then the two individuals have to spend Rs $c(G)$.

The two agents face the constraint that their total initial wealth cannot exceed their total expenditures on the private good and the public good:

$$x_1 + x_2 + c(G) = w_1 + w_2.$$

We consider a Pareto-efficient provision of the public good. The provision is Pareto-efficient if agent 1's utility is maximized given the utility level of agent 2. We must remember that both agents consume the same amount of the public good. The problem can then be written as

max $u_1(x_1, G)$,
x_1, x_2, G
subject to $u_2(x_2, G) = u_2^*$ and $x_1 + x_2 + c(G) = w_1 + w_2$.

Let us form the Lagrangean

$$L = u_1(x_1, G) + \lambda_1 \{u_2^* - u_2(x_2, G)\} + \lambda_2 \{w_1 + w_2 - x_1 - x_2 - c(G)\}.$$

The first order conditions are

(1) $\partial L/\partial x_1 = \partial u_1/\partial x_1 - \lambda_2 = 0$
(2) $\partial L/\partial x_2 = -\lambda_1 \partial u_2/\partial x_2 - \lambda_2 = 0$
(3) $\partial L/\partial G = \partial u_1/\partial G - \lambda_1 \partial u_2/\partial G - \lambda_2 c'(G) = 0$
(4) $\partial L/\partial \lambda_1 = u_2^* - u_2(x_2, G) = 0$
(5) $\partial L/\partial \lambda_2 = w_1 + w_2 - x_1 - x_2 - c(G) = 0$

From (1), we get $\lambda_2 = \partial u_1/\partial x_1$ and from (1) and (2), eliminating λ_2, we get $\lambda_1 = -(\partial u_1/\partial x_1)/(\partial u_2/\partial x_2)$. Using these values in (3), we get the condition

$$(\partial u_1/\partial G)/(\partial u_1/\partial x_1) + (\partial u_2/\partial G)/(\partial u_2/\partial x_2) = c'(G).$$

This condition for the optimal provision of a public good can be written more succinctly as

$$MRS_{G1} + MRS_{G2} = MC_G.$$

that is, the *sum* of the marginal rates of substitution between the private good and the public good for the two individuals must equal the marginal cost of providing the public good.

If the efficiency condition is violated, we can show that at least one of the agents can be made better off and nobody made worse off. The mode of reasoning follows that developed in chapter 4. Suppose, for example, that the sum of the MRSs is less than the marginal cost. Let $MC = 1$, $MRS_{G1} = \frac{1}{2}$ and $MRS_{G2} = 1/3$. Then agent 1 would be willing to accept $\frac{1}{2}$ more rupees of the private good for the loss of Re 1 of the public good and agent 2 would be willing to accept $1/3$ more rupees of the private good for the loss of Re 1 of the public good. Suppose we reduce the amount of the public good by Re 1. Then we can compensate the two agents by giving them Rs 5/6, and still have Rs 1/6 left to distribute to the two individuals and make them better off. Thus if the sum of the MRSs is less than the MC, less of the public good and more of the private good should be provided.

Another way to interpret the Pareto-efficiency condition is to think of the MRS as measuring the *marginal willingness to pay* for an extra unit of the public good. Then the efficiency condition simply says that at the margin, the sum of the willingnesses to pay must be equal to the cost of providing an extra unit of the public good.

The efficiency condition for a private good is that the MC should be equal to the MRS of each person separately. People can consume different amounts of the private good, but they must all value it the same at the margin for efficiency. In the case of a public good, all individuals have to consume the same amount of the good, but they can value it differently at the margin.

The public good efficiency condition is illustrated below. The MRS curves are added *vertically* because both agents must consume the same amount of the public good. The efficient provision of the public good, G^*, is obtained at the point of intersection of the MC and the $MRS_{G1} + MRS_{G2}$ curve.

14.6 Private Provision of a Public Good

The efficiency condition tells us how much of the public good should be provided. The public good is provided in equal amounts to all agents and it might seem natural to seek contributions from each individual to fund the public good. Yet, if it is left to the self-interest motive of individuals on a society to finance public goods, it seems likely that too little of it would be provided.

Let us consider a model similar to the one developed in Section 14.5. Individual i can spend her initial wealth w_i on either the private good (x_i) or as contribution to the public good (g_i). The total

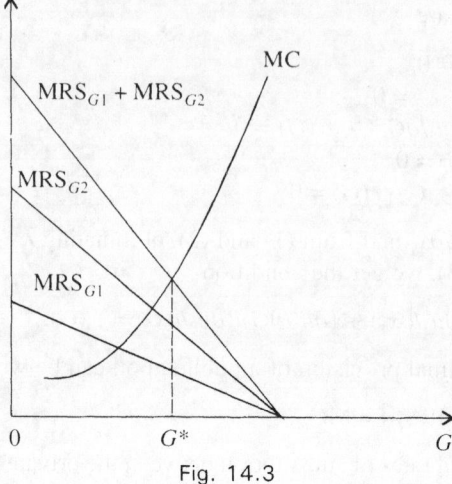

Fig. 14.3

amount of the public good will be the result of the contributions from the two agents, $G = g_1 + g_2$. To simplify matters, let $c(G) = G$, so that $c'(G) = 1$.

The choices of each agent will depend on the choices of the other agent. We consider a Nash equilibrium, where each person's choice is optimal against the other person's choices. The problem of individual i is

$$\max_{x_i, G} u_i(x_i, G),$$
$$\text{subject to } x_i + g_i = w_i.$$

We then get

$$\text{MRS}_i = 1, i = 1, 2.$$

Remembering that MC = 1, we see that the sum of the MRSs is more than MC and hence too little of the public good (compared to the Pareto-efficient amount) will be provided when individuals decide privately how much of the public good is to be provided.

This result is not surprising. In the case of positive externalities, individuals do not take account of the benefits to others and hence the private profit motive leads to a suboptimal output of the good conferring positive externalities. In the case of a public good, everyone can enjoy the good in equal amount, but this benefit is not take into account by individuals.

14.6.1 The Free Rider Problem

Once a public good is provided, nobody can be prevented from enjoying its services. If a bridge is built, then all motorists can drive on it. Hence, each person will have an incentive to pay as little as possible towards the construction of the bridge. Each person will hope that the contributions from others will be sufficient to build the bridge.

In general, *free riding* refers to the consumption of a good without paying for it. If five students go to watch a movie and the five tickets are paid for by only four students, then the fifth student is free-riding on the others. The problem is especially acute in the case of public goods, because the free-rider cannot be prevented from consuming the good once it is provided (in the case of cinema tickets, the four students can refuse to pay for the ticket of the fifth one, in which case the latter will not be able to watch the movie).

Excludability depends on two factors—law and technology. Examples of the use of law to exclude others are use of patents and copyrights. For example, consider the formula to manufacture a drug. The formula is a public good because use of it by one company does not affect the availability to other users. But a patent on the formula can make it excludable.

Ideas are generally public goods Patents and copyrights are two forms of rights over intellectual property which is the legal concept for ownership of ideas. One should note, however, that while the law can establish excludability through intellectual property rights, the effectiveness of exclusion depends on the effectiveness of enforcement of these rights.

Technology is also being increasingly used to exclude potential users who are unable or unwilling to pay for something. Content of television programming is a public good. But is the consumption of broadcast television excludable? This depends on the technology of delivery. While consumption of free-to-the-air television is not excludable, with scrambling technology excludability can be achieved in other instances. Only viewers who pay for decoding equipment can watch certain programmes.

Free riding bears a striking similarity to the Prisoner's Dilemma, though the two are not quite the same. Suppose that there are two tenants in a house who are trying to decide whether to construct a collapsible gate at the entrance or not. If the gate is constructed, both tenants will enjoy improved security in equal measure, so this is like a public good.

Suppose that each person has a wealth of Rs 5000, each values the gate at Rs 1000 and that the cost of the gate is Rs 1500. Note that the joint valuation of the gate exceeds its cost. Now, once constructed, the gate will benefit both tenants. Now each tenant must decide whether to buy the gate or not. The payoffs to the tenants are represented below:

		B	
		Buy	Don't Buy
A	Buy	(–500, –500)	(–500, 1000)
	Don't Buy	(1000, –500)	(0, 0)

It can be easily checked that the dominant strategy equilibrium for each player is not to buy the gate. If tenant A decides to buy the gate, then it is in the interest of player B to free-ride: to enjoy the increased security, but not to contribute anything for it. If tenant A does not buy, it is not in tenant B's interest to buy either. The situation is slightly different from the Prisoners' Dilemma. In the latter, the optimal situation is for the two players to take the same decision. In the free-riding situation, the optimal solution is for just one person to buy and both to enjoy the increased security.

A Pareto-improvement can be achieved if one of the tenants buys the gate and the other makes a *side-payment* to her. For example, if tenant A buys the gate and tenant B pays here Rs 501, then tenant A manages to break even and tenant B still enjoys a surplus of Rs 499.

14.6.2 Demand Revelation

If individuals can be made to correctly reveal their preferences for a public good, then society will know (a) whether it is worth providing the public good and (b) how much to charge individuals for it. However, when individuals are directly asked to reveal their preferences, there is an incentive for people to free-ride. Suppose that individuals know that contributions will be levied upon them in proportion to their stated valuation of the public good. Then, if each individual believes that the contributions from others will be sufficient to provide for the good, she will have the incentive to understate her valuation of the benefits from the public good in order to keep down her subsequent contributions.

On the other hand, if everyone's contribution is *predetermined*, then each individual will have an incentive to exaggerate her true valuation. If an individual gets even a small positive gain from the public good, it will be in her interest to say that her valuation is very high: this will ensure that the good will be provided, but the individual will not have to bear any extra cost.

To bypass this problem, it has been suggested that each agent will receive a side-payment equal to the sum of the other bids, if the good is provided. Suppose that the sum of all other bids was negative and that the i-th individual's bid made the total positive and ensured that the public good would be provided. Then the i-th agent would have to *pay* an amount equal to the sum of other bids. With such a system in place, each agent always finds truth-telling to be the dominant strategy. Unfortunately, the total sidepayments may be very large under this scheme and it might be very costly to induce agents to tell the truth.

14.6.3 Lindahl Allocations

Can we develop a price system that will support the efficient allocation of the public good? Erik Lindahl, a Swedish economist, provided an answer to this question in 1919.

Suppose that the cost of the public good is apportioned in the ratio $h:(1-h)$ between the two agents. Agent 1 then solves the problem:

$$\max_{x_1, G} u_1(x_1, G),$$
$$\text{subject to } x_1 + hG = w_1.$$

This reduces to

$$\max_G u_1(w_1 - hG, G),$$

and the first order condition is

$$(\partial u_1/\partial x_1)(-h) + \partial u_1/\partial G = 0, \text{ that is, } \partial u_1/\partial G = h(\partial u_1/\partial x_1).$$

Similarly, for agent 2, the condition is

$$\partial u_2/\partial G = (1-h)(\partial u_2/\partial x_2).$$

From these two equations, $h = (\partial u_1/\partial G)/(\partial u_1/\partial x_1)$, and $1-h = (\partial u_2/\partial G)/(\partial u_2/\partial x_2)$. We get two 'demand' equations for G, $G_1 = G_1(h)$ and $G_2 = G_2(1-h)$. When h is low, agent 1 demands a large G while agent 2 demands a small G. If the utility functions are nicely behaved, then there will be a certain h^* for which $G_1 = G_2 = G^*$, and this is the required solution. Note that h plays a role similar to price in an ordinary market. Given h, the two agents demand a certain amount of G respectively. We can write $h = p_1$ and $1 - h = p_2$, where p_1 and p_2 can be interpreted as the price at which the public good is sold to the two individuals.

Note that at h^*, $h^* + 1 - h^* = 1 = (\partial u_1/\partial G)/(\partial u_1/\partial x_1) + (\partial u_2/\partial G)/(\partial u_2/\partial x_2) = \text{MRS}_{G1} + \text{MRS}_{G2}$, which shows that the *Lindahl solution is a Pareto-optimal solution.*

Example 14.3: Suppose that $u_i = x_i G$, $i = 1, 2$. Then individual 1 selects G to maximize $u_1 = (w_1 - hG)G = w_1 G - hG^2$. From this, $G_1^* = w_1/2h$. Similarly, we can show that $G_2^* = w_2/2(1-h)$. The Lindahl solution requires that $G_1^* = G_2^* = G^*$. Equating $w_1/2h$ with $w_2/2(1-h)$, we get $h^* = w_1/(w_1 + w_2)$ and hence $1 - h^* = w_2/(w_1 + w_2)$. The contributions are in proportion to the initial wealth of each individual in relation to total wealth. Then $G^* = (w_1 + w_2)/2$, $x_1^* = w_1/2$, and $x_2^* = w_2/2$.

Topics for Discussion

1. Consider the following types of resources:

   • Groundwater comes from 'aquifers' lying below the ground. The same aquifer may lie below many plots of land.
   • Information is an intangible resource and has one of the attributes of a public good—non-excludability (also called non-appropriability).
   • Natural gas, found below ground, is called 'fugitive property', because it keeps moving around.

   For each of these resources, discuss why property rights will be difficult to establish. What would be the 'obvious' legal rules for distributing property rights? What would be their shortcomings?

2. A variety of methods have been developed for estimating the value of goods and services for which no markets exist. An example is the *contingent valuation method* that uses surveys to ask people what they would be willing to pay for the things that have no market value. Do you think such a method will be economically useful in putting a value on goods and services that would have no market value otherwise?

Exercise

1. Consider the Pareto-efficiency condition for the provision of a public good. Show that if the sum of the marginal rates of substitution adds up to more than the marginal cost, then more of the public good and less of the private good should be provided.

2. Suppose that individual i has utility of the form $u_i(x_i, G) = x_i + v_i(G)$, $i = 1, 2$. Show that the optimal provision of the public good will be independent of the optimal allocation of the private good.

3. Atal's production of smoke bothers Murli. Atal can produce with or without a filter to reduce the smoke. Below are given the gains to Atal and the losses to Murli:

	With Filter	Without Filter
Gains to Atal	Rs 100	Rs 120
Losses to Murli	Rs 20	Rs 35

   If Atal is not liable for smoke damage and there are no transactions costs then

   (a) Atal will install a filter.
   (b) Atal will not install a filter.
   (c) Murli will pay Atal not to pollute.
   (d) None of the above.

4. An apple orchard is located next to a bee-keeper. If the orchard produces a tonnes of apples and the bee-keeper produces h units of honey, the total cost function for the apple orchard will be $C_a = a^2$ and the total cost function for the bee-keeper will be $C_h = h^2 - a$. Let P_a = Rs 100 and P_h = Rs 50. The apple orchard owner and the bee-keeper both try to maximize profit. Apple production occurs earlier than honey production.

   (a) If the apple orchard owner and the bee-keeper were to decide upon their production plans individually, what will be the outputs of apples and honey?
   (b) What will be the socially optimal levels of apple and honey production? What kind of a tax/subsidy scheme can achieve these?

5. Ramu and Debu live in adjoining apartments. Ramu plays the guitar and this disturbs Debu at his studies. Debu wants to install sound-proofing (the noise of installation will irritate Ramu). Their payoffs are given below (the first payoff in each pair refers to Debu):

		Ramu	
		Be Noisy	Be Quiet
Debu	Install Sound-proofing	(2, 2)	(−1, 1)
	Not install	(1, 3)	(4, 4)

    (i) What are the two Nash equilibria of this game?

    (ii) If Ramu gets to move first, what will be the subgame-perfect equilibrium?

6. The equation of the inverse demand curve in a perfectly competitive market is $p = 450 - 2Q$. The equation of the private marginal cost curve or the supply curve is $MC_p = 30 + 2Q$. The marginal externality cost is $MC_e = Q$.

    (i) What is the price and quantity in competitive equilibrium?

    (ii) What is the socially optimal price and quantity?

    (iii) What rate of Pigovian tax per unit of output will achieve the socially optimal outcome?

    (iv) Suppose instead that a monopolist supplies the product and faces the same demand and cost conditions. What will be the monopolist's price and output?

7. A village has six residents, each of whom has Rs 1000. Each resident may either invest his money in a government bond which yields 11 per cent per year, or use it to buy a one-year old cow, which will graze on the village commons. Year-old cows and government bonds each cost Rs 1000 each. Cows require no effort to tend and can sold at the end of the year for a price that depends on the milk yield per day at the end of the year. This yield in turn depends on the number of cows that graze on the commons. The prices of two-year old cows are given below as a function of the total number of cows:

Number of cows	Price per 2-year old cow
1	Rs 1200
2	Rs 1175
3	Rs 1150
4	Rs 1125
5	Rs 1100
6	Rs 1075

    (i) If village residents make their decisions independently, how many cows will graze on the commons?

    (ii) How many cows would graze on the commons if decisions were taken collectively?

    (iii) What grazing fee per cow would result in the socially optimal number of cows?

8. Villagers graze their cattle on a piece of land. Let c be the number of cattle grazed. The value of milk yield from c cattle is given by $f(c) = c^{0.5}$ (in rupees). The cost of acquiring one cattle is Rs 0.25. How many cattle will be grazed if the land is owned in common? How many if the land is privately owned by an individual?

9. (a) Firm S produces steel, s, while firm F is a fishery producing fish, f. Their total cost functions are $TC_s = s^2$ and $TC_f = f^2 + s$. Steel production occurs before fish production. Both firms are profit-maximizing perfectly competitive firms facing the market prices $P_s =$ Rs 10,000 per tonne and $P_f =$ Rs 2000 per catch respectively.

    (i) If the firms were to decide upon their production plans individually, what will be the outputs of steel and fish?

    (ii) What will be the socially optimal levels of steel and fish production? What kind of a tax/subsidy scheme can achieve these?

10. There are two tenants in a house who are trying to decide whether to construct a gate at the entrance or not. Suppose that each person values the gate at Rs 2000 and that the cost of the gate is Rs 3500. The strategy options for both tenants are either to buy a gate or not buy a gate. Write down the payoff matrix for this game and analyse the nature of equilibrium.

15 Uncertainty and Information

In all our discussions so far, we have abstracted from uncertainty. The economic agents were assumed to operate in situations without any uncertainty. Moreover, everyone had access to all relevant information. In this chapter, we relax these assumptions and discuss the resulting modifications to the theory. First, we discuss how to model uncertainty and then we turn to problems of information.

Two types of situations are possible when there is some uncertainty. First, everyone may face the same uncertainty and have the same information available to resolve this uncertainty. In the morning, if the sky is cloudy, everyone understands that there is a chance of rain. We all can ring up the meteorological office to get more precise information about the likely state of weather. Second, different people may have different information about the same activity or event and this creates some uncertainty. The CEO of a firm may know about the resources of the firm, its plans for expansion and so on. A worker on the shop floor will not know about these things, but will have much better information about the reliability of the particular machine he is operating. This differential access to information creates uncertainty and we address this problem in later sections of this chapter.

15.1 Uncertainty

Three types of questions come up when we discuss uncertainty.

What is the decision-maker uncertain about?
Uncertainty permeates every aspect of our lives. Consider the model of consumer choice. In real life, consumers are often uncertain about incomes, product prices, product qualities, and, in dynamic contexts, about probable interest rates or inflation rates. Firms may be uncertain about production (there may be possibility of random breakdowns in machines), market prices, strategies of rivals, etc. When dealing with firms, governments are uncertain whether there is any collusion. And so on and so forth.

What form does uncertainty take?
This refers to the extent of our knowledge or ignorance. Suppose that a consumer is uncertain about different prices for a commodity being charged by different shops. This uncertainty can take different forms. (a) The consumer may have some objective frequency distribution for prices, based upon her own experience and that of others. For example, she may know that a price of Rs 2 is usually found in 20 per cent of the shops, while a price of Rs 3 is found in 30 per cent. (b) The consumer may only know that certain prices are more probable than others. (c) The consumer may have some subjective beliefs about the probability distribution of prices, and proceed as if these are correct. (d) The consumer may not be able to make any probability estimates, though she will still have some idea of the range of prices that are available. (e) The consumer may be in a new country and have no idea even about the range of prices available.

What, if anything, can be done to act upon or improve the information available?
Faced with uncertainty, the individual may act *passively*, that is, take a decision given the constraints posed by the uncertain environment or try to be *active*, that is, spend resources to acquire additional, more precise, information.

Under uncertainty, the consequences of an action are not known immediately for certain. Over time, as events unfold, more information becomes available and, therefore, uncertainty is resolved by the passage of time.

We specify the following elements of the problem for an individual decision-maker under uncertainty:

(a) A set of states $(1, 2,\ldots s\ldots S)$ of nature.
   A state of nature is a complete description of a possible environment, for example, the possible states of nature may be 'rain', 'cloudy sky', and 'clear sky'. The states of nature may not refer to weather conditions at all. For example, we may be interested in the economy and define a particular state of nature as (high inflation rate, low unemployment rate, high fiscal deficit). In the simplest case, 'Nature' chooses which state of nature will actually materialize.
(b) A set of acts $(1, 2,\ldots x\ldots X)$ available to the individual.
   For example, the acts may be 'buy an umbrella' or 'not buy an umbrella'.
(c) A consequence function $c(x, s)$ showing outcomes under all possible combinations of acts and states. For example, the weather which might materialize together with the act of the individual will determine her payoffs. If the state of nature is 'clear sky', and the act is 'not buy umbrella', the payoff to the individual will be greater than if the state of nature is 'rain', and the act is 'not buy umbrella'.

15.2 Decision Criteria

We begin our discussion of uncertainty by assuming that the individual has no idea about the probabilities associated with the various states of nature. To arrive at a decision, first a payoff matrix is constructed. Second, all acts that are dominated by others in terms of payoffs are dropped. For example, if I have the option of going to a friend's place by a taxi or a bus or a minibus, and whatever be the state of nature, the minibus ride always gives me more comfort than a bus ride, I will drop the act of bus ride from my consideration. Finally, one of a number of criteria is used to select the best act.

To illustrate the various decision criteria, let us assume that there are only two states of nature, s_1 and s_2, and two possible acts, a_1 and a_2. The payoff matrix is as follows:

	s_1	s_2
a_1	15	17
a_2	13	23

15.2.1 The Maximin Rule

The rule is to achieve the best of all worst outcomes. To apply this rule, we first identify the minimum payoffs under any act. Next, the maximum from among these minimum values is chosen.

In the payoff matrix given above, the minimum payoff for act a_1 is 15 and that for act a_2 is 13. The maximin rule tells the individual to select the act that yields the maximum of these minimum, that is, act a_1. The maximin rule therefore implies a very pessimistic view of life. Its aim is to provide protection against large losses.

	s_1	s_2	min	maximin
a_1	15	17	15	15
a_2	13	23	13	

15.2.2 The Minimax Rule

The application of the minimax rule proceeds in three stages. (i) A *regret matrix* is first constructed, based on the original payoff matrix. For any state of nature, for each action, the amount forgone, compared to the best action, will be written down and these numbers form a column in the regret matrix. (ii) The maximum amount forgone for each act will be identified. (iii) The minimum of these is chosen.

The steps are shown below.

Regret matrix

	s_1	s_2	max	minimax
a_1	0	6	6	
a_2	2	0	2	2

Suppose the state of nature that materializes is s_1. Then the best act is a_1, which yields 15 as compared to 13 under a_2. Hence the 'regret factor' if a_2 is undertaken rather than a_1 and s_1 materializes is 2. Similarly, we get the numbers in the other column. The minimum of the maximum regrets is chosen. The aim is to minimize the regret of not choosing the best action.

15.2.3 The Maximax Rule

In contrast to the first two rules, this rule reflects extreme optimism. Under this rule, in the first stage, the maximum payoffs are identified for any action. Then the action with the largest of these payoffs is chosen. The presumption is that the state of nature yielding the maximum payoff will materialize.

In the payoff matrix under consideration, the action a_2 is chosen under the maximax rule.

	s_1	s_2	max	maximax
a_1	15	17	17	
a_2	13	23	23	23

15.2.4 Hurwicz Rule

To apply this rule, with each action, we associate a function which is the weighted average of the maximum and minimum payoffs:

$$h(a_1) = 15r + 17(1 - r)$$
$$h(a_2) = 13r + 23(1 - r), 0 \leq r \leq 1.$$

The decision-maker selects some $r = r^*$ and given this r^*, that act a_k is chosen for which $h(a_k) = \max h(a_i)$ over all i. Thus the decision-maker evaluates an act by some weighted average of the best and worst payoffs under that act. Of course, there is no clear rationale for the choice of r^*.

In our example, $h(a_1) = 17 - 2r$, and $h(a_2) = 23 - 10r$. These can be represented by two straight lines in the Fig. 15.1. Note that for $r < 0.75$, $h(a_2) > h(a_1)$, and the act a_2 are chosen. For $r > 0.75$, the act a_1 will be chosen.

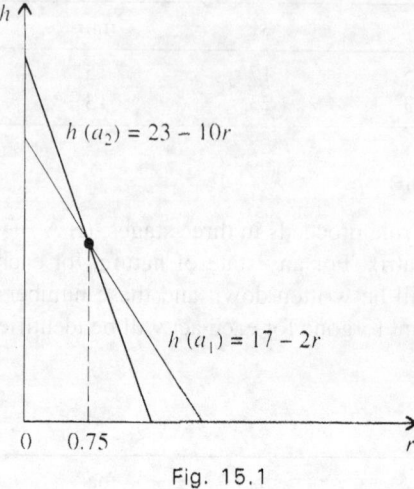

Fig. 15.1

The number $(1 - r)$, associated with the maximum payoff, is called the optimism index. Note that when $r = 1$, the maximin criterion is being used and when $r = 0$, the maximax criterion is being used. Higher the value of $1 - r$, the more optimistic is the decision-maker.

15.2.5 The Principle of Insufficient Reason (Laplace Rule)

Laplace suggested that if nothing is known about the probabilities, then one can simply assume that all states of nature are equally likely. One should then compare the sum of consequences, with each consequence weighted by the same probability. In other words, we either compare the $\Sigma c(a_j, s)$ over all s or $[\Sigma c(a_j, s)]/n$, where n is number of states of nature.

In our example, $\Sigma c(a_1, s)/2 = 16$ and $\Sigma c(a_2, s)/2 = 18$, so that act a_2 is chosen under the Laplace Rule.

15.2.6 Maximization of Expected Value

Suppose that the agent can associate probabilities with states of nature. Then one rule to choose between different alternatives would be to maximize the expected value, that is, the sum of the payoffs weighed by the respective probabilities: $Ec = \Sigma p_s [c(x, s)]$. However, this rule fails to incorporate the individual's attitude towards uncertainty. Let us compare two alternative situations. In one, the individual can win Rs 30 with probability 1. In the other, she can win Rs 50 with probability 1/2 and Rs 10 with probability 1/2. The expected value is the same Rs 30 in both situations. But some people might choose the first situation because in it Rs 30 is a sure outcome. Others may prefer the second situation because there is a possibility of winning Rs 50.

15.2.7 Mean-variance Analysis

Agents who use the expected value rule to choose between alternatives are focusing only on the mean outcome and ignoring the dispersion of the values around the mean. The dispersion of the values represents the risk associated with an alternative. One measure of dispersion that is widely used is the variance V:

$$V(x) = \Sigma p_s [c(x, s) - Ec]^2$$

To calculate variance, we first find out the differences of each value from the mean value, square these differences, weigh them by the respective probabilities and finally sum them up over all possible states of nature. Sometimes, we also use the square root of V, which is called the standard deviation (s.d.).

Since V or s.d. measures the risk of an alternative, one method of taking a decision is to use mean-variance analysis, which employs both the mean and the variance (or s.d.). Given two risky alternatives A and B, the mean-variance rule says:

1. If alternative A has a higher expected value *and* a lower variance (or s.d.) than B, then A should be chosen over B.
2. If both A and B have the same expected value, then the one with the lower variance (or s.d.) should be chosen.
3. If both have identical variances (or s.d.), then the one with the higher expected value should be chosen.

15.2.8 Coefficient of Variation Analysis

Suppose now that two alternatives A and B are such that one has a higher expected value but also a higher variance than the other. In this case, the mean-variance analysis cannot be used. One way out is to use a measure of relative risk called coefficient of variation. The coefficient of variation is defined as (V/expected value), that is, it measures risk relative to the expected value. The coefficient of variation rule then requires agents to choose alternatives with the lowest coefficient of variation.

15.3 The Expected Utility Theory

The expected utility theory, developed by John von Neumann and Oskar Morgenstern, explicitly uses probabilities to help reach decisions in uncertain situations. In addition to states of nature, acts and their consequences, we now introduce the following:

(i) A probability function expressing the beliefs of the individual as to the likelihood of Nature choosing each and every state.
(ii) An elementary utility function $v(.)$ measuring the desirability of the different possible consequences. The function v is called the von Neumann-Morgenstern (*vNM*) utility function.

The expected utility rule says that the individual will choose that act x which maximizes her expected utility of:

$$\text{Max } U(x) = \sum_s p_s v[c(x, s)] \equiv Ev(c),$$

where E is the expectations operator.

This means that in an uncertain environment the individual's utility from an act is equal to the mathematical expectation of the elementary utilities of associated consequences.

15.3.1 Discussion

In an uncertain environment, whenever an act is decided upon, the consequence is not certain; various consequences may follow with different probabilities. Therefore, every act is like a gamble or a lottery. A *lottery* may be defined more formally as follows:

Suppose that a probability p_i can be associated with the state of nature s_i. That is, the probability that state of nature s will occur is p_i. Suppose an act a_i is chosen. This has consequences/payoffs

$c(a_i, 1)$, $c(a_i, 2), \ldots$, with associated probabilities p_1, $p_2, \ldots \ldots$. When we couple these consequences with their associated probabilities, we have a *lottery*:

$$L(a_i) = [\{p_1, c(a_i, s_1)\}, \{p_2, c(a_i, s_2)\} \ldots].$$

Therefore, in an uncertain situation, the individual in essence has to *choose between lotteries*. If we make a number of assumptions[1] about the way individuals rank lotteries (that is, about their preferences over lotteries), then, just as in utility theory under certainty, there will exist a von Neumann-Morgenstern utility function v such that the function U constructed from v as the expected utility

$$U(a) = \Sigma p_i v[c(a, s_i)]$$

will represent these rankings.

Example 15.1: The *vNM* utility function of an individual is $v = \sqrt{w}$, and her initial wealth is 36. Will she accepts a gamble in which she wins 13 with a probability 2/3 and loses 11 with probability 1/3?

The expected utility of the gamble is given by $U = (2/3)(\sqrt{36} + 13) + (1/3)(\sqrt{36} - 11) = (2/3)7 + (1/3)5 = 19/3 > \sqrt{36} = 6$. Hence the gamble should be accepted.

The Allais Paradox

The French economist M. Allais has shown that under situations of uncertainty, people tend to make choices inconsistently. To illustrate, we consider two situations of choice.

Situation 1. *The choice is between (A) a sure win of Rs 30 and (A') an 80 per cent chance to win Rs 45, and 20 per cent chance to win 0.* In this situation, most people tend to choose A, even though A' has an expected payoff of Rs 36. However, the choice is not surprising if the individual is risk-averse.

Situation 2. *(B) A 25 per cent chance to win Rs 30 versus (B') a 20 per cent chance to win Rs 45.* Here, most people tend to choose B'. This, again, is not surprising, because the expected payoff with B' is Rs 9 and that with B is Rs 7.50. Moreover, both are situations of risk.

But the most popular pair of choices (A and B') taken together contradict the assumption of expected utility maximization. To show this, we assume that the *vNM* utility function is $v(.)$ and the initial wealth is w.

Then the choice of A over A' implies
(1) $v(w + 30) > 0.8v(w + 45) + 0.2v(w)$.
The choice of B', on the other hand implies that
$0.2v(w + 45) + 0.8v(w) > 0.25v(w + 30) + 0.75v(w)$, that is
(2) $0.25v(w + 30) < 0.2v(w + 45) + 0.05v(w)$.
Dividing both sides of (2) by 0.25, we get
(2) $v(w + 30) < 0.8v(w + 45) + 0.2v(w)$,

which contradicts (1). Hence there is an inconsistency in the choices under the two situations.

Psychologists Daniel Kahneman and Amos Tversky explain this phenomenon by arguing that 'a reduction in the probability of an outcome by a constant factor has a larger impact when the outcome was initially certain than when it was merely probable'. Thus in the first pair of alternatives, the movement from A to A' represented a 20 per cent reduction in the chances of winning (from 100 per cent to 80 per cent), and so did the movement from B to B' (25 per cent to 20 per cent). But because the first movement was from an initially certain outcome, individuals disliked it much more.

Source: Tversky, A. and D. Kahneman, 1981, 'The framing of decisions and the psychology of choice', *Science*, 211, 453–8.

---

[1] The Independence Axiom together with the Continuity Axiom will guarantee this result. See Varian (1993) or Aliprantis and Chakrabarti (1999).

In uncertain situations, the different consequences can in many cases be expressed in terms of different levels of wealth. Wealth can usually be translated into consumption and hence into utility. From now on, we will analyse situations where $v = v(w)$, so that $U = \Sigma p_i v(w_i)$.

15.3.2 Attitudes Towards Risk

Let us consider another example.

Example 15.2: Suppose that an individual is offered the choice between two gambles. She has to pay Rs 100 to participate in both gambles. In the first gamble, she wins Rs 500 or Rs 100 with equal probabilities. In the second she wins Rs 325 or Rs 136 with equal probabilities.

First suppose that her *vNM* utility function is $v = \sqrt{w}$. Then the expected utility from the first gamble is

$$U = (1/2)(\sqrt{500} - 100) + (1/2)(\sqrt{100} - 100) = (1/2)20 + (1/2)0 = 10.$$

The expected utility from the second gamble is

$$U = (1/2)(\sqrt{325} - 100) + (1/2)(\sqrt{136} - 100) = (1/2)15 + (1/2)6 = 10.5.$$

The individual will therefore prefer the second gamble.

But now suppose that the individual's utility function is different. In particular, let $v = w$. Then the expected utility from the first gamble will be

$$U = (1/2)(500 - 100) + (1/2)(100 - 100) = (1/2)400 + (1/2)0 = 200.$$

The expected utility from the second gamble now is

$$U = (1/2)(325 - 100) + (1/2)(136 - 100) = (1/2)225 + (1/2)36 = 130.5.$$

Hence the second gamble will be preferred.

This example shows that different individuals have different attitudes towards risk and the function v captures these differences.

Definition: The consumer is said to be *risk-averse* if she strictly prefers a certain consequence to a risky prospect whose mathematical expectation of consequences equals the certain consequence. That is, the consumer is risk-averse if $v(r) < Ev(c)$, where $r = Ec$, that is, $v(Ec) > Ev(c)$. Written out more fully, this means that $v(\Sigma p_s c_s)] > \Sigma p_s v(c_s)$, where $c_s = c(a, s)$ for some act a and p_s are the probabilities, $\Sigma p_s = 1$.

The consumer is *risk-loving* if $v(Ec) < Ev(c)$, and is *risk neutral* if $v(Ec) = Ev(c)$.

Therefore a consumer is risk-averse if the following holds: Suppose that the consumer is offered a choice between playing a gamble and getting the expected value of the gamble for sure. Then she will choose the latter option. A risk-neutral consumer will be indifferent between the two options and a risk-lover will prefer the gamble rather than the sure expected value.

If v is twice continuously differentiable function, then it can be shown that $v''(c) < 0 \Rightarrow Ev(c) < v(Ec)$, that is, concavity of v denotes risk-averse behaviour. If v is linear, then the individual is risk-neutral, and if it is convex, then she is risk-loving. To simplify matters, from now on we assume that the consequence function is denominated in terms of just one variable—wealth, w. Moreover, the individual always prefers more wealth to less, that is, $v'(w) > 0$. The utility function of a risk-averse individual is shown below. The chord joining two points on the curve always lies below the curve: a point on the utility function represents $v(Ec)$, while the point on the chord vertically below it represents $Ev(c)$.

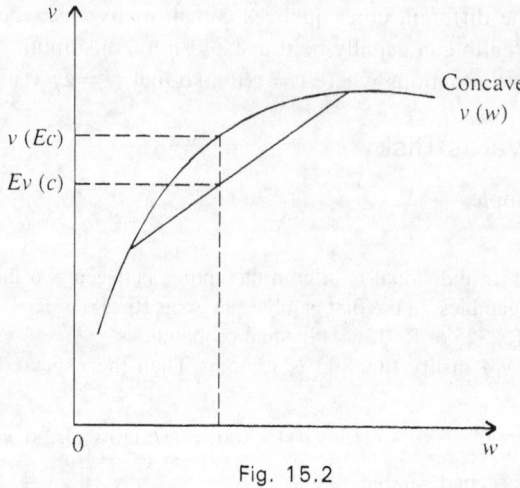

Fig. 15.2

Example 15.3: Suppose that an individual's $v(w) = w^2$. Then $v''(w) = 2 > 0$, and the person is a risk-lover. Will the person accept a gamble where there is a 50 per cent chance of winning 20 and a 50 per cent chance of losing 20, if the person's initial wealth is 100?

If the person does not accept the gamble, then utility is $100^2 = 10,000$. If the gamble is accepted, the expected utility is $0.5(120^2) + 0.5(80^2) = 0.5(14,400 + 6400) = 10,400$. Hence the gamble will be accepted.

It can be shown that if $v = w$, the person is risk-neutral and will be indifferent between accepting or rejecting the gamble.

15.3.3 Measures of Risk-aversion

Now consider two individuals who are both risk-averse. Is there some way of discovering whether one is *more* risk-averse than the other?

One measure might be the curvature of the v curve, that is, $v'(w)$. The more bowed away from the w-axis that the v-curve is, the greater the difference between $v(Ec)$ and $Ev(c)$, and hence the greater the degree of risk-aversion. But the magnitude of $v'(w)$ can be arbitrarily changed by multiplying the utility function by some positive number b. To get over this difficulty, we can use the *Arrow-Pratt measure of absolute risk-aversion*: $R_A(w) = -[v'(w)]/v'(w)$.

An alternative indicator, which has the same properties as $R_A(w)$ for $w > 0$ (except for the fact that it, unlike the absolute measure of risk-aversion, is unaffected by the choice of units of w), is the *Arrow-Pratt measure of relative risk-aversion*: $R_R(w) = wR_A(w) = -[wv'(w)]/v'(w)$.

Example 15.4: In general, both these measures are functions of w. But consider an utility function $v(w) = a - be^{-Rw}$. Applying the definition of absolute risk-aversion, we find that $R_A(w) = -[v''(w)]/v'(w) = -[-R^2b\,e^{-Rw}]/[Rbe^{-Rw}] = R$. The function v is therefore called the constant absolute risk-aversion function.

On the other hand, if $v(w) = a - bw^{-R+1}$, then it can be shown that $R_R(w) = R$, all $w > 0$. The utility function is called the constant relative risk-aversion function.

15.3.4 The Certainty Equivalent

If an individual is risk-averse, we know that $v(Ec) > Ev(c)$. Hence this individual would be willing to pay a *risk-premium*, that is, accept less than Ec for certain in order to be as well off as she would be with $Ev(c)$.

Let g be the risk-premium, and suppose that the individual's initial wealth is w. Then, by definition, $v(w + Ec - g) = Ev(w + c)$. Denote Ec by c^*. The term $Ec - g$ is called the *certainty equivalent* of the random variable c. Let $Ec = 0$ and let $var(c)$ be small and equal to σ^2.

Using Taylor's series expansion, we get the two equations:

(1) $v(w + Ec - g) = v(w - g) = v(w) - gv'(w) + O(g^2)$, and
(2) $Ev(w + c) = E[v(w) + cv'(w) + (c^2/2)v''(w) + O(g^3)]$
$\qquad\qquad\quad = v(w) + (\sigma^2/2)v''(w) + O(g^3)$.

where the O's represent the remainder terms.

Neglecting the remainder terms, and setting the right hand side expressions in (1) and (2) equal to each other, we finally get

$$-gv'(w) \approx (\sigma^2/2)v''(w) \Rightarrow g(w, c) \approx -(\sigma^2/2)v''(w)/v'(w).$$

Now, note that $g(w, c) = g(w + k, c - k)$, where $k = Ec$, since (i) $v(w + k + Ec - g - k) = v(w + Ec - g)$ and (ii) v is a strictly decreasing, continuous function of g, so that g is uniquely determined from $v(w + Ec - g) = Ev(w + c)$. Therefore, we can consider a situation where $Ec \neq 0$ and $w = 0$:

$$g(0, c) \approx -(\sigma^2/2)v''(Ec)/v'(Ec).$$

The certainty equivalent then is $\hat{c} = c^* + (\sigma^2/2)v''(c^*)/v'(c^*) = c^* - (\sigma^2/2) R_A(c^*)$.

15.4 Applications

To recapitulate, under uncertainty the individual will choose according to the expected utility of acts if certain assumptions are satisfied. Whether an individual is risk-averse or not depends on the curvature of the elementary utility function. The curvature by itself is not robust enough to measure the degree of risk-aversion, so we developed the absolute and relative risk-aversion measures. Finally, a risk-averse individual is willing to pay a risk-premium to get a certain rather than an uncertain payoff and the difference between the expected value and the risk-premium is the certainty equivalent, which bears some relationship to the coefficient of absolute risk aversion. We next apply these concepts to several models.

15.4.1 Investment in a Risky Asset

A consumer has some wealth w and is considering investing an amount x in a risky asset. We derive the surprising result that investment will be more when earnings from the asset are taxed than when they are not.

The asset will earn a rate of return r_g in a 'good' state and r_b in a 'bad' state of nature. The investor's wealth in the good and bad states will be, respectively,

$$w_g = (w - x) + x(1 + r_g) = w + xr_g, \text{ and}$$
$$w_b = (w - x) + x(1 + r_b) = w + xr_b.$$

Let the probabilities of the two states be p and $1 - p$. The consumer's elementary utility function is v, and $v' > 0$, $v'' < 0$. The utility function is increasing and concave in wealth.

Let us first find out whether the consumer will invest in the risky asset or not. If the consumer decides to invest, his expected utility will be

$$Ev(x) = pv(w + xr_g) + (1 - p)v(w + xr_b)$$

Then $dEv(x)/dx = pv'(w + xr_g)r_g + (1 - p)v'(w + xr_b)r_b$,
and $d^2Ev(x)/dx^2 = pv''(w + xr_g)r_g^2 + (1 - p)v''(w + xr_b)r_b^2$.

We note for later use that if the consumer is risk-averse, $v'' < 0$ and hence $d^2Ev(x)/dx^2 < 0$. The expected utility function is also concave.

If the consumer decides not to invest, then $x = 0$. Now, $dEv(0)/dx = pv'(w)r_g + (1 - p)v'(w)r_b = v'(w)\{pr_g + (1 - p)r_b\}$. This shows us that if $pr_g + (1 - p)r_b < 0$, then $dEv(0)/dx < 0$, which means that expected utility decreases when the first rupee is invested, and continues to decline thereafter. Then the optimal $x = 0$: nothing will be invested.

If $dEv(0)/dx > 0$, then the optimal amount of investment will be found by setting $dEv(x)/dx = 0$, that is $pv'(w + xr_g)r_g + (1 - p)v'(w + xr_b)r_b = 0$. What will be the effect of taxing the investment? Suppose that the individual has to pay tax at the rate of t per rupee of return. Then

$$Ev = pv\{w + (1 - t)xr_g\} + (1-p)v\{w + (1 - t)xr_b\}, \text{ and}$$
$$dEv(x)/dx = pv'\{w + x(1 - t)r_g\}(1 - t)r_g + (1 - p)v'\{w + x(1 - t)r_b\}(1 - t)r_b. \quad (*)$$

For optimal interior solution $(x > 0)$, $dEv(x)/dx = 0$ which means that

$$pv'\{w + x(1-t)\,r_g\}r_g + (1 - p)v'\{w + x(1 - t)r_b\}r_b = 0.$$

Let $x = x^*$ be the optimal solution when $t = 0$, that is, before taxation is introduced, and let $x = x'$ be the optimal solution after taxation is introduced. It can be seen that $x' = x^*/(1 - t)$, because substituting in the left hand side of the expression $(*)$, we get

$$pv'\{w + x^*r_g\}r_g + (1 - p)v'\{w + x^*r_b\}r_b \text{ which is } = 0 \text{ by the optimality of } x^*$$
pre-tax.

Therefore, if $0 < t < 1$, then $x' > x^*$: *more is invested when the asset is taxed.*

15.4.2 Insurance

Individuals can 'reduce' their risks by insuring themselves against risk. They pay a premium against some contingency, for example, an accident. If the accident does not take place, then the individual loses the premium. However, if the accident does take place, the insurance company will reimburse the individual partly or wholly, the associated costs. Therefore, an insurance scheme in effect allows the individual to transfer wealth from a 'good' state ('no accident') to a 'bad' state ('accident occurs') and thereby achieve a greater degree of evenness of wealth across states.

Suppose that an individual has an initial wealth w. He faces a risk of loss L ($< w$) with probability p. In the absence of the insurance, the individual's expected utility is given by $U_0 = pv(w - L) + (1 - p)v(w)$, where v is the individual's *vNM* utility function, $v' > 0$, $v' < 0$.

Suppose that by paying a premium h, the individual can fully cover the loss, that is, he will be paid L if the loss occurs. His expected utility when he takes out the insurance is $U_1 = pv(w - L + L - h) + (1 - p)v(w - h) = v(w - h)$. The individual will take out this insurance if $U_1 > U_0$. How much premium is the individual willing to pay for full coverage?

Since the individual is risk-averse, there exists some risk-premium k such that $U_0 = v(w - k)$. Let $w - k = w^*$. Then the individual will take out the insurance if $v(w - h) > v(w^*)$, that is $w - h > w^*$. Now, $dU_1/dh = v'(w - h)(-1) < 0$. Hence the *maximum payoff* h^* that the individual is willing to pay for total coverage must satisfy $U_1 = U_0$. That is, $v(w - h^*) = pv(w - L) + (1 - p)v(w)$. Since $v(w - h^*)$ is a linear combination of $v(w)$ and $v(w - L)$, we must have

$$v(w) > v(w - h^*) > v(w - L).$$

Since $v' > 0$, from this we can conclude that $w - h^* > w - L$, that is, $L > h^*$. The individual is prepared to pay a maximum premium h^* which is less than the probable loss L.

From the definition of the maximum premium, we can now carry out a number of comparative static exercises. Consider again $v(w - h^*) = pv(w - L) + (1 - p)v(w)$. Taking total differentials of both sides, we get

$$v'(w - h^*)(-1)dh^* = v(w - L)dp + pv'(w - L)(-dL) + v(w)(-dp).$$

First, we examine what happens when p, the probability of loss, alone varies. Setting $dL = 0$, and manipulating the expressions, we can show that

$$\partial h^*/\partial p = -\,[v(w - L) - v(w)]/v'(w - h^*) > 0.$$

Similarly, setting $dp = 0$, and solving, we can show that

$$\partial h^*/\partial L = p[v'(w - L)]/v'(w - h^*) > 0.$$

Therefore, an increase either in the probability of loss or in the amount of the loss increases the maximum premium that the individual is prepared to pay for complete coverage.

In practice, individuals have to pay a 'deductible' when taking out insurance, that is, the coverage is not complete and the individual has to bear part of the loss. We try to model this. Let y be the amount that can be reclaimed from the insurance firm and D the deductible, that is, $D = L - y$. Also suppose that the insuring firm calculates the premium h so as to cover the expected cost. Let there be an administrative cost of Rs k per rupee of payout because of paperwork. Then the expected cost has two components—the expected payout in the event of a loss and the associated administrative cost. The premium must cover the expected cost:

$$h = py + kpy = (1 + k)py.$$

Hence $h = (1 + k)p(L - D)$ and $dh/dD = -p(1 + k) < 0$. Expected utility now is

$$U_D = pv(w - L + y - h) + (1 - p)v(w - h) = pv(w - D - h) + (1 - p)v(w - h).$$

The consumer chooses D to maximize utility, taking h, which is set to cover expected costs, as given. Noting that h depends on D through $h = (1 + k)p(L - D)$, we get $dU_D/dD = pv'(w - D - h)$ $[-1 + p(1 + k)] + (1 - p)v'(w - h)[p(1 + k)] = 0$. Let the solution be D^*. We can then write the first order condition as

$$v'(w - D^* - h)/v'(w - h) = [1 + k - p(1 + k)]/[1 - p(1 + k)] = 1 + k/[1 - p(1 + k)] > 0,$$
{assuming $1 - p(1 + k) > 0$.}

From this, it follows that $v'(w - D^* - h) > v'(w - h) \Rightarrow w - D^* - h < w - h$ (since $v' < 0$), and hence, $D^* > 0$. *The individual will choose to cover himself less than fully against loss.* Why is this so? Note that if $k = 0$, $h = py$: the premium is equal to the expected payment by the insurance firm. The premium is then called an *actuarially fair* premium. In this case, $v'(w - D^* - h) = v'(w - h)$, which shows us that $w - D^* - h = w - h$, that is, $D^* = 0$. We are back to the situation where the individual covers himself against the loss fully. It is the administrative cost that drives up the premium rate and makes it too expensive for the individual to get complete coverage against loss.

15.5 Information

One aspect of uncertainty is that people do not have perfect information about all the factors that can possibly affect them. For certain types of consumer goods, it is easy to gather information. If one is planning to buy a TV, one needs only to visit a reputed dealer to find out the range of TVs available or their prices. On the other hand, when I enter a fish-market, I do not have prior information about all the different types of fish that are going to be available. Nor do I know which prices will be charged by which sellers, or the extent to which they will be prepared to bargain. I have to spend some time moving around the market to *search* for the best bargain. Of course, this process cannot continue indefinitely, since there is a time constraint and I have to return home in time for the fish to be cooked.

In the fish-market, the sellers are usually better informed about the qualities of their wares than the buyers which means that there is *asymmetric information*. Sellers of both good quality and bad quality fishes must convince the customers that their fishes are of exceptional quality. They sometimes try to do this by describing the supposed quality of their fishes at the top of their voices. Others try to send a *signal* about the quality in more subtle ways, for example by refusing to engage in any sort of bargaining, and even suggesting that customers trying to bargain are not overly concerned with quality and might as well go to the cheaper sources.

15.5.1 The Principal–Agent Framework

In general, situations of asymmetric information are those in which one agent knows something that another does not. We usually employ the *principal–agent framework* to model situations of asymmetric information. One person, the principal, wants to induce another person, the agent, to undertake some action that is costly to the agent. Thus the shareholders of a firm want the CEO to maximize the value of shares by maximizing profits. This involves the CEO working long and arduous hours—quite costly from the CEO's point of view. Unless appropriate incentives are given to the CEO, she will not put in the needed amount of effort.

The incentives to the CEO will be given by means of a contract. A *contract* is a mutual agreement between people to act in some specified way. A common form of contract is an agreement to pay a sum of money on the occurrence of some event that may or may not be controlled by one of the parties. For example, a bookie may agree to pay you a certain sum of money if a particular horse wins at the races or if a particular team wins a tournament. In this case, neither party to the agreement controls the occurrence of the stipulated event. On the other hand, a CEO may be offered a bonus plan: if the profit of the firm exceeds some level, a part of the profits would be paid to the CEO. In this case the CEO can control the stipulated event to some extent.

When a transaction takes place at a single point of time, the contract does not have to deal with uncertain events. Spot contracts usually remain implicit/unwritten. When I buy fish, a part of the contract is that I should not be cheated on the weight of the fish bought. But the fish seller and I do not sit down to write out a contract on a piece of paper. The terms of the contract tend to be unambiguous and therefore the problem of verification or enforcement of the contract is not severe.

Contracts become important when the agreement and the events to which they refer are separated by time or space. Fire insurance is bought before any fire accident actually occurs, but the insurance company cannot reimburse the loss until after the fire actually occurs. A bank lends to a firm to expand its operations, but cannot know beforehand with certainty whether these expansions will be profitable or involve a loss leading to bankruptcy.

A contract is entered into voluntarily by persons who think that they will make mutual gains from the contract. Contracts therefore provide an instrument for gains from trade to be realized. However, people will not enter into a contract unless it is *enforceable*. Courts are thought to provide a mechanism for the enforcement of contracts. However, sometimes contract clauses are contingent on certain things happening and courts may find it difficult to assess whether these things have happened. For example, if a patient suffers additional illnesses while in the hospital, a court will find it difficult to assess whether this was due to the hospital's negligence or because the patient's immunity was low as a result of the original illness. Moreover, courts often take a long time to decide upon cases and court cases can be very expensive.

Non-enforceability in the courts does not make contracts valueless. It becomes necessary to design contracts such that each party chooses to stick to the terms of the contract. Such contracts are said to be *self-enforcing*.

In the simplest principal–agent framework, the principal offers the agent a contract. The agent then accepts or rejects it. Typically, the contract consists of a pai—a payment schedule and a specification of the performance schedule on which the payments depend. For example, the contract may consist of wage rates together with rates of output.

Attention has been focused on two types of constraints that are imposed on agents in self-enforcing contracts. The first is the *individual rationality* or *participation constraint*. The principal has to make sure that the agent agrees to the contract. If the contract falls through, then the agent gets a utility level (say) of u'. Then if the contract is to be accepted by the agent, the agent must get at least u' level of utility from the contract.

The second type of constraint is called the *incentive compatibility constraint*. The principal must take into account the fact that whatever be the terms of the contract, the agent will maximize his own utility, which will generally be different from the principal's. For example, suppose that a shop (the principal) stocks shirts. It knows that richer buyers in general are willing to pay a higher price than poorer buyers. It must then offer a contract which couples the quality purchased with price for that quality. This contract must be offered to any buyer who comes into the shop. The shop must then take into account the fact that faced with the contract; a buyer will maximize his/her utility. In particular, even a richer buyer may choose a (low quality, low price) shirt aimed more at the poorer buyers, if this gives her greater utility than a (high quality, high price) shirt.

15.5.2 A Full Information Model

To illustrate these concepts, we consider a model of full information. A landlord has to devise an incentive scheme for a tenant. The tenant expends effort x, which leads to an output $y = f(x)$ that can be sold on the market by the principal at a price of Re 1. Let $s(y)$ be the payment to the tenant if the output is y. The tenant incurs a cost $c(x)$ if x amount of effort is expended.

The utility of the tenant then is $u(x) = s(y) - c(x) = s(f(x)) - c(x)$. If the tenant does not work for the landlord, he can get u' in an alternative occupation. The tenant will agree to work for the landlord if and only if $s(f(x)) - c(x) \geq u'$. This is the individual rationality constraint that the landlord must take into account while devising the optimal incentive constraint.

Second, given any $s(y)$, the tenant will choose x to maximize his own utility. That is, the tenant will choose x to maximize $u(x) = s(f(x)) - c(x)$. This is the incentive compatibility constraint.

The principal's problem then becomes:

$$\max_{s(y)} f(x) - s(f(x))$$

subject to $\quad s(f(x)) - c(x) \geq u'$ and
$$\max_x u(x) = s(f(x)) - c(x).$$

We can break up this problem in two parts. First, ignore the incentive compatibility constraint and consider the x that will maximize the principal's profit subject to the participation constraint. The principal will pay the tenant only enough to meet the participation constraint: $s(f(x)) - c(x) = u'$. Then the principal's problem is to choose a x to maximize $f(x) - c(x) - u'$. The first order condition is $f'(x) = c'(x)$ and the solution is x^* (say).

Next, the principal has to pick a function $s(.)$ such that it is in the tenant's interest to choose x^*, given $s(.)$. That is, s must be such that $s(f(x^*)) - c(x^*) \geq s(f(x)) - c(x)$ for all x.

There are various ways of devising an appropriate incentive scheme.

Rent. The tenant pays the landlord a fixed sum R as rent and gets to keep the rest of the value of the output. Then $s(f(x)) = f(x) - R$. Hence, $u(x) = f(x) - R - c(x)$, and when the tenant maximizes this, $f'(x) - c'(x) = 0$, which shows that the solution is indeed x^*. R is determined from the participation constraint: $f(x^*) - R^* - c(x^*) = u' \Rightarrow R^* = f(x^*) - c(x^*) - u'$.

Wage labour. The worker is paid $s(f(x)) = wx + K$, that is, a wage of w per unit of effort and a lump sum K. The worker will maximize $wx + K - c(x)$, and this implies $w = c'(x)$. Then if w is set equal to $f'(x^*)$, the worker will choose x^*. K is determined from the participation constraint.

Take-it-or-leave-it. The landlord pays the tenant B^* if he puts in x^* amount of effort, 0 otherwise. B^* is determined from the participation constraint. Thus $B^* - c(x^*) = u' \Rightarrow B^* = u' + c(x^*)$. If the worker chooses any $x \neq x^*$, then he gets $-c(x) < 0$. If $x \neq x^*$, $u = B^* - c(x^*) = u'$. Hence the worker chooses x^*.

Sharecropping. The tenant gets a fixed proportion a of the output. The incentive function is $s(x) = af(x) + K$ where $a < 1$ and K is some constant. The worker's utility function then is $af(x) + K - c(x)$ and the first order condition yields $af'(x) = c'(x)$. Let $\hat{x}$ be the effort level chosen. Since $c'(\hat{x}) = af(\hat{x})$, it is clear that the tenant cannot choose an x such that $f'(x) = c'(x)$. Hence, under sharecropping, the efficiency condition $f'(x) = c'(x)$ cannot be satisfied.

15.5.3 Asymmetric Information

Sharecropping as an institution is widely observed in practice. If it is inefficient compared to the systems of wage labour or renting out, we would expect to see the latter systems rather than sharecropping. One possible explanation is the presence of asymmetric information. The tenant will know how much effort he has put in, but the landlord will, in general, be unable to observe effort. Since the quantum of 'effort' is difficult to measure and therefore unverifiable, the landlord may base the incentive scheme on the output. Output depends on the tenant's effort, but it may also depend on weather, the quality of pesticides, and availability of fertilizers at the right time etc. A system of wage labour is ruled out on this score.

Agricultural operations always suffer from some uncertainties, that is risk. Now, the landlord can be assumed to be less risk-averse than the tenant because he is the 'big guy' and can diversify away risk. Optimal risk-sharing requires that the party least bothered by risk bear the risk. Optimal risk-sharing therefore requires that the tenant, the risk-averse party, be insured against risk more than the landlord. A rent contract, in which the tenant pays a fixed amount to the landlord, violates this, because the risk-averse party bears all the risk. What is needed is a contract in which the landlord bears more of the risk. This is the 'take-it-or-leave-it' contract. But here again, if the target output is missed by a small amount, the tenant forgoes all the payment. So in a sense, again, the tenant bears all the risk.

Sharecropping seems to be the golden mean. Payment depends on observed output. The tenant and the landlord both share in the risk of output fluctuations. This may explain the existence of the institution of sharecropping.

We can distinguish between two types of problems in asymmetric information. A *moral hazard* problem arises when a party to a contract can, after the contract is agreed upon, take an action that might affect the outcome. However, the action is not verifiable.

An example is of a person taking out car theft insurance, and then becoming more careless in locking the car doors. In the absence of insurance, the person would have been sufficiently careful. But with the insurance available, the car-owner no longer has to bear the full cost of the car theft and hence becomes less careful, thereby increasing the probability of theft. Now consider the problem of the insurance company. The insurance company gets its income from the premium payments of its policyholders. In addition to administrative costs, it must bear the cost of insurance payments in those cases where car thefts occur:

$$\Pi = np - qnW - A$$

Here n refers to the number of policy holders, p to the premium paid by each in every period, q the proportion of cases where car thefts occur, W the insurance payment in such cases, and A the administrative expenses.

It is clear that from the insurance company's point of view, it is very important to assess q. The moral hazard problem, by pushing up q, tends to erode the profits of insurance companies.

What is the solution to this problem? One might think that the insurance company should raise p. However, this will tend to lower n. Insurance companies therefore employ the concept of *co-insurance* or *deductibles*: insurance coverage tends to be less than 100 per cent of the loss. This means that if car theft occurs, a part of the loss is borne by the individual insured and this provides an incentive to her to exert due care.

15.5.4 Moral Hazard Problem: An Example[2]

To illustrate the moral hazard problem, consider a principal who wants to employ an agent. Let the agent's utility be of the form:

$$U(w, e) = w^{0.5} - (e - 1)$$

It can be seen that $d^2U/dw^2 = -(0.25)w^{-1.5} < 0$, which shows that the agent is risk-averse. The term $(e - 1)$ captures the disutility of effort; obviously, $e - 1 \geq 0$ for $e \geq 1$. To simplify, assume that only two levels of effort are possible: $e = 1$ (low effort level/shirking) or $e = 2$ (high effort level).

Assume that the agent's reservation utility level is 1. If her U is less than 1, she will refuse to work for the principal.

How does the agent's effort level affect the principal? Suppose that the agent's action can result in revenue of either 10 or 30 for the principal. The agent can influence the probability associated with these revenues by choosing her effort level. When she works hard, the probability of the revenue being 30 is 2/3. When she shirks, it is 1/3.

Action	Revenue = 10	Revenue = 30
$e = 1$	$p = 2/3$	$p = 1/3$
$e = 2$	$p = 1/3$	$p = 2/3$

Thus, for $e = 1$, expected revenue = $(2/3)(10) + (1/3)(30) = 50/3$, while for $e = 2$, expected revenue = $(1/3)(10) + (2/3)(30) = 70/3$. Let us remember that since the only cost to the principal is that of the wage paid to the agent, expected profit = expected revenue $- w$. The principal is assumed to be risk-neutral and to try to maximize profit.

As a benchmark case, let us first see what happens when the principal can observe the agent's effort level, that is, e is observable. We can easily think of a take-it-or-leave-it kind of contract to ensure $e = 2$. The principal must ensure that the agent is willing to work for her, that is the participation constraint is satisfied. Therefore the wage rate w must be such that the agent gets at least her reservation utility level: $U = w^{0.5} - (2 - 1) \geq 1$ which implies that $w^{0.5} \geq 2$, which in turn requires $w \geq 4$.

[2] The following example is taken from Milgrom and Roberts (1992).

If the principal wants to maximize profit, she will try to pay the agent the minimum wage possible. Hence contract offered to the agent will be

$$w = 4 \text{ if } e = 2 \text{ (or slightly above 4)}$$
$$= 0 \text{ otherwise}$$

The principal expects to get $70/3 - 4 = 58/3$ from this employment contract. Is this contract worthwhile for the principal? It can be checked that the principal wants to ensure $e = 2$ because this will yield a higher profit. If $e = 1$, $U = w^{0.5} - (1 - 1) \geq 1$ requires $w \geq 1$.

The contract will be: $w = 1$ always. The agent will shirk and the principal gets $50/3 - 1 = 47/3$ which is less than $58/3$.

Suppose now that e is unobservable and that only the level of revenue is observable. The principal must pay agent more for a good outcome than a bad outcome. Suppose that the principal wants to ensure that $e = 2$. Now the contract must satisfy two types of constraints.

- *Incentive compatibility constraint:* Agent's payoff from $e = 2$ must be greater than the payoff from $e = 1$

    Let y = wage when revenue = 10

    z = wage when revenue = 30

    Hence if the agent chooses $e = 2$, her expected utility will be $(2/3)(z^{0.5} - 1) + (1/3)(y^{0.5} - 1)$, whereas if she chooses $e = 2$, her expected utility will be $(2/3)(y^{0.5} - 0) + (1/3)(z^{0.5} - 0)$. Then incentive compatibility requires:

    $$(2/3)(z^{0.5} - 1) + (1/3)(y^{0.5} - 1) \geq (2/3)y^{0.5} + (1/3)z^{0.5}$$
    $$\Rightarrow (1/3)z^{0.5} - 1 \geq (1/3)y^{0.5}$$
    $$\Rightarrow (1/3)z^{0.5} - (1/3)y^{0.5} \geq 1 \tag{1}$$

- *Participation constraint*

    The agent must get the reservation utility level by selecting $e = 2$:

    $$(2/3)(z^{0.5} - 1) + (1/3)(y^{0.5} - 1) \geq 1$$
    $$\Rightarrow (2/3)z^{0.5} + (1/3)y^{0.5} \geq 2 \tag{2}$$

The principal's problem then is to find values of y and z that

(a) satisfy (1) and (2)
(b) are non-negative
(c) give maximum expected profits to the principal.

Let $z^{0.5} = m$, $y^{0.5} = n$. The constraints then can be written as

(1) $m - n \geq 3$
(2) $2m + n \geq 6$
(3) $m \geq 0, n \geq 0$

The cross-hatched area in Fig. 15.3 represents the region where all the constraints are satisfied.

The principal's expected profit is $(1/3)(10 - y) + (2/3)(30 - z) = 70/3 - (1/3)y - (2/3)z$. Since both y and z have negative coefficients, the principal should try to minimize both z and y in the cross-hatched area. It is then apparent that the solution is $n = 0$, $m = 3$, that is, $y = 0$, $z = 9$. The expected payoff for the principal is $70/3 - (2/3)9 = 52/3$. This is less than $58/3$ which the principal obtains when effort is observable. However, if $e = 1$, principal gets $47/3$, so the contract that makes the wage contingent on observable performance yields higher profit and offers a higher wage for higher levels of performance does better in terms of expected profits.

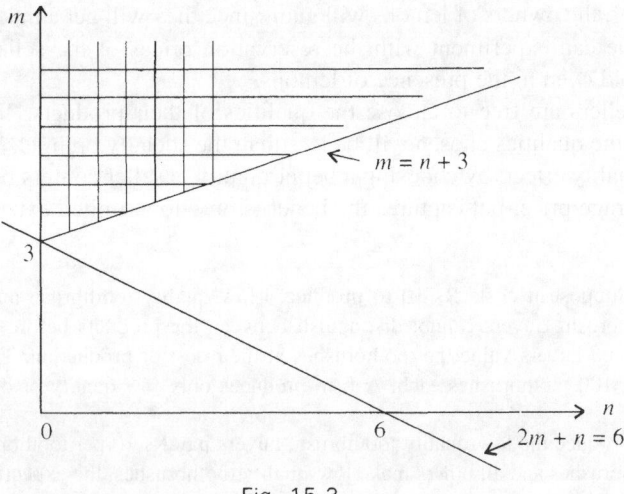

Fig. 15.3

15.5.5 Adverse Selection: The Lemons Problem

Adverse selection occurs when one party to the contract has information relevant to the contract that is not known to the other party before the contract is signed and not verifiable afterwards. A firm when hiring a worker is never absolutely sure whether the worker will turn out to be hard-working or lazy, though the worker himself has this information in advance. A person taking out a medical insurance may have a past history of illnesses which the insuring firm finds difficult to discover. The basic aspects of this problem can be illustrated employing the *lemons problem* scenario developed by George Akerlof.

Consider a market where 100 people want to sell their used Maruti cars and there are many potential buyers of used cars. Used cars may either be 'plums', that is, good quality cars, or 'lemons', that is, bad quality cars. Everyone knows that 50 of the cars are plums and 50 are lemons. The owner of a lemon is willing to sell it for Rs 50,000, while the owner of a plum wants to get at least Rs 100,000. Buyers are willing to pay a maximum of Rs 60,000 for lemons and Rs 110,000 for plums.

If the quality of a car is easily verifiable, then there is no problem in the market for used cars. Lemons will sell for some amount between Rs 50,000 and Rs 60,000, while plums will sell for a price between Rs 100,000 and Rs 110, 000. But now suppose that only the owners know whether their cars are plums or lemons. A buyer can discover the quality of a car only after purchasing the car and driving it around for some time.

In this case, buyers will have to guess how much a car is worth. Let us make the simplifying assumption that a buyer is willing to pay the expected value of a car. This turns out to be $0.5 \times 60,000 + 0.5 \times 110,000 = $ Rs 85,000. But at this price, the owners of plums will not sell their cars. The only cars on the market will be the lemons. However, if the buyers are certain that only lemons will be sold, they will not be prepared to pay more than Rs 60,000. The price in the market will be between Rs 50,000 and Rs 60,000 and no plum will come on the market.

Note that the end-result depends on two variables:

– the reservation prices of the sellers
– the proportion of lemons to plums

In the above example, if four-fifths of the cars were plums, then the buyers would be willing to pay a maximum price of $(0.8)(110,000) + (0.2)(60,000) = 100,000$ and the sellers of plums will sell their cars. However, the owners of lemons will gain, since they will get a much higher price for their cars. Similarly, one can experiment with the reservation prices of the sellers to demonstrate that plums might be sold even in the presence of lemons.

Suppose that sellers are free to choose the qualities of their products. Then in the presence of adverse selection, the qualities chosen will be less than the socially optimal. The reason is that there is a positive externality effect: by choosing a better quality, a seller confers benefits on all sellers by increasing the average price, but captures the benefits only to a limited extent.

Example 15.5: Suppose it costs Rs 10 to produce a low-quality toothbrush and Rs 20 to produce a high-quality toothbrush. Buyers cannot distinguish between the products before purchase, there are no repeat purchases and buyers value the toothbrushes at their cost of production. There are 5 firms in the market producing 100 toothbrushes each. A firm produces only low-quality or only high-quality toothbrushes.

If all 5 firms produce the low-quality toothbrush, buyers pay Rs 10 per toothbrush. If one firm makes high-quality toothbrushes and all others make low-quality toothbrushes, the expected value per toothbrush to buyers is

$$(10)(0.8) + (20)(0.2) = 12$$

Thus if one firm raises the quality of the product, all firms benefit because toothbrushes sell for Rs 12 rather than Rs 10. The high-quality firm receives only a fraction—Rs 2 pr toothbrush—of this extra benefit, while it costs Rs 10 extra to make the high-quality toothbrush. The other Rs 8 is shared by all the other firms. Hence there is no incentive for a firm to improve its quality.

Various means may be adopted to solve the problems arising from adverse selection.

1. Restrict the scope of opportunistic behaviour.
   - The government may require all drivers to carry auto-insurance
   - A company may pay all its employees lower wages but require everyone to enroll under a group medical insurance scheme
   - The government can enact product liability laws, so that if a consumer is saddled with a lemon, she can go to the court for redress. However, the high transaction cost of redress often acts as a deterrent to consumers.

2. Equalization of information between the agents:
   - The *uninformed party* can engage in *screening*. That is, the uninformed party can take steps to gain more information about the product. However there is a cost of collecting information and the uninformed party will try to screen for the good types only if the cost of doing so is less than the benefit.
   - The *informed party* can try to *signal* the quality of the product. Thus potential employees try to signal their abilities and attitudes. But signalling must be credible, that is, the signal should emanate from a high-quality type and it must be impossible for a low-quality type to mimic the signal. For example, owners of plums may try to *signal* the quality of their cars. One way of doing this is to issue a warranty. The owner of a plum will undertake to pay the bill of any subsequent repairs. She can do this, because she knows that this will not really be needed. An owner of a lemon cannot afford to undertake such a warranty. Therefore, the warranty signals the quality of the car and a market for plums can exist. On the other hand, providing full warranty can create a moral hazard problem. The buyer can drive the car roughly after purchase and when repairs are needed, present the repair bills to the seller under the warranty.

- The government can insist on standards and certification to provide information about reliability of a product to consumers. The catch is that this process distinguishes only between products that meet a certain standard and those that do not. It may also drive out low quality products. If there are some consumers who prefer cheaper, lower quality products, then this is a loss from society's point of view.

2. Use third party comparisons.

While buying a car, for example, a consumer can buy auto reports and try to get information about the relative performance of various cars. One important issue here is that of credibility of the information provided. To ensure credibility, the producers of the reports may refuse to carry advertisements from auto manufacturers. But enough of such third party information may not be provided. Information is like a public good, in that it is non-rivalrous. A copy of the same report can be read by many different people, so that the revenue from report generation will be much less, and provide less incentive to produce the report.

15.6 Screening to Solve the Adverse Selection Problem

The following example is intended to give you an idea about how screening can be used to solve the adverse selection problem. The example relates to adverse selection in recruitment of suitable employees. Employers want employees who are intelligent, hard-working and have acquired analytical and quantitative skills. But not all candidates for a position are going to possess these qualities. How does the employer screen out the plums from the lemons? The employer can use a proxy variable to capture some of these qualities in employees.

Suppose that potential employees are of two types—'good' (G) and 'bad' (B) types. The employer is going to hire on a contract basis for one year and is willing to pay a salary of Rs 150,000 for the year to the good types and Rs 100,000 to the B types. When potential employees come for an interview, the employer cannot distinguish between the two types. However she knows that the two types differ in their tolerance for taking 'tough'[3] courses. For a G-type, the 'cost' of taking one of the tough courses at college is Rs 6000 (in terms of the disutility of additional studies required) and for a B-type, it is Rs 9000.

The employer can then use n (number of tough courses) as a screening device. If a candidate has taken less than (say) n^* courses, then this is taken to be indicative of the fact that the candidate is a B-type, and the candidate will be offered a salary of Rs 100,000. Then n^* should be chosen keeping in mind the following conditions:

1. B types can try to take a sufficient number of tough courses to mimic the G-types. To discourage this, n^* should be such that B-types do not find it worthwhile taking so many courses. If B-types take n^* or more courses, they get a net income of $150,000 - 9000n^*$. If they take less than n^* tough courses, they will get 100,000. Hence the condition is

$$100,000 \geq 150,000 - 9000n \Rightarrow n^* \geq 6$$

2. On the other hand, n^* should not be so high that G-types are deterred from taking n^* courses. This requires

$$150,000 - 6000n \geq 100,000 \Rightarrow n^* \leq 8$$

[3] A tough course is presumably one in which regular quizzes and exams necessitate hard work and require analytical approach to problem-solving.

Thus employers can check whether a particular candidate has taken at least 6 courses. If she has, she cannot be a B-type. This screening mechanism will ensure that B-types will not take *any* tough courses and G-types will take exactly 6 tough courses.

If types could have been verified, G-types would have earned 150,000. But now they can earn only up to 150,000–36,000 = 114,000. The existence of B-types imposes a negative externality on G-types.

Topics for Discussion

1. It is difficult for consumers to inspect the quality of goods like wristwatches directly. Why is it that consumers are more prepared to buy such goods from established shops rather than 'hawkers'? Do the same considerations apply when people go to Nepal and buy watches from sidewalk vendors?
2. Businessmen sometimes grumble that graduates from Indian Institutes of Management (IIMs) are not really taught the skills they need to run actual businesses. However, for recruitment purposes, most companies still prefer to tap the IIMs rather than other management institutes. How do you explain this?
3. 'The importance of conspicuous consumption as signal of ability will be different for different occupations'. Discuss.
4. What kind of adverse selection problems would you expect insurance companies to face, and why? Do you think that this can lead to a lemons problem in the insurance market, too?

Exercise

1. Suppose that a farmer is trying to decide which crop to produce. There are three possible states of nature and the payoff matrix is as follows:

| | Rainfall | | |
	Substantial	Moderate	Light
Crop A	7000	3500	1000
Crop B	2500	3500	4000
Crop C	4000	4000	3000

Which crop would you advice the farmer to plant under the maximin, minimax, maximax, Hurwicz, and Laplace criteria?

2. A firm can invest in either of two projects A and B (it cannot invest in both). The possible profits from the two projects along with the respective probabilities are given below:

Profit	Project A (probabilities)	Project B (probabilities)
30	0.05	0.10
40	0.20	0.25
50	0.50	0.30
60	0.20	0.25
70	0.05	0.10

Which project would the firm select using the coefficient of variation measure?

3. Suppose that an individual has an initial wealth of Rs 100. He can lose his entire wealth through theft with a probability of 0.5. Theft insurance is available at a premium of Rs h. The insurance company has an administrative cost of Rs 0.50 per rupee of payout and sets the premium to cover the expected payout plus the expected administrative cost.

If the individual has a *vNM* utility function $v = \ln$ (wealth), where ln is the natural logarithm, calculate the deductible for this individual. How much premium will the individual pay for his insurance coverage?

4. A risk-neutral manager can invest in either Kolkata or Mumbai. The possible profits, the corresponding utilities to the manager and the probabilities associated with the profit levels in the two cities are given below:

Profit (Π)	$U(\Pi)$	Mumbai (probabilities)	Kolkata (probabilities)
1000	0	0	0.1
2000	0.2	0.2	0.15
3000	0.4	0.3	0.15
4000	0.6	0.3	0.25
5000	0.8	0.2	0.2
6000	1.0	0	0.15

Which project would the manager select to maximize her expected utility?

5. It is known that a fraction d of all new cars is defective. Defective cars cannot be identified as such except by the people who own them. Each consumer is risk-neutral and values a non-defective car at Rs 600,000. New cars sell for Rs 400,000 each, used ones for Rs 100,000. If cars do not depreciate physically with use, what is d?

6. Suppose that one in every four new personal computers is defective. The defective ones can be identified only by those who own them. Consumers are risk-neutral and value non-defective computers at Rs 40,000 each. Computers do not depreciate physically with use. If used computers sell for Rs 12,000 each, how much do new ones sell for?

7. Your current wealth level is 49 and you engage in the following wager: if a fair coin comes up heads, you get 15, otherwise you lose 13. Your *vNM* utility function is $v = W^{0.05}$.

(a) What is the expected value of this gamble?
(b) What is the expected utility of this gamble?
(c) Should you have engaged in this gamble?

8. Suppose that your current wealth is 100, and your utility function is $v = W^{0.2}$. You have lottery ticket that pays 10 with a probability of 0.25 and 0 with a probability of 0.75. What is the minimum amount for which you would be willing to sell this ticket?

16 General Equilibrium and Welfare Analysis

In all our discussions so far, we have employed the method of *partial equilibrium analysis*. In this method, the analysis of equilibrium in the market for a particular commodity is carried out in isolation from other markets. For example, we assumed that the supply and demand functions for a commodity depend parametrically on the prices of related products. We ignored the fact that equilibria in different markets are determined simultaneously. If tea prices are high, people shift to coffee, thereby raising coffee price which in turn increases the demand for tea. We need to solve for tea and coffee prices in equilibrium together, taking account of the links in the two markets.

General equilibrium analysis seeks to determine equilibrium prices simultaneously in all markets. We have already come across an example of general equilibrium analysis in the Chamberlinian model of monopolistic competition, where equilibria in product and labour markets are considered together. The present chapter will lay out the basic *GE* framework and point out the welfare results applicable in such a framework.

16.1 A Pure Exchange Model

The basic model to be considered is a pure exchange model, where no production takes place. Consumers have initial bundles of goods—*initial endowments*—which they want to exchange with each other according to their respective preferences. For example, I may have a lot of apples to start with, but if I have a craving for oranges, then I will try to exchange some of my apples for oranges. Of course, I can only do this if there are individuals possessing oranges who want to consume apples.

A number of conceptual clarifications will help us to appreciate and evaluate better the analysis that follows.

Treatment of time. The interval of time over which economic activity takes place is divided into a finite number of elementary intervals of equal length. All instants within each interval are indistinguishable from the point of view of analysis.

Treatment of space. Similarly, the region over which economic activity takes place is divided into a finite number of elementary regions. All locations within each region are indistinguishable from the point of view of analysis.

The economy is considered at a given moment, (called the present moment) in a given region.

Commodity. A commodity is then characterized by (a) its physical properties, (b) the date at which it will be available and (c) the location at which it will be available.

Uncertainty. There is no uncertainty. If uncertainty is present, we will need to characterize a commodity further by the associated state of nature. For example, an umbrella when it is raining will be a different commodity from an umbrella when it is sunny.

It is important to develop an appropriate notation to be able to carry out an analysis of issues in general equilibrium. Let us assume that there are n consumers and k commodities in the economy. Each consumer i is characterized by two things:

- Her *initial endowment vector* $W_i = [w_i^1, w_i^2, \ldots w_i^j, \ldots w_i^k], j = 1, 2, 3 \ldots k$. The symbol w_i^j refers to the amount of the j-th commodity held by the i-th consumer initially. We assume that $w_i^j \geq 0$ for all i and all j.
- Her *preferences* represented by an utility function $U_i = U_i(x_i^1, x_i^2, \ldots x_i^j, \ldots x_i^k)$, where $X_i = (x_i^1, x_i^2, \ldots x_i^j, \ldots x_i^k)$ is the i-th agent's consumption bundle.

Therefore, an individual i starts life with a bundle W_i. She tries to consume a bundle X_i which is derived from utility maximization. The modification to the initial bundle is achieved through purchase and sales in the relevant markets.

A set X of consumption bundles, one for each individual, is called an *allocation*:

$$X = (X_1, X_2, \ldots X_n).$$

An allocation $X = (X_1, X_2, \ldots X_n)$ is said to be *feasible* if

$$\sum_i^n X_i \leq \sum_i^n W_i.$$

This means that $[\Sigma x_i^1, \Sigma x_i^2, \ldots \Sigma x_i^j, \ldots \Sigma x_i^k] \leq [\Sigma w_i^1, \Sigma w_i^2, \ldots \Sigma w_i^j, \ldots \Sigma w_i^k]$, that is, $\Sigma x_i^j \leq \Sigma w_i^j$, for all j. In other words, feasibility means that the total consumption demand for each commodity cannot exceed the total initial endowments of the commodity.

To analyse the equilibrium in this model, we need to introduce a price system p:

$$p = (p_1, p_2, \ldots p_k).$$

Price. The price of a commodity is the amount that must be paid now for the availability of one unit of the commodity at a particular date in a particular location. Thus, comparing prices at the same location but at different intervals of time, we get *interest rates*. Comparing prices at the same date in different locations (countries), we get *exchange rates*.

What does 'payment' mean? There is no money in our economy, and hence no rupee notes with which consumers can pay for their purchases. Payment here takes place in a purely book-keeping sense. Each consumer has a balance sheet. If the consumer commits to accept delivery of x_i^j units of good j at price p_j, then $p_j x_i^j$ amount is debited to her. If she commits to deliver, then $p_j x_i^j$ amount is credited to her.

The i-th consumer tries to

$$\max_{X_i} U_i(X_i)$$

subject to her budget constraint

$$p \cdot X_i \leq p \cdot W_i.$$
that is, $\Sigma p_j x_i^j \leq \Sigma p_j w_i^j$ (the sums being over all j).

Let us assume that the marginal utilities from all commodities are strictly positive for all individuals. Then each consumer will be selecting a bundle on the budget line, $p \cdot X_i = p \cdot W_i$. The solution of the problem

$$\max_{X_i} U_i(X_i)$$

subject to $p \cdot X_i = p \cdot W_i$

yields the demand functions $X_i = X_i(p, p \cdot W_i)$, $i = 1, 2, \ldots n$. The demand for each commodity can depend on *all* prices and the initial endowment.

A *Walrasian Equilibrium* (WE) then is a pair (p^*, X^*), (a set of prices and consumption bundles) such that

$$X_i^* = X_i(p^*, p^* \cdot W_i) \text{ and}$$
$$\sum_i^n X_i^* \leq \sum_i^n W_i.$$

The first condition means that each individual is maximizing utility by choosing the appropriate bundle at the price system p^*, and the second condition means that the demand for each commodity is less than or equal to the total initial endowment of the commodity. We note that all consumers are supposed to act as price-takers. That is, we are assuming all markets to be perfectly competitive and the Walrasian equilibrium can also be called a *competitive equilibrium*.

The Walrasian equilibrium is different from the types of equilibrium we have been discussing so far. It is an equilibrium concept not for one market in particular, but for all markets together. Take any good j. The demand for good j is an aggregation of the demands from all the agents and this cannot exceed the aggregate stock of the good in the economy. Moreover, the incomes are not given. For any price system, income is generated from the sales of some commodities in the initial endowment bundle, and used to buy other commodities. Hence income is not independent of prices. An example is the endowment of labour power. The individual's income from sale of labour will depend on the market wage rate as well as the quantity of labour supplied.

Implicit behind this characterization of the equilibrium is a *free disposal assumption*: commodities can be thrown away free of cost. This ensures that in a Walrasian equilibrium, all prices are non-negative: $p_j \geq 0$ for all j. A negative price for a commodity will mean that an agent trying to sell that commodity will have to give up some other commodities. If the option of free disposal is available, the commodity can be simply thrown away. If I can throw my garbage on the street free of cost, the 'price' of garbage cannot be less than zero. If I have to pay a garbage company to dispose of my garbage, the price of garbage will be negative.

Example 16.1: Suppose that an economy has just two consumers, A and B, and two commodities, labelled 1 and 2. The endowments of the two agents, respectively, are $w_A = (w_A^1, w_A^2)$, and $w_B = (w_B^1, w_B^2)$. The utility functions are Cobb-Douglas: $u_A = (x_A^1)^a (x_A^2)^{1-a}$, and $u_B = (x_B^1)^b (x_B^2)^{1-b}$. We assume that $0 < a, b < 1$.

Agent A maximizes u_A subject to the budget constraint $p_1 x_A^1 + p_2 x_A^2 = p_1 w_A^1 + p_2 w_A^2$. The desired consumption bundle will be $x_A^1 = a(p_1 w_A^1 + p_2 w_A^2)/p_1$, $x_A^2 = (1-a)(p_1 w_A^1 + p_2 w_A^2)/p_2$. Note that we can write these as $x_A^1 = a w_A^1 + a(p_2/p_1)w_A^2$, $x_A^2 = (1-a)(p_1/p_2)w_A^1 + (1-a)w_A^2$. Thus the consumption demands are functions only of the relative price p_1/p_2.

Similarly, $x_B^1 = b w_B^1 + b(p_2/p_1)w_B^2$, $x_B^2 = (1-b)(p_1/p_2)w_B^1 + (1-b)w_B^2$.

Having obtained the desired consumption bundles as functions of the relative price, we use the feasibility conditions to solve for the relative price. Take commodity 1. Feasibility requires that the total demand for 1 not exceed the total initial endowment of 1. Let us see what happens if the demand for 1 is exactly equal to the initial stocks of 1, that is, $x_A^1 + x_B^1 = w_A^1 + w_B^1$. Substituting the expressions for x_A^1 and x_B^1 and solving, we get $p_2/p_1 = [(1-a)w_A^1 + (1-b)w_B^1]/(a w_A^2 + b w_B^2)$.

We have therefore obtained a solution for the relative price. This will be the equilibrium price ratio if the feasibility condition for commodity 2 is satisfied at this price. We can check that $x_A^2 + x_B^2 = (1-a)(p_1/p_2)w_A^1 + (1-a)w_A^2 + (1-b)(p_1/p_2)w_B^1 + (1-b)w_B^2 = (p_1/p_2)[(1-a)w_A^1 + (1-b)w_B^1] + (1-a)w_A^2 + (1-b)w_B^2 = (a w_A^2 + b w_B^2) + (1-a)w_A^2 + (1-b)w_B^2 = w_A^2 + w_B^2$.

We therefore get two interesting results:

1. If there is equilibrium in the market for one commodity, then in Walrasian equilibrium the remaining market will also be in equilibrium.

2. One can only solve for the relative prices in this model. If we want to solve for absolute prices, we must employ some kind of *normalization*. This might involve making the additional assumption that one of the prices, say p_1, is equal to 1. Another commonly employed normalization is to assume that $p_2 + p_1 = 1$. Then if $p_1/p_2 = p^*$, say, $1 + p^* = 1/p_2 \Rightarrow p_2 = 1/(1 + p^*)$. Hence $p_1 = p^*/(1 + p^*)$.

16.2 The Aggregate Excess Demand Function

The aggregate excess demand function is defined as

$$Z(p) = \sum_i^n X_i(p, p \cdot W_i) - \sum_i^n W_i \ .$$

where the X_i's are the demand functions for the i-th individuals. $Z(p)$ is a vector, a typical component of which is $Z^j(p) = \Sigma X_i^j(p, pW_i) - \Sigma W_i^j$: $Z^j(p)$ is the *aggregate excess demand for the j-th commodity*, which is equal to the total demand for the commodity minus the total initial endowments of the commodity. Note that by the feasibility condition of Walrasian equilibrium, in a WE each $Z^j(p) \le 0$: there cannot be excess demand for any commodity in a WE, though there might be excess supplies of some commodities.

We can prove a number of results now.

1. The aggregate excess demand function is homogeneous of degree zero in all prices.

The proof is simple. The budget set for each individual is $B_i = \{X_i \mid p \cdot X_i \le p \cdot W_i\}$. Suppose we multiply all prices by some $t > 0$. Then $(tp) \cdot X_i \le (tp) \cdot W_i \Rightarrow p \cdot X_i \le p \cdot W_i$. Hence the budget set remains unchanged, and the consumer demands the same bundle with the price system tp as she did with p. This means that $X_i(p, p \cdot W_i) = X_i(tp, tp \cdot W_i)$ and hence $Z(tp) = Z(p)$. It therefore follows that if (p^*, X^*) is a WE, then so is (tp^*, X^*).

Consider any price system p'. If we set $t = 1/\Sigma p'_j$, note that we can work with prices $p_j = p'_j/\Sigma p'_j$, since if the price system p' is an equilibrium set of prices, so is p. But $\Sigma p_j = 1$. Therefore, essentially, we can work with the normalization that all prices add up to 1. Hence we can restrict our attention to the set $\Sigma = \{p \ge (0, 0 \dots .0) \mid \Sigma p_j = 1\}$. The set S is called the $(k - 1)$ dimensional *unit simplex*.

2. Walras' Law.

For any $p \in S$, $p \cdot Z(p) = 0$, that is, the value of aggregate excess demand is equal to zero for *all* price systems.

Proof: $p \cdot Z(P) = p \cdot [\ \Sigma X_i(p, p \cdot W_i) - \Sigma W_i] = p \cdot \Sigma X_i(p, p \cdot W_i) - p \cdot \Sigma W_i = \Sigma p \cdot X_i - \Sigma p \cdot W_i = \Sigma (p \cdot X_i - p \cdot W_i)$ $= 0$, by the budget constraint of the i-th individual.

Example 16.2: Consider a two-agent, two-commodity economy. Then $p_1 Z^1 + p_2 Z^2 = p_1(x_A^1 + x_B^1 - w_A^1 - w_B^1) + p_2(x_A^2 + x_B^2 - w_A^2 - w_B^2) = (p_1 x_A^1 + p_2 x_A^2 - p_1 w_A^1 - p_2 w_A^2) + (p_1 x_B^1 + p_2 x_B^2 - p_1 w_B^1 - p_2 w_B^2) = 0 + 0 = 0$.

3. If for some price system p such that all prices are strictly positive, $(k - 1)$ markets clear, then the k-th market also clears.

By Walras' Law, $(p_1 Z^1 + p_2 Z^2 + \dots + p_{k-1} Z^{k-1}) + p_k Z^k = 0$. If the first $k - 1$ markets clear, then $Z^1 = Z^2 = \dots = Z^{k-1} = 0$. Hence, $p_k Z^k = 0$. If $p_k > 0$, this implies that $Z^k = 0$, that is, the k-th market also clears.

Thus, suppose that there are two markets. Then equilibrium in one market will imply equilibrium in the other market, too. In this case, partial equilibrium analysis is equivalent to general equilibrium analysis. In general, we can work with one less market in our analysis, and this can prove to be quite convenient. In standard macroeconomic models, attention is focused on equilibria in the commodity, money and labour markets, and the bond market is ignored on the ground that equilibrium in the other markets implies equilibrium in the bond market, too.

The Composite Commodity Theorem (developed by Hicks and Leontief) also derives its useful-ness from this result. The Composite Commodity Theorem states that if relative prices of some commodities remain unchanged, then for all analytical purposes, the set can be regarded as a single commodity. If we know that there is $k - 1$ commodity whose relative prices remain unchanged, then they can be treated as a single 'composite commodity'. Equilibrium in the market for the k-th com-modity will then imply equilibrium in the market for the composite commodity.

4. If (p^*, X^*) is a WE, and $Z^g (p^*) < 0$, then $p_g^* = 0$. In other words, if a commodity is in excess supply in a WE, then its price must be zero in equilibrium.

Proof. Since (p^*, X^*) is a WE, $Z(p^*) \leq O$. Also, $p^* \geq O$. (We use O to denote the vector $(0, 0,\dots0)$). Hence $p_j^* Z^j (p^*) \leq 0$ for all j.

But by Walras' Law, $p^*Z(p^*) = 0$. If $Z^g (p^*) < 0$ and $p_g^* > 0$, then $p_g^* Z^g(p^*) < 0$. All other terms $p_j^* Z^j (p^*) \leq 0$ and hence we will have $p^*Z(p^*) < 0$ which contradicts Walras' Law.

16.3 Existence of a Walrasian Equilibrium

One of the first questions to be addressed by economists was under what conditions at least one WE will exist. That is to say, under what conditions will there exist at least one set of prices for which (i) when individuals maximize their utilities subject to their budget constraints, (ii) the resulting demands can be met by the existing stocks of the commodity in the hands of the consumers?

We will give a proof of existence for the case when there are only two commodities in the economy. Let these be commodities 1 and 2. There are n consumers in the economy. The set of all equilibrium price vectors is $E = \{p|Z(p) \leq O, p \in S\}$. This is the set of all price vectors for which the aggregate excess demands are non-positive and the prices add up to 1. We want to show that E is non-empty, that is, there is at least one p^* such that $p^* \in S$ and $Z(p^*) \leq O$.

Consider two price vectors $p' = (0, 1)$ and $p'' = (1, 0)$. Both these belong to the set S, since $0 + 1 = 1 + 0 = 1$. Assume that neither p' nor p'' is in E (otherwise there is nothing to be proved). We will then show how to construct a price vector p from p' and p'' which will belong to E.

First, we note that if p' and $p'' \notin S$, then $Z^1(p')$ and $Z^2(p')$ will both be strictly positive (> 0). The reason is that by Walras' Law, $0. Z^1(p') + 1. Z^2(p') = 0 \Rightarrow Z^2(p') = 0$. If $Z^1(p') \leq 0$, then $p' \in E$, which is a contradiction. Therefore, $Z^1(p') > 0$. Similarly, $Z^2(p') > 0$.

Let us now define a price vector $p(t) = tp' + (1 - t)p'' = (1 - t, t)$, where $0 \leq t \leq 1$. Since $1 - t + t = 1$, $p(t) \in S$. By Walras's Law, $(1 - t) Z^1(p(t)) + t Z^2(p(t)) = 0$. If $0 < t < 1$, then one of the numbers $Z^1(p(t))$, $Z^2(p(t))$, must be positive and the other negative. Without loss of generality, assume that $Z^1(p(t^0)) < 0$ for some $t^0 \neq 0, 1$.

Also note that $t = 1 \Rightarrow p(t) = p' \Rightarrow Z^1(p') > 0$.

We plot the $Z^1(p(t))$ function against t. We use the results that $Z^1(p(t^0)) < 0$ and $Z^1(p(1)) = Z^1(p')$ > 0. As $t > 0$, $Z^1(p(t))$ must change sign from positive to negative somewhere. But if Z^1 is continuous, it cannot change sign without becoming zero somewhere. Suppose that $Z^1(p(t^*)) = 0$. Then, since $0 < t^* < 1$, $Z^2(p(t^*)) = 0$. Hence $p(t^*)$ is an equilibrium price vector.

We have therefore been able to prove that there is at least one price vector for which all markets clear when individuals maximize their utilities subject to their budget constraints. Note that in this proof, the continuity of the excess demand functions is very important. If Z^1 is not continuous, then we may have a situation where there is no t^* such that $Z^1(p(t^*)) = 0$, as Fig. 16.1b shows.

If there are more than two commodities, then the procedure we used for proving existence cannot be used and more advanced mathematical tools must be employed. The idea of a basic proof can be sketched as follows.

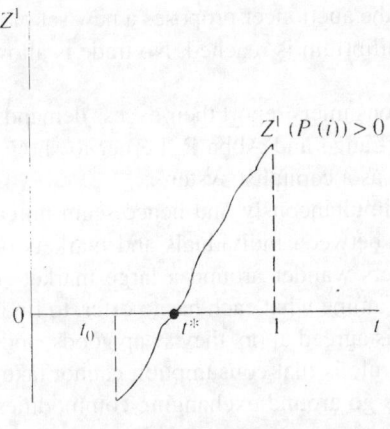

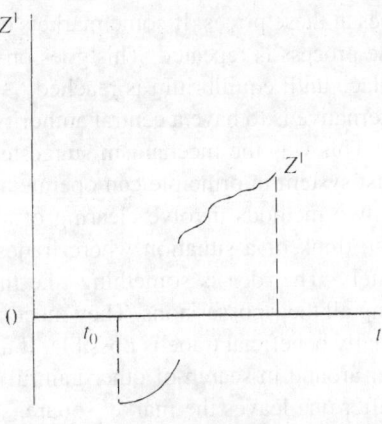

Fig. 16.1a   Fig. 16.1b

Start with an arbitrary price system p in the unit simplex at which the economy is not in equilibrium. Some commodities may be in excess supply, some in excess demand, while some markets may clear at the price vector p.

Construct a new price system with the help of p, following these rules: (a) raise the price of a good in excess demand, (b) lower or at least do not raise the price of a commodity in excess supply, (but never lower it below zero), (c) do not change the price of a good in zero excess demand. One can do this by constructing a new price p'_j for the j-th commodity, where $p'_j = p_j + \max(0, Z^j(p))$. Then, if $Z^j(p) \leq 0$, $p'_j = p_j$, while if $Z^j(p) > 0$, $p'_j = p_j + Z^j(p) > p_j$.

Multiply each p'_j by a scalar to ensure that the resulting price vector is in the $(k-1)$ dimensional unit simplex. The scalar to be employed is $1/[1 + \Sigma\max(0, Z^j(p))]$. It can be checked that the prices $M^j(p) = [p_j + \max(0, Z^j(p))]/[1 + \Sigma\max(0, Z^j(p))]$ add up to 1. Let $M(p)$ be the vector whose j-th component is $M^j(p)$. M represents the rule by which we start with a p in the unit simplex and generate another price vector in the unit simplex and is therefore called a *mapping from the unit simplex to itself*.

We next use some mathematical properties of the unit simplex to show that there will exist a price system p^* such that $p_j^* = M^j(p^*)$ (that is, $p^* = M(p^*)$); such a p^* is called the *fixed-point* of the mapping M). This p^* satisfies the condition (a) p^* is in the unit simplex.

We can also quickly prove that (b) $Z^j(p^*) \leq 0$ for all j. Let $Q = \Sigma\max(0, Z^j(p))$. Then since $p_j^* = M^j(p^*)$, cross-multiplication yields

$$p_j^* + p_j^*Q = p_j^* + \max(0, Z^j(p^*))$$
$$\Rightarrow p_j^*Q - \max(0, Z^j(p^*)) \Rightarrow p_j^*Q \, Z^j(p^*) = \max(0, Z^j(p^*)) \, Z^j(p^*)$$
$$\Rightarrow Q\Sigma p_j^*Z^j(p^*) = \Sigma[\max(0, Z^j(p^*))] \, Z^j(p^*).$$

By Walras' Law, $\Sigma p_j^*Z^j(p^*) = 0$. Hence $\Sigma[\max(0, Z^j(p^*))] \, Z^j(p^*) = 0$. Now, each term of this expression is either 0 or $[Z^j(p^*)]^2$, hence non-negative. Since the sum of all the terms is equal to zero, each term must be equal to zero. This can only happen if $Z^j(p^*) \leq 0$ for all j.

By proving (a) and (b), we have therefore proved that p^* is an equilibrium price vector.

16.3.1 Mechanisms for Attaining a WE

Proving the existence of at least one WE is not the same as showing that the economy will be able to attain this WE. In the literature, various mechanisms for reaching the WE have been proposed.

1. The most famous process is the tatonnement process. A hypothetical auctioneer calls out a price vector and agents respond by providing informatic to the auctioneer about their demands and

supplies at these prices. If some markets do not clear, the auctioneer proposes a new set of prices, and the process is repeated. This goes on until an equilibrium is reached. No trade is allowed to take place until equilibrium is reached.

2. An alternative is to have a central authority to which consumers report their excess demands at all prices. This was the mechanism suggested by Oskar Lange and Abba P. Lerner to show that a socialist system in principle can operate as efficiently as a capitalist system.

3. These two methods involve clearing of all markets simultaneously and hence seem unrealistic. We can think of a situation where trades take place between individuals and markets operate separately. The idea is something like this. Consumers wander around a large market square, carrying all their possessions. They meet others and examine what each has to offer, to find out if a mutually beneficial trade is possible. If an exchange is agreed upon, they swap goods, and again wander around in search of other gainful trades. The rule is that consumption cannot take place until after one leaves the market square, so consumers go around exchanging commodities until they are satisfied with what they possess. Note that in this scenario, speculative trades are possible, so that consumers can initially try to obtain commodities which they do not like, but which may secure them good terms later.

We can also imagine the existence of market-makers, that is, specialists in trades of commodities. An individual or a number of individuals can set up stalls for buying and selling so that others do not have to wander around in search of trading opportunities.

16.3.2 Problems with the Concept of WE

There are a number of features of a WE that we ought to worry about.

• Existence of a WE requires that each consumer be aware of all the prices. However, some goods trade at different prices at different locations. Moreover, in an uncertain world. today's choices depend on forecasts of tomorrow's prices and trading opportunities. Consumers often cannot correctly forecast these.

• Consumers must be able to buy as much or as little they want to at the going prices. But consumers might want to transact such large quantities that they affect the prices. Also, in many economies, commodities are sometimes in excess demand and rationing is not unknown.

• Consumers may not act rationally, that is, try to maximize their utilities subject to the budget constraint. One might question whether utility functions exist at all or whether consumers have utility maximization as their goal.

16.3.3 Uniqueness and Stability

We now know that under certain conditions, at least one WE will exist. However, there may possibly be a large number of Walrasian equilibria. In other words, the equilibrium may not be *unique*. This is not a desirable situation, because it allows us to say very little about the economy. Ideally, we would like to have each exchange economy (characterized by a set of preferences and endowment vectors) to have only one equilibrium. Then, starting from any set of initial conditions, we can predict exactly what will happen if we change some of the parameters, because there will be only one equilibrium corresponding to the new situation. If there are multiple equilibria, we will have no idea as to where the economy will land up.

To ensure that the WE is unique, additional assumptions have to be made. One assumption that has been made is that all goods are gross substitutes for all prices. Two commodities i and j are gross substitutes at a price vector p if $dZ^j(p)/dp_i > 0$. It can then be shown that the WE will be unique.

Another problem is that the mere existence of a WE does not guarantee that the economy will eventually arrive there through some dynamic processes of adjustment. The *stability* issue has to do with the endogenous processes operating within the economy that bring it back to equilibrium. Again, additional assumptions about the process of adjustment must be made.

16.4 Graphical Representation: The Edgeworth-Bowley Box Diagram

Most of the issues raised so far can be conveniently illustrated by means of the Edgeworth-Bowley box diagram.

First, let us consider an agent whose budget line is given by the equation $p_1 x_1 + p_2 x_2 = p_1 w_1 + p_2 w_2$, where (w_1, w_2) is the initial endowment bundle. Note that the budget line always passes through (w_1, w_2), since $x_1 = w_1$ and $x_2 = w_2$ satisfies the budget constraint.

In Fig. 16.2, E is the initial endowment point. The consumer's best choice point is C. The line segment EB represents the offer of x_1 by this consumer while the line segment BC represents her demand for x_2. Now, consider a different set of prices, with (say) a higher p_1. Note that the equation of the budget line can be written as $x_2 = -(p_1/p_2)x_1 + \{(p_1/p_2)w_1 + w_2\}$, which means that the budget line rotates around E to the right. The new best choice point is C'.

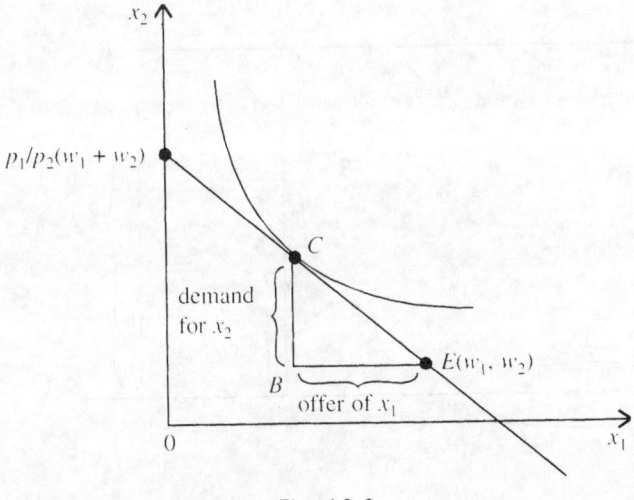

Fig. 16.2

Continuing is this way, and joining the best choice points, we get an offer curve passing through E, C, C', etc. This is shown in Fig. 16.3. At each point on the offer curve, MRS $= p_1/p_2$.

Next, consider a pure exchange economy with two consumers A and B and two commodities 1 and 2. Let $w_1 = w_1^A + w_1^B$, $w_2 = w_2^A + w_2^B$. One can then draw a rectangular box with these dimensions. The horizontal arms of the box refer to commodity 1 and the vertical arms to commodity 2. Hence the length of the horizontal arm is the total initial endowment of commodity 1. This is found by adding A's and B's endowments of commodity 1 together. Similarly, the length of the vertical arm is the total initial endowment of commodity 2. A's endowments are measured from the southwest corner, and B's from the northeast corner. As a result, the same point E represents the initial endowments of both agents. It can be taken as the starting point. Note that all points within or on the boundaries of the arc are feasible, that is, represent consumption bundles such that $x_1^A + x_1^B \le w_1^A + w_1^B$, and $x_2^A + x_2^B \le w_2^A + w_2^B$.

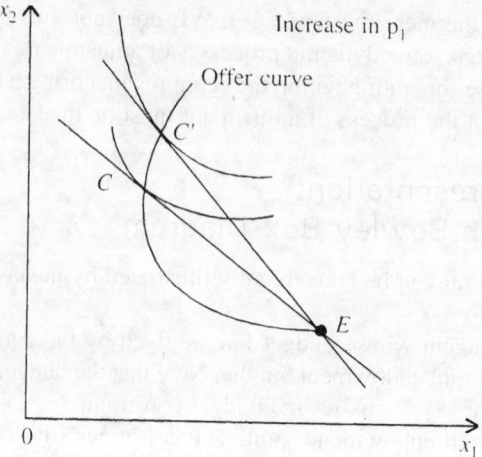

Fig. 16.3

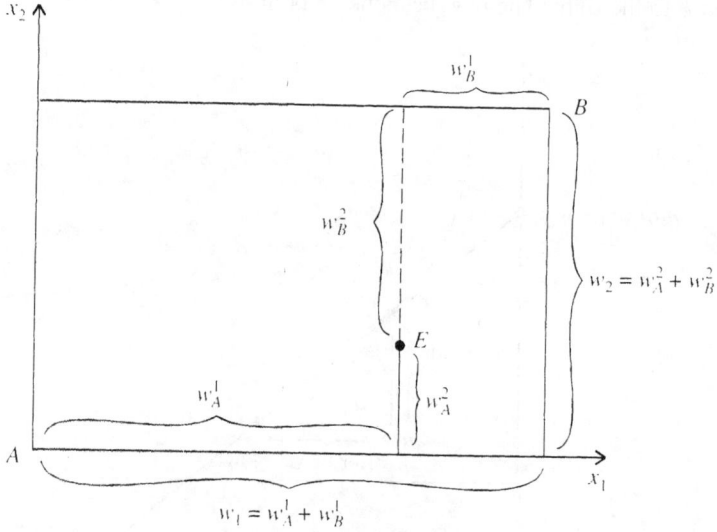

Fig. 16.4

·   From E, by taking different price ratios, we can generate the offer curves EO_A and EO_B of the two agents, respectively. Fig. 16.5 shows how B's offer curve is generated. The two offer curves intersect at the point W in Fig. 16.6. At W, the demand for each commodity is exactly matched by the corresponding offer, which means that markets clear. Moreover, on their corresponding offer curves, the two consumers are making their best choices. Hence the point W represents the Walrasian equilibrium. The equilibrium price ratio is given by the slope of the line EW.

It is easy to illustrate the problems of existence, uniqueness and stability in the $E–B$ box diagram. In Fig. 16.7, the two offer curves do not intersect even once within the box. Hence no WE exist. In Fig. 16.8, the offer curves bend so much that they cross thrice. Points W_1, W_2, and W_3 are all WE points. Moreover, W_1 is not stable by the criterion that any excess demand for a commodity should drive up its price and close the gap between supply and demand.

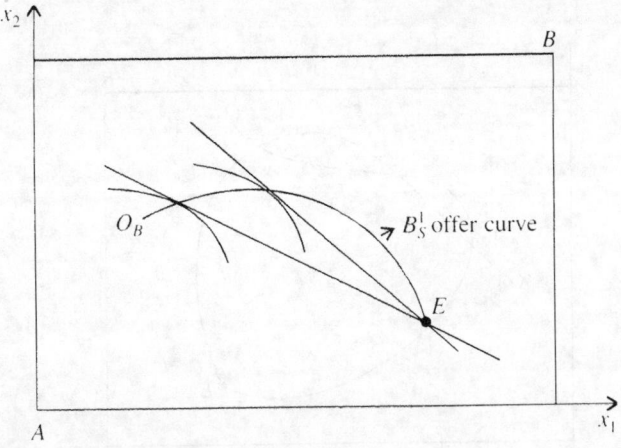

Fig. 16.5

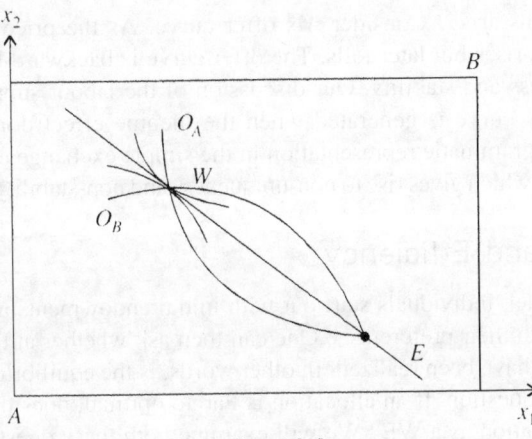

Fig. 16.6

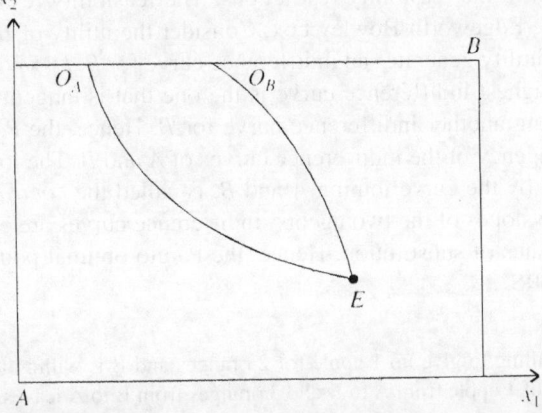

Fig. 16.7

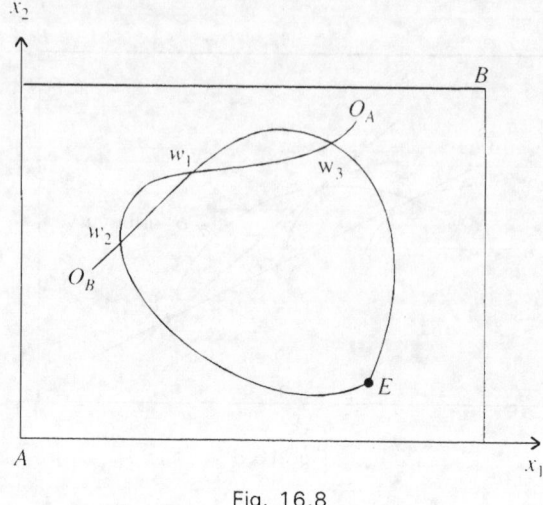

Fig. 16.8

Why do these problems arise? Consider A's offer curve. As the price of 1 rises, the offer of commodity 1 by A at first rises but later falls. The offer curve is backward-bending and this creates the problems of uniqueness and stability. Our discussion of the labour supply curve showed that a backward-bending supply curve is generated when the income effect dominates the substitution effect. In terms of our diagrammatic representation in the simple exchange economy, it is this dominance of the income effect which gives rise to non-uniqueness and non-stability of Walrasian equilibria.

16.5 Equilibrium and Efficiency

In the pure exchange model, individuals start out with initial endowments and then exchange these bundles in accordance with their preferences. One can then ask whether at the resulting WE, all the potential gains from trade have been realized. In other words, is the equilibrium Pareto optimal? One can also ask the opposite question. If an allocation is Pareto optimal, does there exist a set of prices that can support this allocation as a WE? We will examine both these questions for the case where there are two agents and two commodities.

An allocation will be Pareto optimal when one person's utility is maximized, holding the other's utility level fixed, subject to the feasibility restrictions. The feasibility restrictions are satisfied for any point inside or on the Edgeworth-Bowley box. Consider the utility of B to be fixed at a certain level. This fixed level of utility generates an indifference curve for B, I_B, say, in Fig. 16.9. Given this indifference curve, A's highest indifference curve is the one that is tangential to I_B. We can repeat the exercise by considering another indifference curve for B. Hence, the Pareto optimal points are given by the points of tangency of the indifference curves of A and B. The locus of all such points in the E-B box, represented by the curve joining A and B, is called the *contract curve*. At each point on the contract curve, the slopes of the two agents' indifference curves are equal. But the slopes are the respective marginal rates of substitution. Hence, the Pareto optimal points are characterized by the condition $MRS_A = MRS_B$.

Example 16.3: If A is willing to give up 1 apple for 2 oranges and B is willing to give up 1 apple for 3 oranges, then the transfer of 1 apple from A to B and 3 oranges from B to A leaves B as well off as before, but makes A strictly better off.

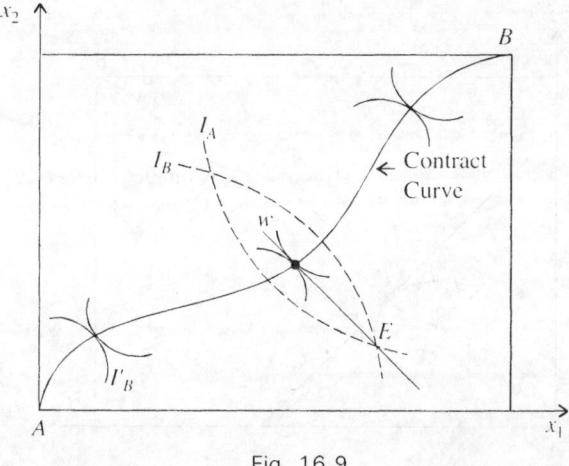

Fig. 16.9

If each consumer maximizes utility subject to the budget constraint, we know that $MRS_A = p_1/p_2$ and $MRS_B = p_1/p_2$. On each point of EO_A, $MRS_A = p_1/p_2$ and on each point of EO_B, $MRS_B = p_1/p_2$. In Fig. 16.6, the two curves intersect at the point W and it is only at this point that $MRS_A = p_1/p_2 = MRS_B$. The point W lies on the contract curve and hence, the Walrasian equilibrium is Pareto optimal. This result is called the First Fundamental Theorem of Welfare Economics:

The First Fundamental Theorem of Welfare Economics. If an allocation (x_1, x_2) is an equilibrium relative to a price system (p_1, p_2), then it is Pareto optimal. In other words, at the equilibrium, all the potential gains from trade are realized.

The relationship between an equilibrium and the set of all Pareto optimal allocations is shown in Fig. 16.9. Note that there is an indifference curve for each agent passing through the initial endowments point E. They are labelled I_A and I_B respectively. These represent the utility levels that the two agents will have if they do not trade with each other and only consume their respective endowments bundles. Therefore, these utility levels are called the *reservation levels of utilities*. The two agents will trade only if they can attain higher indifference levels by trading. Thus mutual gains from trade are possible only in the lens-shaped area contained within the two reservation level curves. W is the point of equilibrium defined by the intersection of the two offer curves. The price line is the line joining E with W.

A number of assumptions are needed to prove the First Fundamental Theorem. First, no externalities must be present. We have seen that in the presence of externalities, individuals acting in their own self interest will not achieve Pareto optimal outcomes. For example, if a negative externality like pollution is present, there will be too much pollution in equilibrium, and a Pareto superior outcome is possible with government intervention. Second, there must be a large number of agents so that no agent thinks that she can affect the market outcome. All agents must be price-takers. Third, at least one equilibrium must exist.

We now turn to the other side of the picture. Consider a point on the contract curve. This is a Pareto optimal allocation. Then we can ask the following question. Does there exist a set of prices such that when agents maximize their utility at these prices and markets clear, the original Pareto optimal bundle is replicated? The answer is yes and Fig. 16.10 shows why. At the point P on the contract curve, two indifference curves I_A and I_B, are tangent to each other. Hence we can draw a straight line BB that is the common tangent passing through P. The slope of BB defines a particular price ratio $(p_1/p_2)^*$. Let the initial endowment be any point on BB, say E. BB is then the budget line

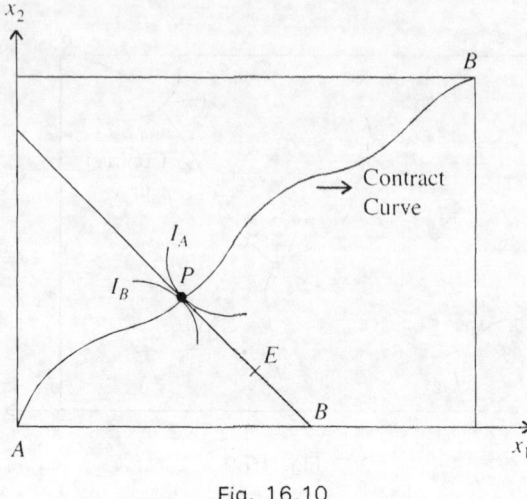

Fig. 16.10

for both agents, and if they maximize their utility subject to the $(p_1/p_2)^*$, then the resulting equilibrium is at point P. This can be stated as the Second Fundamental Theorem.

The Second Fundamental Theorem of Welfare Economics. If agents have convex preferences, then there will exist a set of prices such that a Pareto optimal allocation is an equilibrium allocation for an appropriate assignment of endowments.

Fig. 16.11 shows what can go wrong if indifference curves are not convex to the origin. Given the line budget line BB, A wants to consume at Y rather than at P. B wants to consume at P. Hence markets do not clear.

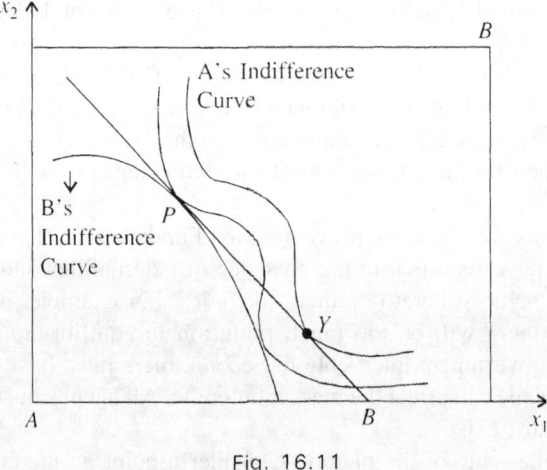

Fig. 16.11

The Second Welfare Theorem essentially states that the problems of efficiency and distribution can be separated. Suppose we know that a particular allocation is Pareto-optimal, that is, efficient. Then there will exist a set of prices at which agents will achieve this allocation in equilibrium. One can then start with a redistribution of endowments (on the line BB) to determine how much wealth each agent should have.

16.6 The Social Welfare Function

One problem with Pareto-optimality as an efficiency criterion is that it does not take account of distributional considerations. Thus a situation in which only one person owns all the wealth of the economy is Pareto optimal, because any attempt to improve the lot of the rest of the population by redistributing wealth will hurt this person and make her worse off.

The Pareto-optimality criterion bypasses completely the necessity of comparing one person's utility with another. Interpersonal comparisons of utility require value judgements to be made. Society may feel that providing food and shelter to a poor man by taxing a rich man is better than letting the poor man starve and not taxing the rich man.

Suppose that there is a set of alternatives available to every individual in the society. Each individual has a preference ordering P_i over these alternatives, and makes a choice according to this ordering from the set of alternatives (the relation P_i is to be interpreted as 'strictly preferred to by i'). The problem now is to take the preference profile $(P_1, P_2, \ldots P_n)$ and use a 'social choice rule' (SCR) to arrive at a *social preference relation* P_s. That is, if different individuals make different choices, then how do we arrive at a 'social choice' from the same set of alternatives?

Some examples of social choice rules are the following:

1. *Dictatorship*. Here the social welfare is identified with the welfare/utility of a single person, say individual 1: $P_s = P_1$.
2. *Simple majority rule*. Here a is socially preferred to b ($a \, P_s \, b$) if and only if the number of individuals strictly preferring a to b is at least half of the total population, that is, if and only if number $\{a \, P_i \, b\} \geq n/2$.
3. Rank ordering method (de Borda's rule). Suppose there are m alternatives. Then each individual is asked to rank all the alternatives in order of preference and then assign points to them. The first-ranked alternative gets m points, the second-ranked gets $(m-1)$ points and so on. The alternatives are then socially ranked on the basis of the total points assigned.

16.6.1 Arrow's Impossibility Theorem

Since the social choice rule is to be constructed out of the utilities of the many individuals in the society, we expect the task of constructing a SCR to be a difficult one. Arrow proved an extreme result, that it is impossible to construct a SCR possessing some 'reasonable' properties.

Let Pi be the 'strictly preferred to' relation for agent i. Let us make two assumptions about P_i:

(a) There is no pair x and y from the consumption set X_i for the agent i such that $x \, P_i \, y$ and $y \, P_i \, x$. (P_i is an asymmetric relation). The consumer cannot strictly prefer 2 apples to 3 oranges and at the same time strictly prefer 3 oranges to 2 apples.

(b) If $x \, P_i \, y$, then for any third element z, either $x \, P_i \, z$ or $z \, P_i \, y$ (P_i is negatively transitive.)

Arrow laid down four conditions that any 'reasonable' SWF should satisfy.

Unrestricted domain. The SCR should prescribe an asymmetric and negatively transitive ordering over social outcomes for *every* array of individual preferences, that is, every preference profile.

This condition is satisfied by the dictatorial rule, but violated by the simple majority rule, as the paradox of cyclical voting shows.

The paradox of cyclical voting. Let there be three individuals x, y, and z, who have to choose from three alternatives a, b, and c. Their preference rankings are:

For x, $a \, P_x \, b$ and $b \, P_x \, c$.
For y, $b \, P_y \, c$ and $c \, P_y \, a$.
For z, $c \, P_z \, a$ and $a \, P_z \, b$.

Suppose voting is between two alternatives at each stage. First, the voting is between a and b. There are two individuals who prefer a to b (individuals x and z) and one who prefers b to a (individual y). By the simple majority rule, a is socially preferred over b ($a P_s b$). Next, there is voting between b and c and it can be shown that $b P_s c$. Then, by transitivity, we should have $a P_s c$. However, if there is a third round of voting between a and c, it is seen that $c P_s a$. Hence P_s is not transitive.

Pareto or unanimity rule. If $a P_i b$ for every i, then $a P_s b$. If everyone in the society prefers a to b, then society must also prefer a to b.

This condition is satisfied by all three rules—the dictatorial, the simple majority, and de Borda's rule.

Independence of irrelevant alternatives. For any two preference profiles $(P_1, P_2, \ldots P_n)$ and $(P'_1, P'_2, \ldots P'_n)$ such that $a P_i b$ if and only if $a P'_i b$ for all i, $a P_s b$ if and only if $a P'_s b$. Thus take any two alternatives a and b from the choice set X. The social ranking between a and b should not change with changes in the array of consumer rankings over *other* outcomes. The preferences between a and b should depend only on how people rank a versus b, and not on how they rank other alternatives.

As an example, consider two elections in both of which all voters prefer Mr Akbar to Mr Anthony. Then in a contest between the two, Mr Akbar should win. It should make no difference that Mr Amar was preferred by all voters to Mr Akbar in the first election and that Mr Anthony was preferred by everyone to Mr Amar in the second election.

This condition is satisfied by both the dictatorial rule and the simple majority rule, but violated by de Borda's rule.

Example 16.4: Suppose that the two individuals x and y rank alternatives a, b, and c as follows:

> For x, $a P_x b$ and $b P_x c$.
> For y, $b P_y c$ and $c P_y a$.

First, suppose that only alternatives a and b are available. Then x assigns 2 to a and 1 to b. The individual y does just the opposite. Aggregating, we see that a is given 3 and so is b, so that there is a tie. But now introduce a third alternative c. Then x assigns 3 to a and 2 to b, while y assigns 3 to b and 1 to a. The alternative a gets 4 while b gets 5, and b is chosen. This happens merely because c is introduced, even though preferences between a and b remain the same.

Non-dictatorship. There should exist no individual i such that $P_s = P_i$ for all preference profiles $(P_1, P_2, \ldots P_n)$.

Arrow's Impossibility Theorem. If the number of alternatives is greater than or equal to three, then there does not exist a SCR satisfying the above four conditions.

Thus Arrow has shown that three 'reasonable' features of a social decision mechanism are inconsistent with democracy. If we want to construct a social preference relation to aggregate individual preferences, we must give up one of the four requirements laid down by Arrow.

16.6.2 Social Welfare Function

Suppose that the preferences of any individual i in the society can be represented by means of an utility function u_i. If the individual strictly prefers a to b, then $u_i(a) > u_i(b)$. The task is to construct a *social welfare function* (SWF) which provides a way of starting with a set of individual utility functions and assigning a social welfare to these:

$$W = W(u_1, u_2, \ldots u_n).$$

There are a number of ways of generating a SWF:

Classical utilitarian welfare function. The SWF is simple the sum of the individual utilities: $W(u_1, u_2, \ldots u_n) = \Sigma u_i$.

Weighted-sum-of-utilities function. This is a generalization of the classical utilitarian welfare function: $W(u_1, u_2, \ldots u_n) = \Sigma a_i u_i$. Here the a's are supposed to be weights indicating how important each agent's utility is to the social welfare. For example, if $a_i = 1$, say and all other $a_j = 0$, then the i-th agent is the dictator.

Rawlsian or minimax welfare function. Here the social welfare is identified with the welfare of the worst-off agent: $W(u_1, u_2, \ldots u_n) = \min(u_1, u_2, \ldots u_n)$.

Whatever be the mode of aggregation of individual utility functions to arrive at the SWF, it seems reasonable to impose the restriction that the SWF should be increasing in each person's utility, given the levels of other persons' utilities: $\partial W/\partial u_i > 0$ for all i. This is called the *Pareto-condition* on the SWF.

Given a SWF, society's task is to choose an allocation $X^* = (X_1^*, X_2^*, \ldots X_n^*)$ that maximizes W subject to the feasibility conditions.

Result. If X^* maximizes a social welfare function, then it is Pareto optimal.

Proof: If X^* is not Pareto optimal, then it will be possible to strictly increase the utility of at least one agent, and not leave anybody worse off. But by the Pareto-condition, this means that social welfare will be higher, which contradicts the assumption that X^* maximizes the SWF.

16.6.3 Fair Allocations and Fair Net Trades

We can now try to specify some specific value judgements and examine their implications.

First, let us consider the concept of fairness. A feasible allocation X^* is *equitable* or *envy-free* if there is no agent who desires another agent's consumption vector more than his own, that is, if there does not exist i and j such that i desires j's bundle more than his own, (which we write as $X_j^* \succ_i X_i^*$). A *fair* allocation is an allocation that is both envy-free and Pareto optimal.

Result. If $X^* = (X_1^*, X_2^*, \ldots X_n^*)$ is an equilibrium relative to a price system p and $p \cdot X_i^* = k$ for all i, then X^* is a fair allocation.

Proof: By the First Fundamental Theorem, X^* is Pareto optimal.

Suppose it is not envy-free. Then there exist i and j such that $X_j^* \succ_i X_i^*$. This must imply that $p \cdot X_j^* > p \cdot X_i^*$. Why? Because, if i prefers j's bundle, yet does not purchase it in equilibrium, this can only be because she cannot afford it at the equilibrium prices.

But this contradicts our assumption that $p \cdot X_i^* = p \cdot X_j^* = k$. Hence X^* must be a fair allocation.

Therefore, if the value of consumption bundle in equilibrium is the same for all agents, then nobody will 'envy' another's bundle. We do not have to provide identical bundles to all agents to rule out envy.

The notion of fair allocations can be extended a bit further. Suppose that $X = (X_1, X_2, \ldots X_n)$ is a feasible allocation. Now, $X_i = W_i + (X_i - W_i)$, for all i. This shows that the consumption bundle is a sum of the initial endowment bundle W_i and the *net trade* $(X_i - W_i)$. A feasible allocation is a *fair net trade* if it is Pareto optimal and there does not exist i and j such that $W_i + (X_j - W_j) \succ_i W_i + (X_i - W_i)$. Thus given initial endowments, each agent must be satisfied with the net trade she has arranged.

Result. If $X^* = (X_1^*, X_2^*, \ldots X_n^*)$ is an equilibrium relative to a price system p, then it represents a fair net trade.

Proof: The proof is similar to the one given earlier. First, equilibrium implies Pareto-optimality of X^*. Next, suppose that it does not represent a fair net trade. Then there exist i and j such that $W_i + (X_j^* - W_j) \succ_i W_i + (X_i^* - W_i) \Rightarrow p \cdot W_i + p \cdot (X_j^* - W_j) > p \cdot W_i + p \cdot (X_i^* - W_i) \Rightarrow p \cdot (X_j^* - W_j) > p \cdot (X_i^* - W_i) = 0$, (by the budget constraint of the i-th individual). But this means that $p \cdot X_j^* > p \cdot W_j$, which shows that the budget constraint for the j-th individual is violated. This is a contradiction. Hence X^* must represent a fair net trade.

16.7 Production

In this section, we briefly discuss how production is incorporated in general equilibrium models. Productive activities are carried out by l 'firms'. We abstract from all legal types of organizations (corporations, partnerships, and sole proprietorships) and different types of activities (agriculture, mining, manufacturing, etc.). We introduce the abstract notion of a firm or a producer, who chooses and carries out a *production plan*.

A production plan is simply a vector of numbers, one for each commodity in the economy. Positive numbers denote the levels of outputs, while negative numbers denote the level of inputs. The set Y_j of all feasible production plans y_j for the j-th firm is called the *production set* of the j-th firm. Note also that the convention of using negative numbers for inputs and positive numbers for outputs means that the profit of the firm, for a price system p, is $p_j = p \cdot y_j$. All firms act as price-takers, and all firms try to maximize their profits. Again, therefore, we are ruling out imperfectly competitive markets.

> **Example 16.5:** Suppose there are just three commodities, labour, gun, and butter. Then if a vector $(-1, 0, 2)$ for a firm represents a feasible production plan, this means that the firm can produce 2 units of butter with 1 unit of labour. At the price system $(3, 4, 2)$, the firm's profit is $3(-1) + 4 \times 0 + 2 \times 2 = 1$.

Once production is introduced into the picture, we have to tackle the question of the distribution of profits. In a capitalist economy, consumers own firms and are entitled to a share of the profits. Let T_{ij} be the share of the i-th consumer in the j-th firm's profit. If $T_{12} = 0$, say, this means that individual 1 does not share in the profit of firm 2. The i-th consumer's budget equation then becomes $p \cdot X_i = p \cdot W_i + ST_{ij}(p \cdot y_j)$, summing over j. The consumer maximizes utility subject to this budget constraint.

A feasible allocation then refers to all allocations that can be supported by the existing endowment bundles plus feasible production plans. That is, the total demand for a commodity can now be met from the initial endowments as well as through production. Among the initial endowments, we now include the endowments of factors of production.

Debreu has shown that existence of an equilibrium can be proved even after introducing production into the model by making a number of assumptions on the production sets. Three of these deserve special mention. One assumption is that the j-th producer always has the option of doing nothing, which is, using 0 inputs to produce 0 outputs. Second, production processes are supposed to be irreversible. If one can make egg-rolls out of eggs, it should never be possible to produce eggs out of egg-rolls. Third, a production process that uses inputs but produces zero outputs is possible. In other words, we assume free disposal.

One can also prove the two fundamental theorems of welfare after introducing production into the model.

In the pure exchange model, efficiency or Pareto-optimality is achieved when the consumption bundles cannot be redistributed among the agents to make at least one person strictly better off and nobody worse off. This requires the equality of the marginal rates of substitution of all the agents. In a competitive equilibrium, each agent maximizes utility by equating MRS with the price ratio, and since there exist a common set of price ratios, all MRSs are equalized.

When production is introduced into the picture, two more possibilities for improving some agents' utility arise. First, we have to see whether inputs are being properly utilized. Is it possible to redistribute inputs to increase the production of at least one output, keeping others fixed? The answer is yes, if the marginal rates of technical substitution are different between firms. We however know that profit-maximizing firms must also minimize costs. This requires each firm to equate the MRTS between any two inputs to the corresponding factor price ratio. In equilibrium, there is a common set of factor prices, and hence all MRTS are equated.

Second, if the product-mix is inappropriate, then by changing the product-mix, the economy can reach a Pareto-superior allocation. The economy might produce a lot of clothing and very little rice (in terms of our example in Chapter 1) efficiently. But everybody in the economy will be happy if more rice and less clothing is produced. Given the inputs, we know that the efficient product-mixes can be represented on a production possibilities curve. The slope of the PPC at any point is called the *marginal rate of transformation* (MRT) at that point, and measures the opportunity cost of rice in terms of clothing. For Pareto-optimality, we require that this be the same as the MRS, that is, the rate at which individuals are willing to give up rice for clothing (see Appendix).

Why is this so? Suppose that the product-mix is such that MRT = 1 while the MRS at the consumption bundle for Kumar is 2. This means that Kumar is willing to give up 2 units of rice in order to obtain an additional unit of clothing. But this additional clothing can be produced at the cost of only one unit of rice. With the capital and labour saved by producing 2 fewer units of rice for Kumar, 2 additional units of clothing can be produced. Kumar can be given 1.5 units of this extra clothing, and the remaining to other members of this community, making everybody better off. Therefore the original product-mix was not efficient.

How is this equality achieved with competitive equilibrium? First, MRT is equal to the ratio of marginal costs, because this ratio reflects the opportunity cost. Second, with perfect competition, these marginal costs are equal to the prices. Hence, MRT is equal to the ratio of the prices and therefore to the MRS for every individual.

Topics for Discussion

1. One suggested mechanism for arriving at a Walrasian equilibrium is for an auctioneer to call out a set of prices, examine the demands and supplies at these prices, and announce a new set of prices accordingly. An alternative method is to have a centrally planned economy where a central planner operates in the same manner as the auctioneer. Do you think that these two methods are equivalent? Give reasons for your answer.

2. Do you feel that the representatives of the people elected through a system of voting act according to an 'adequate' social welfare function? What alternative would you suggest?

3. Suppose that a system is devised in which the 'perfect happiness' of everyone else in the society could be assured through just one person living in complete misery. Would you say yes to such a system? (This question is poised poignantly by Ursula Le Guin in her short story 'The ones who walk away from Omelas'.)

Exercise

1. Suppose that a pure exchange economy has just two consumers, A and B, and two commodities, labelled 1 and 2. The endowments of the two agents, respectively, are $w_A = (w_A^1 = 10, w_A^2 = 10)$, and $w_B = (w_B^1 = 8, w_B^2 = 4)$. The utility functions are: $u_A = (x_A^1)^{.05}(x_A^2)^{.05}$, and $u_B = (x_B^1)^{.25}(x_B^2)^{.75}$.
   Solve for the Walrasian equilibrium in this model.

2. Let $E_i(p)$ be the excess demand function for good i. Which of these following sets of excess demand functions satisfy Walras Law?

   (a) $E_1(p) = -p_2 + 10/p_1$, $E_2(p) = p_1$, $E_3(p) = -10/p_3$
   (b) $E_1(p) = (p_2 + p_3)/p_1$, $E_2(p) = (p_1 + p_3)/p_2$, $E_3(p) = (p_1 + p_2)/p$

3. A consumer's utility function is $U = a\ln x_1 + (1 - a)\ln x_2$, where ln refers to the natural logarithm. She has an endowment of 10 units of commodity 1 and 0 of commodity 2. If p is the price of commodity 1 in terms of commodity 2, derive the consumer's demand for the two commodities in terms of p and a. What is her offer curve in this case?

4. In an economy, clothing and food are produced with the help of labour and capital. Suppose that $w = r =$ Rs 4/hr. Suppose also that in clothing production, $MP_L^C/MP_K^C = 2$ and that in food production $MP_L^F/MP_K^F = 1/2$. Is this economy efficient in production? If not, how should it reallocate its inputs?

5. Consider an economy with two goods food and clothing and two consumers, Ayan and Brinda. For a given initial endowment, when $P_F/P_C = 3$, Ayan wants to buy 6 units of clothing while Brinda wants to sell 2 units of food. Is $P_F/P_C = 3$ an equilibrium price ratio? If so, why? If not, in which direction will it tend to change?

Appendix

Pareto optimality. Suppose that an economy has just two consumers, A and B, and two commodities, labelled 1 and 2. Let X^1 and X^2 represent the total amount of goods 1 and 2 produced and consumed: $X^1 = x_A^1 + x_B^1$ and $X^2 = x_A^2 + x_B^2$. Let us now consider the bundles (X^1, X^2) which lie on the production possibility frontier and represent the functional relationship between them by the transformation function T: $T(X^1, X^2) = 0$.

A Pareto optimal allocation is one that maximizes any one person's utility, given the level of the other person's utility and subject to the transformation function. It can be written as

$$\max_{x_A^1,\, x_A^2,\, x_B^1,\, x_B^2} u_A(x_A^1, x_A^2)$$

subject to $u_B(x_B^1, x_B^2) = u^*$ and $T(X^1, X^2) = 0$.

The Lagrangean for this problem is

$$L = u_A(x_A^1, x_A^2) - z[u_B(x_B^1, x_B^2) - u^*] - y\, T(X^1, X^2).$$

The first order conditions are:

$$\partial L/\partial x_A^1 = \partial u_A/\partial x_A^1 - y\partial T/\partial X^1 = 0,$$
$$\partial L/\partial x_A^2 = \partial u_A/\partial x_A^2 - y\partial T/\partial X^2 = 0,$$
$$\partial L/\partial x_B^1 = -z\partial u_B/\partial x_B^1 - y\partial T/\partial X^1 = 0,$$
$$\partial L/\partial x_B^2 = -z\partial u_B/\partial x_B^2 - y\partial T/\partial X^2 = 0.$$

From the first two equations, we get

$$(\partial u_A/\partial x_A^1)/(\partial u_A/\partial x_A^2) = (\partial T/\partial X^1)(\partial T/\partial X^2)$$

and from the third and fourth equations, we get

$$(\partial u_B/\partial x_B^1)/(\partial u_B/\partial x_B^2) = (\partial T/\partial X^1)(\partial T/X^2).$$

The left hand sides in both these expressions are the MRSs, while the right hand sides are the marginal rate of transformation (MRT). We therefore have MRS$_A$ = MRS$_B$ = MRT.

Mathematical Appendix

Vectors

A *set* is a well-defined collection of *elements*, considered together or as a whole. These elements, in particular, can be numbers. Thus $(1, 2)$ is a set consisting of the elements 1 and 2. We write $1 \in (1, 2)$.

Sometimes a set can be specified by listing explicitly all its elements. For example, $S = (1, 2, 3, \ldots 100)$. At other times, it is not possible to carry out such a complete listing, and we have to define the set by mentioning a defining property possessed by all elements of the set. For example, suppose we want to define the budget set B of a consumer. This consists of all the bundles (F, C) he can buy with his income, and bundles are of non-negative quantities of the goods (see Chapter 3). We write $B = \{(F, C) \mid I \geq P_F F + P_C C \text{ and } F \geq 0, C \geq 0\}$. The symbol $\mid$ stands for 'such that'.

A set C is said to be *convex* if for any two elements $x, y \in C$, the element $z = \lambda_1 x + \lambda_2 y$, where $\lambda_1, \lambda_2 \geq 0$ and $\lambda_1 + \lambda_2 = 1$, also belongs to C. Note that z can also be written as $z = \lambda x + (1 - \lambda)y, 0 \leq \lambda \leq 1$. Intuitively, a convex set is one in which the straight line joining any two points in the set lies completely within the set.

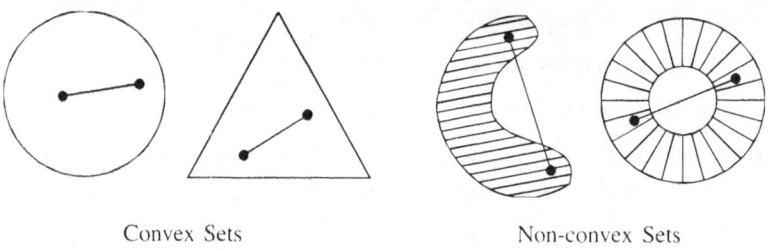

Convex Sets   Non-convex Sets

Fig. 1

A *vector* is an ordered set. As sets, $(1, 2)$ and $(2, 1)$ are the same. But as vectors, they are different, because the order of the elements is different. Elements of vectors are often written with subscripts to denote this order: $x = (x_1, x_2, \ldots x_n)$ is a vector whose i-th element is x_i.

Let us consider vectors whose elements are real numbers. We can *add* two vectors by adding their corresponding elements. If $x = (x_1, x_2, \ldots x_n)$ and $y = (y_1, y_2, \ldots y_n)$, then $x + y = (x_1 + y_1, x_2 + y_2, \ldots x_n + y_n)$.

We can perform *scalar multiplication* by multiplying every element of a vector by a fixed real number r: $rX = (rx_1, rx_2, \ldots rx_n)$. In particular, if $r = -1$, then we get the vector $-x = (-x_1, -x_2, \ldots -x_n)$.

Vector *subtraction* can then be defined: $x - y = (x_1 - y_1, x_2 - y_2, \ldots x_n - y_n)$.

The *inner product/dot product* of two vectors is a number obtained by multiplying corresponding elements of the two vectors and then adding them up:

$$x \cdot y = x_1 y_1 + x_2 y_2 + \ldots + x_n y_n = \Sigma x_i.$$

Inequalities and equalities. $x \geq y$ means $x_1 \geq y_1, x_2 \geq y_2, \ldots x_n \geq y_n$. Similarly for $x \leq y$. Also, $x = y$ if and only if $x_1 = y_1, x_2 = y_2, \ldots x_n = y_n$.

Example: (i) Let $x = (4, 3)$ and $y = (1, 2)$. Then $x + y = (4 + 1, 3 + 2) = (5, 5)$. $x - y = (4 - 1, 3 - 2) = (3, 1)$. $x \cdot y = 4 \times 1 + 3 \times 2 = 10$.

(ii) Consider the pure exchange model in Chapter 16. There are k commodities. Let the initial endowment vector of the i-th consumer be $W_i = [w_i^1, w_i^2, \ldots w_i^j, \ldots w_i^k]$, $j = 1, 2, 3 \ldots k$. The symbol w_i^j refers to the amount of the j-th commodity held by the i-th consumer initially.

Let $X_i = (x_i^1, x_i^2, \ldots x_i^j, \ldots x_i^k)$ be the i-th agent's consumption bundle. Note that

$$\sum_i^n X_i = (\sum_i^n X_i^1, \sum_i^n X_i^2, \ldots \sum_i^n X_i^j \ldots \sum_i^n X_i^k) \text{ and } \sum_i^n W_i = (\sum_i^n W_i^1, \sum_i^n W_i^2, \ldots \sum_i^n W_i^j \ldots \sum_i^n W_i^k).$$

Let $p = (p_1, p_2, \ldots p_k)$, $p_j \geq 0$ for all j, be a price system. If we denote the vector whose n elements are all zeros as $O = (0, 0, \ldots 0)$, then we can write $p \geq O$.

We see that $p \cdot X_i = \sum p_j x_i^j$ and $p \cdot W_i = \sum p_j w_i^j$.

Functions

Let there be two non-empty sets A and B. Suppose that with each element $x \in A$ is associated, in some manner, one and only one element of B, which we denote by $f(x)$. Then f is said to be a *function* or a *mapping* from A to B. We often write $f: A \to B$. A is called the *domain* of the function, B its *codomain*, and the elements $f(x)$ are called the values of f. The set of all values of f is called the *range* of f.

Example: $y = 10 - x$. This rule tells us that when $x = 1$, $y = 9$, when $x = 2$, $y = 8$, etc.

Note that (i) the rule must be applicable to each and every element of A, (ii) with any element x of A, a unique element $f(x)$ of B can be associated (iii) different elements of A can get mapped to the same element of B and (iv) not every element of B need be associated with elements from A.

For example, let $A = (1, 2)$ and let $B = (3)$. Then if f associates 1 with 3 and also 2 with 3, it is a function. But if $A = (3)$ and $B = (1, 2)$, and f associates 3 with *both* 1 and 2, then it cannot be a function.

We shall often use *real-valued functions*, which map elements from some set to the set of real numbers. The set A will also often be the set of real numbers. In this case, the function can be represented by means of a graph.

A function is *continuous* if its graph does not have any breaks or discontinuities. A *strictly increasing* (decreasing) function is one that always increases (decreases). That is, if $a, b \in A$ and $a > b$, then f is strictly increasing if $f(a) > f(b)$. If a function is strictly increasing or decreasing, it is said to be *strictly monotonic*.

A strictly monotonic function associates a separate y with each and every x. For example, let $A = (1, 2, 3)$ and $B = (4, 5, 6)$. Then if f associates 1 with 4, 2 with 5 and 3 with 6, it is strictly monotonic. We can then define an *inverse function* g which associates 4 with 1, 5 with 2, and 6 with 3, that is, we can start with y values and get back to x values. Another example is $y = 2x$. This can be written as $x = y/2$, and allows us to recover x values from y values. Note that this is not possible if, for example, f associates 1 with 4 and 2 also with 4. Then starting from 4, we cannot unambiguously go back to x values.

A function f of one variable x is differentiable at a point x^* if the derivative of f exists at x^*. We denote the derivative at x^* by $df(x^*)/dx$ or $f'(x^*)$. The function f is twice differentiable at x^* if both the first order and second order derivatives exist at x^*. That is both $df(x^*)/dx$ and $d^2f(x^*)/dx^2$ exist. The second order derivative is sometimes written as $f'(x)$ (see section on Calculus).

Let f: $A \to B$, where A is a convex set. Then f is said to be a *concave function* (or, simply, convex), if for any x and y in A, and a number r such that $0 \leq r \leq 1$.

$$f(rx + (1 - r)y) \geq rf(x) + (1 - r)f(y).$$

Let R_+ be the set of all non-negative real numbers and let R be the set of all real numbers. Consider a concave function $f: R_+ \to R$. If f' is differentiable, then f is concave if and only if $f'(x) \leq 0$ for all x. Another property of concave functions is that $f(a) \leq f(b) + f'(b)(a - b)$ for all a and b.

A function f is *strictly concave* if the strict inequality holds in each of these three expressions, that is,

$f(ra + (1 - r)b) > rf(a) + (1 - r)f(b)$ for all a and b and for all r such that $0 \leq r \leq 1$,

$f''(x) < 0$ for all x in the domain of f,

$f(a) < f(b) + f'(b)(a - b)$ for all a and b in the domain of f.

A *convex* function satisfies

$f(ra + (1 - r)b) \leq rf(a) + (1 - r)f(b)$ for all a and b and for all r such that $0 \leq r \leq 1$,

$f''(x) \geq 0$ for all x in the domain of f,

$f(a) \geq f(b) + f'(b)(a - b)$ for all a and b in the domain of f.

A *linear function* is the equation of a straight line. It can be written as $ax + by = z$. A linear function is both convex and concave. Two alternate ways of writing this equation are useful:

$x/(z/a) + y/(z/b) = 1$. The terms z/a and z/b represent respectively the intercepts on the x and the y axis.

$y = -(a/b)x + (z/b)$. Here $-(a/b)$ represents the slope of the line with the positive direction of the x axis.

A function $z = f(x, y)$ is linearly homogeneous or *homogeneous of degree one* if $f(tx, ty) = tz$, for $t > 0$.

Calculus

The (first) derivative of a function f at x^*, if it exists, is

$$df(x^*)/dx = \lim_{h \to 0}[f(x^* + h) - f(x^*)]/h.$$

The second derivative of f at x^* is the derivative of the first derivative.

Example: Let $f(x) = ax$. Then $[f(x^* + h) - f(x^*)]/h = [a(x^* + h) - ax^*]/h = a$. Hence

$$\lim_{h \to 0}[f(x^* + h) - f(x^*)]/h = a.$$

In the text, we often use $f'(x)$ to denote df/dx and $f''(x)$ to denote $d^2f(x^*)/dx^2$. Some basic results on differentiation are often used in the text:

If $f(x) = x^n$, then $df/dx = nx^{n-1}$. For example, if $f(x) = x^3$, then $df/dx = 3x^2$.

If $f(x) = ag(x)$, where a is a constant, then $df/dx = a(dg/dx)$.

If $f(x) = \ln x$, then $df/dx = 1/x$, for $x \neq 0$.

Let $g(x)$ and $h(x)$ be both functions of h.

If $f(x) = g(x) + h(x)$, then $df/dx = dg/dx + dh/dx$.

If $f(x) = g(x) - h(x)$, then $df/dx = dg/dx - dh/dx$.

The product of the two functions is $f(x) = g(x) \cdot h(x)$. The *product rule* gives the derivative of f as a function of the derivatives of the g and h functions:

$$df/dx = h(x)(dg/dx) + g(x)(dh/dx).$$

Example: Let $g(x) = ax$ and $h(x) = \ln x$. If $f(x) = g(x)h(x)$, then $df/dx = (\ln x)(a) + (ax)(1/x) = a\ln x + a$.

Given two functions $y = g(x)$ and $z = h(y)$, the *composite function* is $f(x) = h(g(x))$. The *chain rule* of differentiation is $df/dx = (dh/dg)(dg/dx) = (dh/dy)(dy/dx)$.

Example: Let $g(x) = x^3$ and $h(y) = 5y$. Then $f(x) = h(g(x)) = 5x^3$. We can directly differentiate this to get $df/dx = 15x^2$. Or we can notice that $df/dx = (5)(3x^2)$ by the chain rule.

Let $f(x) = g(x)/h(x)$. That is, $g(x) = f(x) \cdot h(x)$. By the product rule, $dg/dx = f(x)(dh/dx) + h(x)(df/dx)$. This implies that

$df/dx = [dg/dx - f(x)(dh/dx)]/h(x) = [h(x)(dg/dx) - g(x)(dh/dx)]/[h(x)]^2$,

substituting for $f(x)$. (We assume that $h(x) \neq 0$.)

Example: Let $g(x) = \ln x$, $h(x) = x$. Then $f(x) = (\ln x)/x$ and $df/dx = [x(1/x) - (\ln x)]/x^2 = [1 - \ln x]/x^2$.

Let us now consider a function of two variables: $y = f(x_1, x_2)$. Then the *partial derivative* of f with respect to x_1 is

$$\partial f(x_1, x_2)/\partial x_1 = \lim[f(x_1 + h, x_2) - f(x_1, x_2)]/h.$$
$$h \to 0$$

It is just the derivative of f with respect to x_1, holding x_2 constant. Similarly, we can define the partial derivative of f with respect to x_2, holding x_1 constant.

Example: Let $f(x_1, x_2) = x_1 x_2 + x_1$. Then $\partial f(x_1, x_2)/\partial x_1 = x_2 + 1$.

The function f is *continuously differentiable* if its partial derivatives exist and are continuous. The function f will then possess total derivatives or differentials everywhere. The differential of $f(x_1, x_2)$ is

$df = [\partial f(x_1, x_2)/\partial x_1]dx_1 + [\partial f(x_1, x_2)/\partial x_1]dx_2$.

Optimization

If $y = f(x)$, then $f(x)$ attains a *global maximum* at x^* if $f(x^*) \geq f(x)$ for all x. It attains a *global minimum* at x^* if $f(x^*) \leq f(x)$ for all x.

Suppose that f is differentiable in a small set containing x^* (called a neighbourhood of x^*). It can then be shown that if f reaches a maximum at x^* in the sense that $f(x^*) \geq f(x)$ for all x in this set,

$$df(x^*)/dx = 0 \text{ and } d^2f(x^*)/dx^2 \leq 0.$$

These expressions are referred to as the *first order* and *second order* condition respectively for a *local maximum*. The first order condition says that the function is flat at x^* while the second order condition says that the function is concave *near* x^*. These are necessary conditions for a local maximum. The two conditions assure us that the function has reached a peak in a small 'neighbourhood' of x^*.

[For a *local minimum*, the second order condition becomes $d^2f(x^*)/dx^2 \geq 0$.]

However, this might be consistent with the function reaching a higher value than at x^* outside the neighbourhood of x^*. One way of ruling this out and ensuring that the maximum at x^* is a global maximum is to assume that the function is concave everywhere and not just in the neighbourhood of x^*. [For a global minimum, the function must be convex everywhere.]

Example: Let $f(x) = x - x^2$. Then $df/dx = 1 - 2x$. By the first order condition, $df/dx = 0$ which implies that $x^* = 1/2$. Now $d^2f(x^*)/dx^2 = -2 < 0$. Hence x^* is a maximum. Note also that $f'(x) < 0$ always, so that this is a global maximum.

Now let $y = f(x_1, x_2)$. Then a necessary condition for f to attain a local maximum or minimum at (x_1^*, x_2^*) is

$$\partial f(x_1^*, x_2^*)/\partial x_1 = \partial f(x_1^*, x_2^*)/\partial x_2 = 0.$$

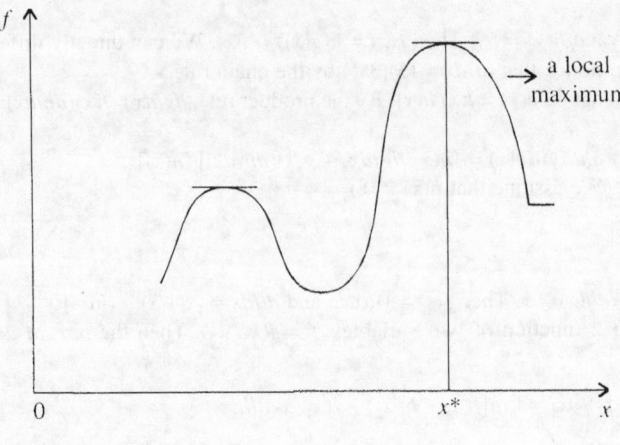

Fig. 2

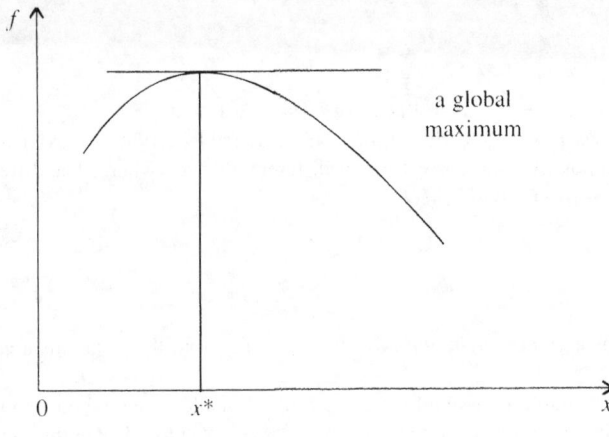

Fig. 3

Constrained Optimization

Consider the constrained optimization problem:

$$\max f(x_1, x_2) \text{ subject to } g(x_1, x_2) = b.$$

The problem is sought to be solved by maximizing the *Lagrangean* function:

$$L = f(x_1, x_2) + \lambda[b - g(x_1, x_2)].$$

where λ is the Lagrange multiplier. Note that when the constraint is satisfied with equality, the term multiplied by λ becomes zero.

The first order conditions are:

$$\partial L/\partial x_1 = \partial f/\partial x_1 - \lambda \partial g/\partial x_1 = 0,$$
$$\partial L/\partial x_2 = \partial f/\partial x_2 - \lambda \partial g/\partial x_2 = 0, \text{ and}$$
$$\partial L/\partial \lambda = b - g(x_1, x_2) = 0.$$

Random Variables

A variable x is a *random variable* if it can take on the values $x_1, x_2, \ldots x_n$ with the probabilities $\pi_1, \pi_2, \ldots \pi_n$. The expectation of x is defined to be $Ex = \Sigma x_i \pi_i$. If a is a fixed number, $Ea = a$.

The *covariance* of two random variables x and y is defined as $\text{cov}(x, y) = E(x - Ex)(y - Ey)$, while the *variance* of x (say) is given by $\text{var}(x) = E(x - Ex)(x - Ex) = E(x - Ex)^2$. If a is a fixed number, $\text{var}(a) = 0$.

Let a and b be fixed numbers. Then $E(ax) = aEx$ and $E(ax + by) = aEx + bEy$. In particular, $E(x + y) = Ex + Ey$.

Also, $\text{cov}(x, y) = E(xy - xEy - yEx + ExEy) = E(xy) - (Ex)(Ey) - (Ex)(Ey) + (Ex)(Ey) = E(xy) - (Ex)(Ey)$, since Ex and Ey are fixed numbers.

$\text{Var}(ax) = E(ax - aEx)^2 = a^2 E(x - Ex)^2 = a^2 \text{var}(x)$.

References

Akerlof, G. (1970). 'The market for lemons: quality uncertainty and the market mechanism'. *Quarterly Journal of Economics*, 89, 488–500.

Aliprantis, Charalambos D. and Subir Kumar Chakrabarti (1999). *Games and Decision Making*. Oxford University Press.

Arrow, K. (1951). 'An extension of the basic theorems of classical welfare economics', in P. Newman (ed.), *Readings in Mathematical Economics*. Baltimore: Johns Hopkins University Press.

Arrow, K. and F. Hahn (1971). *General Competitive Analysis*. San Francisco: Holden Day.

Averch, H. and L.L. Johnson (1962). 'Behavior of the firm under regulatory constraint'. *American Economic Review*, 52, 1052–69.

Axelrod, R. (1984). *The Evolution of Cooperation*. New York: Basic Books.

Bailey, E.E. and A.F. Friedlander (1982). 'Market structure and multiproduct industries'. *Journal of Economic Literature*, 20: 1024–48.

Bain, J. (1956). *Barriers to New Competition*. Cambridge, Mass.: Harvard University Press.

Baumol, William J. (1966). *Economic Theory and Operations Analysis*. New Delhi: Prentice-Hall.

————— (1993). *Entrepreneurship, Management, and the Structure of Payoffs*. Cambridge, MA: The MIT Press.

Baumol, W.J., J.C. Panzar and R.D. Willig (1988). *Contestable Markets and the Theory of Industry Structure*. Harcourt Brace Jovanovich Publishers.

Berle, A.A. and G.C. Means (1932). *The Modern Corporation and Private Property*. New York: Macmillan.

Bhole, L.M. (1992). *Financial Institutions and Markets: Structure, Growth and Innovations*, 2nd edition. Tata McGraw-Hill.

Budhiraja, S.B. and M.B. Athreya (1996). *Cases in Strategic Management*. New Delhi: Tata McGraw-Hill.

Cable, John, and M. Dirrheimer (1983). 'Hierarchies and Markets: An Empirical Test of the Multidivisional Hypothesis in West Germany'. *International Journal of Industrial Organization*, 3, 43–62.

Cable, John, and Hirohiko Yasuki (1985). 'Internal organization, business groups, and corporate performance: An empirical test of the multidivisional hypothesis in Japan'. *International Journal of Industrial Organization*, 3, 421–38.

Carlton, D.W. and J.M. Perloff (1994). *Modern Industrial Organization*. Second Edition. HarperCollins.

Chamberlin, E. (1962). *The Theory of Monopolistic Competition*. Cambridge, Mass.: Harvard University Press.

Chandler, A. (1966). *Strategy and Structure*. New York: Doubleday & Co.

Coase, R. (1937). 'The nature of the firm'. *Economica*, 4, 386–405.

————— (1960). 'The problem of social cost'. *Journal of Law and Economics*, 3: 1–44.

Cookenboo, Jr., L. (1971). 'Costs of operation of crude oil trunk lines', in H. Townsend (ed.), *Price Theory*. England: Penguin Books.

Cooter, R. and T. Ulen (1988). *Law and Economics*. Glen View, Illinois: Scott, Foresman and Company.

d'Aspremont, C., J.J. Gabszewicz and J.F. Thisse (1979). 'On Hotelling's "Stability in Competition"' *Econometrica*, 47, 1145–50.

Debreu, G. (1959). *Theory of Value*. New York: Wiley.

Dixit, A. (1979). 'A model of duopoly suggesting a theory of entry barriers'. *Bell Journal of Economics*, 10: 20–32.

Dixit, A. (1990). *Optimization in Economic Theory* (2nd edn). Oxford: Oxford University Press.

Dixit, A. and B.J. Nalebuff (1991). *Thinking Strategically.* New York: W.W. Norton.

Doeringer, P.B. and M.J. Piore (1971). *Internal Labor Markets and Manpower Analysis.* New York: M.E. Sharpe, Inc.

Fisher, Anthony C. (1981). *Resource and Environmental Economics.* Cambridge: Cambridge University Press.

Frank, Robert H. (1994). *Microeconomics and Behavior.* New York: McGraw-Hill.

Friedman, J. (1971). 'A noncooperative equilibrium for supergames'. *Review of Economic Studies,* 38, 1–12.

Friedman, M. (1962). *Price Theory.* Chicago: Aldine.

Gupta, Devendra B. (1985). 'Urban housing in India'. *World Bank Staff Working Papers,* No. 730.

Gylfason, T. and A. Lindbeck (1994). 'The interaction of monetary policy and wages'. *Public Choice,* 79, 33–46.

Hotelling, H. (1929). 'Stability in competition'. *Economic Journal,* 39: 41–57.

Hemenway, D. (1988). *Prices and Choices: Microeconomic Vignettes.* 2nd edn. HarperBusiness.

Hey, John D. (1979). *Uncertainty in Microeconomics.* Oxford: Martin Robertson.

———— (1989), *Current Issues in Microeconomics.* London: Macmillan.

Hicks, J. (1932). *Theory of Wages.* London: Macmillan.

Kerr, J.M. et al. (1997). *Natural Resource Economics: Theory and Application in India.* New Delhi: Oxford and IBH.

Kreps, D. (1990). *A Course in Microeconomic Theory.* Princeton: Princeton University Press.

Lange, O. and F.M. Taylor (1976). *On the Economic Theory of Socialism.* New Delhi: Tata McGraw-Hill.

Leibenstein, H. (1950). 'Bandwagon, snob, and Veblen effects in the theory of consumer's demand'. *Quarterly Journal of Economics.*

Lindahl, E. (1919). 'Just taxation—a positive solution', in R. Musgrave and A. Peacock (eds), *Classics in the Theory of Public Finance.* London: Macmillan.

McKenna, C.J. (1986). *The Economics of Uncertainty.* New York: Oxford University Press.

Milgrom, P. and J. Roberts (1992). *Economics, Organization and Management.* New Jersey: Prentice-Hall.

Miller, Roger LeRoy and P.H. Raymond Fishe (1995). *Microeconomics: Price Theory in Practice.* Harper Collins.

Mookherjee, D. (1995). *Indian Industry: Policies and Performance.* New Delhi: Oxford University Press.

Mukhopadhyay, Swapna (1992). 'Casualization of labour in India: Concept, incidence and policy options'. *The Indian Journal of Labour Economics,* Vol. 35, No. 2.

Nash, J. (1951). 'Non-cooperative games'. *Annals of Mathematics,* 54, 286–95.

Perloff, J.M. (2001). *Microeconomics.* 2nd edn. Delhi: Pearson Education Asia.

Porter, M.E. (1980). *Competitive Strategy.* New York: Free Press.

Rasmusen, E. (1989). *Games and Information.* Oxford: Basil Blackwell.

Reddy, V.N. and A. Bose (1995). 'Domestic Consumption of Tea in India: A State Level Analysis'. A Project Sponsored by Tea Board, Calcutta.

Samuelson, P. (1947). *Foundations of Economic Analysis.* Cambridge, Mass: Harvard University Press.

———— (1948). 'Consumption theory in terms of revealed preference'. *Econometrica,* 15, 243–53.

———— (1954). 'The pure theory of public expenditure'. *The Review of Economics and Statistics,* 64, 387–9.

Scherer, F.M. and D. Ross (1990). *Industrial Market Structure and Economic Performance.* Boston: Houghton Mifflin.

Sen, A. (1996). *Readers in Economics: Industrial Organization.* New Delhi: Oxford University Press.

Shapiro, C. and J.E. Stiglitz (1984). 'Equilibrium unemployment as a worker discipline device'. *American Economic Review,* 74/3, 433–44.

Shy, Oz (1995). *Industrial Organization.* Cambridge, Mass: The MIT Press.

Spulber, Daniel F. (1995). 'Economics and management strategy: a survey', Part I. *Journal of Economics and Management Strategy.*

Stonier, A.W. and D.C. Hague (1980). *A Textbook of Economic Theory.* London: ELBS and Longman.

Thomas, Christopher R. and S.C. Maurice (2001). *Managerial Economics: Concepts and Applications.* 8th edn. New Delhi, Tata McGraw-Hill.

Tirole, J. (1988). *The Theory of Industrial Organization*. Cambridge: The MIT Press.

Tversky, A. and D. Kahneman (1981). 'The framing of decisions and the psychology of choice'. *Science*, 211, 453–8.

Varian, H. (1989a). 'Price discrimination', in *Handbook of Industrial Organization*, Amsterdam: North-Holland.

Varian, Hal R. (1992). *Microeconomic Analysis*. 3rd edn. W.W. Norton.

————— (1993). *Intermediate Microeconomics: A Modern Approach*. 3rd edn. New York: W.W. Norton.

Williamson, O.E. (1981). 'The modern corporation: origins, evolutions, attributes'. *Journal of Economic Literature*, 19: 1537–70.

Index

---

[1] The numbers within brackets refer to the chapters in which the word occurs.